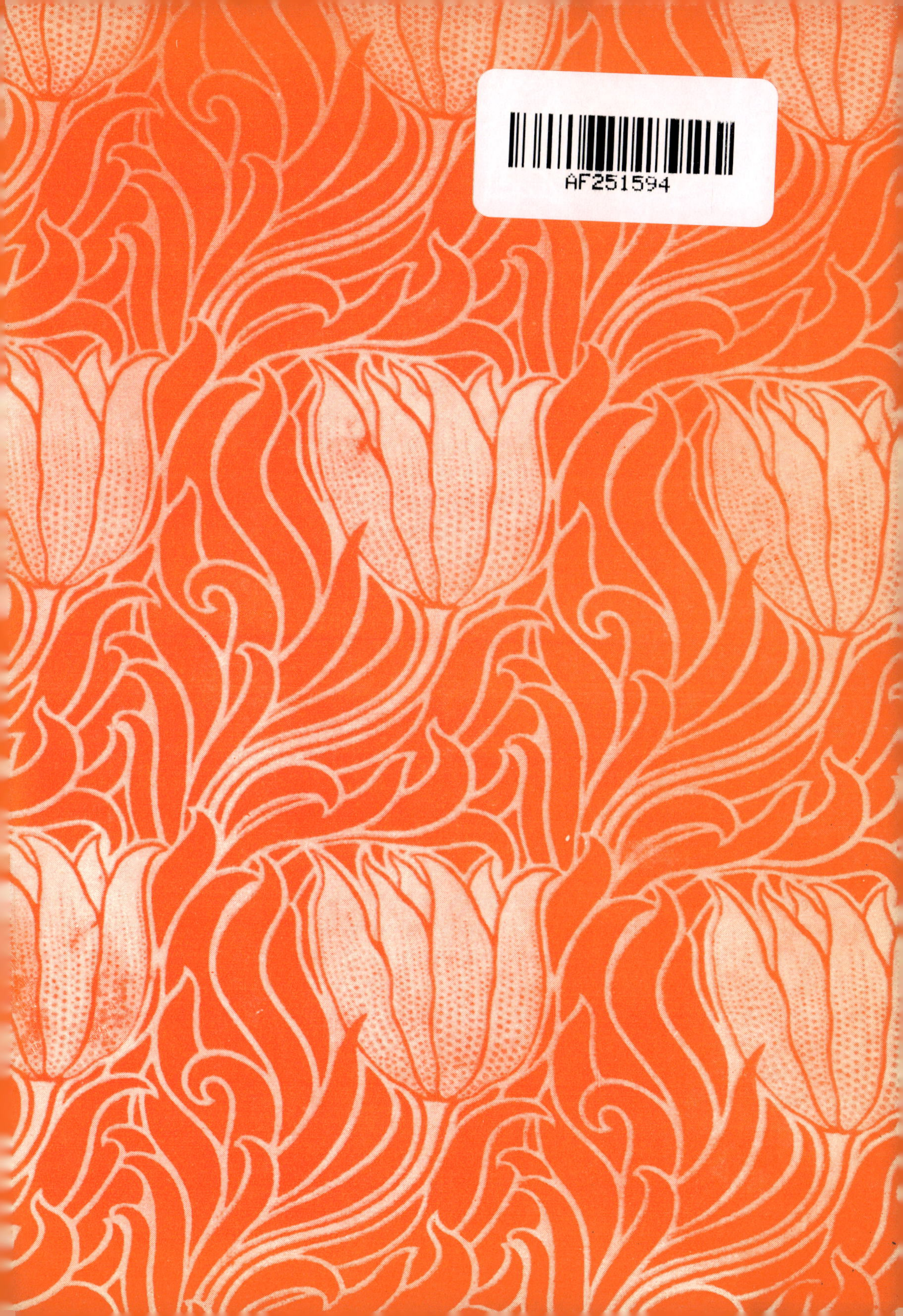
AF251594

ART NOUVEAU

ART NOUVEAU

by

Bernard Champigneulle

Translated from the French by
Benita Eisler

Barron's Educational Series, Inc.
Woodbury, New York

Library of Congress Catalog Card No. 76-8467

Paper Edition

International Standard Book No. 0-8120-0667-4

Cloth Edition

International Standard Book No. 0-8120-5111-4

Library of Congress Cataloging in Publication Data

Champigneulle, Bernard, 1896-
    Art nouveau.

    Includes index.
    1. Art nouveau.   2. Art, Modern — 19th century.
I. Title.
N6465.A7C5213   709'.03'4   76-8467
ISBN 0-8120-5111-4
ISBN 0-8120-0667-4 pbk.

contents

significant dates in art nouveau

1883   First glass is made by Gallé in Nancy. Mackmurdo's title page is done for *Wren's City Churches*.

1885   Construction begins on Gaudí's Church of the Sagrada Familia in Barcelona.

1886   Arts and Crafts Society is founded by Walter Crane, under the influence of William Morris.

1887   Seurat paints *The Cancan*.

1888   Albums of Japanese decorative prints are published in Europe.

1889   Gauguin's first ceramics are made. First meetings of the Nabis.

1892   Horta begins work on the Tassel House in Brussels.

1893   Posters are made by Toulouse-Lautrec for the Moulin Rouge. Lithographs are done by Bonnard for *La Revue Blanche*. Paintings and engravings are done by Toorop. Solvey residence is begun by Horta.

1894   Beardsley illustrates *Salomé* by Oscar Wilde.

1895   Van de Velde designs, furnishes, and decorates his own house, Uccle, Brussels. Posters are designed by Mucha for Sarah Bernhardt.

1896   Bing opens his Galerie Art Nouveau in Paris. The review *Jugend* is founded in Munich. Designs are done by Obrist. Decor and furniture are done by Eckmann.

1897   Sezession group is founded in Vienna (Olbrich, Hoffmann, and Klimt). Mackintosh begins work on the Glasgow School of Art.

1898   Castel Bérenger, designed by Guimard, is the first architectural
        example of art nouveau (to be known in France as Modern
        Style) in Paris. Lalique designs jewelry. Illustrations, furniture,
        and designs are done by Grasset.

1899   Furniture is designed by Horta, Van de Velde, Mackintosh, and
        Majorelle. Lamps and other objects completed by Tiffany.

1900   Art Nouveau Pavilion opens at the World's Fair. Guimard
        designs the entrances for the Paris Métro.

1901   School of Nancy is founded, under the directorship of Gallé,
        with Prouvé, Daum, and Majorelle on the faculty.

1902   Van de Velde is named Artistic Advisor to the Grande-Duchy
        of Saxe-Weimar.

1905   Gaudí continues work on the Church of the Sagrada Familia,
        the Güell estate, and he finishes the Casa Mila in Barcelona.

an aesthetic revolution

The term is banal. What it describes is extraordinary. Art nouveau appears, in the history of the arts, as a singular phenomenon. Its fluid forms often elude our grasp, and its boundary lines are imprecise. A complex but self-conscious phenomenon, nourished by fertile cultural terrain, art nouveau illuminates with its fireworks that period, christened in playful nostalgia, *la Belle Epoque.*

To many critics, art nouveau is a stylistic detour, an avatar without issue which only interrupted the course of artistic evolution: others see in it the resurgence of the baroque, an innovation, a long-awaited revolution, a realization of the spiritual yearnings of a society which, at the juncture of two centuries, seemed to herald a new order.

The subtle music of symbolism, its ironies and tender lyricism, was about to have the graceful preciousness of its songs translated into a design for living. Symbolist poetry had rejected the straightjacket of the Alexandrine, abandoning itself to the voluptuous seduction of free verse . . . The artists and craftsmen of the period listened carefully to the message—a message which had already been whispered to them by earlier generations, and from which they constructed a philosophy and a style. The symbolist poets were their brothers. If symbolism did not actually give birth to art nouveau, the two movements were in perfect harmony; symbolist songs were sung amid hangings where climbed the sinuous vine, among glass the color of a storm at sea, and in surroundings lit by lamps in the shape of morning glories.

Despite its ephemeral existence in the life of the arts, no other style has been called by so many different—and varied—names. Now, there is nearly unanimous agreement by art historians on the term *art nouveau.* The words first appeared on the shop sign of a gallery which Samuel Bing opened in Paris in 1896. The French, however, in their anglophile snobbery, persisted in using the term *Modern Style,*

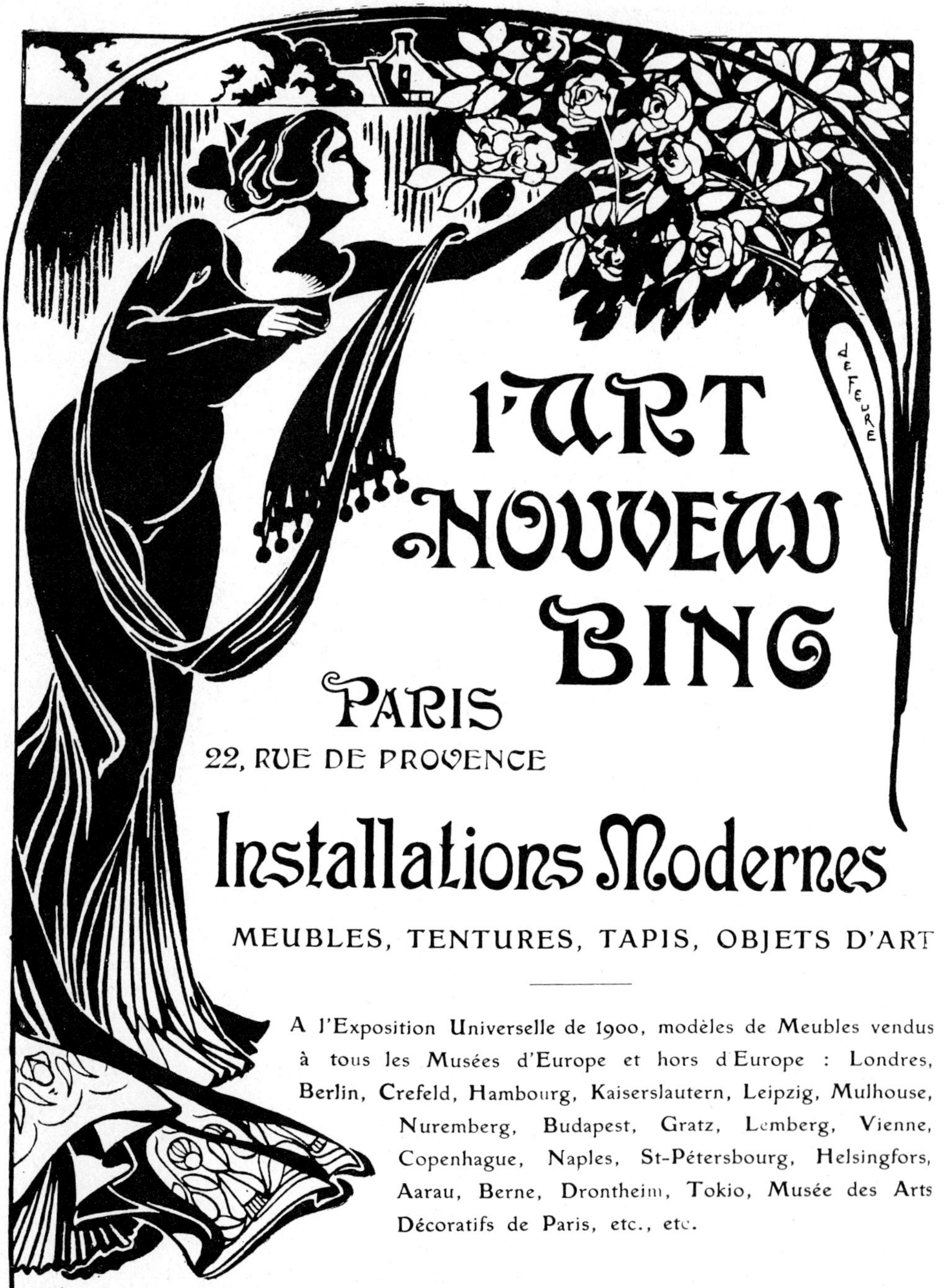

GEORGES DE FEURE   Shop sign for Samuel Bing's gallery, l'Art Nouveau, ca. 1895

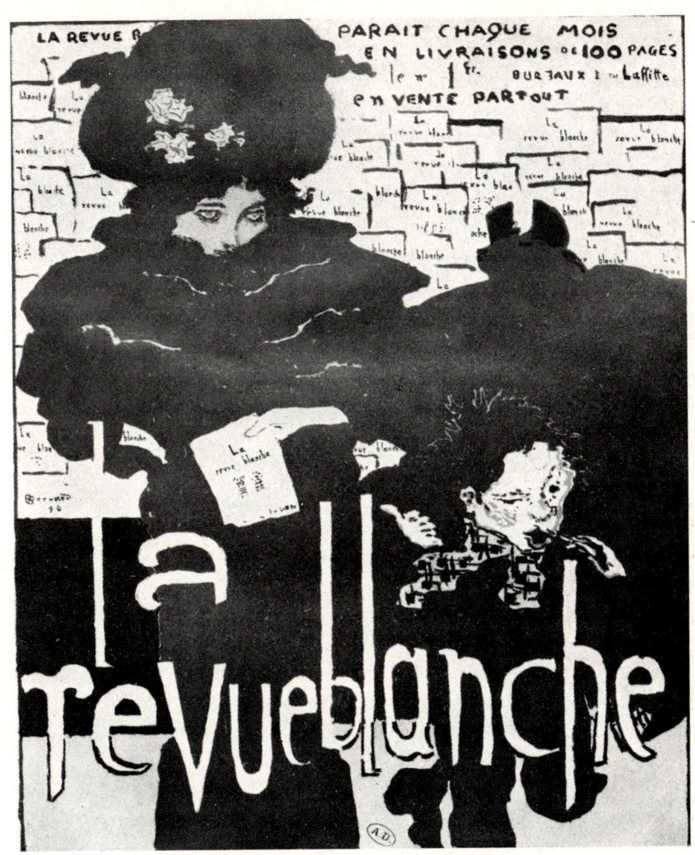

PIERRE BONNARD   Poster for *La Revue Blanche*, 1894

while the Germans gave to the new aesthetic the name *Jugendstil*, from the review *Jugend* which popularized it. At the same time, the term *Sezessionstil* recalled the avant-garde *Sezession*, which was born in Vienna, and spread from there throughout central Europe. The Italians adopted *Stile Liberty* or *Stile Nuovo*, and the Americans, *Tiffany Style*, from the name of its best-known designer. The Spanish spoke of *Modernista* or *Arte Joven* until the fame of the great Spanish architect defined the *Style Gaudí*. There were also numerous descriptions which started as terms of derision, and then became current idiom: the *noodle* style, the *whiplash*, and, later on, *la Belle Epoque* style. The Germans did even better in finding the name *Bauchwurmstil*, or *tapeworm* style. Parisians spoke of a *Style Métro*, involuntary homage to Guimard; *fin de siècle;* or *style 1900*. All these referred to the

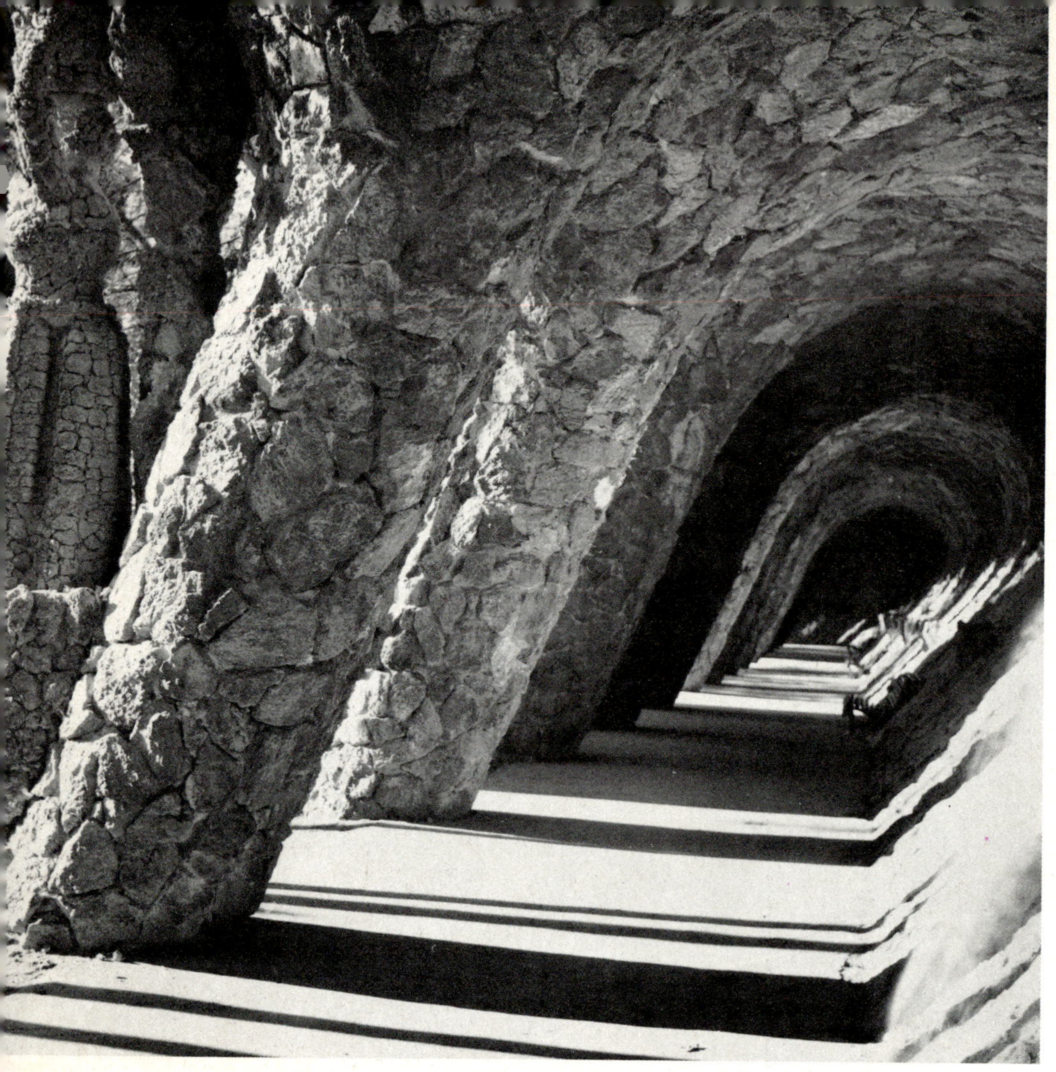

ANTONI GAUDÍ The Güell Estate, 1900–1914

novelties which emerged just about the time of the Paris World's Fair of that year, while the *Style Loubet* was used to publicize the Republic (Loubet being the name of the president at the time), by trying to create a stylistic analogy to those previously named for kings.

All of this points clearly to the vitality of a mode of expression whose effervescence did not dissipate unnoticed. It was certainly a concept which could have only started with aesthetes and developed from the meeting of original minds. Some of these artists and architects had borrowed from the symbolist poets a particular method of calling attention to their work: adopting an eccentric life-style, designed to

12

infuriate the conventional. Earlier architects had perceived and expressed the shift which would lead modern construction toward its new destiny. But only exceptionally did the facades of their houses reveal this aesthetic.

The poster now seized on the new style at just the time when commercial publicity had started to capture markets by virtue of its colorful imagery. Fashion and beauty products were the first to be

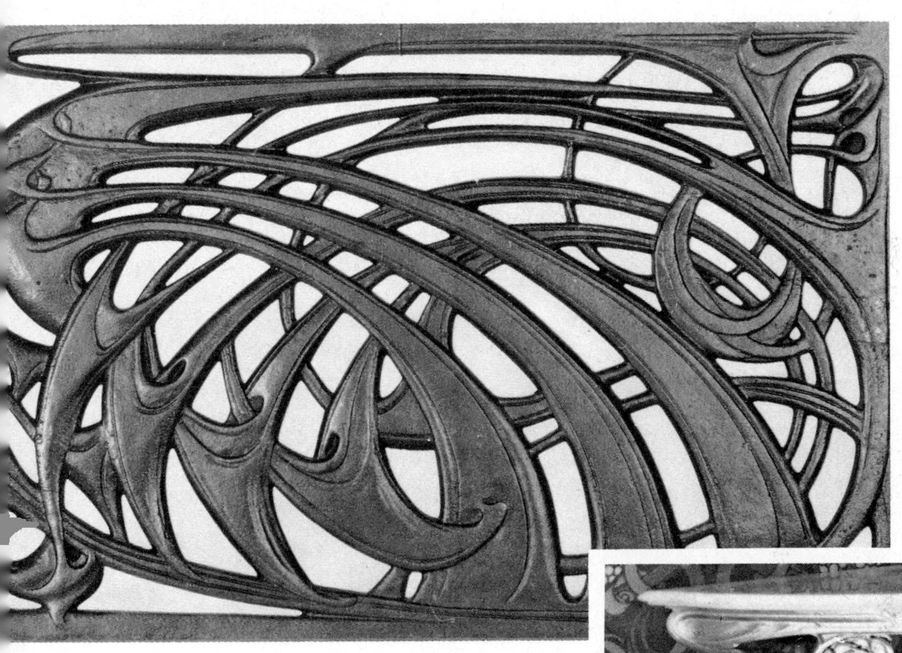

HECTOR GUIMARD   Lead panel for a balcony, 1898–1900

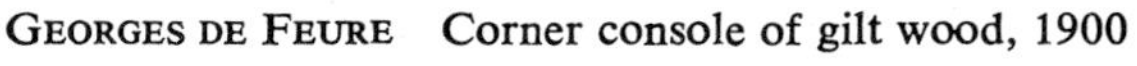

GEORGES DE FEURE   Corner console of gilt wood, 1900

influenced. And women themselves became living propaganda for the new movement. The female body, stylized by the corset, was now liberated by clothes whose skirts fluttered as freely as petals.

Art nouveau was essentially a decorative movement: it boasted no great sculptors or painters who could, strictly speaking, be considered proponents of its theories and disciplines. Nonetheless, all of the artistic currents of the period were profoundly influenced by its creativity. In order to understand its real significance and evolution, art nouveau must be seen within the larger aesthetic context which characterized the end of the nineteenth century, in the plastic as well as decorative arts. For there is no schism between what we call "applied arts," by which we mean "applied from industry," and Art, with a capital *A*. Most creators of objects and designers promulgating the renaissance of the decorative arts at this time were also painters and engravers. We must always repeat, and indeed proclaim, that the division established by nineteenth century art historians between fine arts and minor arts never in any way corresponded to reality. There is more fine art in a Ming pot than in many pretentious pictorial compositions. The greatest periods in art, Dynastic Egypt or the Gothic period, never made the hierarchical distinction among the various disciplines, all of which contributed to a common artistic enterprise.

If we fail to consider its goals and their significance, art nouveau is difficult to define as an art form. It is, first of all, an event in European art. Known by different names, depending upon the country in question, and different national characteristics, more or less clearly articulated, art nouveau became almost synonymous with the last years of the nineteenth century and the first years of the twentieth, to the point of being, for some, a philosophy, an ethic, and a way of life.

the arts in society at the end of the 19th century

Art nouveau responded, first, to the will and the desire for transcendance, on both a social and an artistic plane. In the second half of the nineteenth century, art had come more and more to resemble merchandise produced to satisfy the lowest level of taste of its clientele. To be sure, we are speaking only of the art market, and of those who stood to profit handsomely from the preferences of individual patrons, or from state commissions for the large number of public works; for we should not forget that, side by side with impressionism, during this most astonishing period of French painting there flourished a less glorious kind of art.

Painters, sculptors, architects, decorators accommodated—occasionally, with considerable talent—the laws of supply and demand.

And just what was the nature of this demand? A prosperous society, fond of luxury and comfort, wanted to see the reflection of its own image. Never was the full-length portrait, the sitter in equally full-dress regalia, produced in such numbers, while busts of government bureaucrats adorned the mantelpieces of every official administrator's office. This society also wanted to see images faithful to nature in the last detail; landscapes decorated all sitting rooms. They liked genre painting and historical subject matter, selected either from biblical or from classical antiquity, or from the repertory of medieval subjects made fashionable by the romantic movement. There was a widespread demand for anecdotal scenes from contemporary life. The taste of the bourgeoisie was identical to that of the state. Official commissions went to Bonnat, Bouguereau, Cormon, and Luc-Olivier Merson. The Franco-Prussian War was illustrated by Detaille and Alphonse de Neuville.

The basis for this understanding between society and the painters it employed was, undoubtedly, the desire to create a common culture.

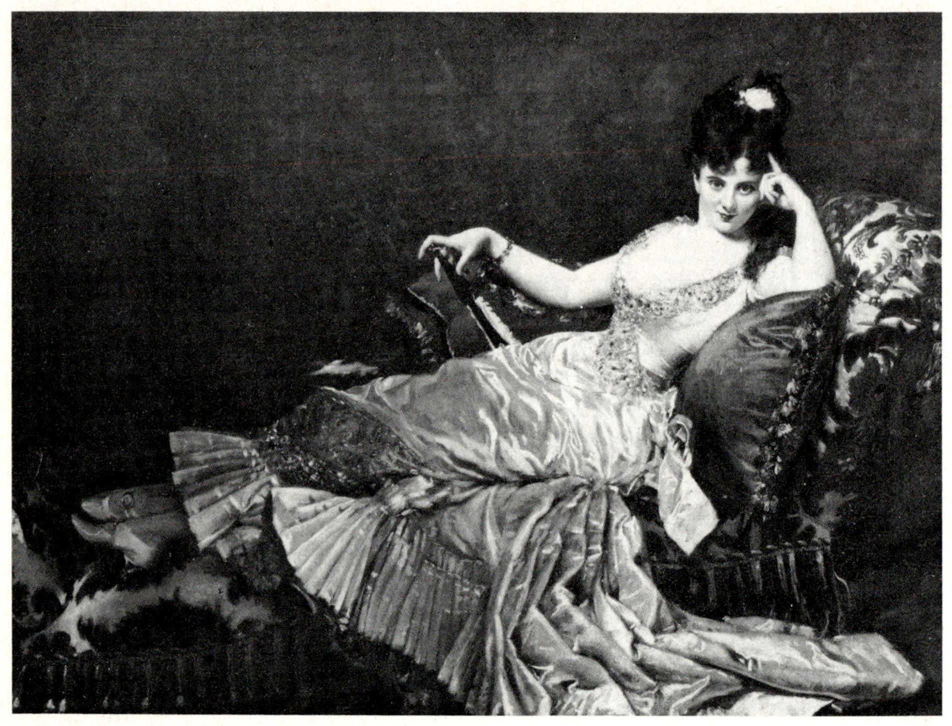

Émile-Auguste Carolus-Duran *Portrait of Madame de Lancey,* ca. 1885

They both sought fidelity of pictorial representation in the interest of exalting the contribution of history and mortality, particularly when tempered with superficial references to the Old Masters.

These same principles were at work everywhere. They inspired Lenbach in Germany, Lord Leighton in England, Maccari in Italy, Répine in Russia, Fortuny throughout Europe. These paintings all deferred to subject matter, above all else, which today we would call *anecdote,* but which, at this period, was much more than anecdote, as we define the term: these artists were attempting to translate sentimental values, to represent an ideal, or a symbol. They were masters of allegory who covered acres of wall surface in official residences, university buildings, theaters, and churches. At this time, a frenzy of building was taking place in cities whose rapid rate of population growth and economic development has never been equaled. Within these new monuments, painters were called upon to decorate walls and ceilings— representing thousands of square feet.

We have been too quick to heap scorn upon the "bourgeois" who

16

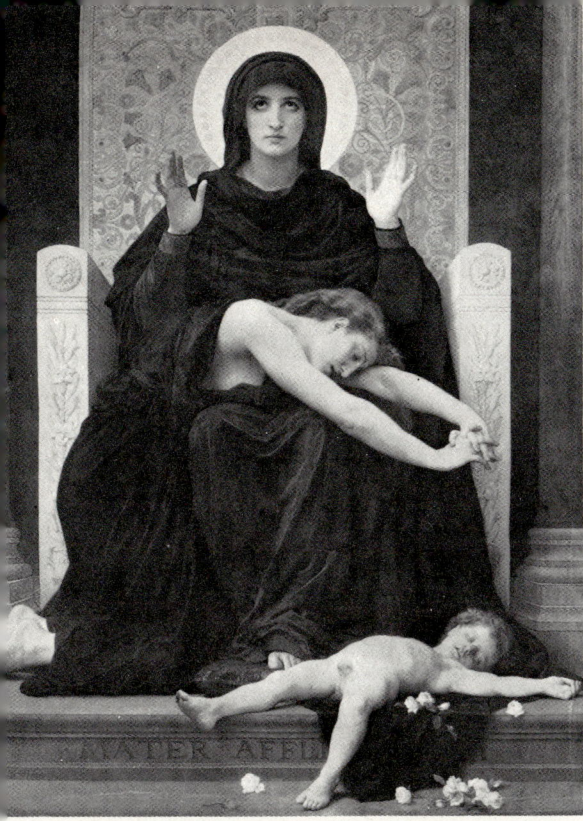

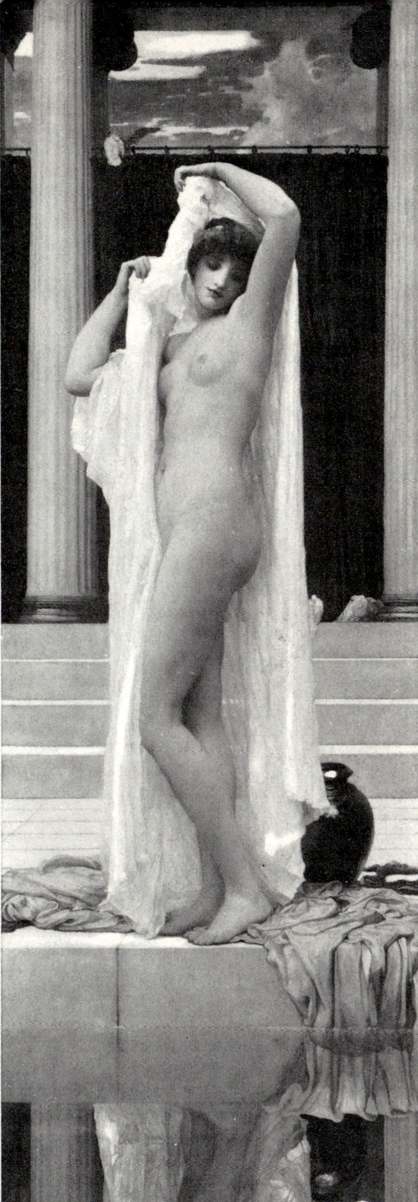

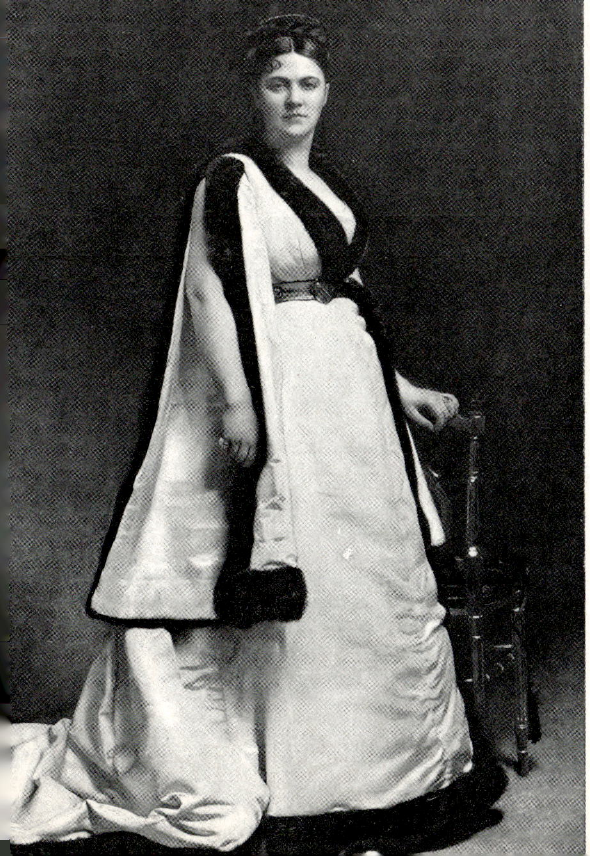

William Bouguereau *Consoling Virgin,* 1877

Léon Bonnat *Portrait of Madame Pasca,* 1874

Frédérick Leighton *Psyche's Bath,* ca. 1880

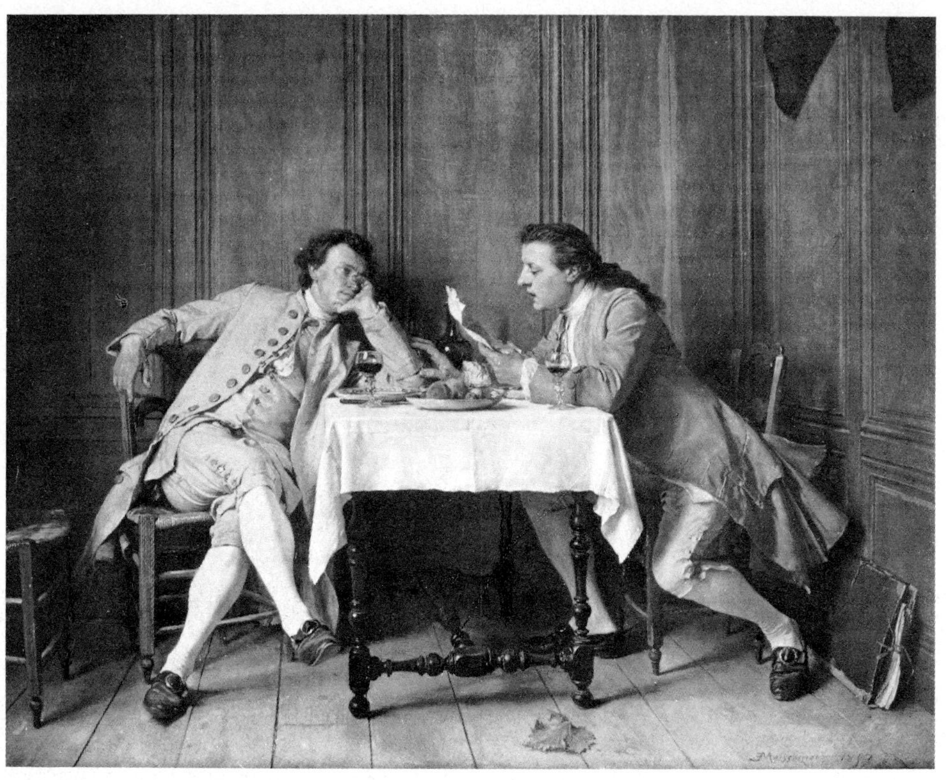

JEAN-LOUIS-ERNEST MEISSONIER *The Secret,* 1857

delighted in these paintings that we find so dull today. We have forgotten that an art critic as acute as Baudelaire often praised fulsomely
works which seem valueless to us; that these paintings were purchased
by museum curators of enormous culture; that Delacroix said of Meissonier: "Of all of us, he is the one whose fame is most certain to
endure"; that Marcel Proust, when he created a painter for his literary
universe — the character of Elstir — took as his model Helleu!

At this same time, the great upheavals which were to transform
in depth and breadth the world's way of seeing had begun. Impressionism, an art of sensibility and spontaneity, challenged every accepted
idea about art. And, not surprisingly, it met with indifference from the
public and with hostility from academic painters — that is, from all
the other painters — who rejected and denigrated this new way of
painting all the more ferociously, as they must vaguely have perceived
that this celebration of color and light was fated to eclipse whatever

18

remained of surface vitality in their own compositions, composed of formulas learned by rote.

A European phenomenon, art nouveau has no ties or references to the impressionist school (which is completely French and totally individualistic), whose artists had no aspiration to transform society. The new style was directed toward precisely the reverse form of plastic expression; its graphic line was the complete antithesis of the discoveries of the impressionists, their studies of the vibrations of light, their brush strokes. The impressionists were landscape painters who became aware of their personal sensations as they observed changes in nature, whereas the protagonists of art nouveau were "abstract naturalists" and analysts; they drew their inspiration from the description of natural elements, particularly from vegetation, which they tried to transpose into a decorative repertory, destined to provide their con-

CESARE MACCARI   *Cicero and Cataline in the Senate,* ca. 1885

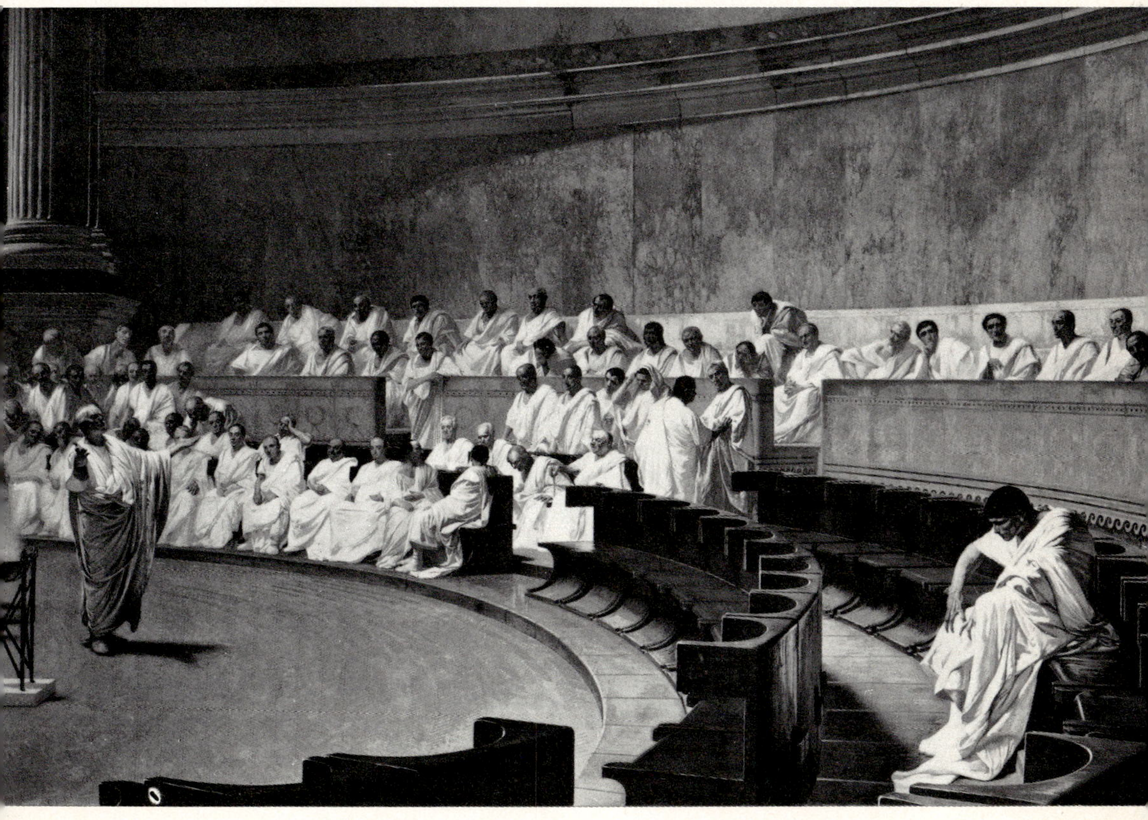

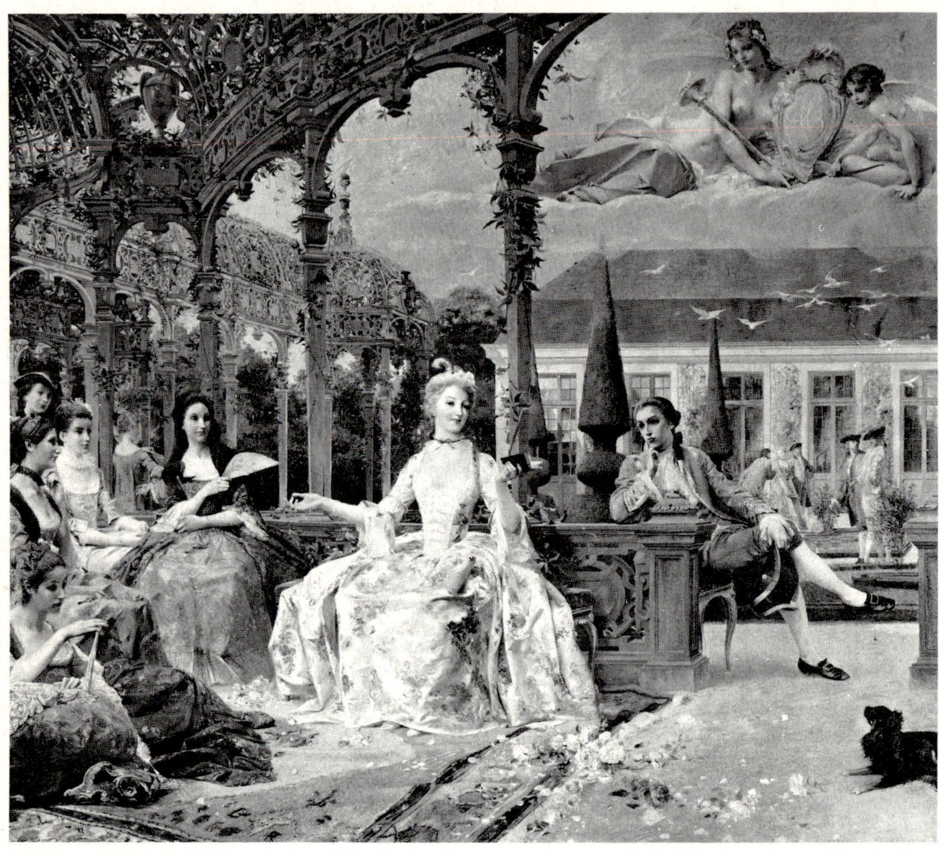

LUC-OLIVIER MERSON *Mlle. de Clermont*

temporaries with a modern style. Indeed, the term *Modern Style* gives a fairly exact description of their goals.

The state of sculpture, at the turn of the century, was even more discouraging. With the exception of Rodin, whose genius transcends period, sculptors expressed themselves in imitations which, on occasion, reached the heights of the absurd. Statuary in public spaces proliferated, as it proclaimed to passers-by — who, in any case, remained oblivious to the message — that the decline of a noble art turns into grandiloquent parody. In every country, monuments of overstatement multiplied, whose gesticulations, aimed at transcribing the reality of life in picturesque detail, forgot that the sculptor's art is an art of synthesis which must recast life within a harmony of forms and the exemplary quality of their inner meaning. Cities were inundated with monuments

20

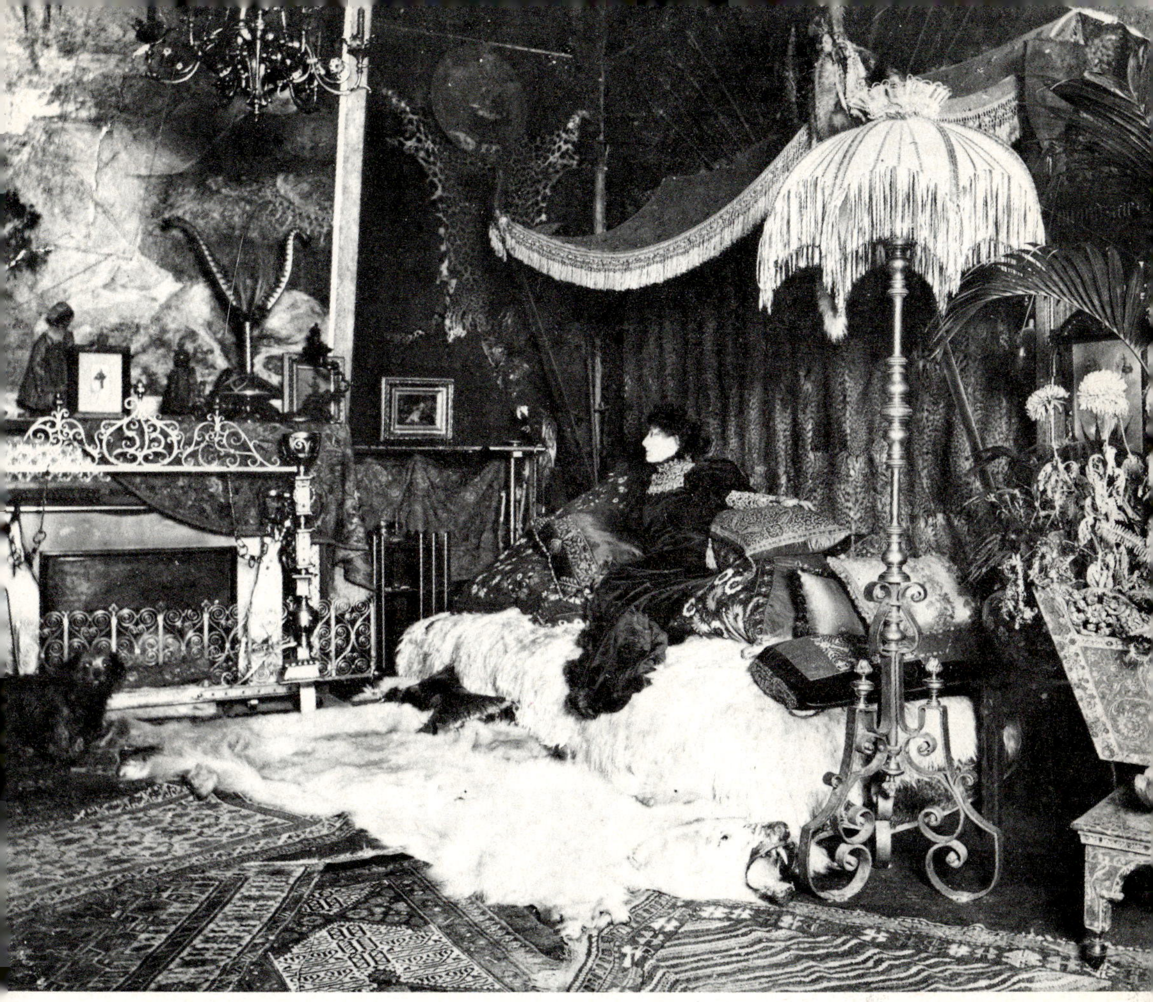

Sarah Bernhardt at home

which, only a few years later, would lose any value of intimate communication with the viewer.

Architecture, too, stagnated under the weight of homage to the styles of the past, vaguely reinterpreted for contemporary use. Archaeological discoveries and the revelations of history paralyzed the spirit of invention. Architecture schools in the Beaux-Arts tradition handed down, as Holy Writ, a doctrine considered untouchable, whose basis was the classical orders established by the Renaissance. And any deviation was deemed sacrilege. Lacking the capacity to create new forms, European culture turned to its past, in an attempt to rediscover its own traditions. These traditions, however, were inevitably recast by external and artificial means, leading to utterly inert monuments. The English Gothic style of the fifteenth century took on a newly sublime character in the hands of the Victorians, thus giving the Gothic Revival its unquestionable legitimacy. But the German pastiches of this same period, inspired by German myths and past military glory, assumed a dreary, ponderous character. Everywhere there reigned an eclecticism which hopped from Romanesque to Gothic to Renaissance.

When we come to interior decoration, we find an outlandish confusion of history and geography. The Henri II dining room of the working classes corresponded to the Louis XV sitting room of the *petit bourgeois*. Upper bohemians and artists prided themselves on their exotic surroundings, a heady mix of Turkish and Chinese carpets, water pipes, and buddhas. There was an avalanche of plush cushion backs and poufs, divans, and sofas. Windows were framed by massive hangings which unfurled over moldings. Fringes and tassels abounded. It was the apotheosis of the upholsterer, who disguised with his fabric the poverty of structure. Stamped leather imitated the tooling of Cordova; cabinets and dressers aped the Italian Renaissance.

the first stirrings of reaction

The evolution of the arts throughout history bears witness to the fact that each style in due course engenders another. Had the sap finally run dry? Whether the cause was a failure of intelligence or the desire to stabilize all forms within an immutable order, the result was an impression that all creative energy seemed to have atrophied.

At the time of Louis-Philippe, there were still enough stray ideas left to evolve a Louis-Philippe style. But after that, it was all over. Taste plunged — but not without shudders of delight — into overstuffed interpretations of the Gothic, or of Louis XVI, which the "elite" loved and whose makers it patronized.

A mania for the antique and the Gothic, allied to local traditionalism, held sway throughout Europe. Established powers rested not only upon a soporific conservatism, but upon a body of aesthetic and moral ideas which can be traced to erudite architects like Viollet-le-Duc and most of the writers of the time. England, the earliest industrialized country, took pains to disguise every new building. Her banks, markets, and stations did not give any evidence of having been designed for use by industrialists or merchants, but for use by knights or monks of the Middle Ages. America, which had no history but already boasted

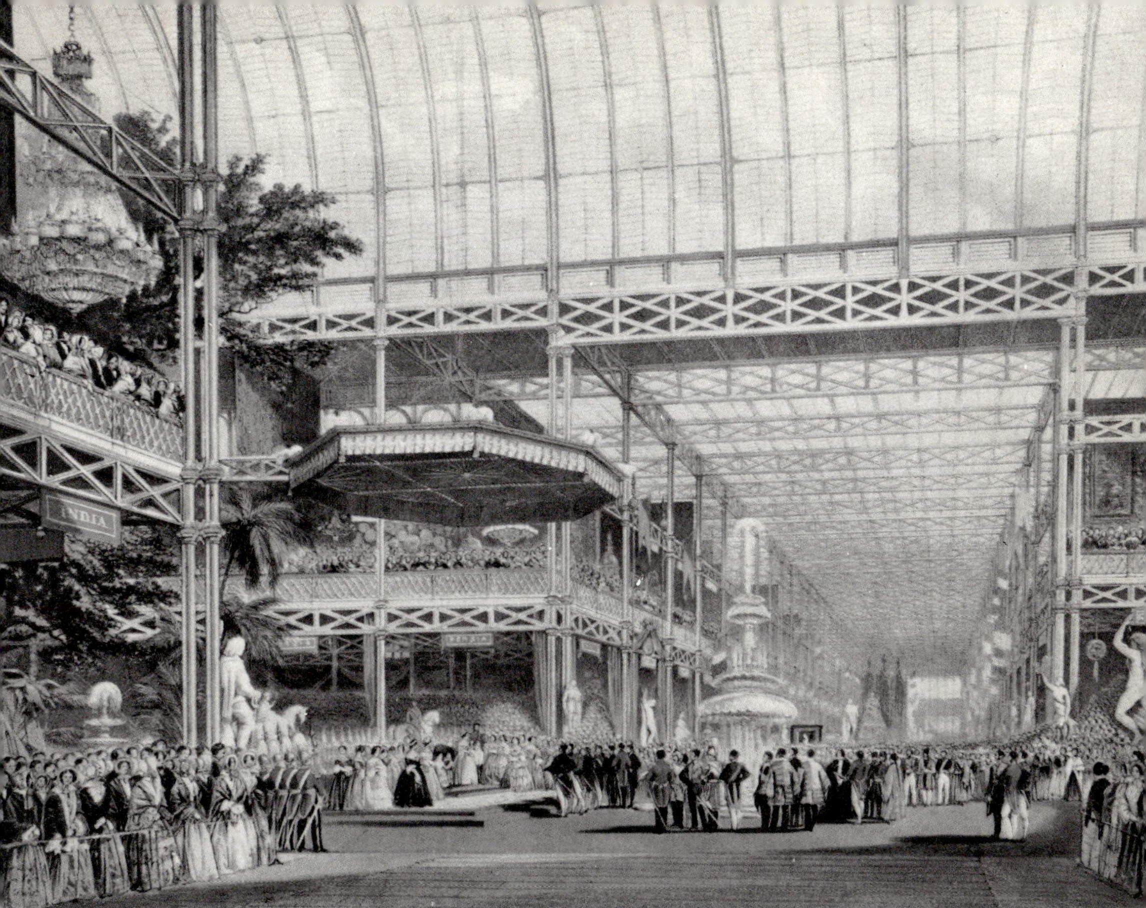

Interior of the Crystal Palace, designed by Sir Joseph Paxton, 1851

a large number of millionaires, was, even more than Europe, disposed to create a brand-new past. Economic wealth, relative social stability, faith in the benevolent march of progress and well-being conferred a sense of security and optimism that resisted change.

Warning signs of reaction, however, were not lacking. A diverse group of contemporaries had perceived that the new industrial civilization would have to produce art forms which would take into account the possibilities of mechanical production. The Crystal Palace, built for the London Exhibition of 1851, was an extraordinary prefiguration of the future, but it housed only objects which clung to the past. Henry Cole deplored the stagnation and mediocrity of its ornamentation. The report of the French representative to that Exhibition, Count Laborde, reveals a visionary who sought to remedy the absence of a repertory of original forms and ornamental vocabulary, the latter until then nonexistent, except as borrowings from the past. "The future of the arts, sciences and industry," he wrote, "is in their alliance." He wanted architecture and the arts which were dependent upon it "to benefit from every kind of innovation made possible by the inventions of our century and way of life." He predicted that the new technology would create a new standard of living which must, in turn, engender appropriate forms. He noted the absurdity of transforming chandeliers meant for candles into fixtures for gas or kerosene.

When engineers and architects collaborated, they pioneered the use of iron in architecture. But Eiffel, like most of his engineer contemporaries, had not the slightest aesthetic concern: his bridges and tower acquired their purity of form from their perfect adaptation to function. But it is not quite accurate to speak of "functional forms" in this context. Before being used as a radio transmitter, the Eiffel Tower had no function whatever. It stood as a symbol of French invention, a monument to prestige, for the World's Fair.

the pioneers of art nouveau ~ revolutionaries

It is to the honor of a few men that they reacted, and were reactionaries, at the same time as they were revolutionaries. For this role they needed faith and a spirit of adventure. Against them was arrayed another double power: money in league with entrenched conservatism. The dissidents were up against a fortress, an official art protected by the highest authorities of a society closed to anything new. The paradox of this society was that it was bursting with pride over everything that showed the spirit of scientific discovery and invention in the technical domain, while in the realm of art the new inspired only fear.

In 1890 the Exposition celebrating the centenary of the French Revolution exhibited the most astounding scientific discoveries, but, conversely, the arts seemed to have atrophied. However, in his Nancy workshop, Gallé continued to create glass which caught the essence of plants and skies; in Brussels, Horta designed the first Modern Style house for a university professor; in Vienna, artists joined forces to found the Sezession group; while, in Barcelona, a very young architect named Gaudí designed for a tile manufacturer a house constructed entirely of ceramic tile and cast iron — the strangest house ever seen.

These men were unknown to one another. But they were each inspired by the same ambition. A "modernity," the evidence of certain distinct creative ideas, emerged simultaneously in various centers of artistic activity, in various countries. But it would not be called a movement, since it was not a collective enterprise. Each artist in his own orbit, each in his own professional sector sought to contribute to his time an *art nouveau*. They were, at one and the same time, workers who loved their work and visionaries who saw beyond what they had been taught.

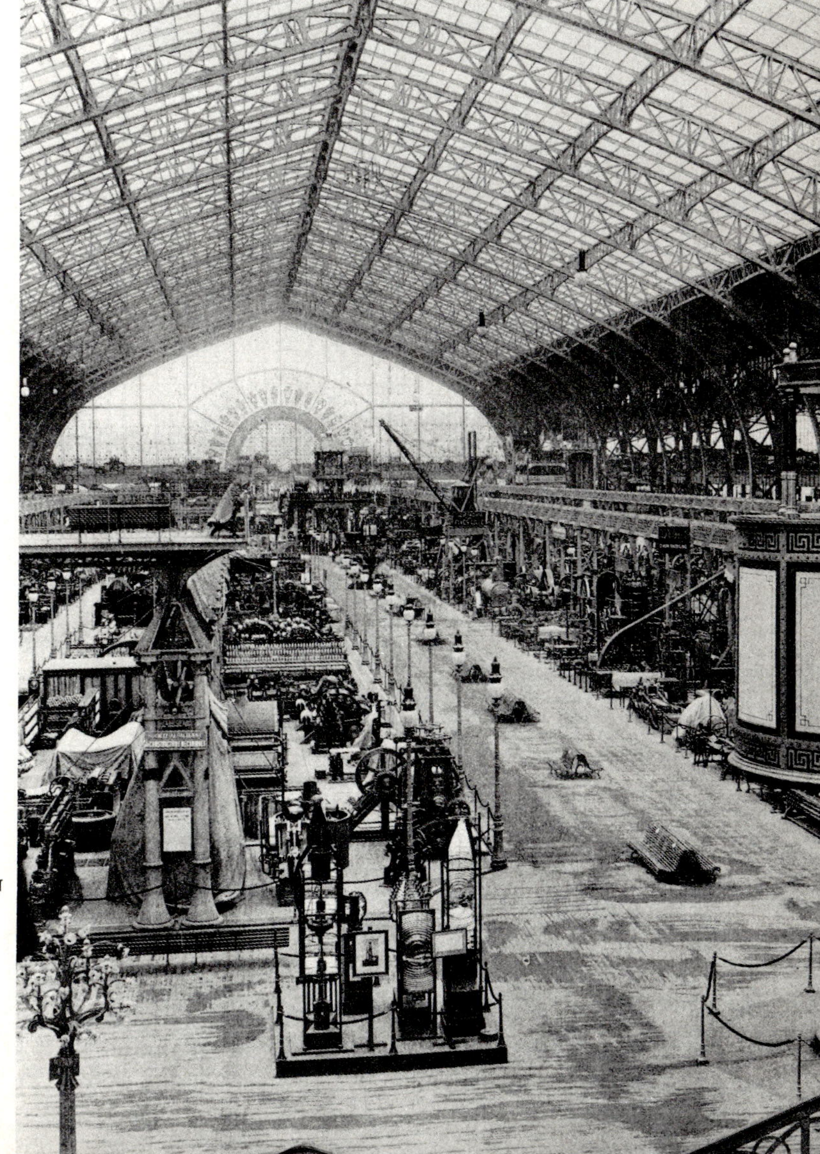

Dutert and Contamin
The Hall of Machines
built for the World's
Fair, Paris, 1889

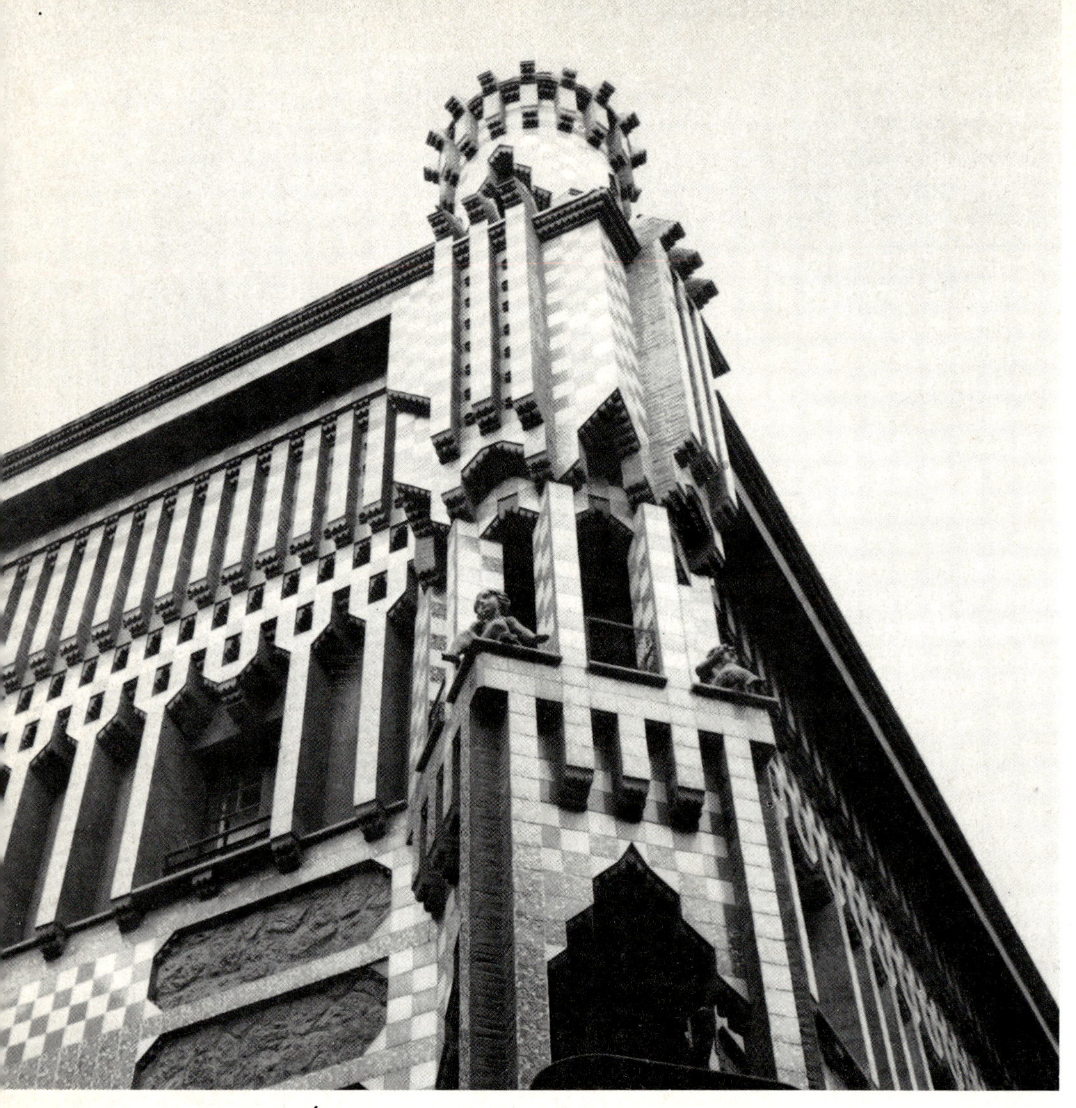

Antoni Gaudí Detail of Casa Vicens, Barcelona, 1878–1880

Because today art nouveau is greeted with faintly patronizing smiles, because it appears, half a century later, as a backdrop in theater and music hall, adding to the clichés about *la Belle Epoque,* it is easily mistaken for whimsy, for a diversion whose exaggerations were intended for the pleasure of a brilliant and jaded society, for a harmless joke whose very name Modern Style consigned it to mere snobbery.

Nothing could be less accurate. Art nouveau was developed with intense faith and dedication. It was the result of passionate experimentation, whose impulse was the determination to escape the yoke of rules, and of a mysterious, mystical calling. There was, indeed, a mystical source of the new art. It was also an art of great daring. With no support at all, these men decided that they would strip the houses of the bourgeoisie of their anachronistic trappings, and give them a new style adapted to present-day living. To achieve this goal, they struggled unceasingly.

This concept of a new style was not only an aesthetic revolution. It was at the same time a poetic and philosophic movement of humanitarian beliefs (the poor were to benefit, as fully as the rich, from the superior quality of their surroundings). Its creators were apostles who believed themselves invested with a social mission. In this respect the

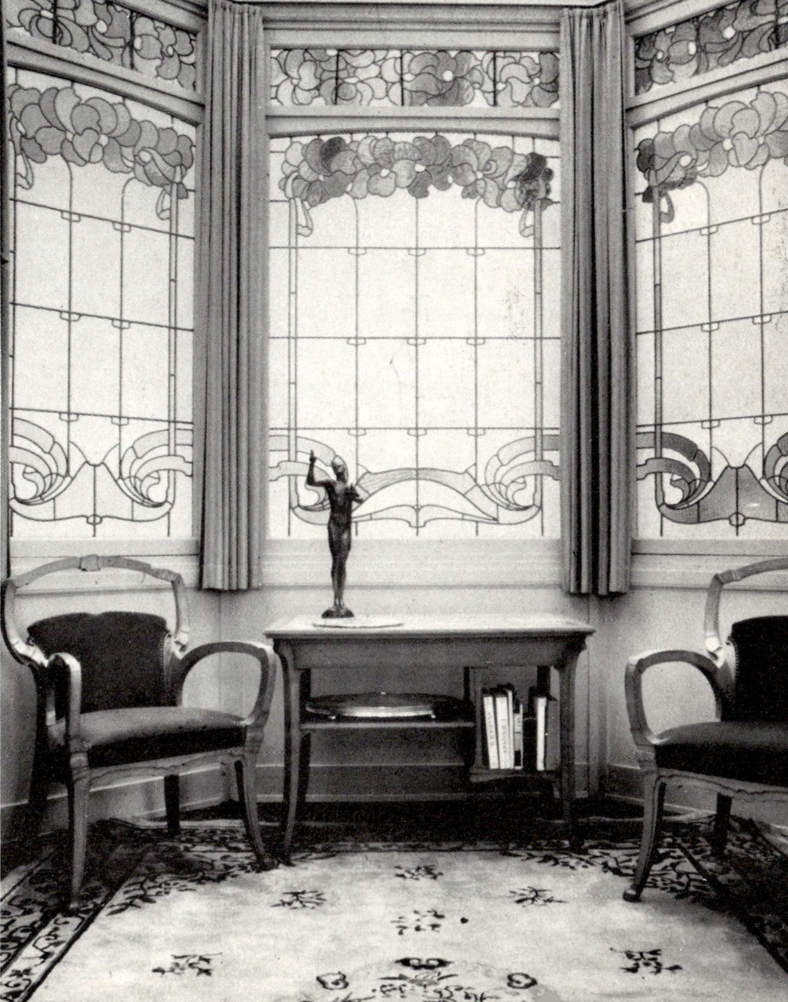

VICTOR HORTA
Glass and furniture
for an apartment,
1898–1900

movement failed, since its creations, original and expensive to produce, could only find patrons — with a few rare exceptions — in the world of industry and finance. But this is not to deny these men their generous aspirations and insistence upon the highest standards of workmanship.

Because today it is difficult to restore art nouveau to its original climate, difficult to define it other than by its after-effects (amusing décors, witty accessories, tea tables, or hat pins), we forget that it was a serious matter, that these artists created and overcame a hostile public. Art

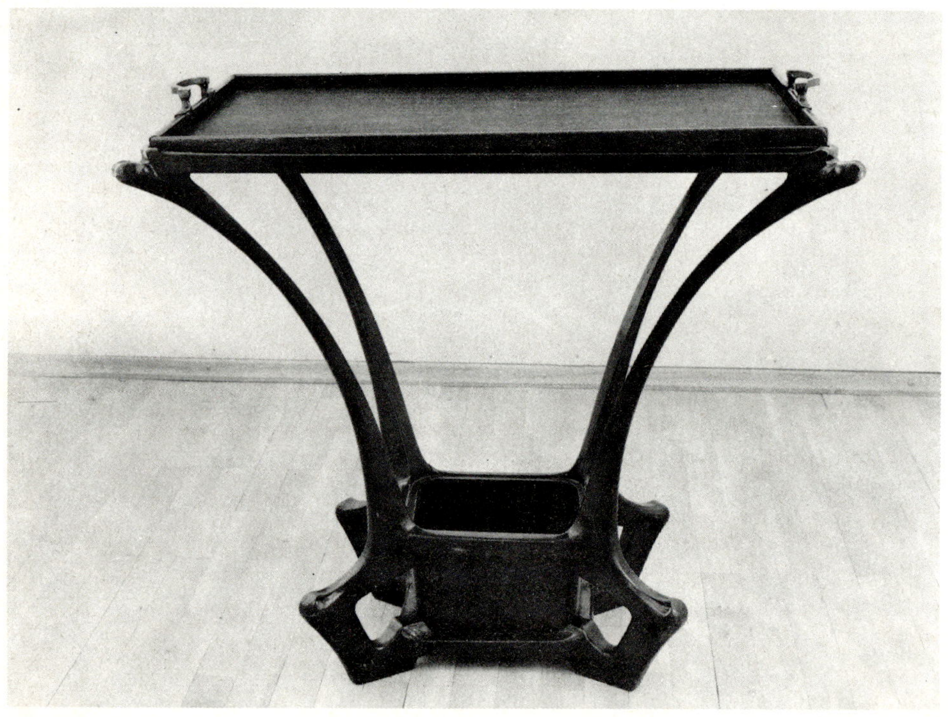

HERMANN OBRIST   Tea table, 1900

nouveau was not a self-contained phenomenon; it developed with a multiplicity of implications, in the interlocking relationships of man to the arts and of art to society.

28

the precursors
of art nouveau

The creators of art nouveau sought to sever ties with the past — that past which had weighed so heavily upon the work of their immediate predecessors — and to invent art forms which would utilize the new techniques and materials. Its expression was a style of unprecedented originality. But nothing is born in a vacuum. The growth of art nouveau is more or less direct, more or less overt; it was most influenced by the historical period closest to it, whose forces shaped the origins of the style and quickened the inspiration of the artists. Consciously or unconsciously, these artists had absorbed the old formulae and were ready to engender a new repertory of forms, a new figurative vocabulary. This is a natural and constant phenomenon throughout the ages which in no way detracts from that felicitous spontaneity which is one of the distinctive qualities of art nouveau.

These influences did not come only from earlier works of art — architecture, the plastic, graphic, or decorative arts — they derived from the realm of ideas, from spiritualist writings, from poetry. It was far from being a movement whose leader handed down to his disciples the principles of a new aesthetic. Quite the reverse: there were no incendiary articles, no proclamations or manifestoes. Rather, art nouveau was the unstructured encounter of artists of every background, of every discipline, who shared common aspirations and whose central concern was to create outside the terrain surveyed by academicism. They consecrated their work to everyday objects designed to renew the man-made environment, while sustaining an almost sacred respect for the work of art.

The primordial — and sometimes exclusive — source of inspiration was nature. But here we must be careful to make an essential distinction. To the practitioners of this new style, the discovery of nature differed radically from that of the impressionists, even to the point of antithesis; with art nouveau, the goal was not to transcribe the sensations that Nature produces in us, but to analyze them in detail, in the manner of a botanist, then to subject them to decorative metamorphoses which express this synthesis. Among the artists whose works and ideas may have changed the course of this evolution should be mentioned the Pre-Raphaelites, and symbolists, along with the contemporary discovery, by Europe and the United States, of the arts of Japan.

the mania for the medieval

In order to explain the origins of art "nouveau," or "modern," we must go back to those first reactions against the debasement of architecture and to the general decadence of artistic production throughout the nineteenth century. Augustin Pugin (1813–1852) was born in England of a French father who was a draftsman. Pugin's conversion to Catholicism was to shape his architectural career. He had the proselytizing zeal of the convert, and it was with the exaltation of an ardent mysticism that he preached the gospel of a renaissance, based upon the principles of civilizations which had created those monuments worthy of our admiration; that is, medieval civilization. Pugin died at the age of thirty-nine, but his intense creative activity produced many buildings and a ceaseless outpouring of writings in which he propagated and defended his ideas.

The struggle against the architecture of classical antiquity was an uphill battle. By consecrating his career to church architecture and ecclesiastical furnishings, Pugin rediscovered the "functional" logic of the Middle Ages, its norms, its vigorous structures which were the organic source of their ornamentation. His first book was entitled *The True Principles of Pointed or Christian Architecture*. After other works on architecture and a treatise on *Floriated Ornament,* he wrote *Contrasts: or a Parallel between the Noble Edifices of the Middle Ages and the Corresponding Buildings of the Present Day; Shewing the Present Decay of Taste*. There have been few titles as programmatic as this one.

During the greater part of the nineteenth centry, John Ruskin (1819–1900) propounded his ideas in England and throughout the continent. In a language rich with imagery, Ruskin expressed his ideas fulsomely, unafraid of confusion or contradiction. A prominent sherry importer, Ruskin's father was also interested in art and was a frequent host of writers and artists. John Ruskin was educated at Oxford and,

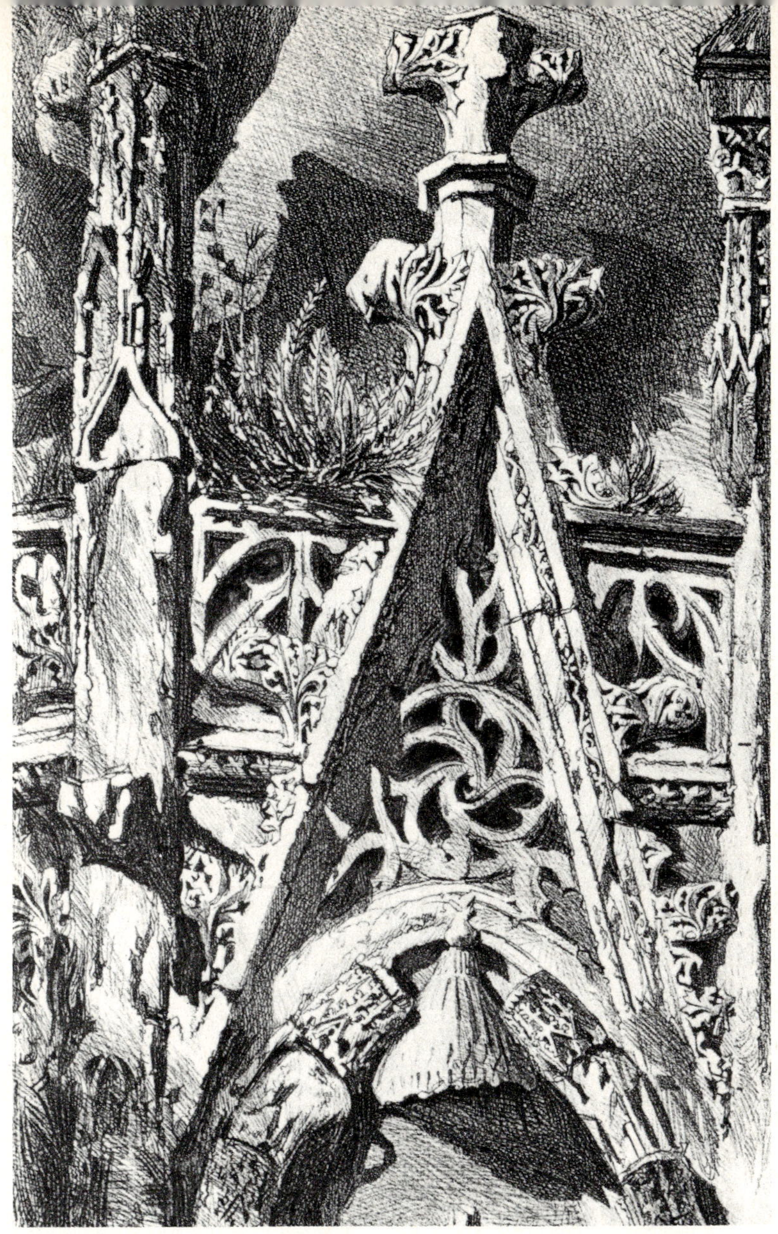

after he had inherited a large fortune, traveled all over Europe, visiting museums and monuments, studying painting, and writing his first book, *Modern Painters,* which brought him instant fame.

Like Pugin, Ruskin wanted his own period to adapt the principles which had governed the architecture and sculpture of the Middle Ages.

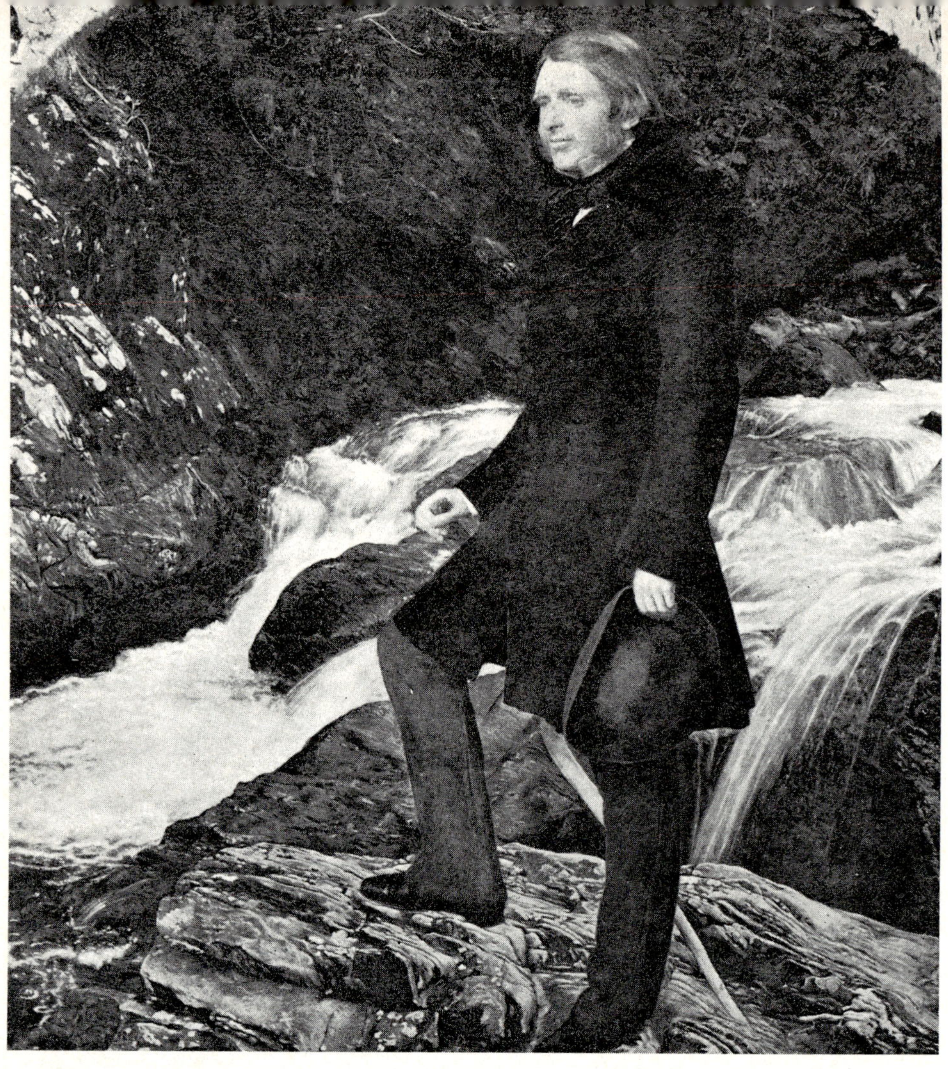

Sir John Everett Millais   Portrait of John Ruskin, 1854

He maintained that the architectonic principles which had made possible the construction of churches and cathedrals of unequaled splendor were intelligent, rational precepts whose vitality in every domain should continue to serve as a guide. His work *The Seven Lamps of Architecture* (1849) is an attempt to demonstrate this belief. "Wherever Church architecture is true and beautiful, it is simply the logical conclusion to the domestic architecture of the same period; as soon as the pointed arch was used in the streets, it began to be used in the churches; when the rounded arch was used in the street, it was used in the church; when the pointed roof was placed above the attic window, it was placed above the belfry tower; when the flat ceiling became the style in the drawing room, it was the style in the nave . . . ." And he recalled that the windows of the houses surrounding the cathedral of Rouen were smaller copies of the architecture in the larger structure. More recent scholarly studies have revealed some of the superficial aspects of Ruskin's eloquent rhetoric. But he had stated the essential truths. For him, it was a brief against the architecture of his time that it had artificially prolonged the life of Renaissance orders. In his own way, he had perceived functionalist principles of construction — but without perceiving at the same time, that it was not possible, without dishonesty, to adapt the techniques and aesthetic of another period. His own period, and the beginning of the twentieth century, could have and should have put into practice the most constructive of his theories, as expressed in a

Sir John Everett Millais   *Ophelia,* 1852

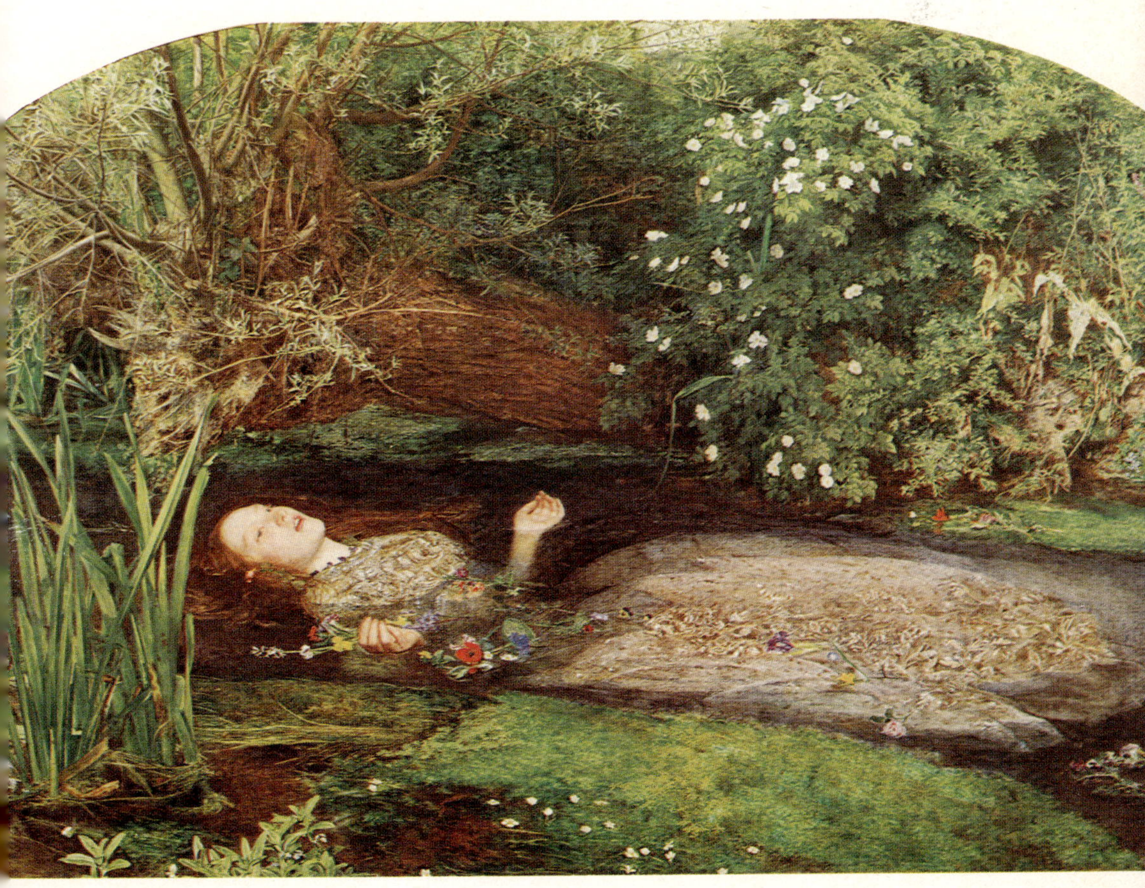

sentence like the following: "The most noble building will be the one where, to the intelligent eye, the vast secrets of its infrastructure are revealed, as animal form is revealed, in such a way that not even the most careless observer can fail to discover them." But in his fascination for the Gothic, Ruskin considered painted or sculptured decoration one and the same as structure — contradicting the entire evolution of the arts.

Ruskin was a sociologist and aesthete at the same time; in this he is a precursor. Indeed, his precepts would lead to the creative revolution of the "new art," art nouveau.

Until this time, reactions to the industrial age took the form of attacks upon the machine, against the ugliness with which it filled everyday life, against a mechanized society where everything was weighed in the light of material gain. It was logical that the first opposition would take place in England, where industrial capitalism had absolute authority over men's lives. Workers were treated, for the most part, like animals, crammed into hivelike structures, in the most sordid conditions. In exalting the artisan class of the Middle Ages, Ruskin was dreaming of a mythical era where architect and craftsman collaborated in a common enterprise whose goal was to edify the soul in its search for supreme beauty. If the aristocracy still lived surrounded by things of the past, the new middle classes had their taste corrupted by the products of commerce.

Ruskin's horror of industrial society led him to an exaggerated exaltation of nature. In a book on the English landscape painters, he has described magnificently nature seen as a benevolent divinity, providing a counterpoise to the infernal machine, to the objects and ornaments it produces, and to the servitude of the industrial worker.

However admirable it was to preach the good and denounce the evil, it would be still more laudable to work toward some remedies. Thus, Ruskin founded a printing press whose operation he entrusted to an intelligent young laborer, inviting artists to collaborate on the books. He created workshops for hand weaving in the heart of the country, and organized small centers of cottage industry. He founded the Guild of St. George, whose program was similar to the cooperatives, and whose principal goal was to allow workers to escape the owners' yoke. Ruskin devoted his entire fortune to these generous projects.

His influence upon English taste was considerable. The Gothic revival stamped modest dwellings and inspired grandiose palaces.

34

Only the Crystal Palace, built by Paxton in London, displayed in its clarity and precision a sense of iron structure and use of glass which announced the future of architecture. But Ruskin referred to this revolutionary structure as a "hothouse for squash."

He has been seduced by the Pre-Raphaelites, for, like him, they worshipped the Middle Ages. Ruskin acquired a disciple in William Morris — who, nonetheless, declined to follow the Master in every aspect of his nostalgia. It was undoubtedly thanks to Ruskin that Morris came to espouse a logical conception of a return to nature, along with the belief in what we would today call a sense of teamwork.

In any event, the crusade which Ruskin led to revive handicrafts — fallen into low estate in England — appears as an essential element in the intellectual movement which resulted in a new future, a new destiny. We should not forget that, before his death in 1900, Ruskin had presided over the beginnings of that movement which he baptized, without realizing it, to be sure, with the ardor of his belief.

william morris vs. industrial society

Not only was William Morris (1834–1896) a writer and poet, he was also a painter and draftsman. But, above all, he was a reformer and organizer. A handsome man of independent means, he could indulge his tastes without worry about the future. If, in his youth, he had been a dilettante, he made up for it later, when, with the fervor of a crusader, he lent his many talents to a lost cause. Morris merely tried to reverse the tide which had placed England at the forefront of industrial powers, assuring her economic supremacy, with all the resulting opulent ugliness. By changing the quality of their environment, Morris hoped to improve the daily life of the workers crammed into slums, whom Taine, in his *Notes sur l'Angleterre,* compared to penitents in "the last circle of Hell."

In his passion for the Middle Ages, inherited from Ruskin, Morris sought to revitalize industrial society by adopting the precepts and mores of an earlier era. He envisioned a golden age to come when artists would replace industrialists, bringing joy and efficiency to the act of labor.

Large cities, with their "slaves and drugged despots," filled him with revulsion. He left London to live in the country. Morris believed that the machine and mass production were calamities for the modern world, on an aesthetic as well as a social level. He abandoned his early studies of architecture for painting, overcome with enthusiasm for the first pictures of Burne-Jones, his Oxford contemporary. The latter had returned from a trip to Italy with a boundless admiration for Botticelli, an admiration which was to leave an indelible mark upon his work.

Dante Gabriel Rossetti, the artist-poet, founded, with a group of friends, the Pre-Raphaelite Brotherhood in 1848. They all shared a distaste for the realism of Raphael and the "carnal character he gave the Saviour." Whether Protestant or Catholic, the Pre-Raphaelites dedicated themselves to the same mission, the renewal of primitive art; this art alone could preach the truth to their contemporaries, degraded by modern civilization.

Internecine strife destroyed the Brotherhood four years later. But

WILLIAM MORRIS   The William Morris Room, London

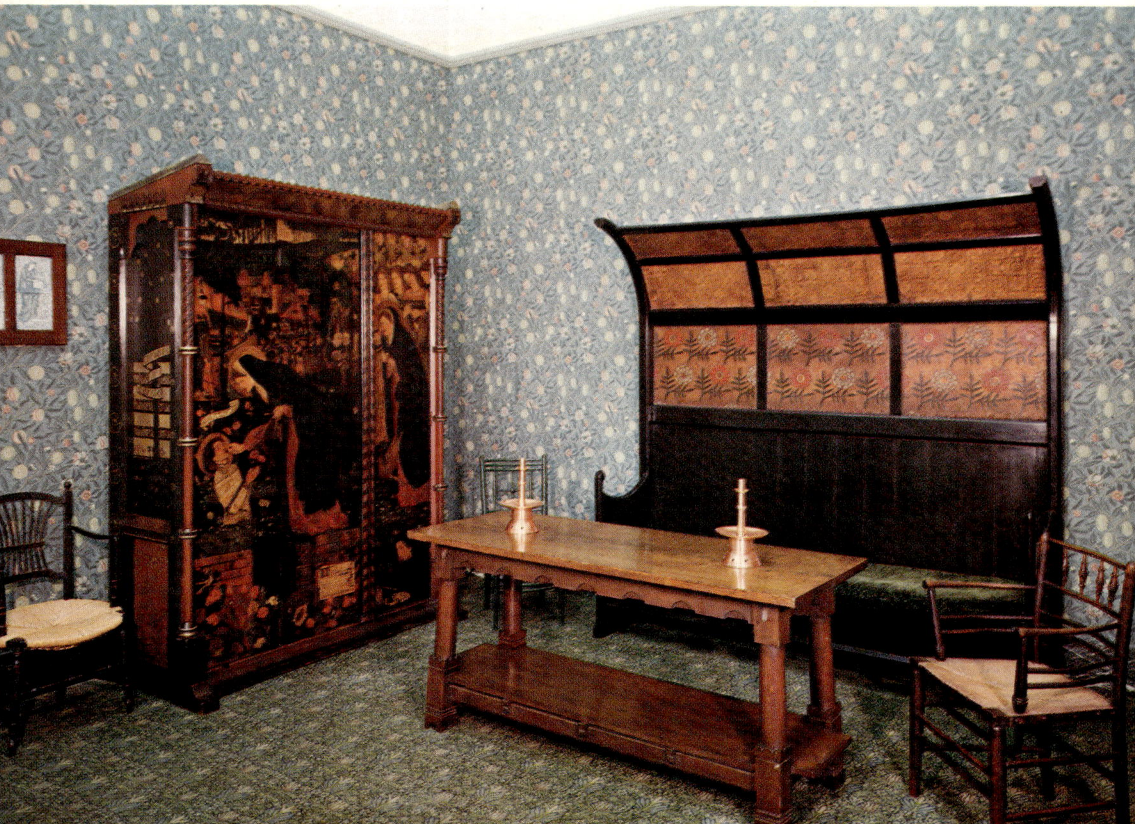

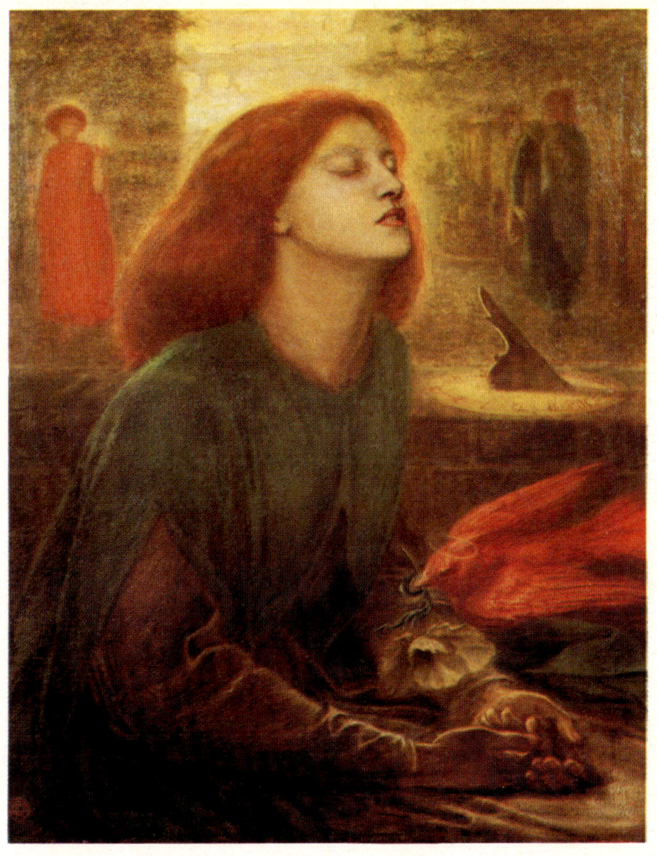

DANTE GABRIEL ROSSETTI *Beata Beatrix*, 1863

its spirit remained. Burne-Jones, the faithful disciple for Morris and Rossetti, was to be one of its last representatives. Filled with religious fervor, the Pre-Raphaelites exalted the works of God in nature and the spirit of heroism and saintliness in men. But the lofty sentiments and nobility of soul were expressed with singular pictorial poverty. These artists tried so hard to render in all its exactitude every detail and the color in nature that the whole managed to look wrong. In trying to depict human spirituality, they succeeded only in creating inexpressive if not fatuous-looking characters. Nonetheless, in an atmosphere enamored of art and avid for novelty, the success of this school of painting kept growing.

Morris was an altogether different artist. His activities and goals were clearly defined, and he lived according to his theories. Fascinated

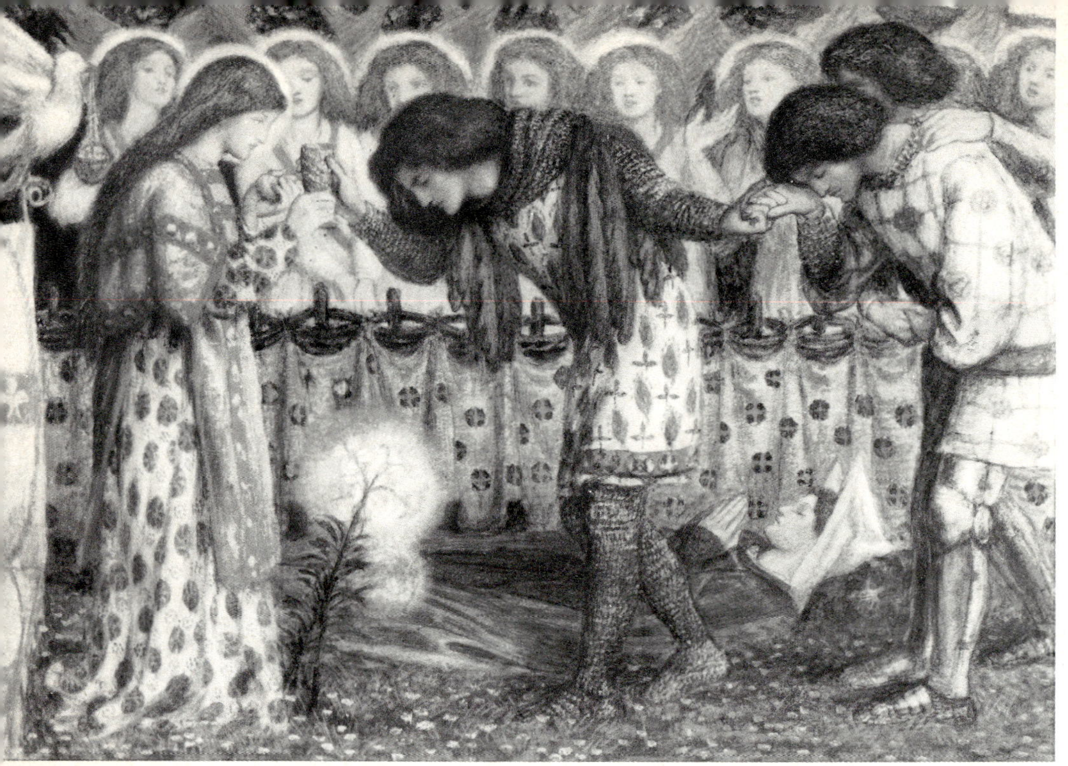

by the Isolde legend, Morris married the model who incarnated, for him, the legendary Queen. But, appearances notwithstanding, he was far from being a frivolous romantic or jack-of-all-trades. His marriage was the decisive factor in a committed and purposeful sense of direction. With the collaboration of his friend Philip Webb, he designed a house on the outskirts of London, the Red House, using local red brick, in which each element is the response to an original concept in planning. This house is one of the first examples of organic architecture; the plan is based upon the logical disposition of rooms, which in turn determines the structure of the different facades. All materials — exterior as well as interior — were handmade. Painter friends decorated the walls while Morris himself assumed the task of designing the furniture and other objects.

This experiment must be considered the first direct step toward art nouveau. And it would shortly be followed by another step, still more important, which would bring the public into contact with utilitarian objects which were also works of art. In 1861, Morris opened a shop in London where, for the first time in history, everything needed in the furnishing of a house could be purchased. Its stock consisted of fur-

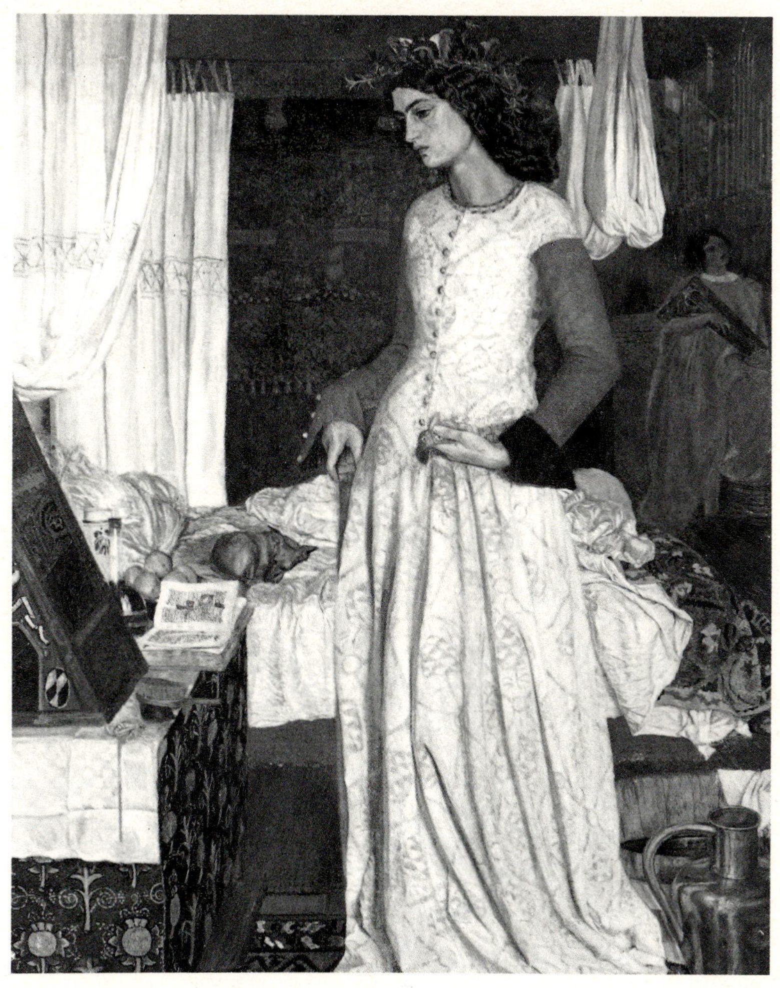

WILLIAM MORRIS   *Queen Guinevere, 1864*

niture, ceramics, decorative glass, upholstery fabric, and works of art.
The nucleus of Morris's close friends became associates in this venture:
Dante Gabriel Rossetti; Burne-Jones, who had assumed the role of
Master to the young "modern" artists (and who had been steered by
Morris toward decorative art with his most impassioned rhetoric); and
still other artists, who, inspired by communal spirit, worked with great
enthusiasm. The activity of this small group is significant, not only for
the novelty of their style, but, above all, because it was the fruit of
cooperation among different artists who agreed to submit to the dis-

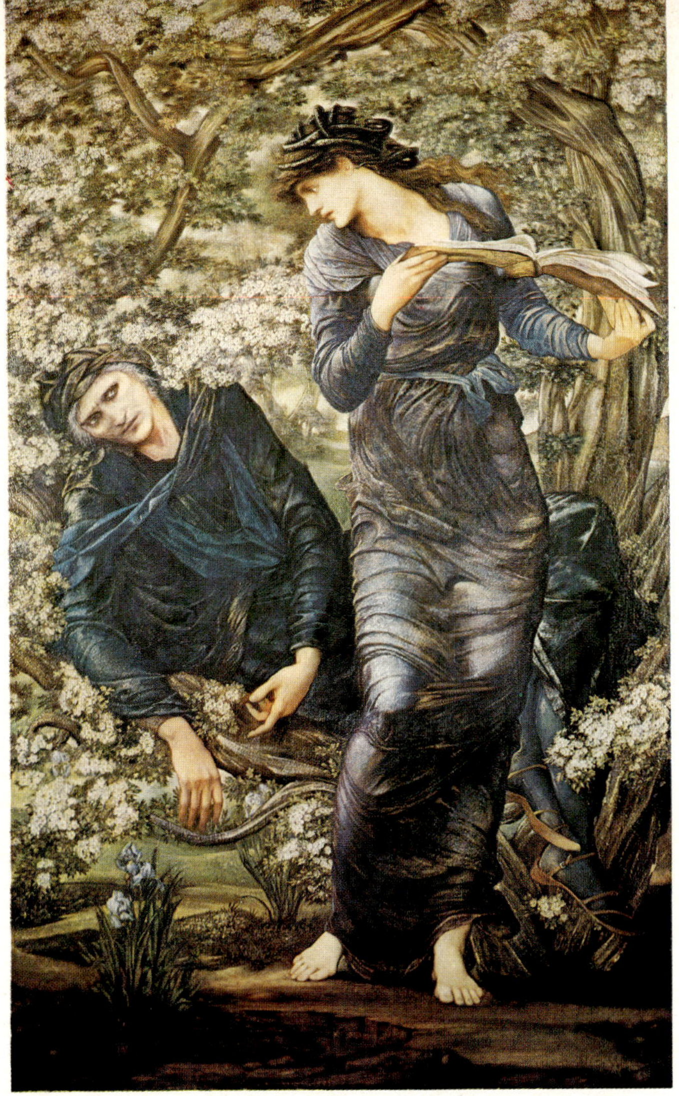

EDWARD BURNE-JONES   *Merlin and Vivien, 1870–1874*

cipline required in fusing the beautiful with the useful. The distinction between fine and decorative arts had been abolished.

The profits from this enterprise were modest. But Morris achieved the results he sought: he had inaugurated the dignity of handicrafts; he had obtained the acknowledgement that the artist could, without debasing himself, contribute to the surroundings of everyday life. On the financial level, which had certainly to be taken into account, Morris quickly perceived that the greatest success of his shop were the fabrics, the "chintz" whose design of leaves and flowers cast a long-lasting and powerful spell over the English. They liked seeing in their cottages the

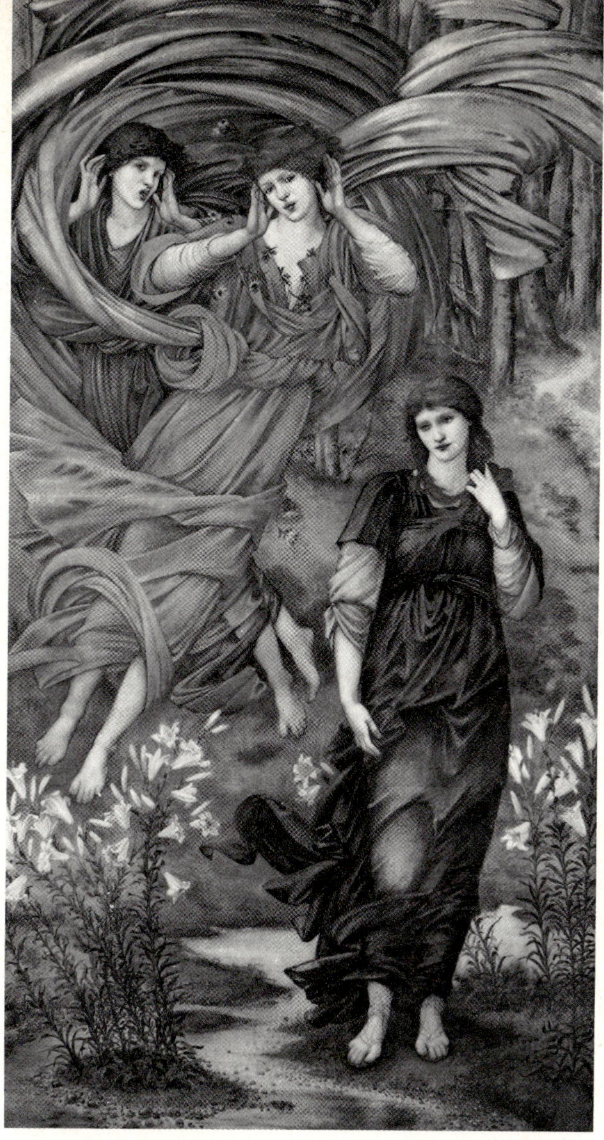

Edward Burne-Jones   *Sponsa di Libano,* 1891

stylized but recognizable motifs of the same flowers they tended so lovingly in the garden. A market was created in England for these textiles, while throughout Europe the English Garden enjoyed its greatest vogue.

Morris then decided to create workshops for hand-loomed textiles and wallpaper, which he established in the countryside of the Thames Valley, thus satisfying both his desire to supervise the proper operation of the project and his horror of living in the city.

Although somewhat vague, the principles that Morris preached constantly are set forth in one of his papers: *The Decorative Arts: Their Relation to Modern Life and Progress*. Albeit fanatic in their fidelity to Medievalism, these precepts nonetheless acknowledged that an art of imitation is a dead art. Therefore, it was the *spirit* of the Gothic that had to be assimilated, while avoiding pastiche — its teachings retained and transposed in accord with the imperatives of contemporary life. Early monuments should be understood and evaluated, while avoiding any "masquerade in the hand-me-down finery of other periods." With pen and spoken word, Morris preached his gospel aggressively, never hesitating to declare that bonfires should be made of "everything owned by the rich."

PHILIP WEBB   The Red House, 1859

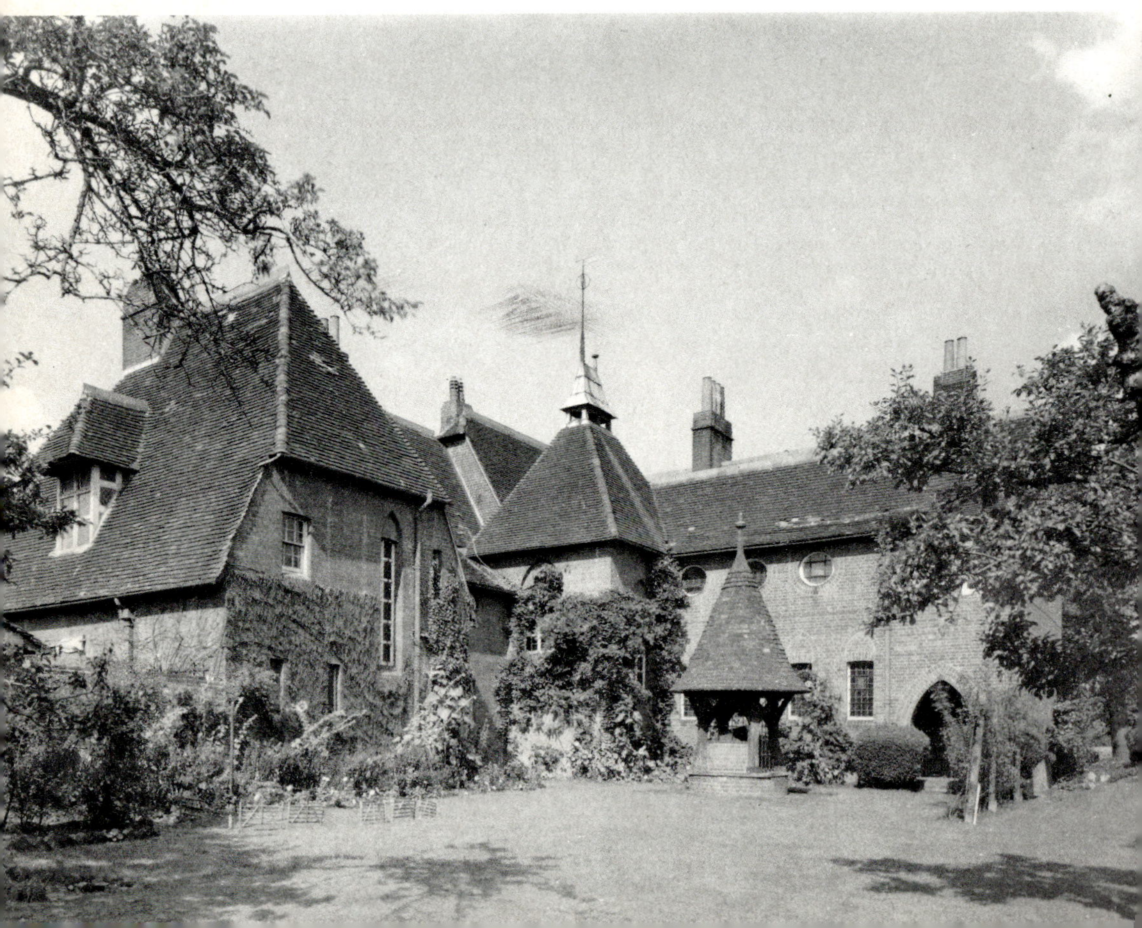

arts and crafts

Medieval architects worked in close collaboration with painters, sculptors, fresco artists, and glassmakers. Thus, it was in complete union with the artists and architects of his own time that the contemporary craftsman should produce useful objects. Together they had to create an architecture and objects adapted to daily life, inventing for these new objects, new forms. Like the artisans of ages past, they would work for love. This was the meaning that Morris gave to art, as he defines it, when he wrote: "Art is the result of man's joy in his achievement." He thus found himself at opposite poles from Pugin, who wanted to understand the architecture of the past in order to imitate it, the result being the Gothic revival. And Morris, more than Ruskin, understood the architectonic principles of Medieval architecture, their logic and decorative determinants.

At the roots of this new aesthetic, there were, as we have already seen, larger social concerns. These may seem naive to us today, and, indeed, they made little impact then. At the same time that Morris started his workshop for hand-printed textiles (Kelmscott Printing Press — 1891) he was the founder of a Socialist League, an indication of his desire to convert the working class to his renewal of the arts: classes for the workingman would liberate him from the slavery of the factory. He would be educated to want surroundings whose honesty and purity would bring him happiness. Unfortunately, experience would prove that there was an inherent — and inescapable — contradiction in this idea. These ideological principles, also espoused by Gallé and the Belgian architects, were denied by reality: the handmade was much more expensive than the mass-produced, making the former affordable to only the well-off middle class. Moreover, the general public was unenthusiastic about objects which were new but looked old-fashioned.

Still sustained by his beliefs, his intellectual energy undiminished, Morris founded the Arts and Crafts Exhibition Society in 1886, which was to have a profound influence upon decorative art, on the continent as well as in England. The Society heralded twentieth-century principles of functionalism: form following function, decoration determined by structure. . . . Morris, to be sure, used an altogether different vocabulary, and his rigid rejection of the machine obviously limited the dissemination of his designs.

Morris had carefully followed the theories expounded by Owen

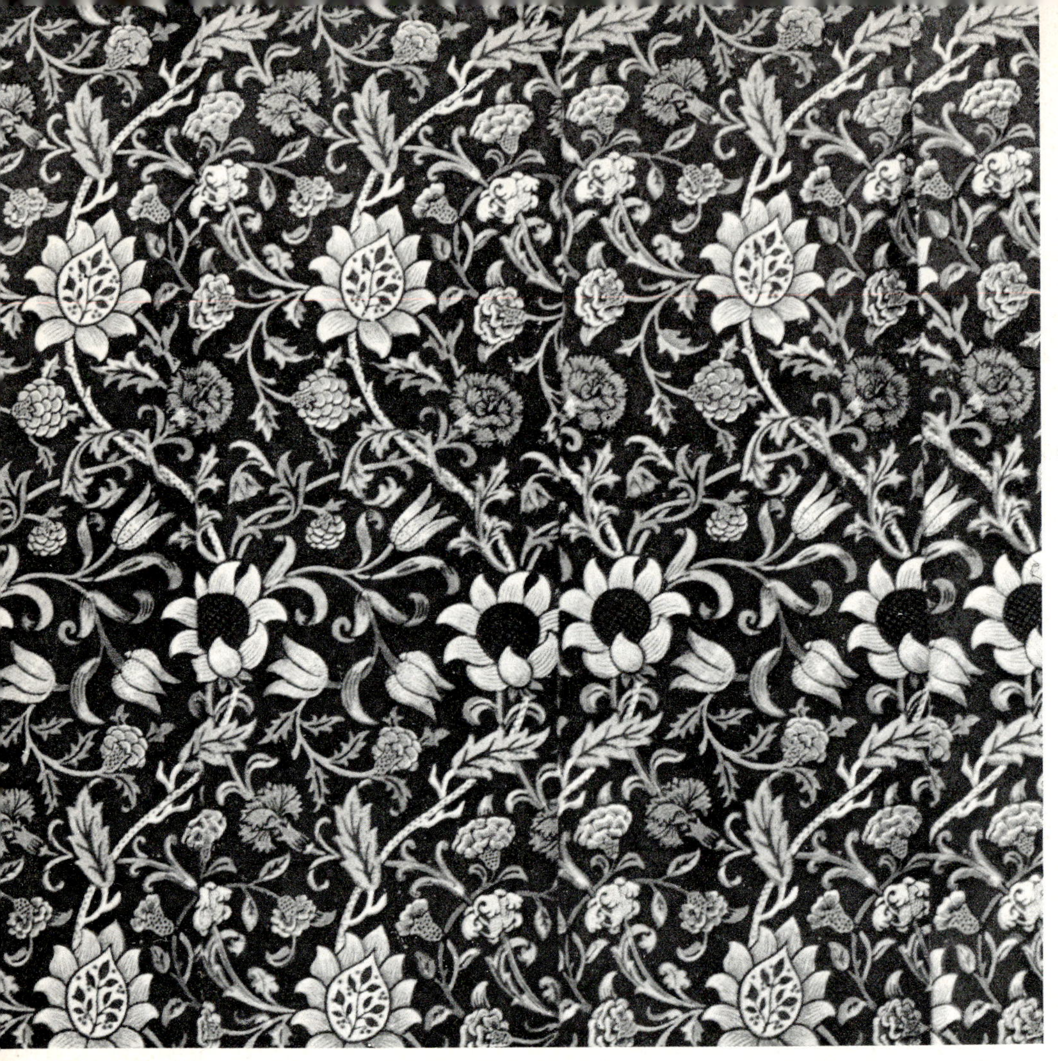

WILLIAM MORRIS   Chintz with "Evenlode" pattern, 1900

Jones in his treatise *The Grammar of Ornament*. From this work, he adapted a basic tenet: "Ornament should be based upon geometric construction." And since nature was devoid of straight lines, it was obvious that ornament of organic inspiration must be conveyed through a geometry of curved lines. Morris and his painter-disciples thus directed all their efforts to transposing plant forms in such a way as to produce lines of pure ornament. They did not translate the appearance of a stem, leaf, or flower, but its "essence," structure, or "geometry," composed of asymmetry, and they organized these elements into decorative compositions of a very special style. It was these principles

44

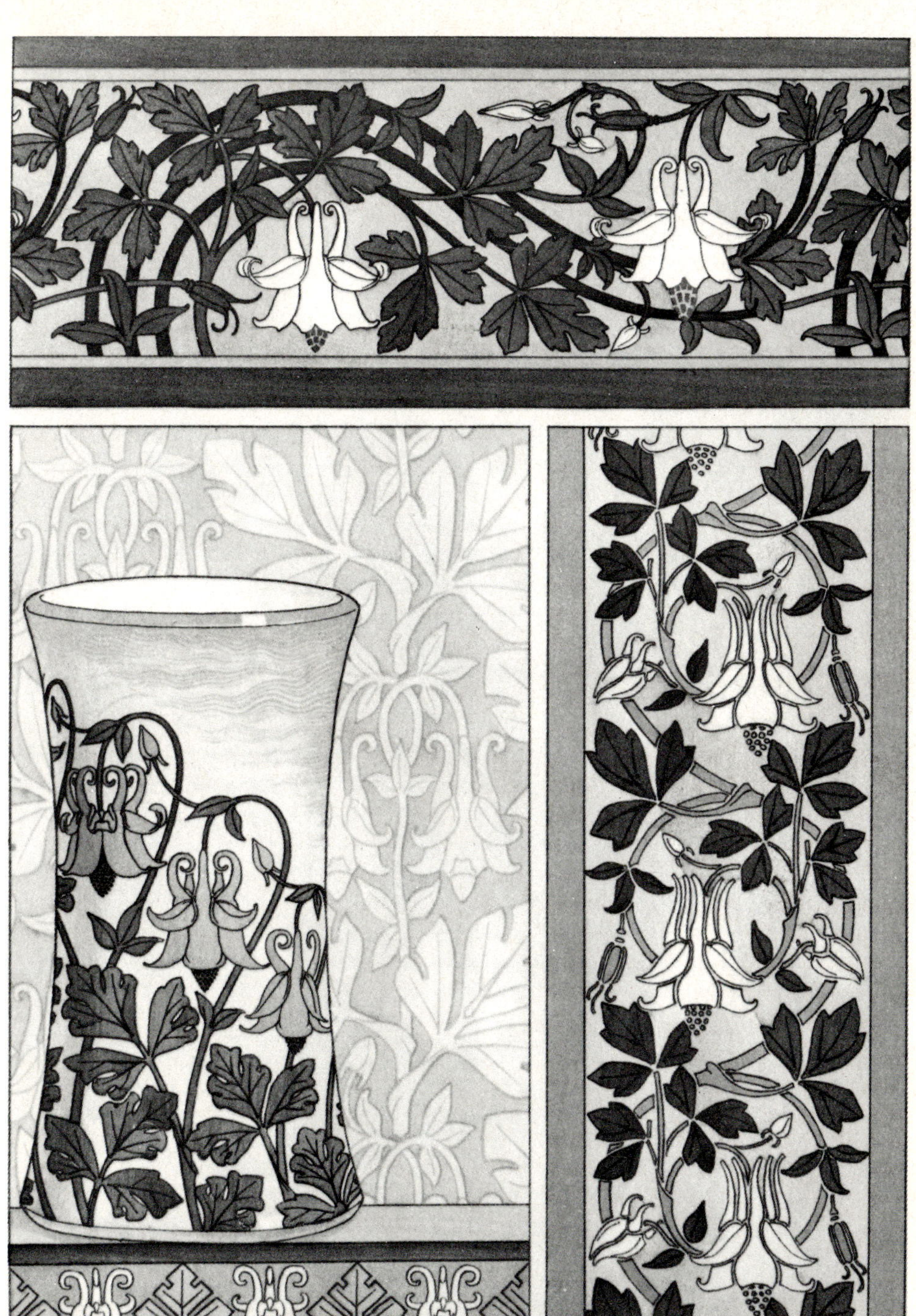

EUGÈNE GRASSET   Illustration from *La plante et ses applications ornementales*, 1896

which were adumbrated by Eugène Grasset in his book *La Plante et ses applications ornementales* (1896) in a much narrower context, closer to the structure which appears in a botanical cross section. This book was to be the French grammar of art nouveau, as it demonstrated how the subject could be reduced to simple schema. We need only compare the decorative drawings of Owen Jones and Morris to drawings by Mackmurdo, Van de Velde, and Modern Style around 1900 to trace the rapid evolution toward geometric stylization.

the reaction against traditional architecture

A movement of architectural reaction gained in strength after Morris's death. His collaborator and faithful disciple Walter Crane (1845–1915) directed the activities of the Society with great inventiveness. The movement had been responsible for a certain architectural vogue known as "the domestic revival," whose principle protagonists were the architect Philip Webb, Morris's boyhood friend, and Richard Norman Shaw. Their houses, primarily country cottages, were typically English: of simple appearance, they suggested virtuous contentment; while their amenities gave them a certain modern note, they remained essentially Jacobean and Tudor re-creations. The owners found intellectual serenity in coming home to a historical setting, while enjoying, at the same time, the benefits of progress. It was in this way that architects became decorators, presiding, for example, over the birth of the rocking chair, whose curvilinear form was so well suited to Modern Style. There were many feeble attempts at innovation, but these tended to resolve themselves into adaptations, as in the case of the oriel windows, characteristic of old English houses.

With all their experimentation, however, the forerunners of art nouveau ignored, disdained, or detested iron construction. Their views notwithstanding, the Crystal Palace (1851) was to become the great example for engineers and architects of metal construction in the nineteenth century. At approximately the same time, Labrouste, in Paris, built the main reading room of the Bibliothèque Sainte-Geneviève, followed, in 1858, by the elegant cupolas of the Bibliothèque Nationale. Shortly thereafter, Hittorff designed the shed of the Gare du Nord,

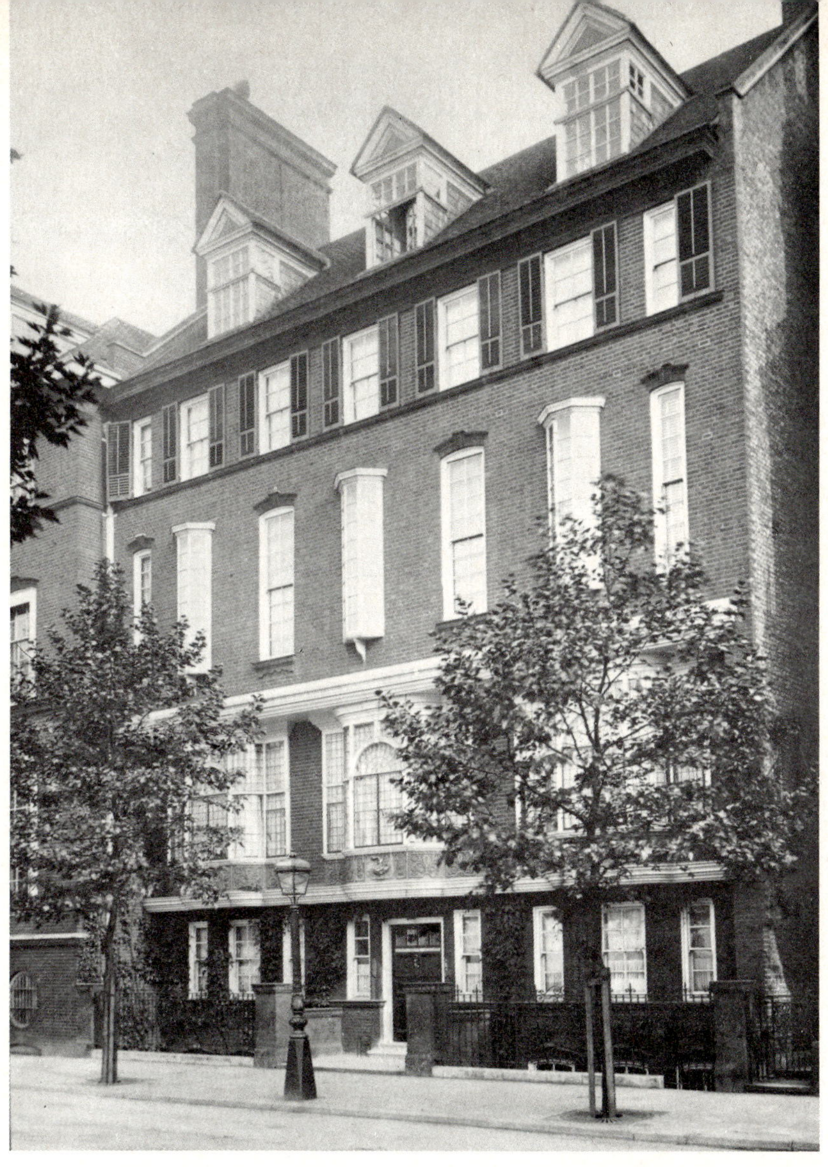

RICHARD NORMAN SHAW   The Old Swan House, 1876

which would serve as a model for so many other stations. The Brooklyn Bridge was begun in 1870. And in 1889, the Eiffel Tower was the tallest structure in the world, while the Hall of Machines (unhappily destroyed) bore witness to the potential of iron in the building of a masterpiece of design.

In architecture, Great Britain remained, for a long while, tied to tradition, perhaps because it was traditionalist at heart. It should be observed, nonetheless, that buildings by Webb and Shaw reveal the

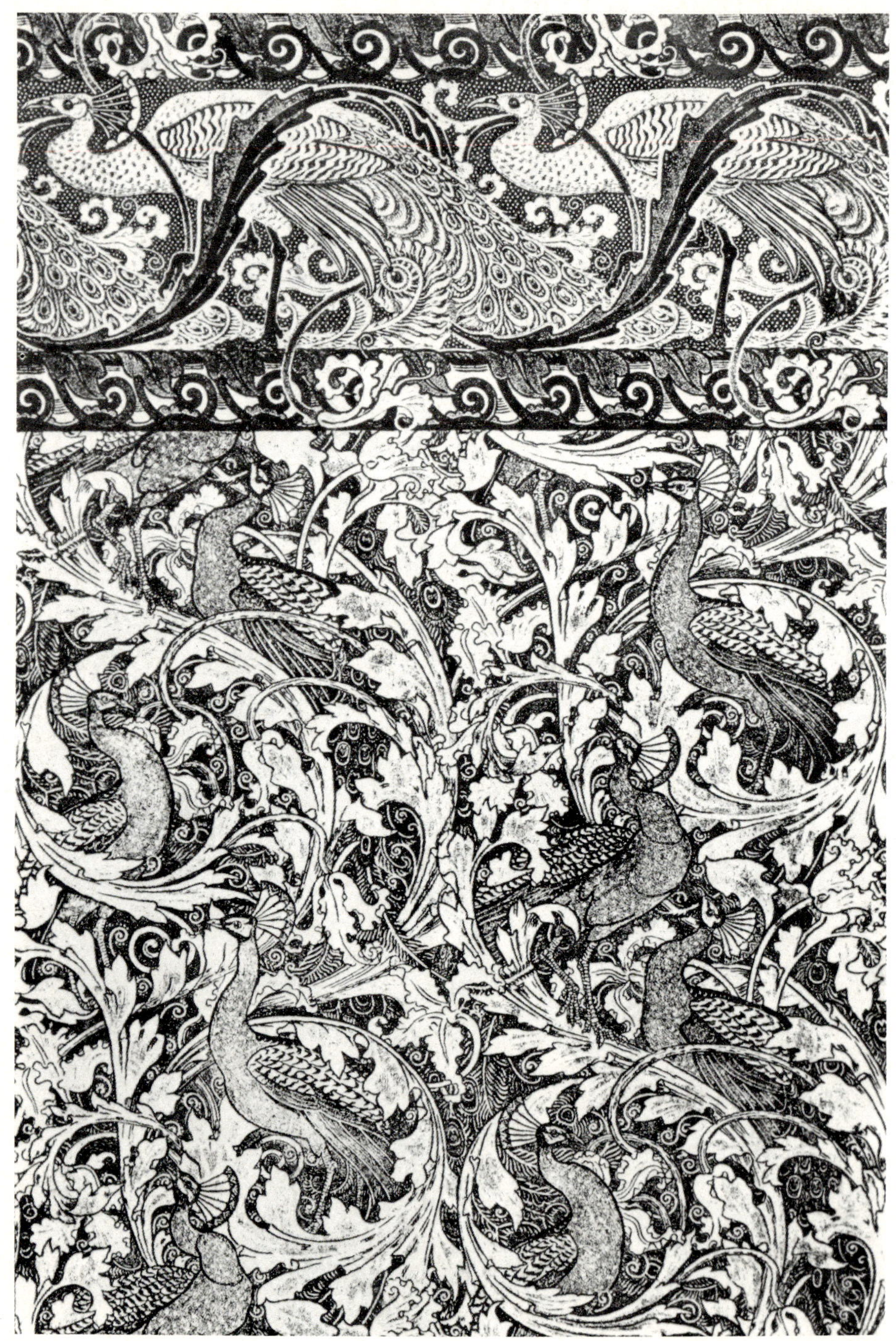

WALTER CRANE   Wallpaper design "The Peacock Garden," 1880

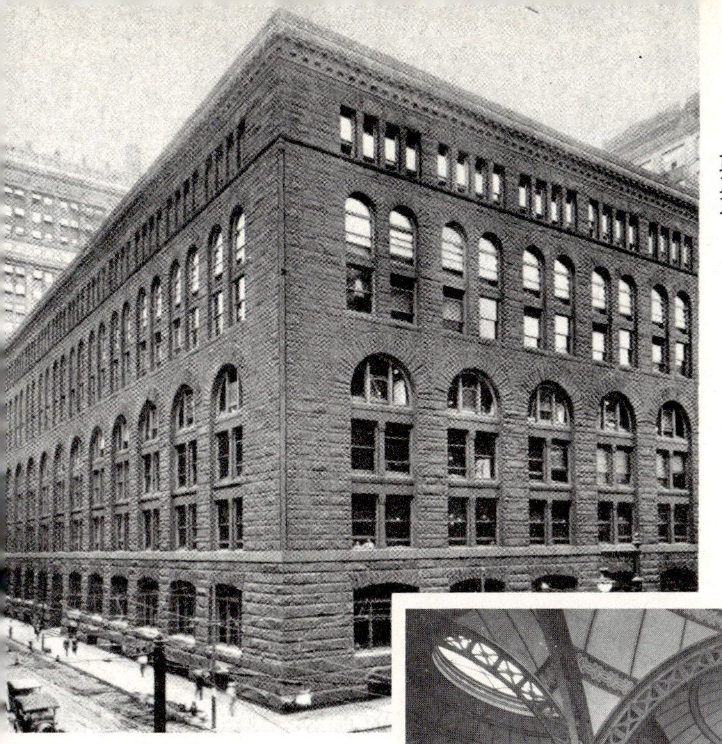

Henry Hobson Richardson Exterior of Marshall Field Department Store, 1885–1887

Henri Labrouste   Domes of the Main Reading Room of the Bibliothèque Nationale, 1858

desire to break with the solemnity of Victorian architecture. Their plans tend to avoid the classic rectangle, while the facades are enlivened with expensive elements which add, despite references to past styles, something new and harmonious. In a similar direction, and to more compelling and inventive effect, Henry Hobson Richardson (1838– 1886) in the United States developed the idea of fusing the old and the new, by combining fieldstone, pebbles, and brick in the building of country houses which were Romanesque in style but asymmetrical in plan. At the same time, Richardson designed in Chicago the first skyscraper (if a building of only twelve stories can be so designated), once again inspired by Romanesque architecture.

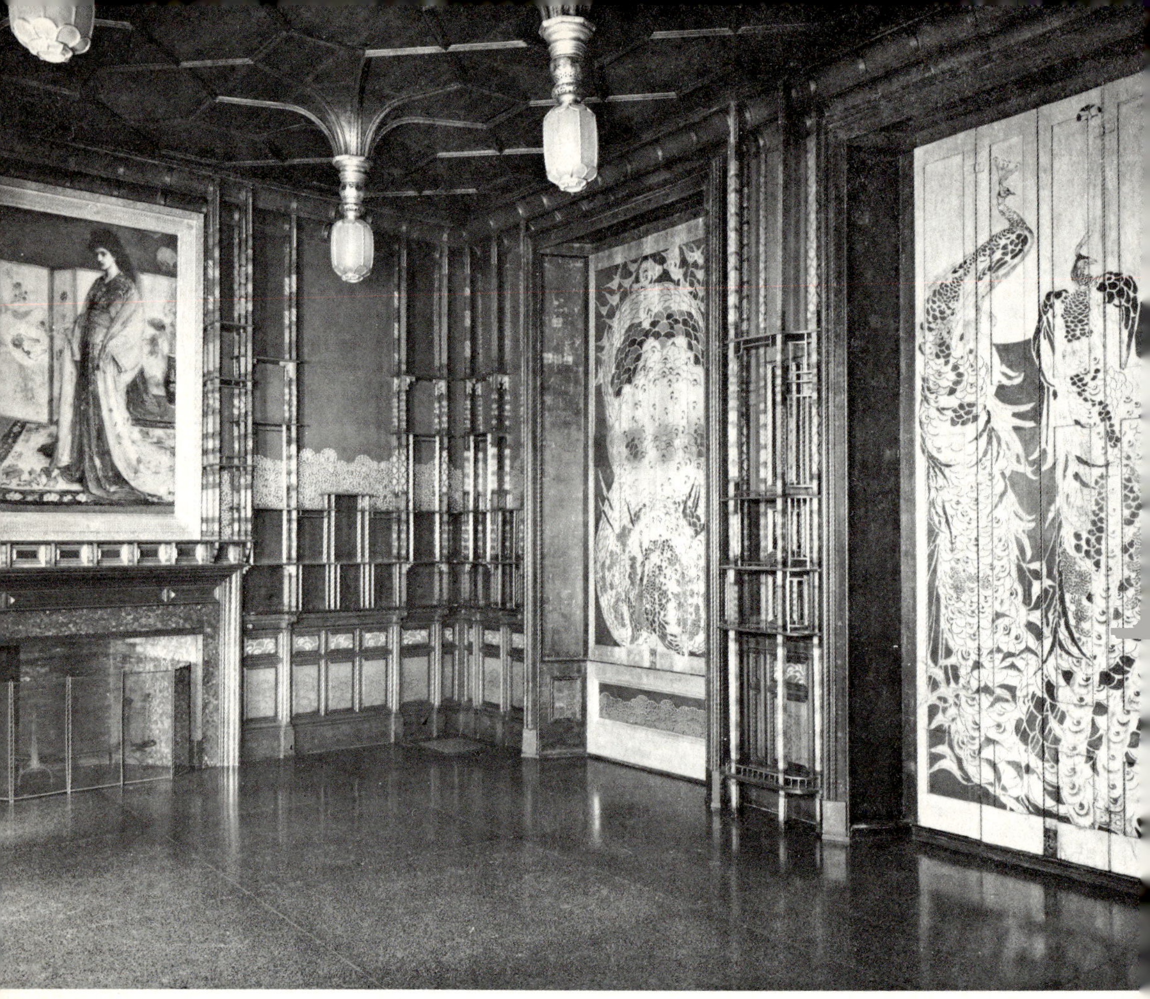

Perhaps these innovators' hostility to the principle of the machine accounts for their contempt toward the heroic age of iron architecture; in any case, however, they concentrated their efforts on domestic architecture, on private houses where iron was used only on the inside; others would design the vast industrial projects whose beauty was a function of the perfect execution of a technical program.

In another realm, there were many signs pointing to the development of an art nouveau. Richard Redgrave, in England, made glass vases from 1847 whose forms remained Victorian, while their decoration of flowers or vines was transformed into naturalistic stylization which escaped the stylistic conventions of the period. The question remains whether Redgrave had seen any Japanese prints. Toward 1870, manufacturers of printed textiles were looking for new ideas; their

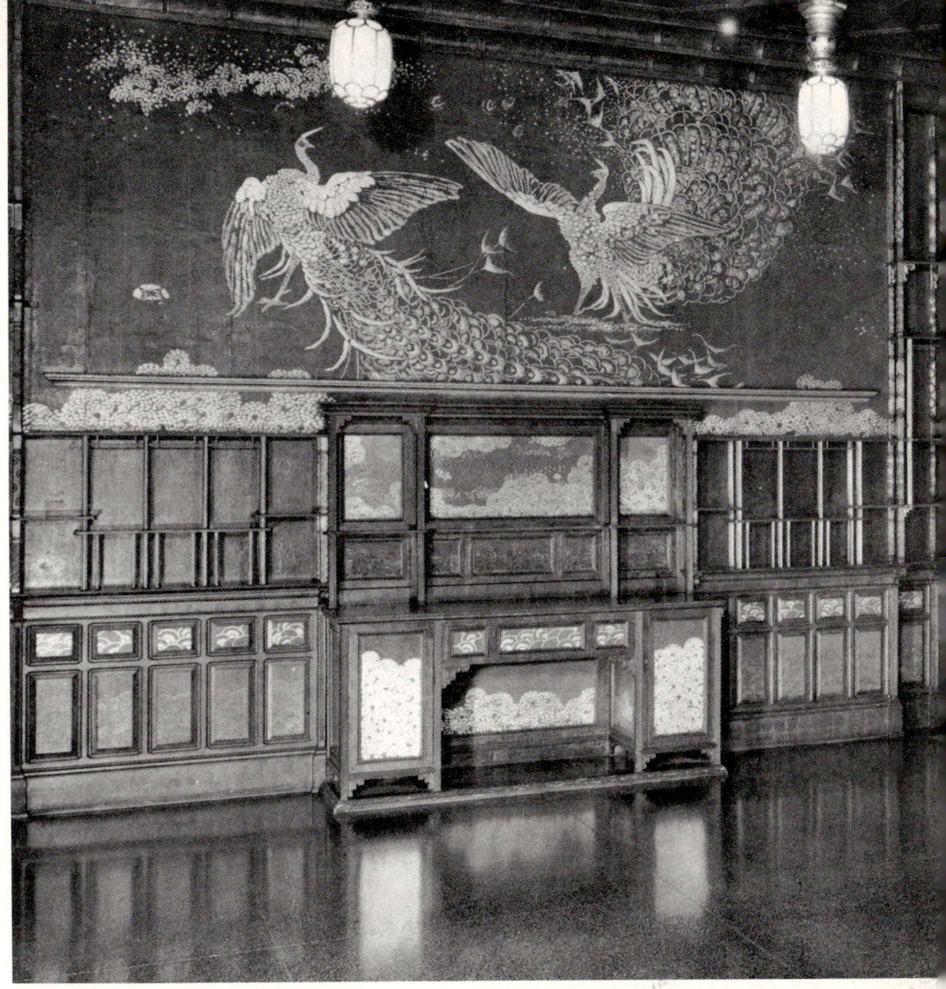

designs began to borrow from the elegance of floral motifs whose linear traceries may be considered anticipations of art nouveau.

The artist who seems to have gone the farthest soonest in the direction of art nouveau is unquestionably Felix Bracquemond (1833–1914), an engraver, decorator, and ceramist who worked for Haviland of Limoges. When he discovered the Japanese woodcut, he evolved a stylized design which was directly inspired by the oriental hallmarks of fidelity to nature and taste for linear asymmetry. The table service that he made in 1867 for the ceramist Eugène Rousseau bears an interpretation of plant and animal forms which anticipates objects made a quarter century later.

The case of Whistler (1834–1903) is more complex. He was a dilettante, a dandy with a brilliant mind and somewhat facile talent, who believed in art for art's sake, while giving evidence in his own work of total eclecticism. This American came to live in Paris when he was twenty-three, then moved to London, finally commuting between the two cities. He was a friend of those masters who transformed style in both literature and the plastic arts: Baudelaire, who translated one of his texts (*Ten O'Clock*), Oscar Wilde, Manet, and Mallarmé.

As a painter, Whistler deeply admired Rossetti, although his own work owes more to the impressionists and to Japanese art.

Whistler's strange mural panels, painted in 1876 for Leyland House in London, were considered an astonishing milestone in decoration (we will be seeing many peacocks in art nouveau). The iridescent plumage of the peacock's tail, painted gold and blue, spread to full width, and covering the entire height of the wall is an almost surrealistic experience. Everything in these wall paintings exhibits sumptuousness of decorative effect and a disdain for naturalism — the influence of Japan, perhaps. But greater evidence points to Persian art, then enjoying a great vogue in England, as more influential in this work than the purity of Japanese calligraphy. Whistler's receptive intelligence was susceptible to everything that was new.

the japanese influence

Beyond the historical influences we have already discussed, there was another, made more remote by geographical distance. The art of Japan would be of major importance to art nouveau. The interest elicited by colored woodcuts, exported after the opening of Japan to the West, was a discovery and a revelation. If Bracquemond was the first to realize the treasure trove of ideas offered by these artists, until now unknown to their Western counterparts, writers interested in art, like Baudelaire and the Goncourts, helped make the Japanese known and admired. Harunobu, Utamaro, Hiroshige all revealed a world of exceptional imagery which would delight Europeans in search of new modes of expression: the fervent love of nature — whether a mountain or blade of grass — rendered in all its truth, subtly arranged but never deformed, the flat colors, with outlines as decorative as they are descriptive, the asymmetrical compositions, the power of suggestion joined to unity of style — all this enchanted Western eyes.

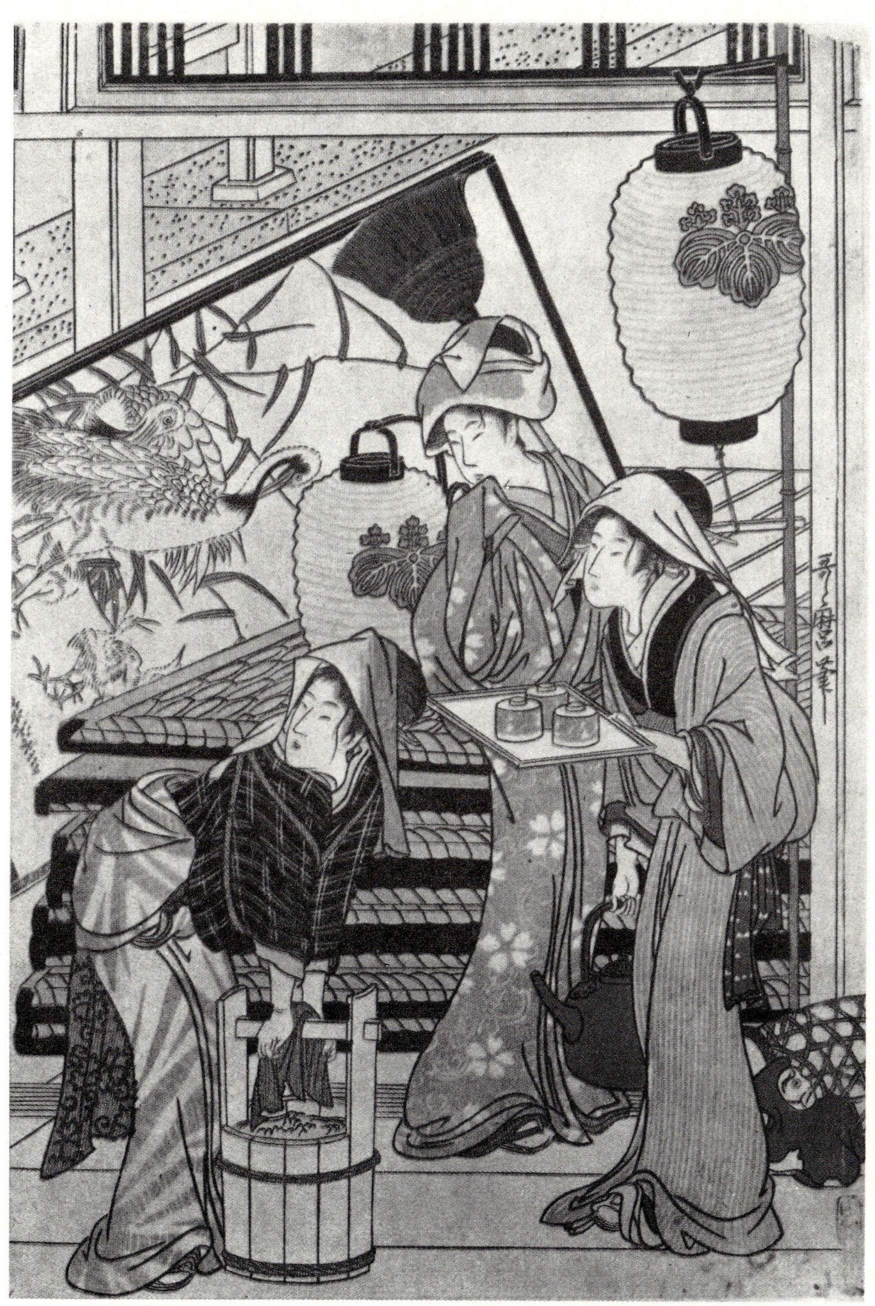

Kitagawa Utamaro *Servants Busy Cleaning*, ca. 1800

These prints were part of a relatively recent form of Japanese folk art. Although executed with care and skill, they were not descendants of the great Japanese art of earlier centuries: these works were nonetheless greeted with wonder, on their arrival in Europe. Japanese ceramics, too, became much sought-after objects, serving as decorative example if not model. Japanese potters produced no work comparable to the great periods of Chinese porcelain. But these objects were still of a quality superior to the work of contemporary European manufacture; they especially appealed to the latent desire of artists involved in the search for a new aesthetic, by whom they were welcomed, even before capturing the public, as an invaluable repertory of form and decorative motif.

The Japanese exhibit at the World's Fair of 1867 was a revelation:

ARTHUR LASENBY LIBERTY   Wallpaper, 1888

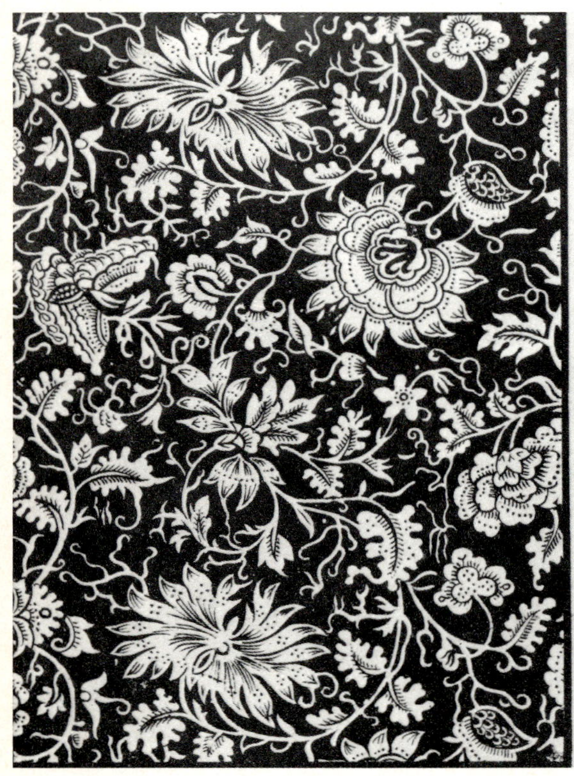
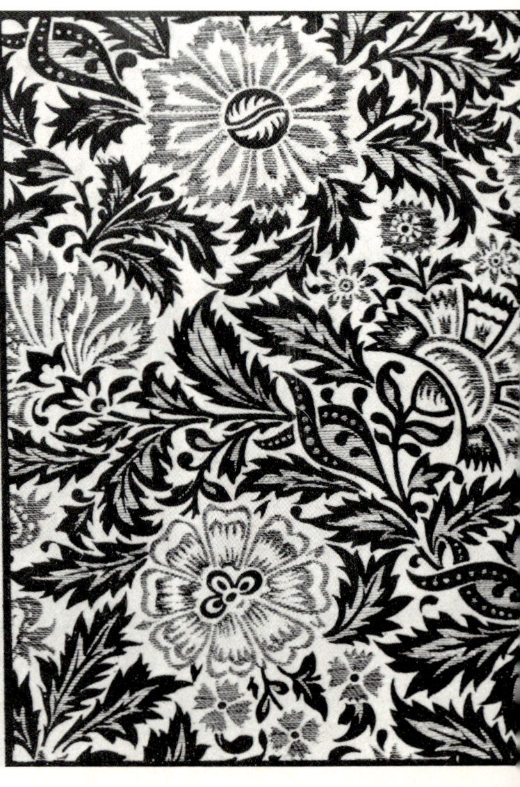

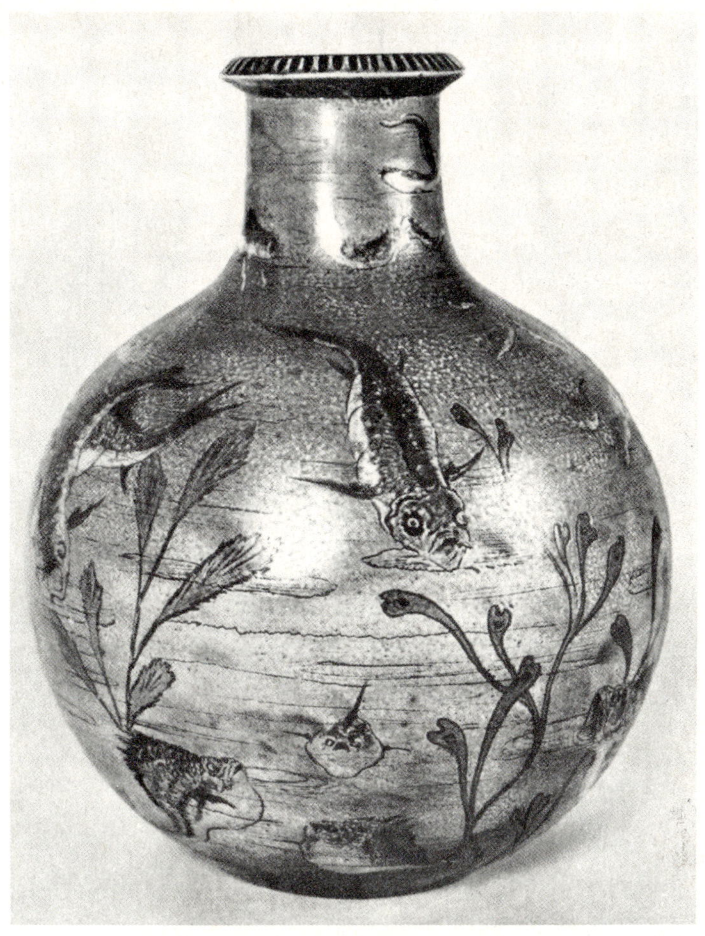

EDWIN MARTIN   Earthenware vase, 1897

William Morris, for example, received from it a sort of creative transfusion, while his disciple Arthur Lasenby Liberty was so inspired that he established a shop dedicated to the products of the Far East and its Western interpretations. Liberty's would shortly open a branch in Paris; the silky printed cotton which soon became — and remained — world famous was woven in Lyons. Its international renown became so phenomenal that the Italians called Liberty Style everything which suggested art nouveau. In 1883, the Union Centrale des Arts Décoratifs organized the first Salon of Japanese Art. In 1889, the artists of the Salon des XX in Brussels set aside a section for Japanese art. In the

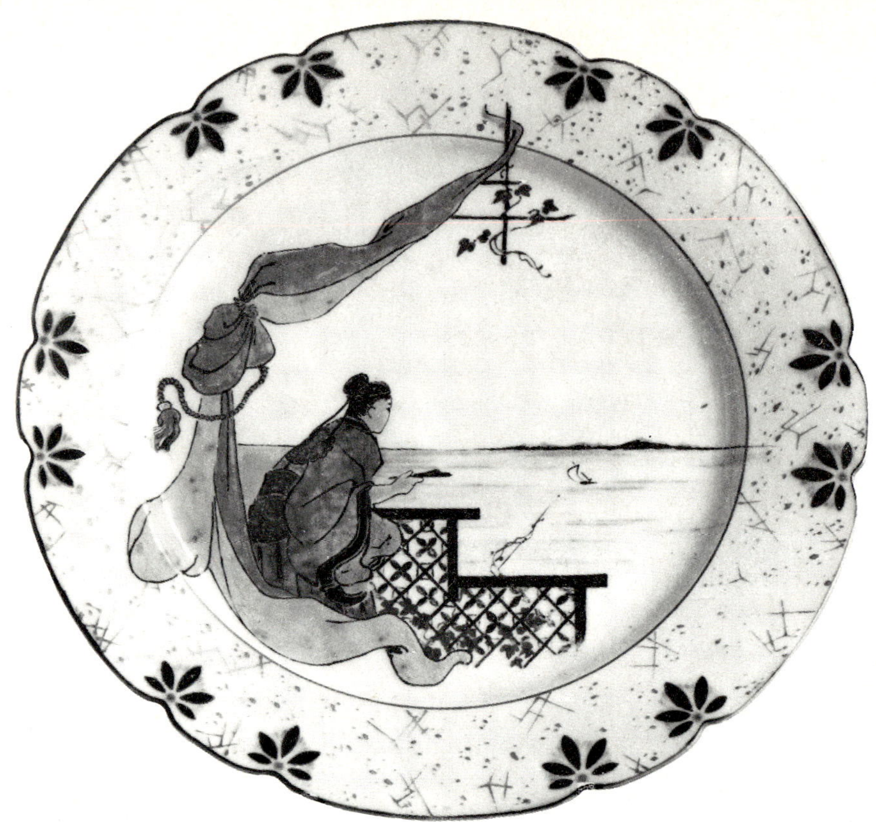
Albert-Louis Dammouse   Plate, 1880

following year, an exhibit of Hokusai art created a sensation in London. Reproductions and books devoted to prints and ceramics distributed Japanese art throughout Europe.

The United States found itself in the forefront of this movement, thanks to Louis Comfort Tiffany, who collected Japanese art, and who was inspired by his collection in the design of his own ceramics and glassware. Tiffany and Company became the most important firm in the world dealing in Near and Far Eastern objects. E. C. Moore, the artistic director of Tiffany, gathered together for the Paris Fair of 1878 a collection whose unusual character aroused a chorus of admiration. His own designs, inspired by Japanese objects, were the basis for an interest in curios which proved long-lasting.

When Samuel Bing, an expert in oriental art, transformed his Paris shop into a gallery of modern objects under a shop sign proclaiming "Art Nouveau" (1896), he sold bronzes, ceramics, jewelry, upholstery fabric, and art glass by Tiffany, whom he represented in Paris, while the former was his dealer in New York. In his gallery, Bing always mixed, in displays, Japanese and contemporary Western objects. In 1897, he exhibited the Goncourt collection. Bing was deeply involved in the artistic activity of the day; he commissioned, for example, a Tiffany glass window, based upon the Bonnard painting *Maternité*. The latter was so captivated by the things he saw in Bing's gallery that his friends nicknamed him the "Japanese Nabi." Like Gallé, who quite independently had become inspired by Japanese art, Tiffany used glass to obtain altogether unexpected — if less overtly oriental — effects.

Samuel Bing   Cover for monthly periodical *The Japanese Artist*, 1896

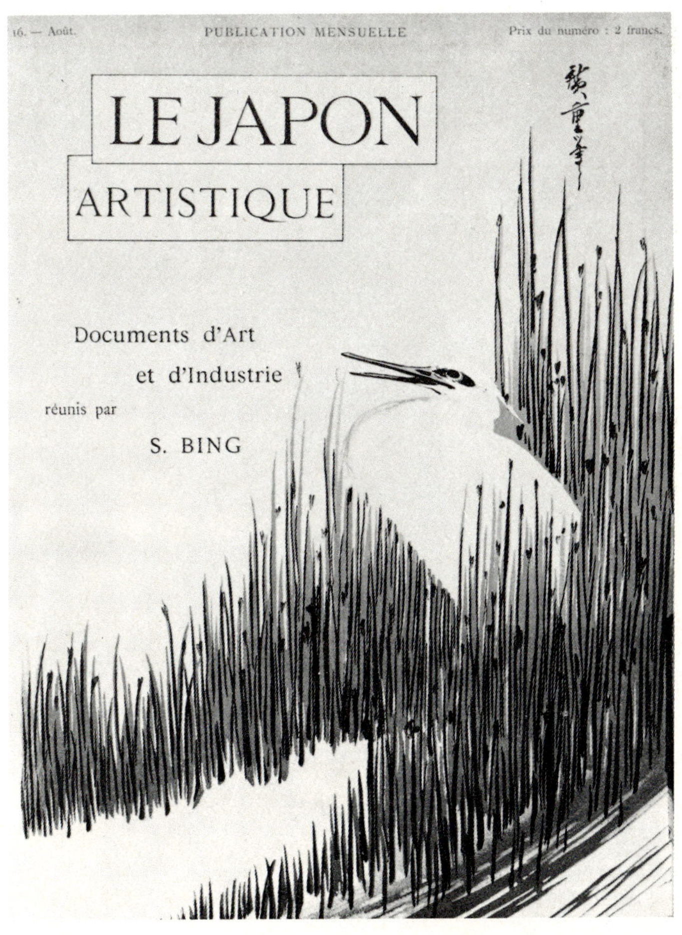

The Japanese vogue caught on everywhere. The distinguished potter Delaherche moved to Cincinnati to polish his craft by studying with Japanese artists working there. The Royal Copenhagen Porcelain factory, as well as the other Danish factory of Bing and Grondhal, experimented with oriental motifs. The moving spirits of Jugendstil in Germany and in Vienna found sustenance in Deneken's album *Japanese Motifs of Surface Ornamentation*.

Many of the greatest painters followed the lead — very influential at a certain point — of Émile Bernard, who claimed to have discovered the principle of partitioning by studying Japanese silk hangings. In the work of the Nabis, especially of Sérusier, we find considerable evidence of Japanese imitation in the lines of the landscapes. Manet depicted Zola in his study, in which we see a Japanese print and screen. In the portrait of *Le Père Tanguy* by van Gogh, the sitter

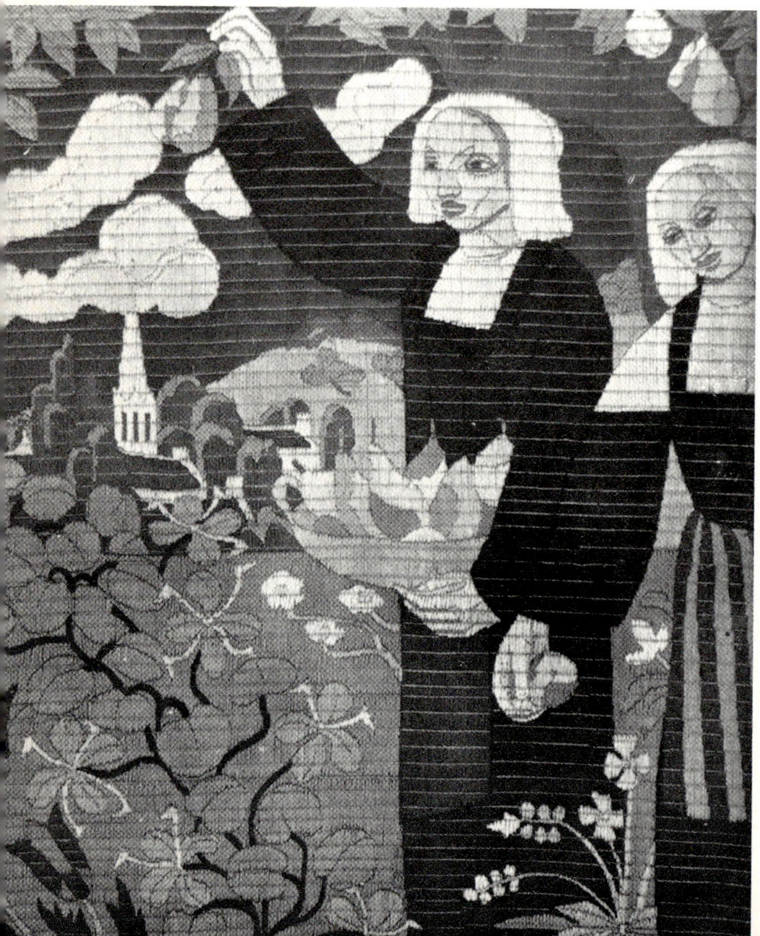

ÉMILE BERNARD   Tapestry, 1888

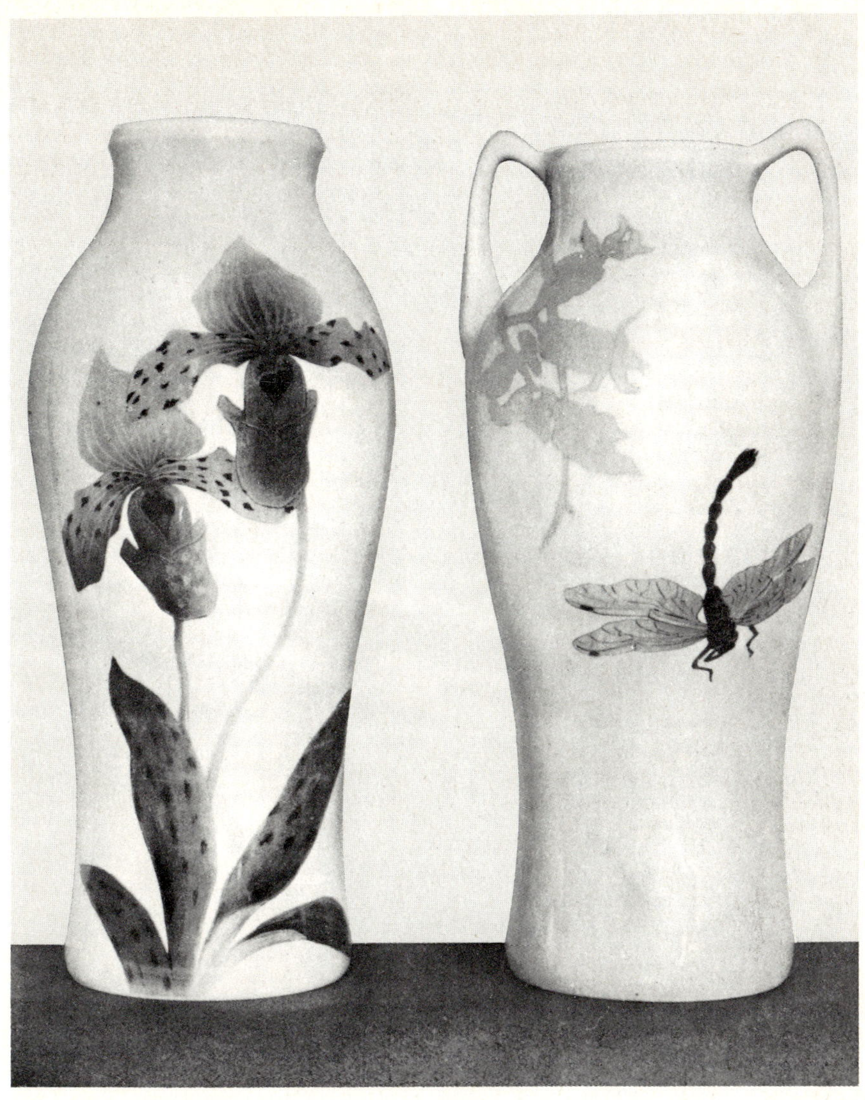

Royal Copenhagen Porcelain Factory   Vases, ca. 1900

emerges from a background similar to a Japanese woodcut. Many van Gogh landscapes of about this time (1886) still manage to reveal, despite their disturbed line, an oriental inspiration in the simple, sensitive renderings of plant forms. Van Gogh faithfully copied Hiroshige prints, like the one of flowering plum trees. When he arrived in Arles, he wrote to Émile Bernard of his joy in seeing a countryside "as beautiful as Japan" — which he had never visited.

Needless to say, it was not the narrative content of Japanese art

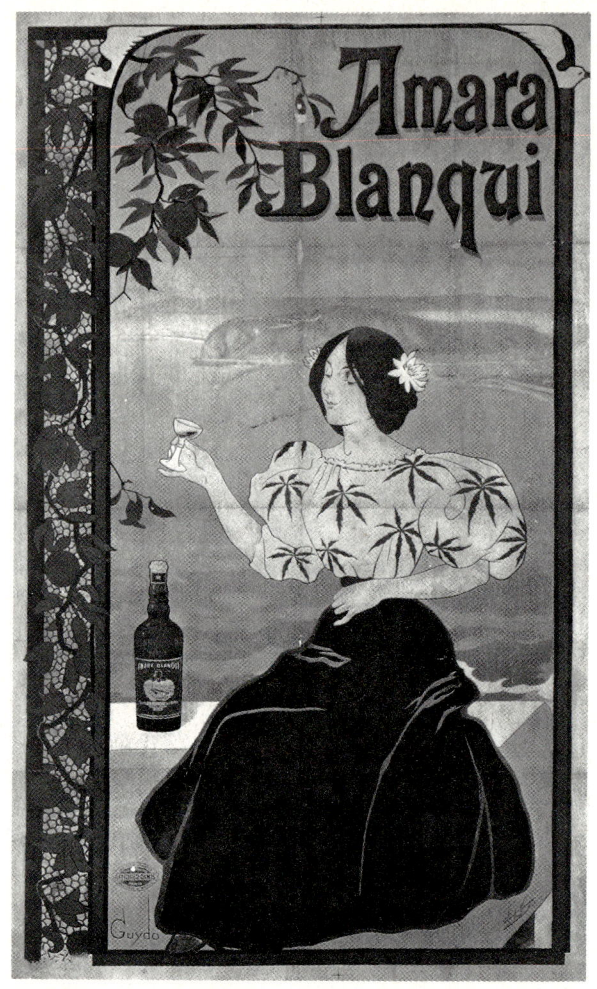

GUYDO   Poster for Amara Blanqui liqueur, 1893

which fascinated Western artists, so much as its linear construction and supreme sensitivity to nature. The Europeans were avid for new methods and sought new thrills. Exoticism gave them all that, but in their rejection of the past and their refusal to copy it they merely fell into another kind of imitation, which led them to still another impasse.

The Japanese vogue did not take long to degenetrate into vulgarity. Furniture manufacturers produced lacquered whatnot tables inlaid with fake ivory and wood, and bamboo screens upon which Samurai embroidered in silk were locked in combat; tea sets decorated with

Vincent van Gogh
Flowering Plum Tree, 1888

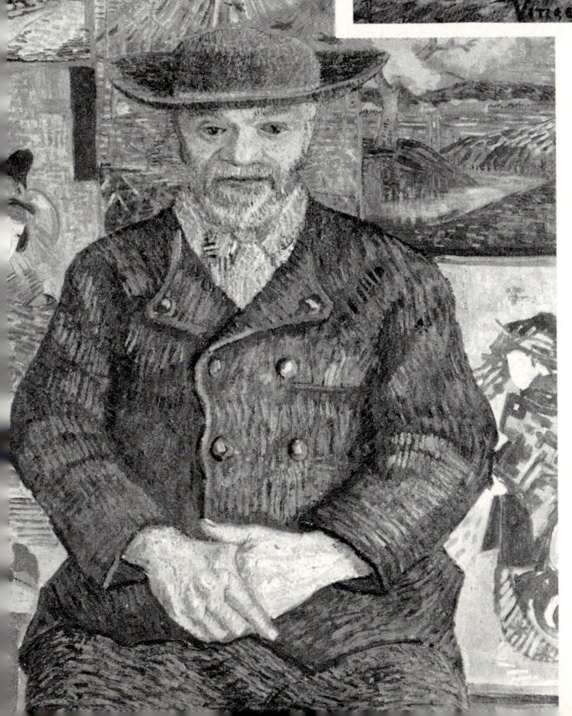

Vincent van Gogh
Le Père Tanguy, 1886–1888

flowering branches were all the rage. It was this last phase of the Japanese vogue which had nothing to do with art nouveau or, indeed, with any other kind of art.

william blake,
a distant forerunner

In the background of this constellation of influences exerting their pressure at the very moment when a new style was emergent, can be seen the strange and distant image of William Blake (1757–1827). This painter-poet was a visionary. His religious exaltation impelled him to explore the invisible world, while reality seems to have remained for him remote. His mind was steeped in the works of Dante, Swedenborg, Milton, and the Bible, and, above all, in a fabulous world created by his own feverish imagination. His life was marked by poverty and, toward its end, obscurity. Were it not for the generosity of a wealthy friend, who ultimately was his only patron, Blake would have died destitute.

Twenty years after his death, he was rediscovered by Rossetti, who felt for Blake a kinship based upon a thousand shared affinities. Rossetti instantly perceived the earlier artist's mystical character, as well as admired the formal qualities of his paintings and engravings, his manner of turning plant forms into ornament, and his use of the flames as background to his compositions. The Pre-Raphaelite painter introduced the works of this *peintre maudit* to his circle, and the Brotherhood immediately adopted William Blake.

It is through their mediation that we must consider Blake a precursor of art nouveau. The earlier artist had done away with perspective. His extreme linear style, all sinuousity, imposed its flexible lines; indeed, Blake prefigures the famous *whiplash* of Modern Style.

His art is all innocence and strangeness, angelic fervor and Satanism. He made engravings of his poems, in which writing and illustration were fused, then heightened them with watercolor *(Songs of Innocence, Songs of Experience, The Marriage of Heaven and Hell)*. Toward 1795, he published small books of fantasies in which he illustrated scenes showing the discord of reason and imagination — the drama of his life. Blake believed passionately in his own genius and suffered from the

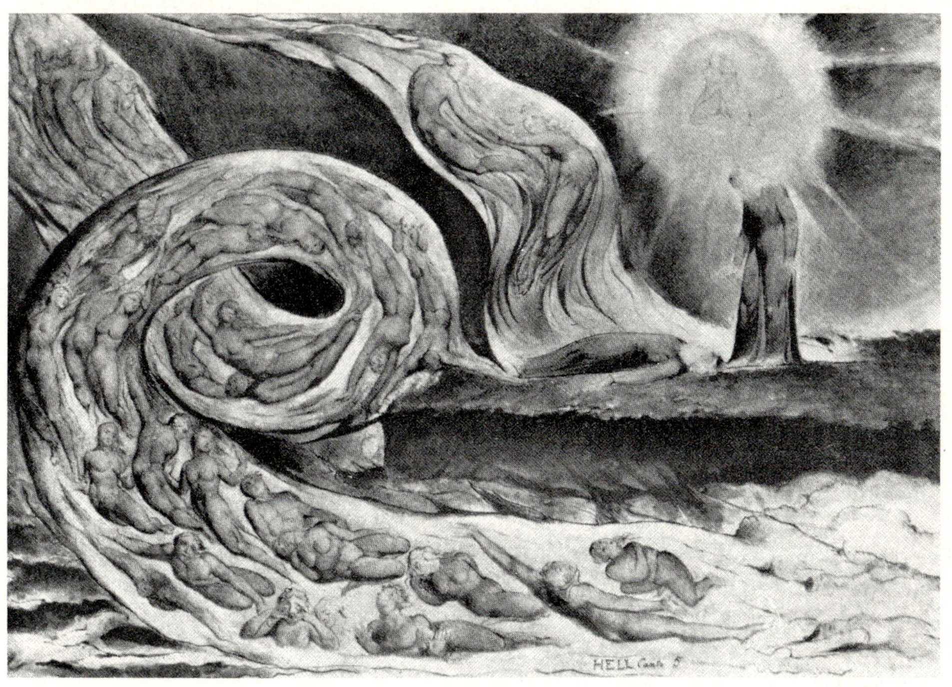

WILLIAM BLAKE   *Paolo and Francesca in the Whirlwind of Lovers in the Circle of the Lustful,* 1824–1827

incomprehension of his contemporaries. In both his paintings and his engravings, everything is exalted into symbolic form. Naked bodies, phantasmagorical figures, like ectoplasm, whirl about in settings which are not of this world. *Jacob's Ladder* is a staircase of light whose spirals are lost as they twist into the night of infinity. His work is full of theories of celestial angels, and the terrifying image of God the Father also appears, who, it is said, had first appeared at the youthful poet's window.

There is often something naive about paintings and engravings laden with metaphysical symbols, but Blake was removed from the mainstream of his time. He comes out of the eighteenth century, and the influence of the rococo is manifest in his asymmetrical ornamentation and convoluted forms. His work has its roots in the baroque and is, at the same time, a prefiguration of art nouveau. It also has a singular power to shock; a hundred years after the artist's death, those artists who were most involved with art nouveau, like Mackmurdo,

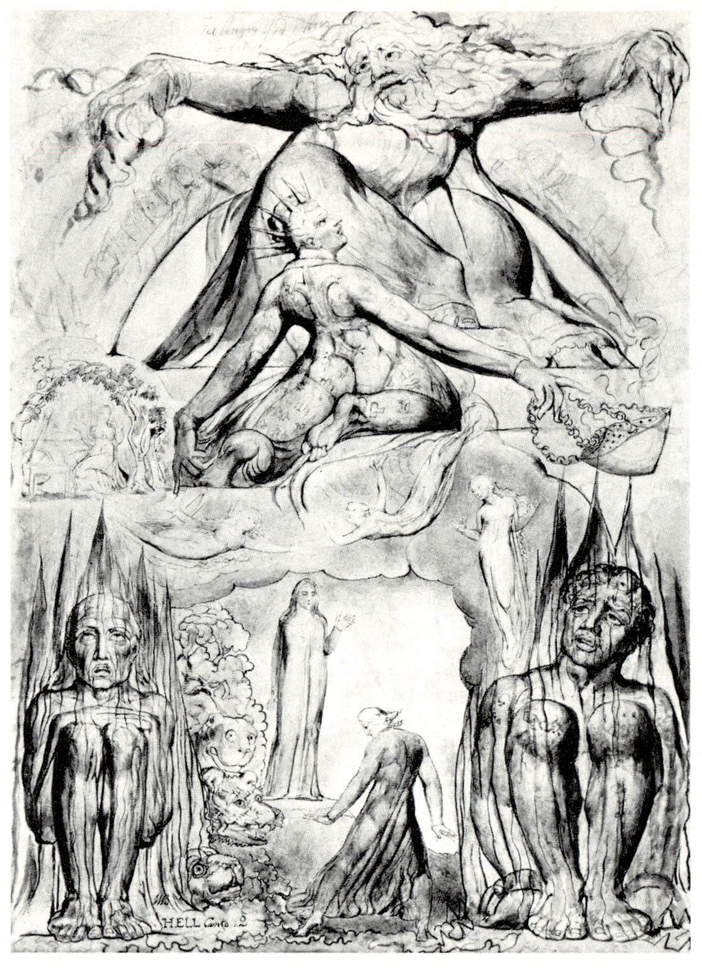

WILLIAM BLAKE   The Mission of Virgil, 1824–1827

Robert Burnes, Walter Crane, Toorop, or Grasset, paid homage to Blake's heavy, swirling lines. Blake had translated into a uniquely ornamental style a totality of spiritual values and mystical visions. He had a highly personal, tragic sense; he was hurled from the darkest shadows to the dazzling light of the apocalypse. Most of his distant disciples of 1900 were less interested in the involved beliefs of this ardent spiritualist; but they carefully studied the originality of his ornamental writing and decorative creativity, using both to forge their own style.

64

painters and poets

During the entire nineteenth century, a current of mystical thought expressed itself in art and literature. We can follow it along the straight and sometimes tangled lines which link the religious Gothic of Pugin to the innovators of the turn of the century, who tried to establish, as Gauguin wrote, "the right to challenge anything." If, today, the Pre-Raphaelites strike us as aesthetes who had read too much and whose pictorial qualities were not equal to their aspirations,

ÉMILE BERNARD *Pont-Aven, 1888*

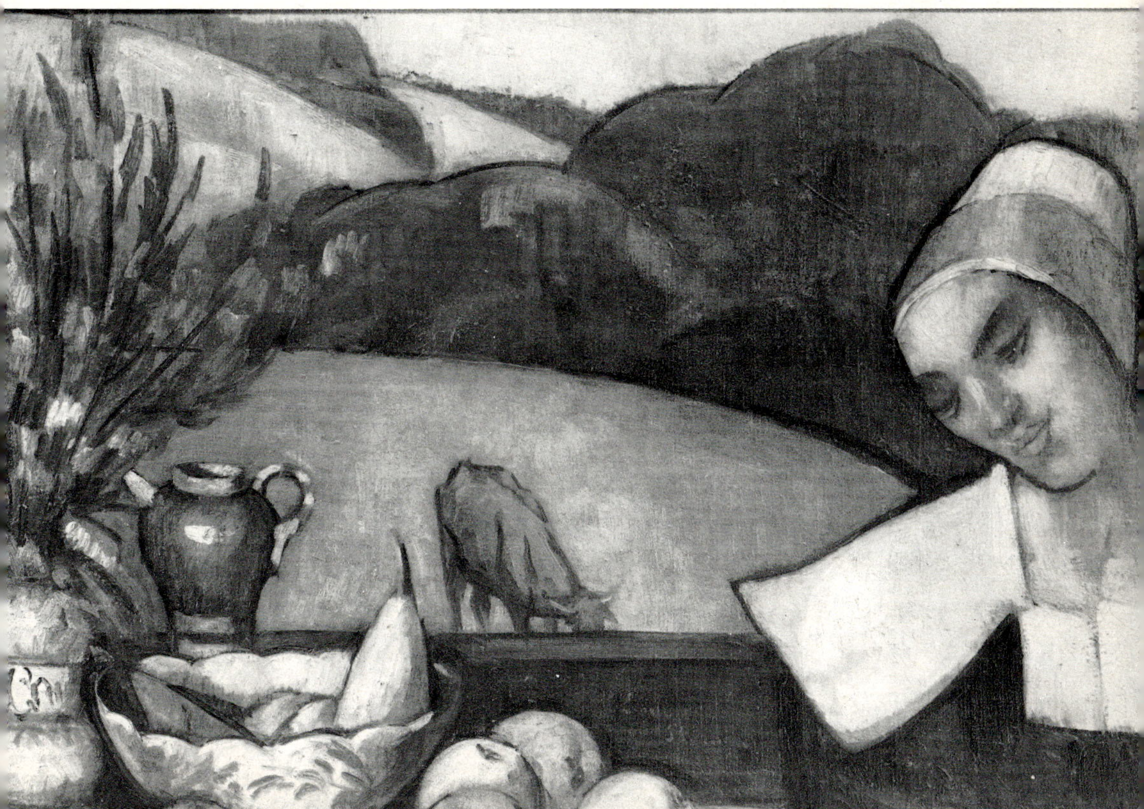

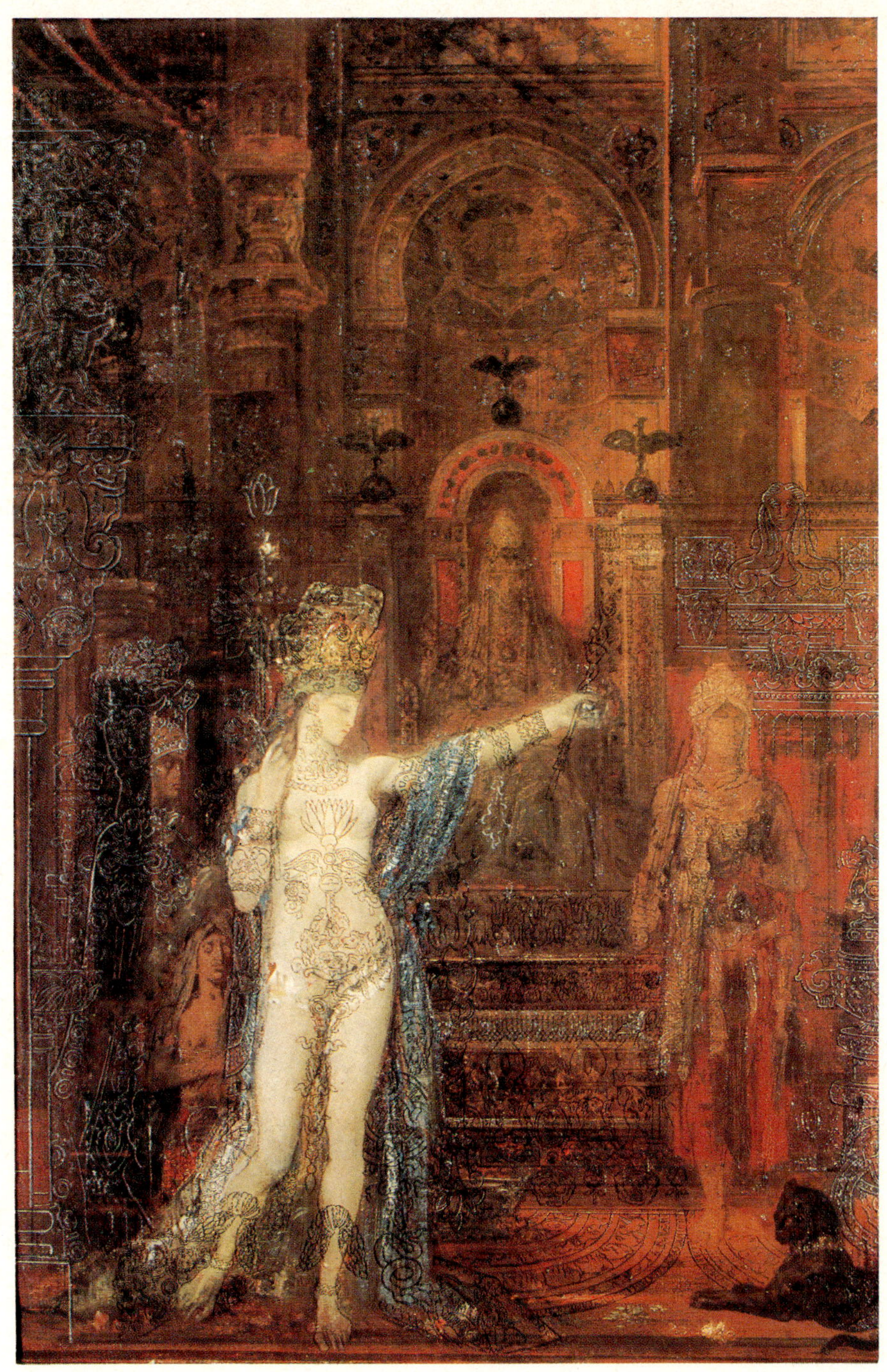

Gustave Moreau *Salome Tatooed*

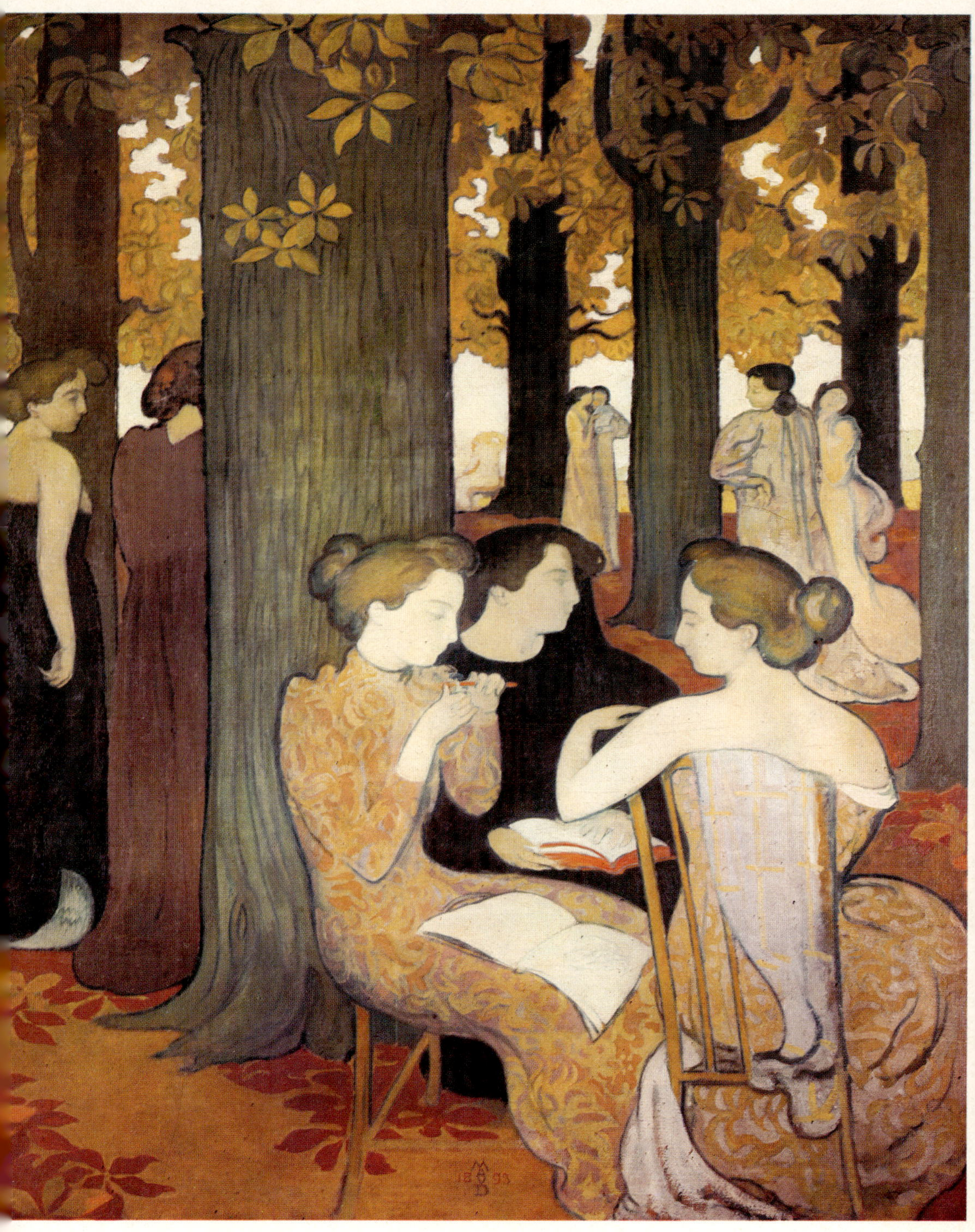

Maurice Denis *The Muses, 1893*

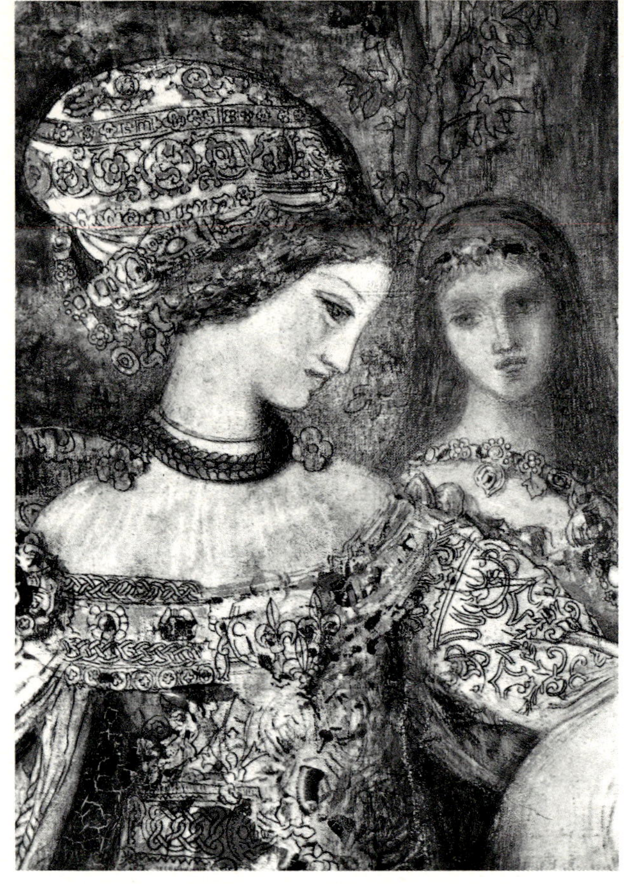

GUSTAVE MOREAU   *The Unicorn*, 1896

they nonetheless contributed, in the midst of the conventional, the confused, and the ugly which seemed to overwhelm the period, a fresh breath of idealism and profound yearning for purity. Their dreams of legends and a paradise lost merged with symbolism and paved the way for art nouveau.

Symbolism played its part in the antirealist movements which united artists and writers. Its name — invented by Jean Moréas — designated a tendency shared by many others, who had in common the searching creative intelligence and "modernity" celebrated by Baudelaire as the essential leavening in a work of art. The painters made less of this programmatic aspect of their art than the poets or musicians, but, as opposed to the strict doctrinal obedience that would later be demanded by surrealism, symbolism did not insist upon rigid boundaries. Along with it, there emerged the *Cloissonisme* of Émile

Bernard, reformulated by Maurice Denis, *Divisionnisme, Synthétisme,* and *Idéisme,* propounded by Albert Aurier, who edited the review *Le Moderniste.* This was the period when such reviews proliferated; more or less ephemeral, with a more or less tiny readership, their texts and illustrations diffused the ideas and images which contributed to the aesthetic of art nouveau. Some of these periodicals, which began

PAUL SÉRUSIER *Libations*

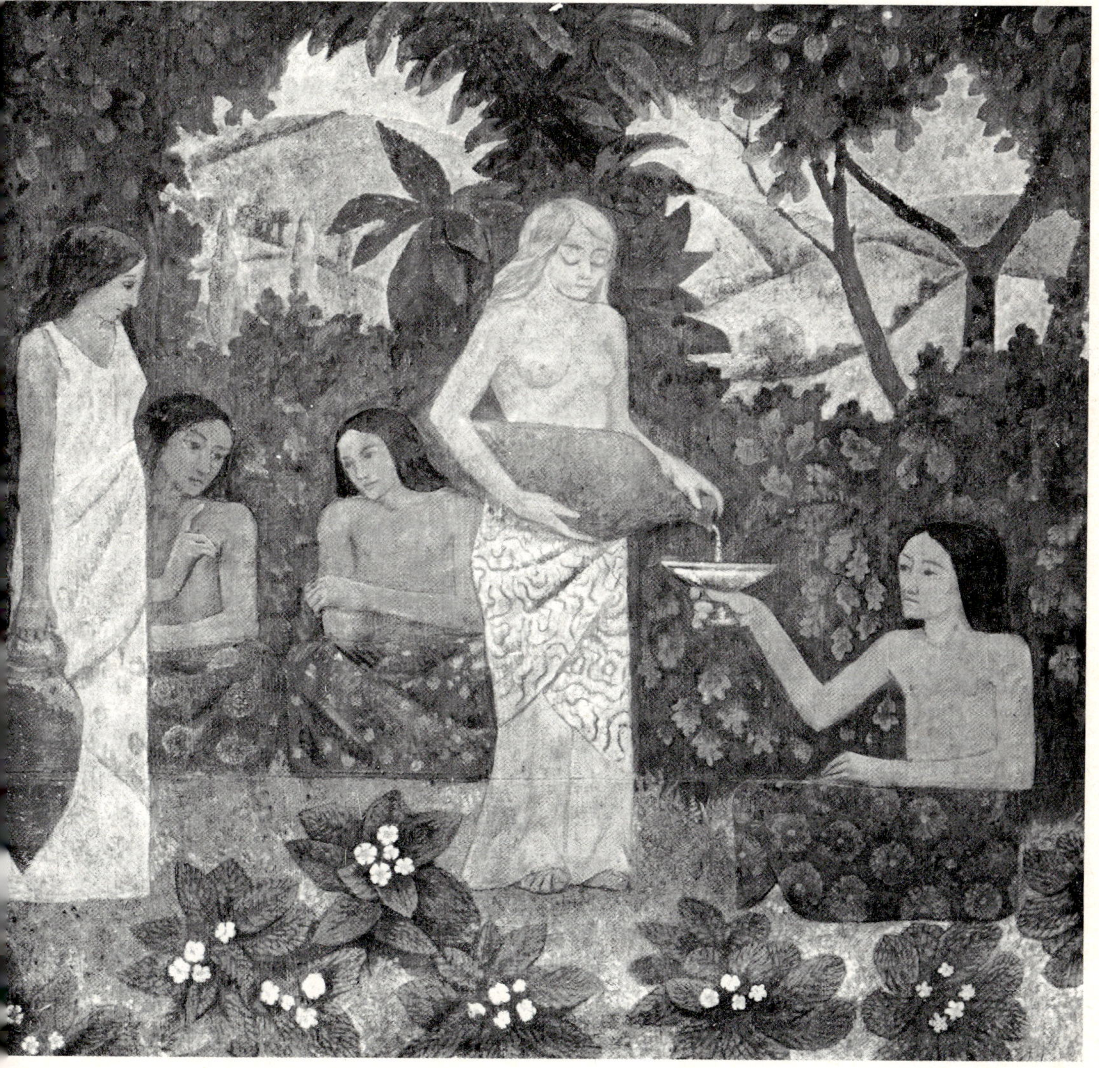

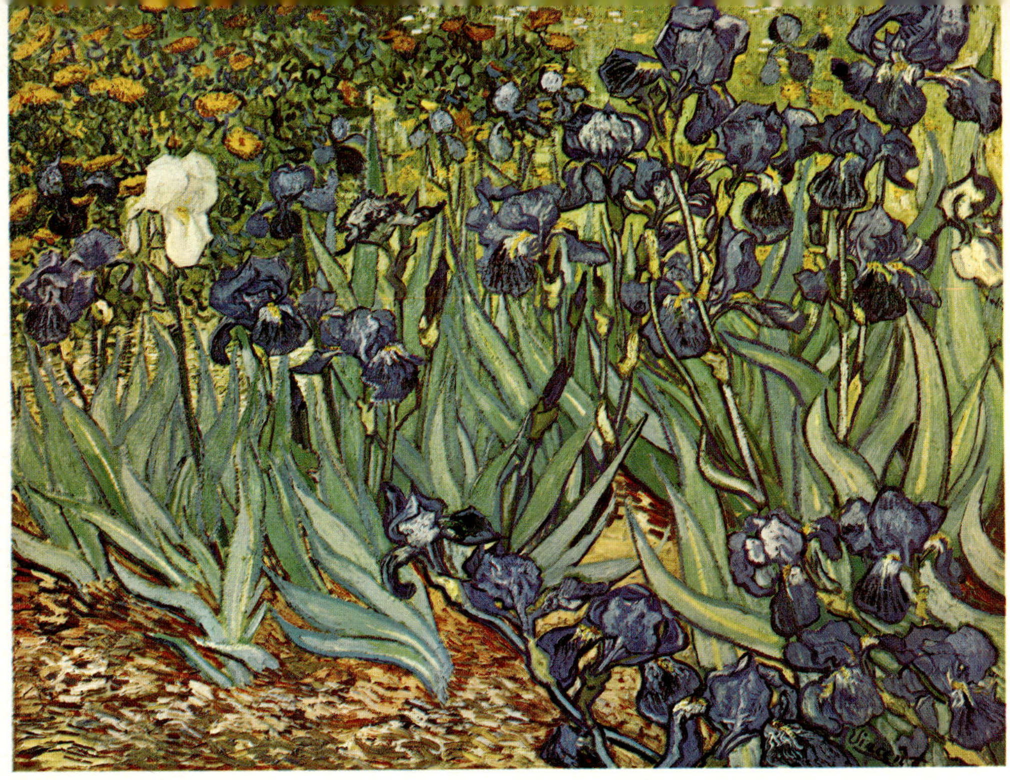

Vincent van Gogh   *Iris,* 1889

to appear around 1884, were the *Hobby Horse,* founded in England by Mackmurdo's Guild; then *La Revue Blanche* in Paris, published by the Natanson brothers, whose graphics were the work of a group of young artists who were to become famous; Beardsley's *The Yellow Book; The Studio,* a primary source for painting, architecture, and decoration; then *Die Jugend* (1896), whose title would baptize the new art in Germany, in response to which appeared *Juvendud* in Barcelona. In Vienna, the Sezession Group was sustained by the review *Ver Sacrum* while in Belgium Van de Velde started *Van Nu en Straks* and in Russia Serge de Diaghilev published the review *Mir Isskustva.* Other publications, too, first saw the light of day at this same time, like *Art et Décoration* and *L'Art Décoratif* in France, and *Deutsche Kunst und Dekoration* in Germany, which gave most of their attention to art nouveau.

The role of *La Revue Blanche* in Paris is particularly important in the history of the arts. In its pages were to be found the art critics Fénéon and Geffroy, as well as illustrations by the painters Vallotton, Roussel, Bonnard, Denis, and Sérusier, whose intimate friendship with Gauguin conferred upon him great authority. The review was buoyed

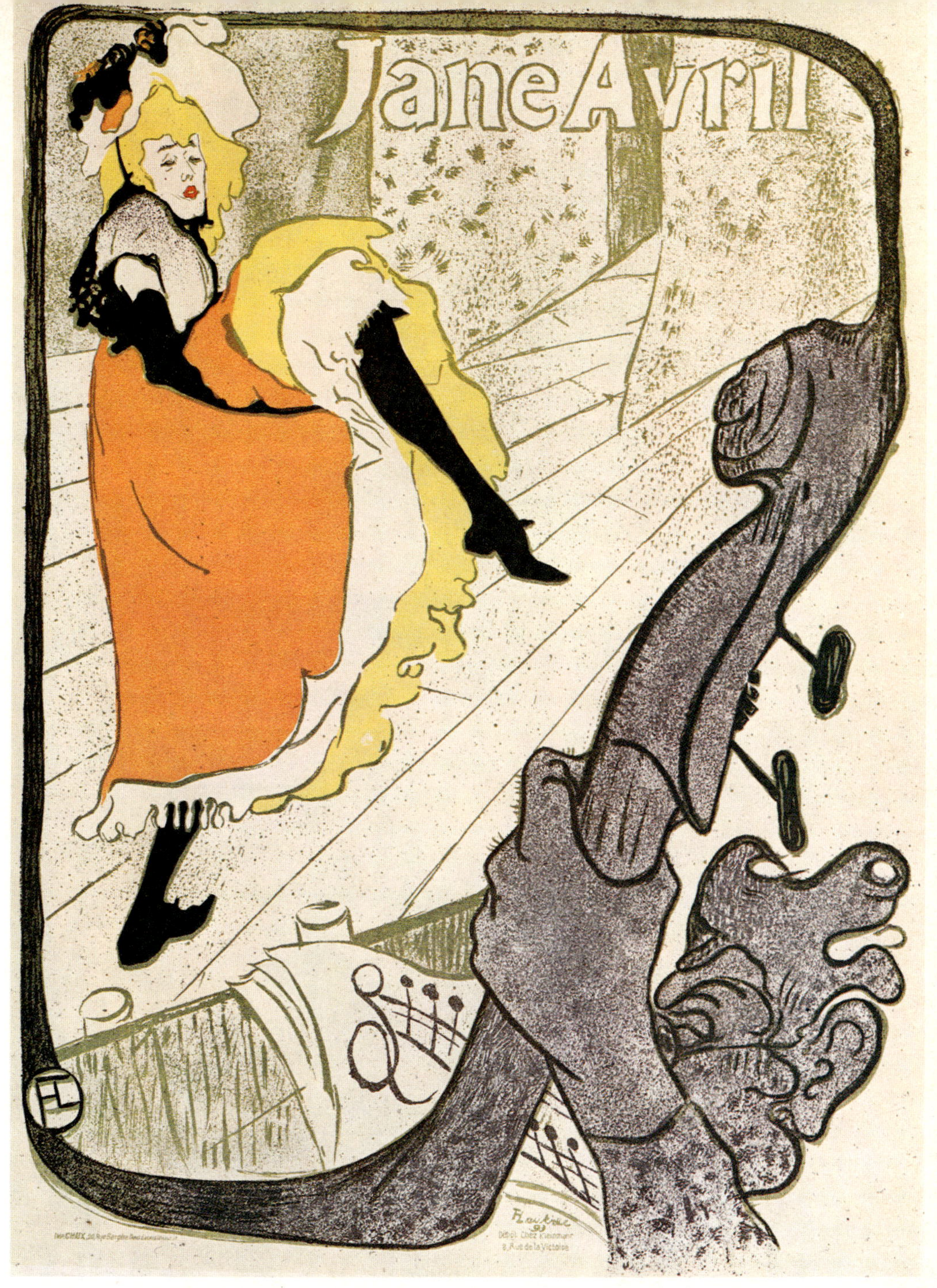

HENRI DE TOULOUSE-LAUTREC   Poster for Jane Avril, 1893

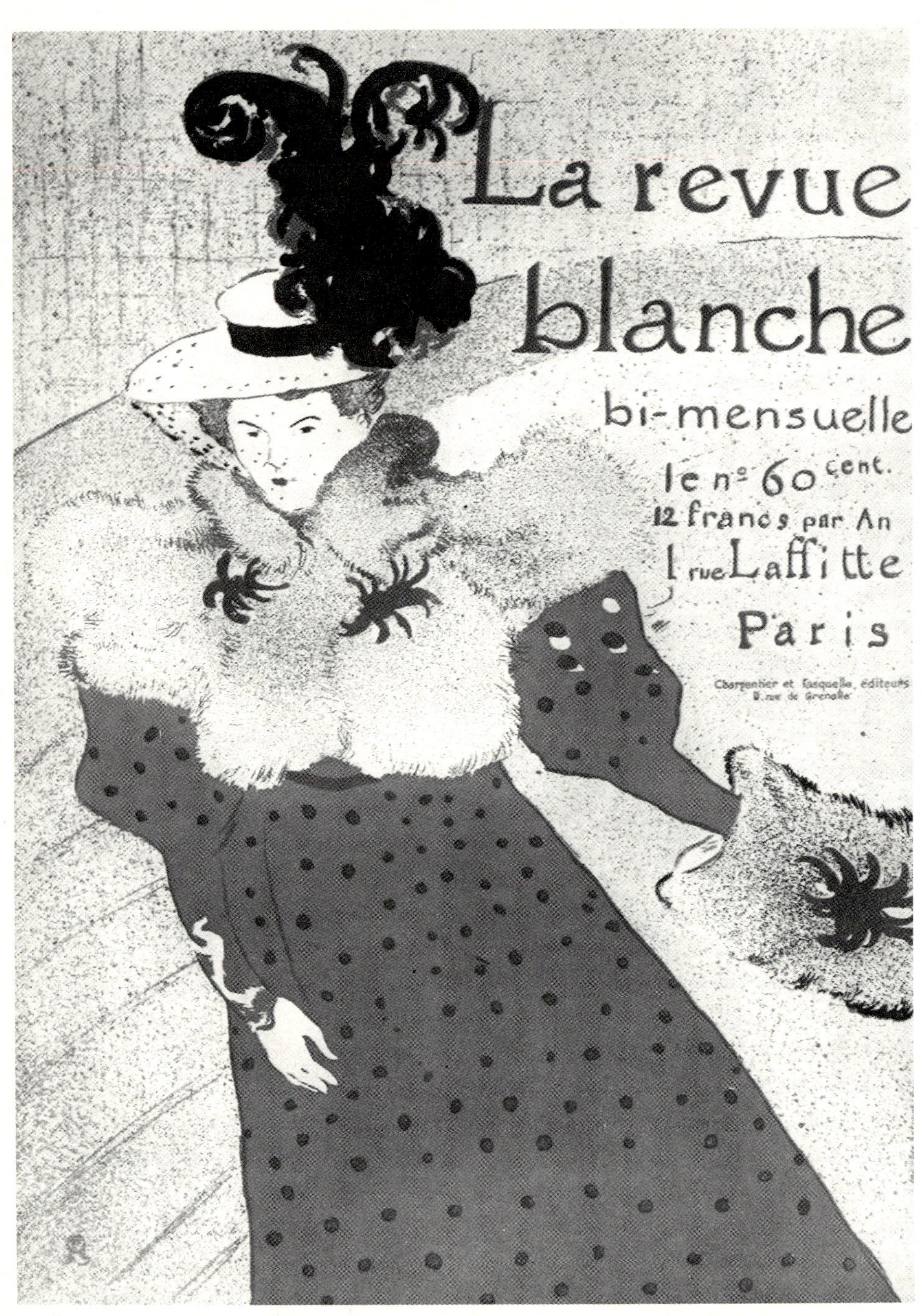

HENRI DE TOULOUSE-LAUTREC   Poster for *La Revue Blanche*, 1895

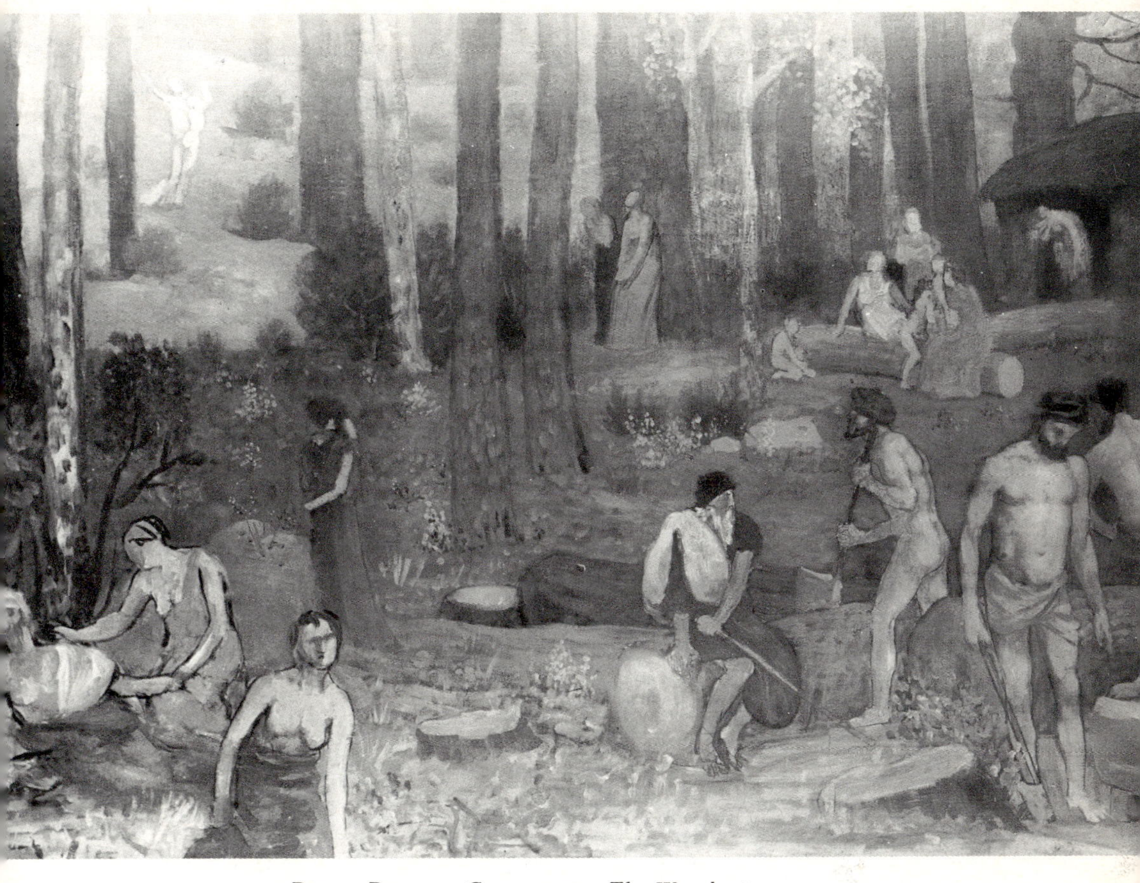

by a wave of new ideas, which, in turn, were quickened by a concept of art parallel to the refinements of the symbolist poets and writers. Without grouping together all those painters who were part of the beginnings of modern art under the banner of art nouveau, it is still hard to deny the similarities, the ties which unite them. There are more than mere affinities, for example, between a Gustave Moreau and a Mallarmé. Hermetism, mystery, and symbol are expressed in both of these artists' work, along with a classical sense of composition.

Gustave Moreau, whose works are as irritating as they are enchanting, and who influenced an entire grateful generation of noted painters, cannot be understood, unless in terms of another generation which reaches back beyond symbolism to William Blake. The surrealists, too,

were quick to claim Blake as a father-figure. The archaizing romanticism of the Swiss Böcklin and his Wagnerian landscapes filled with
dramatic action are in the same Blakean spirit. And the same dream-
like atmosphere and yearnings toward a mythical world are found in
the noble compositions of Puvis de Chavannes.

These names should indicate the extreme diversity of painters
imbued with the same ideal: to escape realism. And to this end they
willingly placed themselves beyond the pale of conventional taste. The

ÉDOUARD VUILLARD   *The Piano*

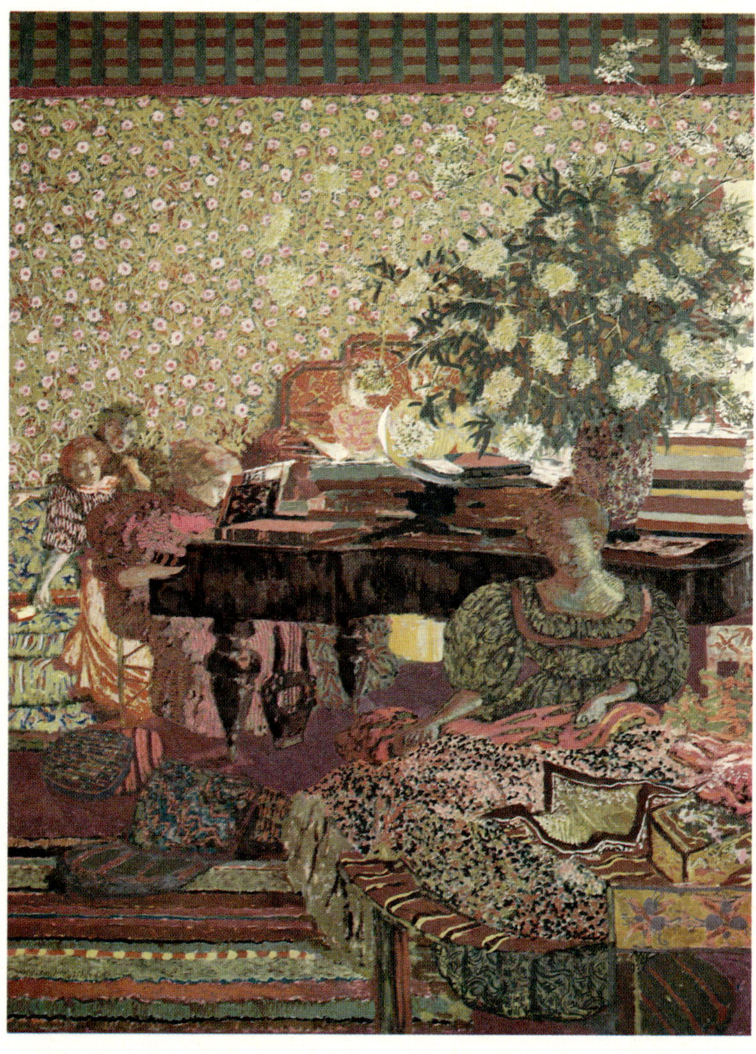

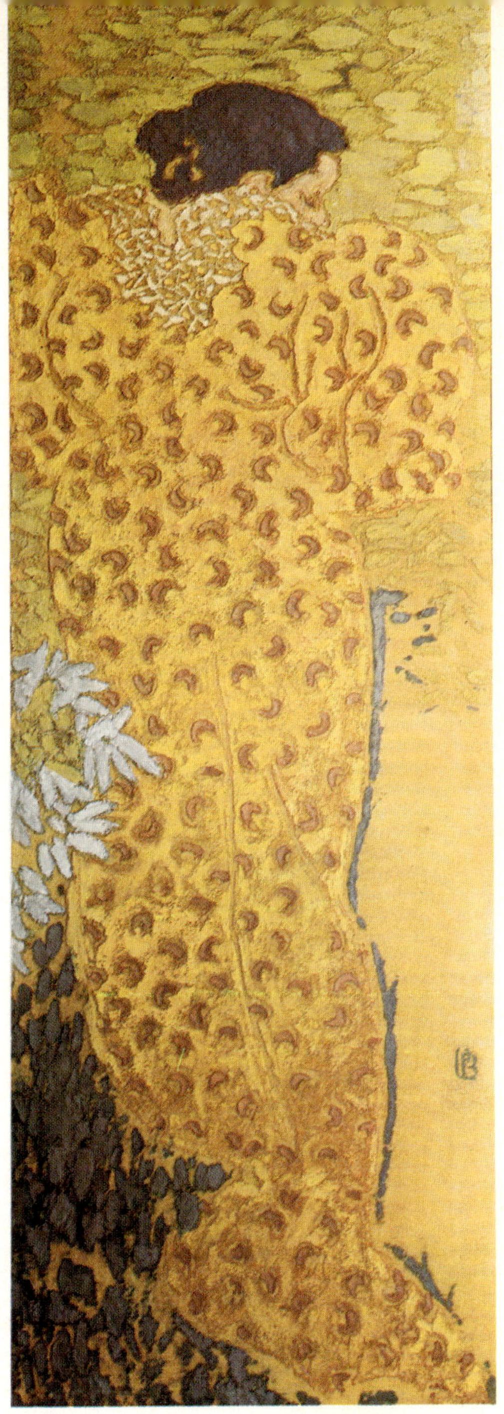

PIERRE BONNARD   *The Dressing Gown*, 1892

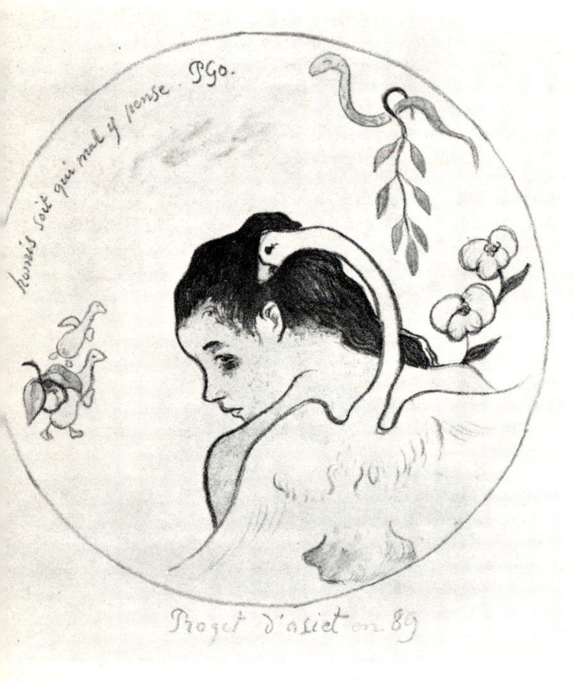

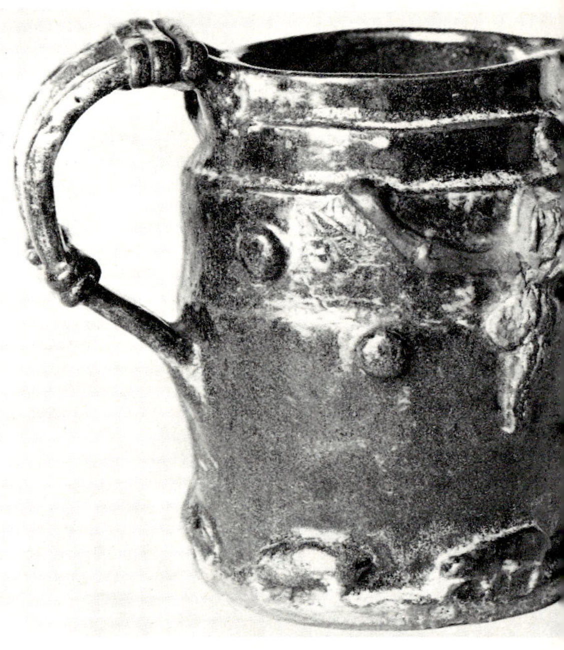

PAUL GAUGUIN   Plate, *Leda and the Swan*, 1889

PAUL GAUGUIN   Clay Pot, 1886–1887

antimaterialist movement consisted of Catholic converts like Léon Bloy or Joris-Karl Huysmans, as well as intimates of the Grand Paladin of the Rosicrucians. The general public, moreover, made no distinction between the odor of incense or burning sulphur.

Some artists and writers thought they could escape the vulgarity of the herd by affecting eccentric and original poses — all carefully studied: the style was supposed to prove that the bearer was not part of ordinary humanity. Swinburne, the author of a penetrating essay on Blake, had already made himself the subject of scandal by his work and way of life. He outraged the entire neighborhood when he settled in Etretat with an adolescent boy, a dwarf, and a monkey. The romantics had been given to red vests. The symbolists favored an

76

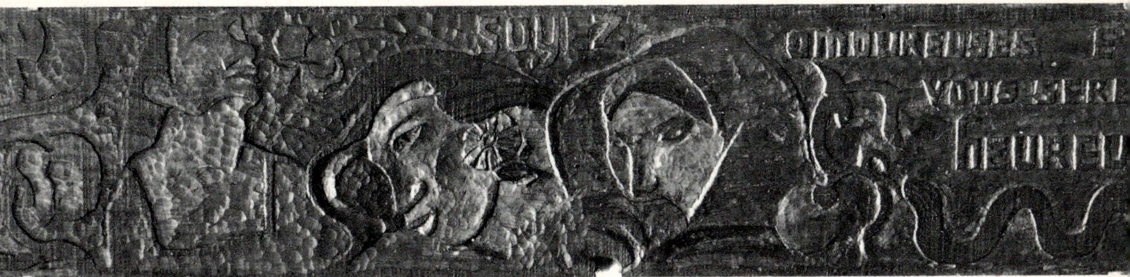

PAUL GAUGUIN   Decorative panel, 1890

"artistic" uniform, consisting of a cape, trailing scarf, and large-brimmed hat. But it all came from the desire to distinguish themselves from the bourgeoisie. The latter, of course, had nothing but contempt or revulsion for these persons who seemed to mock them with their eccentricity, just as they mocked them by their ridiculous and incomprehensible works. Some of these so-called artists even went so far as to flaunt proudly a title of opprobrium, "decadent." Gustave Moreau was viewed as a harmless madman with his sphinxes, demon lovers, *femmes fatales* covered with gold and gems. In Huysmans' *A Rebours,* tortoises with shells encrusted with precious stones wander about the carpets in the house of his hero, des Esseintes. From these images it was but a short step to the extravagances of Modern Style.

Because art nouveau focused essentially on the decorative arts, we too easily forget that it referred to aesthetic principles concerned with all art forms: every medium could have shared in these reciprocal influences. Nor is it to diminish the importance of art nouveau to call it a style. Of what significant phase of art would this not be true? If style sometimes works it ways unconsciously, it can also exercise its powers as an imperative upon the strongest personalities. One example is the astonishing authority of Toulouse-Lautrec, a contributor to *La Revue Blanche,* in drawings which consisted entirely of nervous curved lines and barely modulated colors. A poster like *Jane Avril au Jardin de Paris,* where the dancer's black stocking echoes the curve of the bass fiddle in the foreground, is only one example, among many, of a decorative style which can be dated precisely — 1893. Despite antithetical methods of draftsmanship, we can find meetings and analogies between the new decorative art and the precise, eccentric curves repeated by Seurat in *Le Chahut (the Cancan),* 1890. These painters,

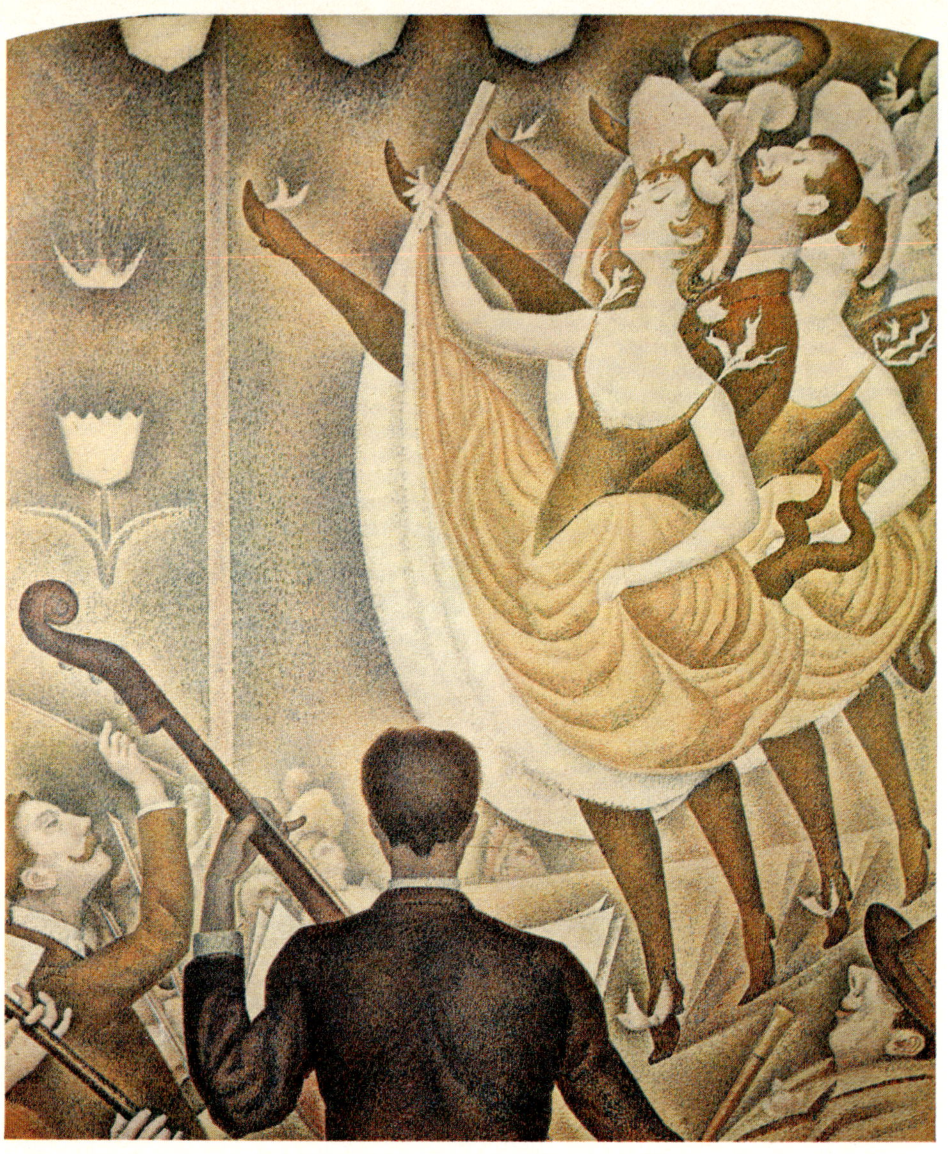

GEORGES SEURAT   *The Cancan, 1889–1890*

by the force of their artistic personality, influenced, at least indirectly, every aspect of art nouveau.

It is particularly interesting, as we look for precursors of art nouveau, to observe the attraction that "decorative" objects held for artists.

Gauguin began making ceramic pitchers, table centerpieces, and furniture. By choosing ordinary objects, he emphasized the evolution

78

which could lead painters — even those with genius — to handicrafts
whose function was merely to enhance life's surroundings. If Gauguin's
vases cannot really be ranked among his masterworks, they nonetheless reveal the turnabout that took place for artists driven by the need
to experiment. Neither a Meissonier nor a Gérome would have been
interested in making pottery. From the friendship of Émile Bernard
and Gauguin was born *Cloisonnisme,* that enthusiastic discovery of

GEORGES SEURAT   *The Circus,* 1891

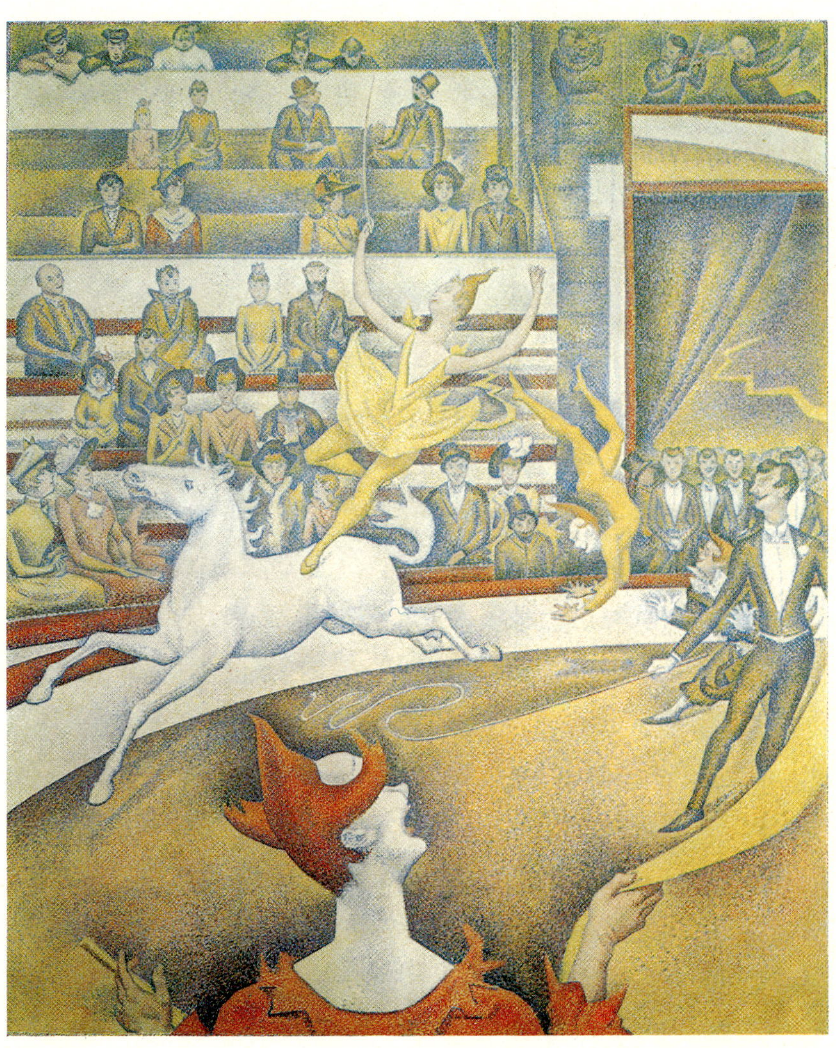

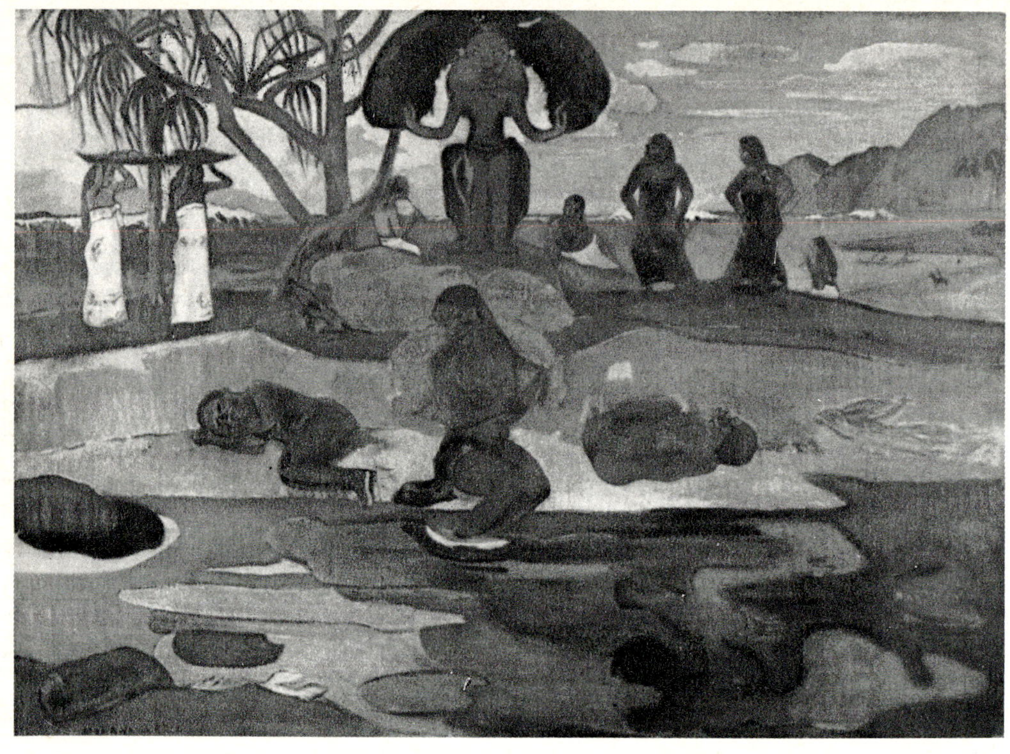

PAUL GAUGUIN   *Le Jour de Dieu*, 1894

"pure tones juxtaposed," which had so much resonance. Émile Bernard was a talented sculptor in wood. And Gauguin, when he lived in Tahiti, made strange wood sculptures to decorate his hut, without being concerned that posterity would relegate these to minor works.

Gauguin preached the suppleness of a fluid line which outlined forms, just as lead had outlined the colored glass of Medieval windows. And when he came to paint works like *Le Jour de Dieu* he outlined on the ground, in front of figures who merge with the tropical landscape, and in the sky arabesques and undulating spots which are only explained by his desire for decoration; some of this stylized decor seems the invention of art nouveau ornamentalists. The sources of inspiration are the same: a linear style borrowed from the Japanese.

The correlation is still more readily discernible in the Nabis painters. At this time, Sérusier would invite fellow painters Ibels, Bonnard, Maurice Denis, Vuillard, Piot, Vallotton, and Maillol to Ranson's studio. The group then discovored Cézanne and Van Gogh at Tanguy's shop. Denis was the intellectual of the circle, whose theories were received like manna from heaven. It is to Denis that we

80

owe the famous definition of a painting: "a flat surface covered with colors arranged in a particular order." Other influences came from Odilon Redon, a close friend of Mallarmé, and the painter-poet of the imaginary, the unconscious, and the symbol. Bonnard and Sérusier painted the sets for *Ubu Roi* by Alfred Jarry, directed by Lugné-Poe.

The group known as the Nabis emerged in the last years of the century, exactly contemporary with the first flowering of art nouveau. Thus, it is hardly surprising to find the same notes in some of their paintings, and especially in their drawings and engravings. Bonnard,

ODILON REDON *Buddha*

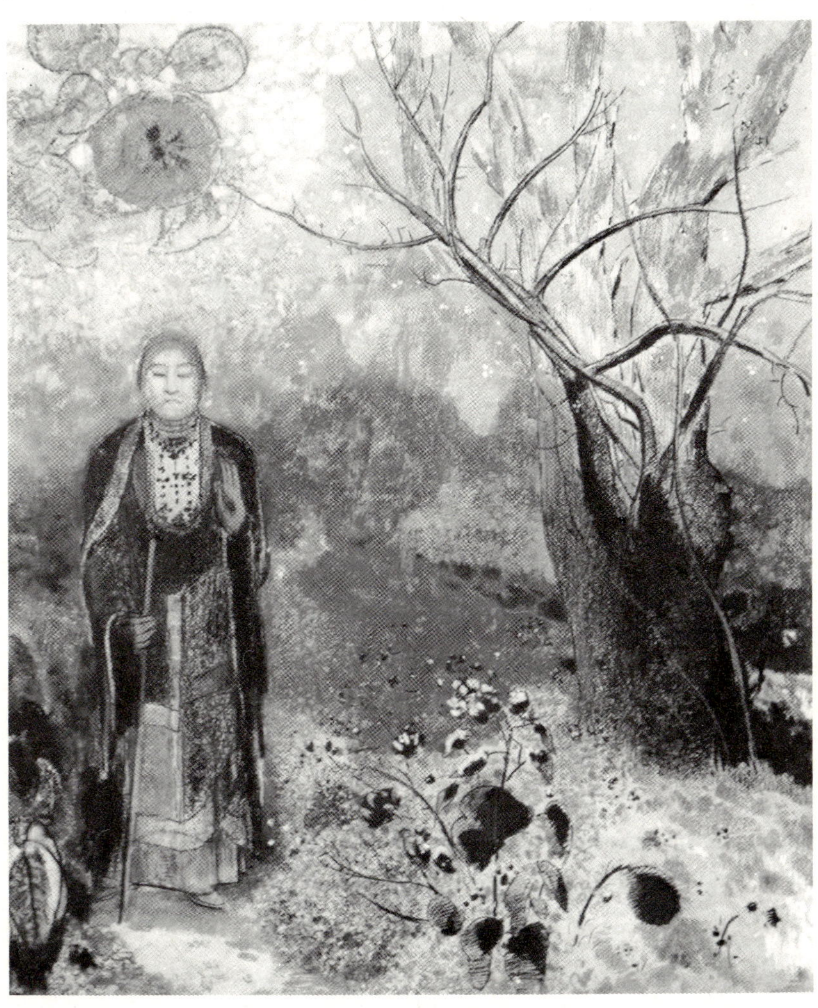

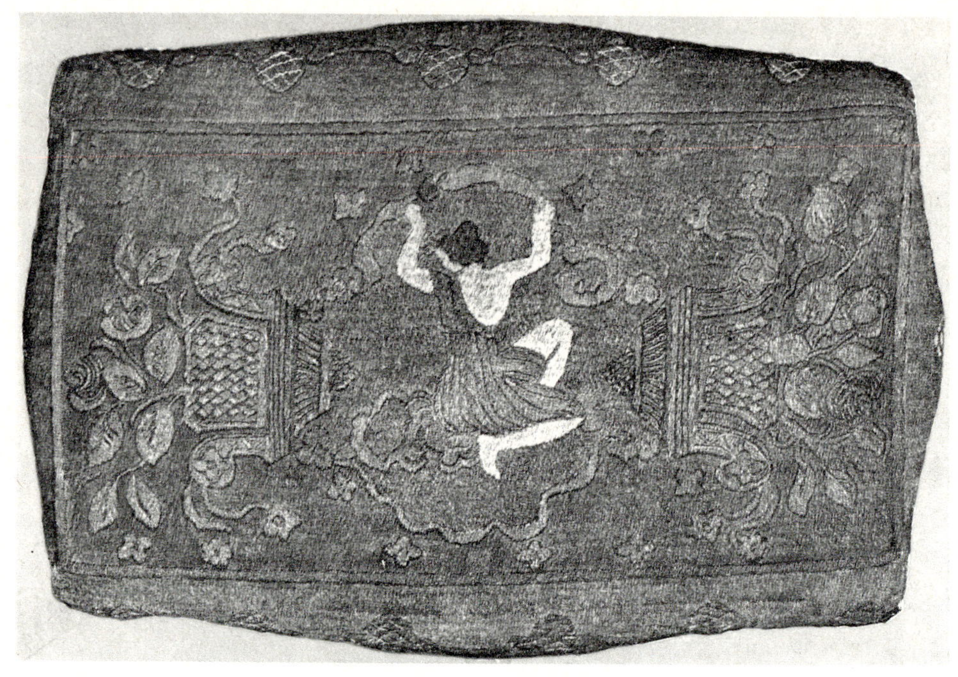

Aristide Maillol   Tapestry, 1904

Vuillard, Maurice Denis, and Lugné-Poe shared a studio at some point around 1890. Sérusier, Vallotton, and Roussel joined forces with them, holding joint exhibitions at the Durand-Ruel gallery. But their alliance was short-lived. Bonnard and Vuillard were too sensitive and individualistic to submit to the doctrinaire recipes of Sérusier. And, accompanied by Roussel, they defected. The philosophy and originality of Odilon Redon makes him an isolated case. And Vallotton worked too much in opposition to all his friends to exhibit with any of them.

Following the example of William Morris — often without realizing it — the major artists of this period illustrated books, and made woodcuts and lithographs. Bonnard's posters for France-Champagne (1892) and for *La Revue Blanche* (1893) must be ranked among the first documents in color published in France for commercial distribution. Maillol neglected painting to devote himself to his tapestries, which are imbued with the spirit of art nouveau, until the loss of his sight, in the first years of the new century, obliged him to turn to other things; he then discovered sculpture. Like Rodin, Maillol was to become a great admirer of Puvis de Chavannes. Sculpture enabled

82

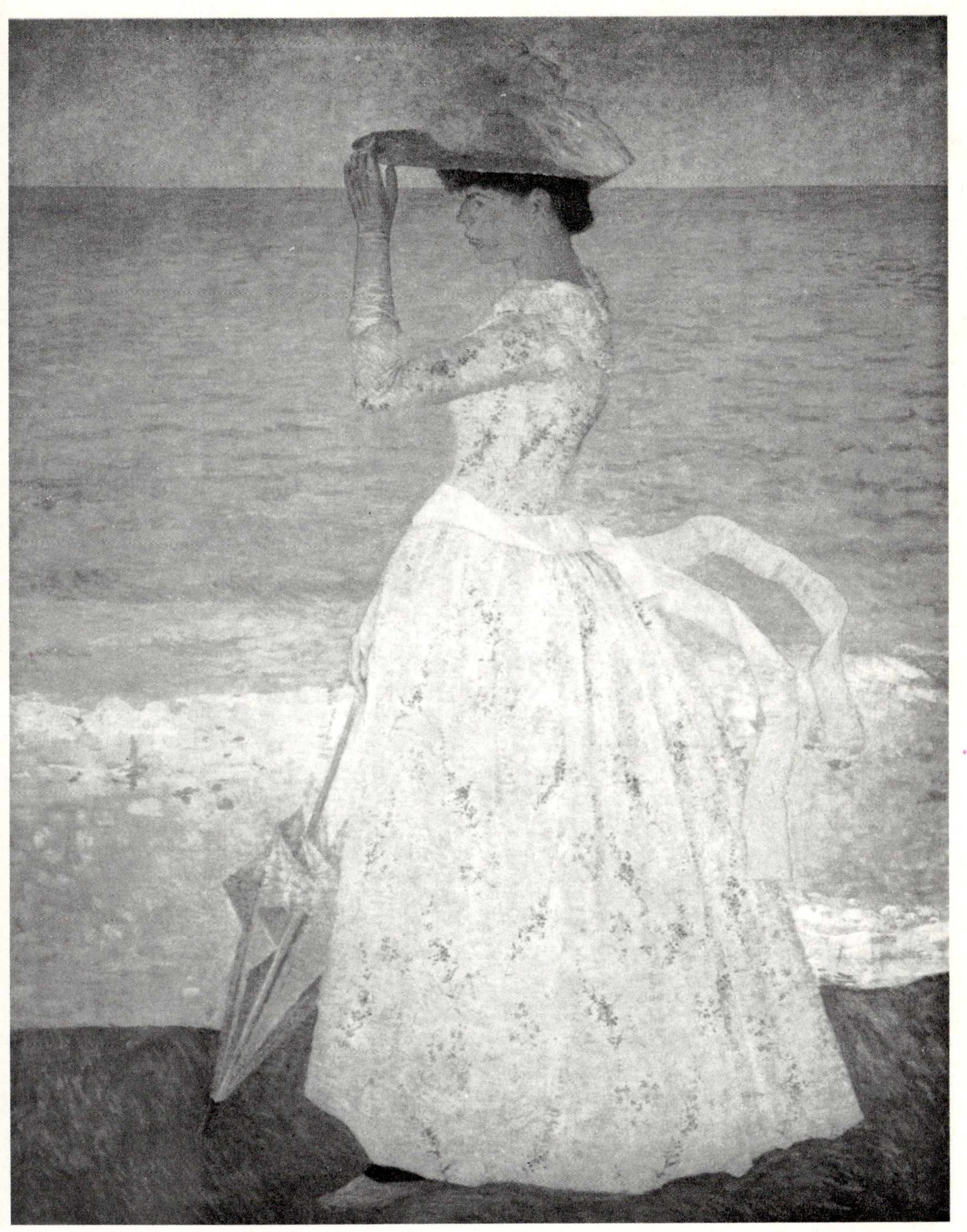

Aristide Maillol *Woman with a Parasol, 1895*

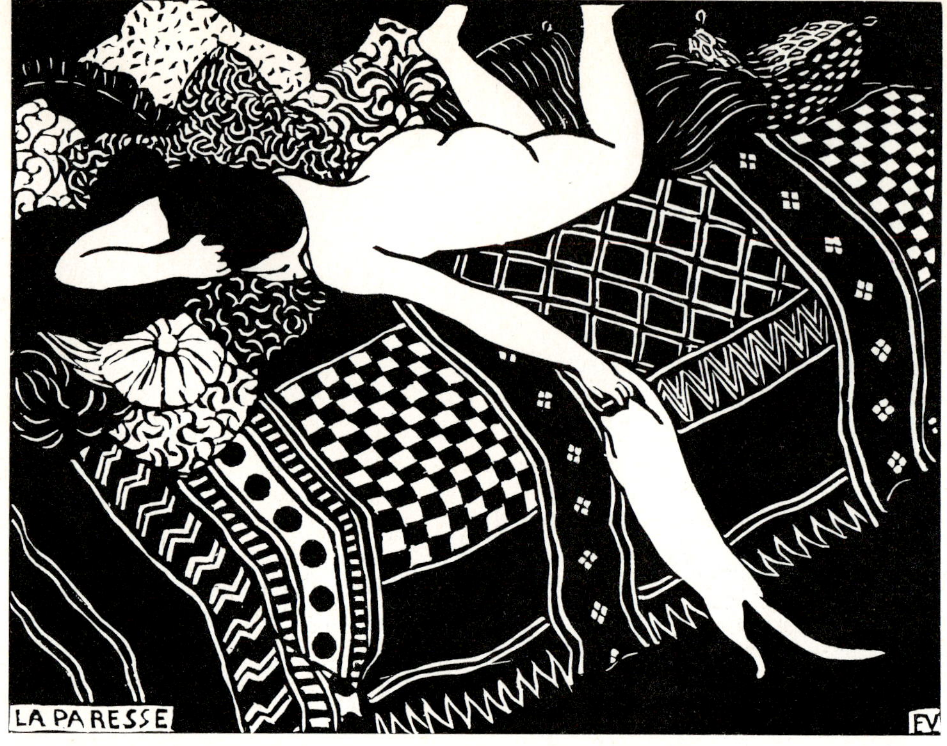

Félix Vallotton *Sloth*, 1896

this Mediterranean artist to rediscover the purity of ancient Greece, recasting it in his own vision of grave sensuality.

Painters and poets shared ideas and discoveries. But if we had to choose one artist who, above all others, most completely translates the atmosphere of this period, the prize would go to a musician. Debussy, all discretion and subtle elegance, upset the laws of harmony and brought hitherto unknown powers to music. The première of *Pelléas and Mélisande,* based upon Maeterlinck's play performed in Paris nine years earlier, took place in 1902. An extraordinary sensibility fused with musical genius enabled this composer to reveal the diffuse shadings and to illuminate the most fleeting sensations, wedding them into something altogether new.

Debussy, Mallarmé, Maeterlinck: all names hallowed by greatness. We forget all too easily the importance of the Maeterlinck influence in Belgium, France, and beyond, on the most diverse personalities in the arts. Kandinsky saw in him a seer, searching for the "spiritual in art." We should mention, in passing, that around 1900, Kandinsky, using juxtaposed colors, painted landscapes whose structure was close to the work of the Jugendstil or art nouveau.

84

forms

It was to be expected that art nouveau would be greeted coldly by that segment of the public which had been lulled for so long by the predictable purring of architects and decorators. Everything about the new style, its choice of lines and forms, seemed to the unenlightened, arbitrary invention or mere provocation. Art nouveau seemed to flaunt its disrespect for tradition, along with its confusion of genres and the irrationality of its adherents. Harsher critics saw it as the fatal conclusion of the *mal du siècle*.

And, indeed, art nouveau lends itself to misinterpretation. Its modes of expression are the profound reflection of the individualism of its creators. These artists felt that they were setting off on a great adventure, each steered by his personal techniques, his sensibilities, his reflections, his turn of mind, and by the resources of his own means of artistic expression. In creating a modern art appropriate to their times, these artists indulged in creative acts of unsurpassed boldness, probably as much to upset the general public as for other reasons.

Without in any way denying their technical virtuousity, we can still quarrel with the vanity displayed in some of their overblown plastic exercises. Even so, we must also acknowledge that the organic structures of Van de Velde, Guimard, or Majorelle were very carefully thought out; they required numerous preparatory plans and sketches which, unlike those of their predecessors, had not been copied from earlier works, and, indeed, did not even refer to earlier architects. None of their contemporaries seemed to realize that it is far more difficult to search for and to find new forms than it is to follow the formulas prescribed by architectural schools, particularly as these modernists were not trying to simplify, as their successors would do, by eliminating all ornamentation; quite the reverse, they gave ornament pride of place, by according it a structural role. Not inaccurately, some of their works have been compared to Gothic architecture, in the sense that the architectural and decorative lines of both merge, with one reinforcing the other.

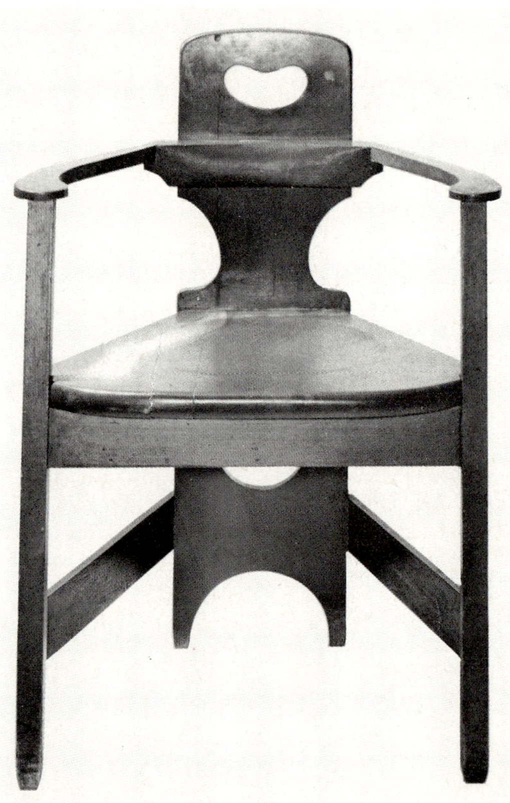

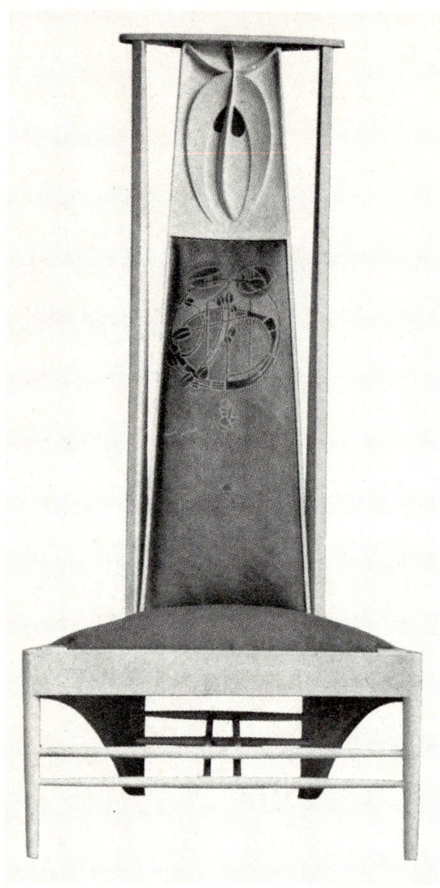

Indeed, this is the most valuable avant-garde quality of art nouveau. As soon as it ceased to invent, repeated itself, became commercialized, it disappeared. "The very elements which made art nouveau so accessible," wrote Nikolaus Pevsner, "caused its rapid decline. The style of Schinkel, Semper, Pearson and the whole Beaux-Arts could be taught and utilized with impunity by anyone who came along. Commercially a Van de Velde or a Tiffany was a disaster. No one would have attempted to commercialize the ideas of a Gaudí. It is this individualism which links art nouveau to the preceding century; its emphasis on craftsmanship, a manifest antipathy towards industry, and, finally, the preference for the precious or, at least, highly expressive material."

In fact, the modernists had established, whatever their individual interpretations, a repertory of forms and vocabulary. Japan had taught them new methods of expression, altogether different from any ideas then known in the West; they now challenged their own tradition with two-dimensional paintings, linear arabesques, and unmodulated color. The Western aesthetic principles which had reigned for two centuries were now overthrown. But, as opposed to the artists of the Far East who were heirs to a long tradition and applied common cultural formulas to all their work, the European modernists remained the heirs of romantic individualism. And this strain only became more pronounced. An obvious diversity of language exists among these artists who shared the same system of ideas. There is no similarity between a Majorelle chair and a Mackintosh chair, or between a Horta house and one designed by Gaudí. Art nouveau had its personal idioms and a national language as well. But one cannot speak of this movement as having schools. The groups which formed here and there all shared their discoveries and inventions with one another; nor did they promulgate elaborate doctrines. They met in a spirit of challenge and comradeship, and exhibited together. And that was all.

naturalization and stylization

The creators of art nouveau had in common, nevertheless, the goal of interpreting nature, and of interpreting it in a very special sense. The stylization of organic forms may appear as a mere detail in the evolution of the new style; but in reality this was its most powerful contribution.

Art nouveau may seem to have exploded like a brilliant but short-lived constellation; in fact, its germination took place slowly over the course of a generation, at least. Its characteristic morphology would start with the first experiments of William Morris and the first anthologies of the plant and its stylized forms. The *Grammar of Ornament* by Christopher Dresser is dated 1856. Botanical reference books

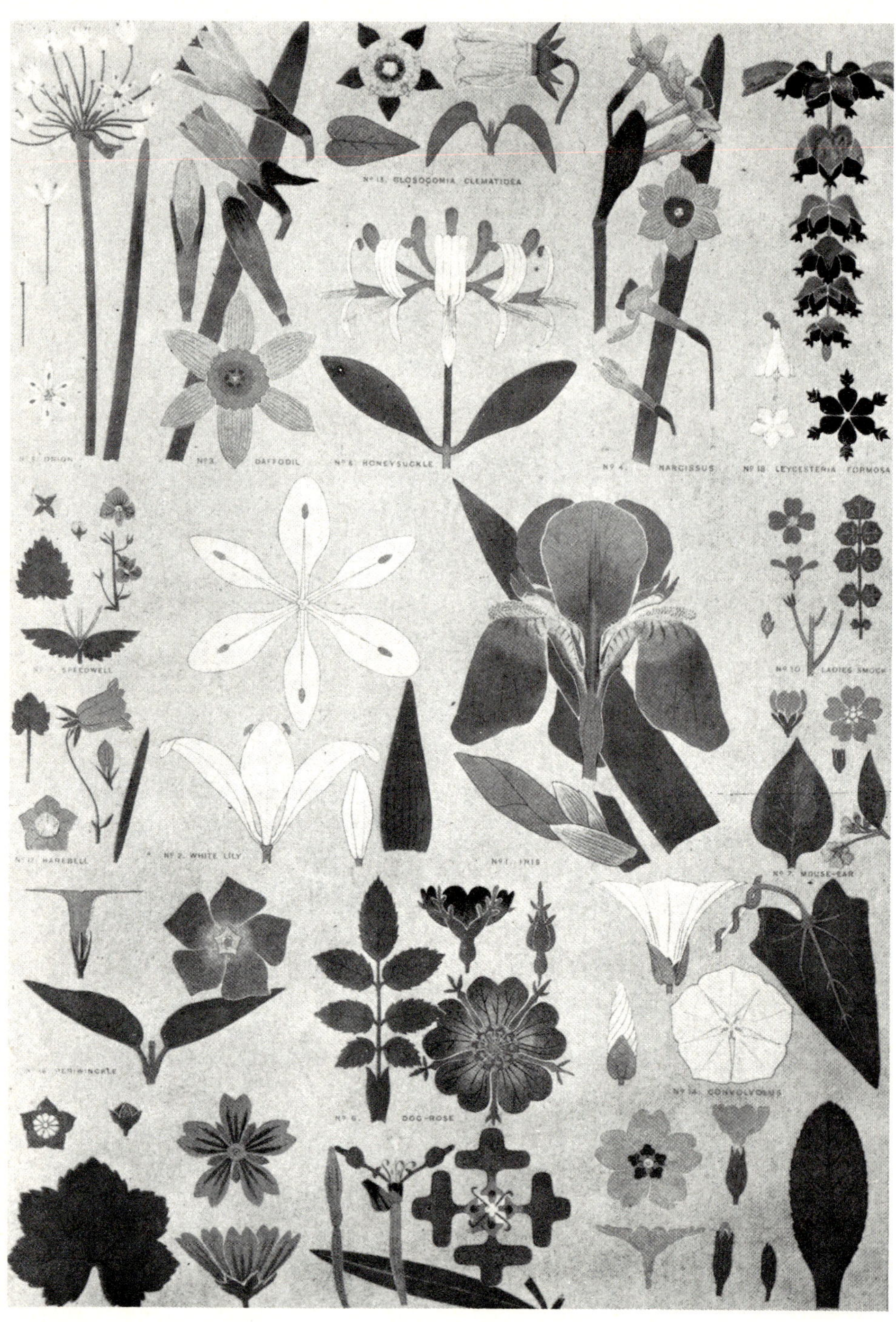

CHRISTOPHER DRESSER   "Plans and Elevations of Flowers," from
The Grammar of Ornament, 1856

schematically illustrated had been consulted in artists' studios for many years.

In these works, naturalism was reduced to its essential lines, at least in the view of artist-decorators, who exulted in their decorative possibilities. The evolution of the modernists is all the more curious as their development paralleled that major artistic event of the nineteenth century, impressionism, its obvious antithesis. The latter, in its experiments with such ephemera as the changing effects of light, is exclusively pictorial, and without any decorative concerns, whereas art nouveau was essentially the work of decorators, or of painters converted to decoration. Gauguin abandoned the impressionists with whom he exhibited in his youth, moving steadily into linear and *cloisonné* paintings. Conversely, Bonnard, whose early work reveals an acute feeling for the decorative, ultimately found his natural environment in the pleasures of "impression."

As opposed to French impressionism, art nouveau was a European event, with an antenna, an active branch in the United States, born as a result of Tiffany's efforts. The new style flowered with the fruit characteristic of the particular country. One could compare this diversity of language, bearing in mind the differences, to the great stylistic waves of earlier centuries, whose expression, although resting upon similar principles, affirmed very varied local contexts.

The impressionists discovered with abandon a body of optical truths which were opposed to realism, and which described a world of luminous vibrations. In order to capture the passage of time, or that which cannot be grasped, Nature was depicted serially. When Monet painted the same haystack or the same cathedral at every hour of the day, he was trying to record the impalpable, and to fix what Nature leaves unfixed and to which it never returns. The method of art nouveau is the reverse, the method of synthesis. It seized Nature in immutable lines. The objective was not to translate things into a transitory truth, but to give them an image capable of transforming truth into a decorative composition, transforming it into an object. Where impressionist art intercepts the instant by spots of pure colors, modernist art is on an altogether different plane; a plane that reduced the vision of the real to a sort of schema, to areas of almost uniform color rigorously enclosed within their contours.

Many of the most talented artists were able to participate in both these phenomena of the period, seemingly poles apart, but which more than overlapped — which explains how a Gauguin or Toulouse-Lautrec can appear in anthologies of impressionism. Gauguin, who had exhibited in his youth with the impressionists, was led ultimately to repudiate the painters of dispersed color values, to espouse a chromatism *cloisonné,* abandoning all attempts at verisimilitude to get closer to the truth. Toulouse-Lautrec, besides paintings composed of patches or stripes of color, like the portraits of the artist's mother, also painted works whose draftsmanship is a sure and precise linear style; his posters, consisting of areas of contrasting color, are masterpieces which rank him among the great masters of art nouveau.

women and flowers

The stylized flower became the favored motif everywhere. The tree with its foliage, the plant and its flowers are evoked, to be changed, pulverized, distended, and bent to the artist's requirements. The latter exercised his choices within a carefully defined framework. Among the principle emblems of art nouveau were the lily, iris, morning glory, fern, and poppy; the peacock, that flower-bird; and those forest vines whose undulating lines would appear in relief on buildings and furniture, evolving into the famous *whiplash* which became a symbol of Modern Style.

Some artists reproduced plants with fidelity, even to their natural setting (in one of his first glass vases, Gallé used the transparent glass to suggest the bottom of a pond where water lilies appear among the reeds). Other artists took such liberties in interpreting the plant world that it is impossible to identify the original models. But whatever the degree of their naturalism, all artists are reference points of the same style.

Floral compositions, in their undulating grace, exude an erotic quality and a tender grace which inevitably suggests woman. And, just as inevitably, woman came to join the flower in scenic representations within the repertory of art nouveau. Her long tresses floated in volutes, echoing the movement of her rounded arms. Feminine types emerge, bringing their joyful dances to Chéret's posters, to Mucha's elegant stylizations, and even to the morbidity of Klimt. The statue of *La Parisienne* dominated the official entrance to the 1900 World's

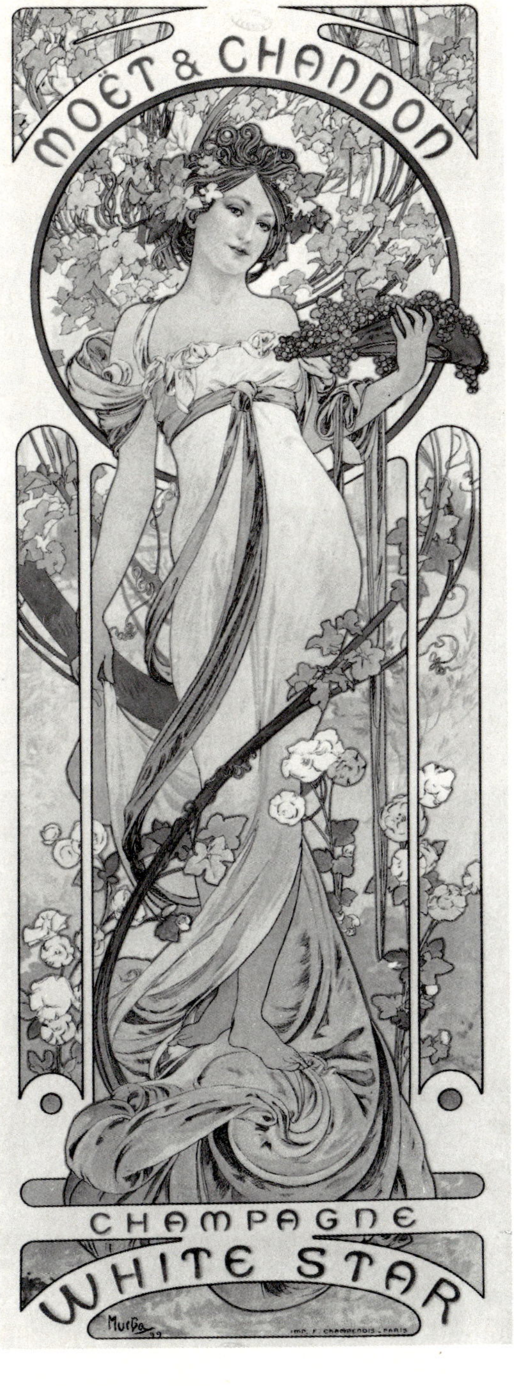

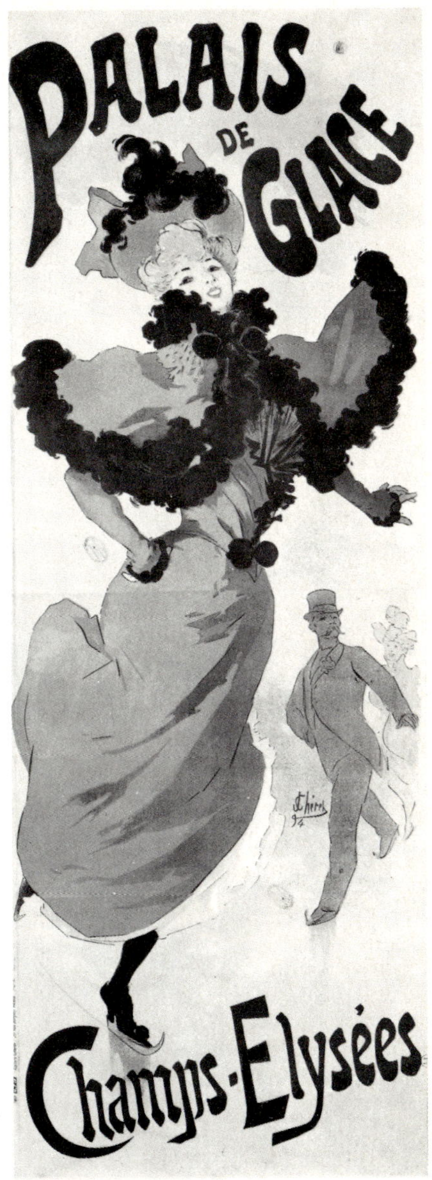

JULES CHÉRET   Poster for the
Ice Palace, 1894

ALFONS-MARIA MUCHA   Poster for
Moet et Chandon Champagne, 1889

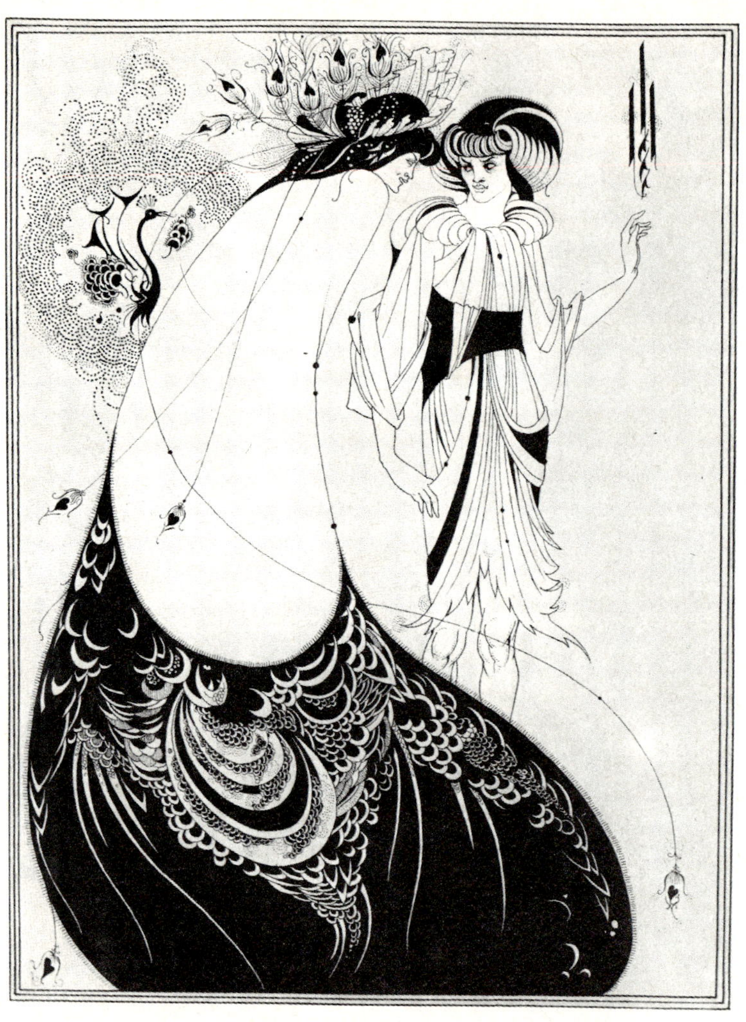

AUBREY BEARDSLEY　*The Peacock's Robe,* 1894

Fair, but the living beauties, in the swish of their trailing gowns, wreathed in feather boas, their large hats like petals, were more like flowers. Sculptors modeled the nude according to the canons of the new style. In England, the tormented bodies of Robert Burnes recalled William Blake, and Beardsley gave form, in a linear style of perverse precision, to the *Salome* of Oscar Wilde. His flowers and women are sometimes sinister, but their stylistic deformation is too mannered, too unrealistic to have any erotic power. If we were to sketch the

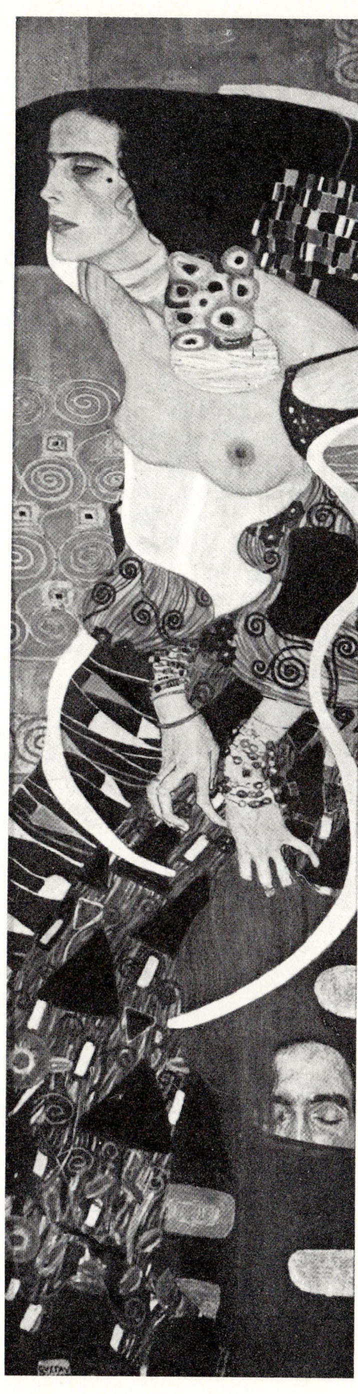

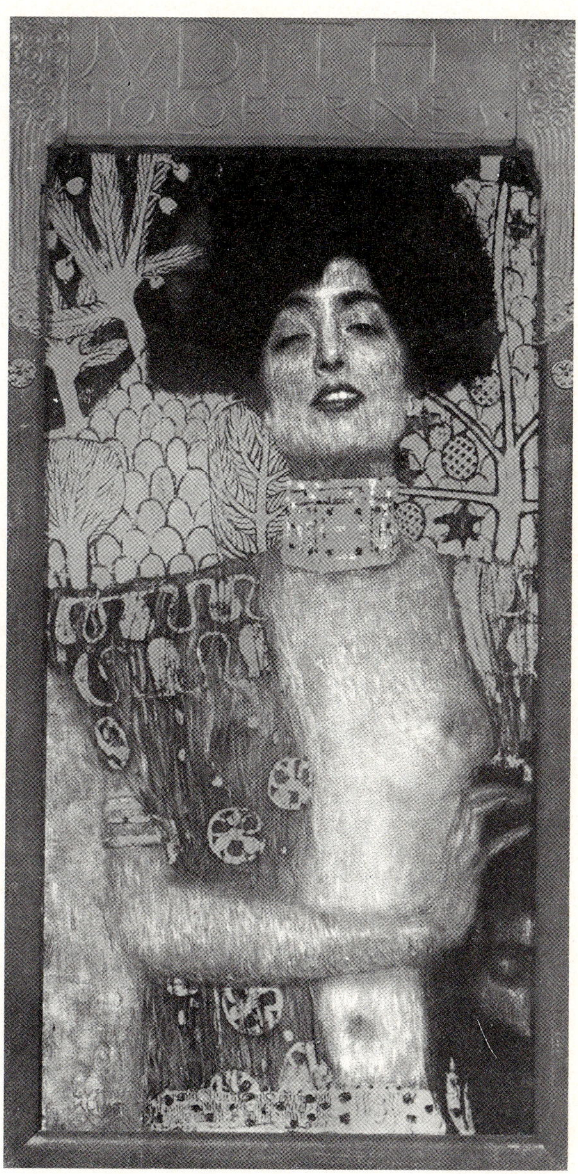

GUSTAV KLIMT   *Judith*, 1901

GUSTAV KLIMT   *Salome*, 1909

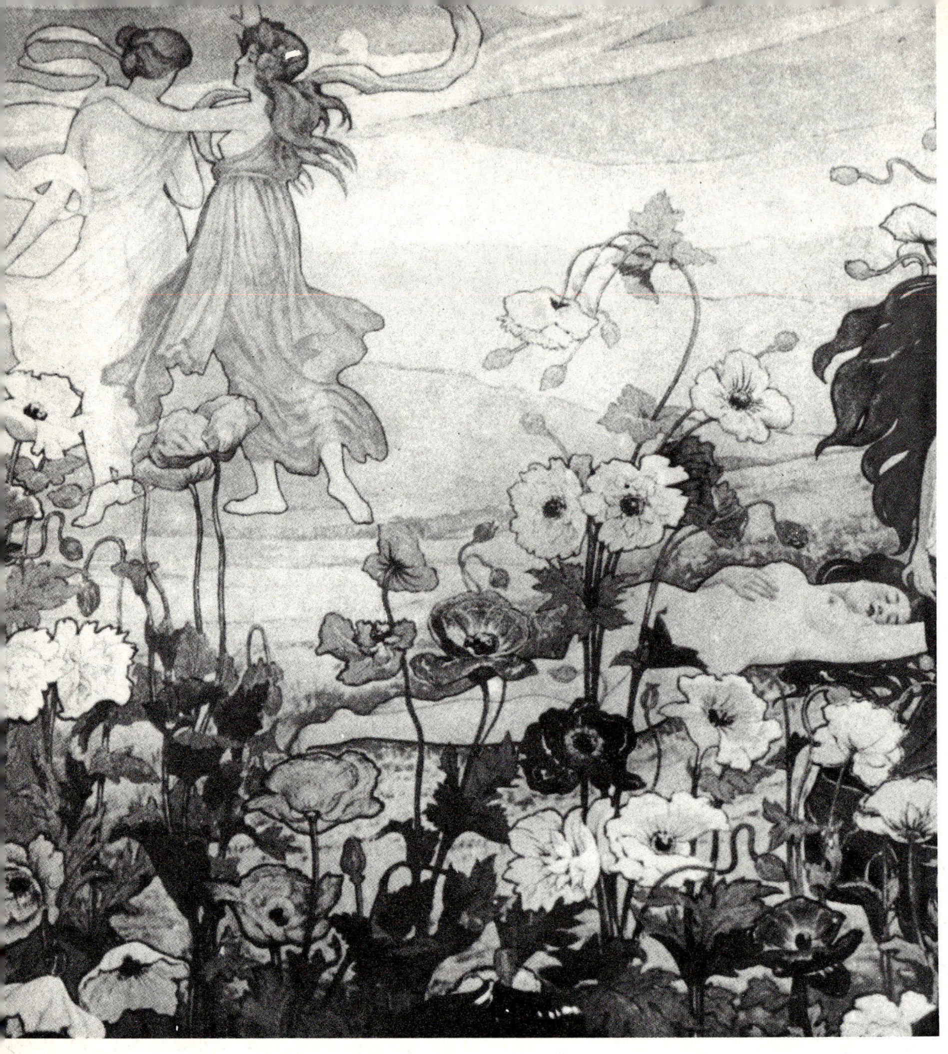

prototype for the art nouveau woman, she would be, at least in France, full-blown, radiant, and vital.

Around 1900, the Parisian woman, whether society beauty or courtesan, was characterized by dazzling elegance; rustling deliciously, and sparkling with wit, she took the center stage, eclipsing her male counterpart. And in an atmosphere of symbolic refinements, these particular embodiments of woman were celebrated by artists with the same conviction that had glorified the Pre-Raphaelites' angels. Boldini, Georges de Feure, very much part of the world of arts, letters, and the theater, never tired of depicting her intoxicating image. Woman entered Modern Style decor by virtue of her artifice. And it is on the

94

level of clever and facile pictorial values that she appears in all the salons.

With these portraits, we come to the peripheries of art nouveau. Their worldliness, like that of drawing-room furniture, bric-a-brac, and jewels, could only serve as a reminder of the high standards of rigor and quality which characterized their more dedicated contemporaries.

This was the precise moment when the flying wedge of art nouveau decoration attacked mere ornament; what they were attacking was, to be sure, primarily that bastardized, historicized ornament which continued to be produced for prominent interiors, both public and private, but also modernist ornamentation — at least whenever it was superfluous. The furnishings designed by Gallé, decorated with painted landscapes; the work by two semiabstract designers, Majorelle and Van de Velde — these furnishings do not, at least in principle, refer

GEORGES DE FEURE   Detail from the poster for the *Journal des Ventes,* 1897

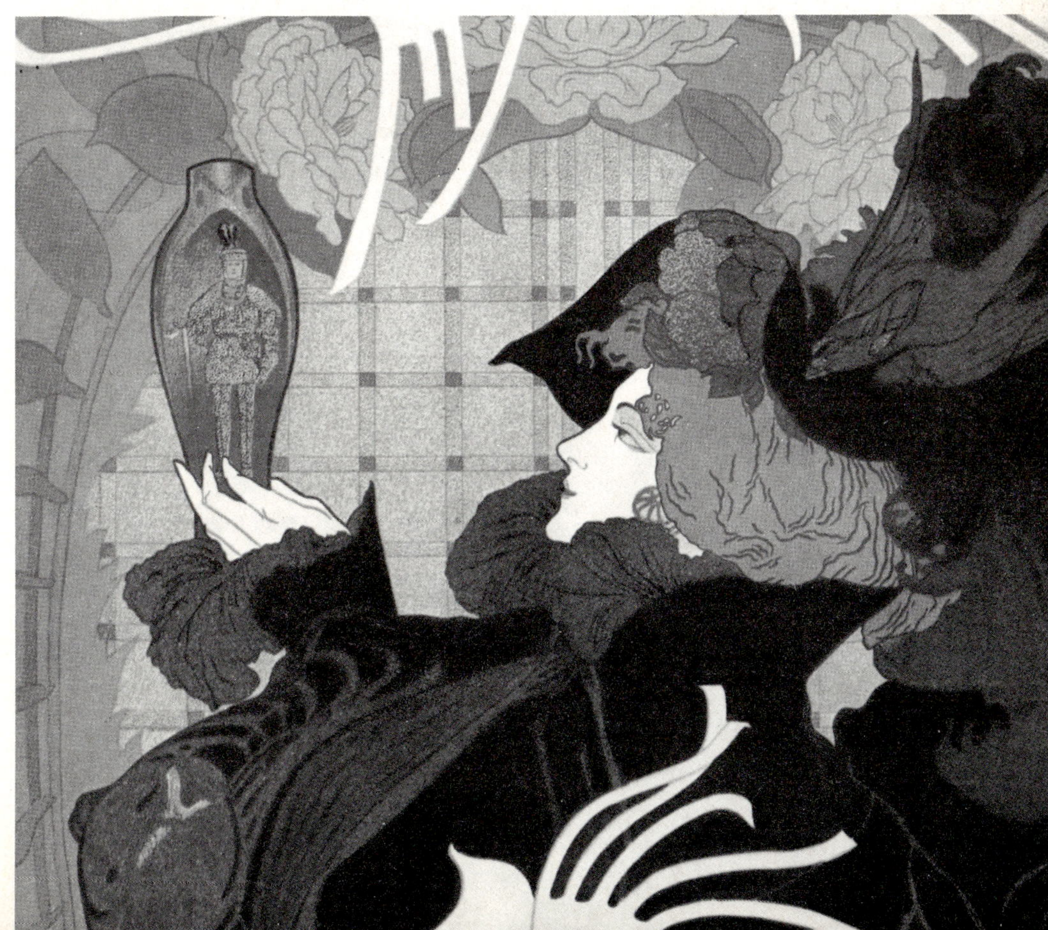

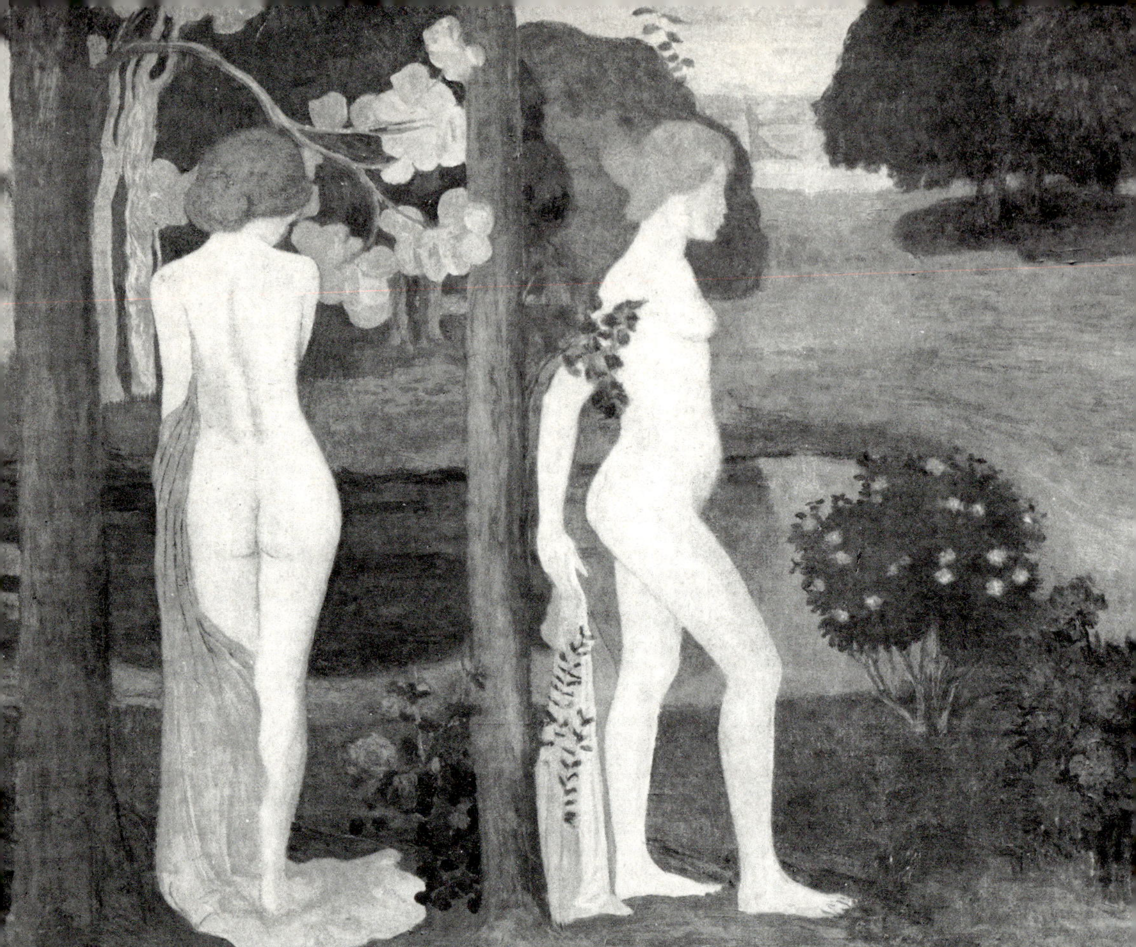

to any example which already existed in the design repertories, or even to forms derived from nature.

All this shows that it is really impossible to categorize the elements of an art nouveau style, to fix its morphological boundaries. The curve? The spiral? But then where do we place a Mackintosh who, believing in art nouveau, nevertheless designed, almost exclusively, buildings and furniture consisting only of angles and straight lines? And what about Van de Velde, who abandoned all decorative elements? And the refined rectilinear decors of Josef Hoffmann and the Viennese school? It may well be stated in reply that these men were exceptions, since art nouveau is defined by many as a neo-baroque style because of its profusion of curves and convexities.

Art nouveau, after all, was concerned with translating the form

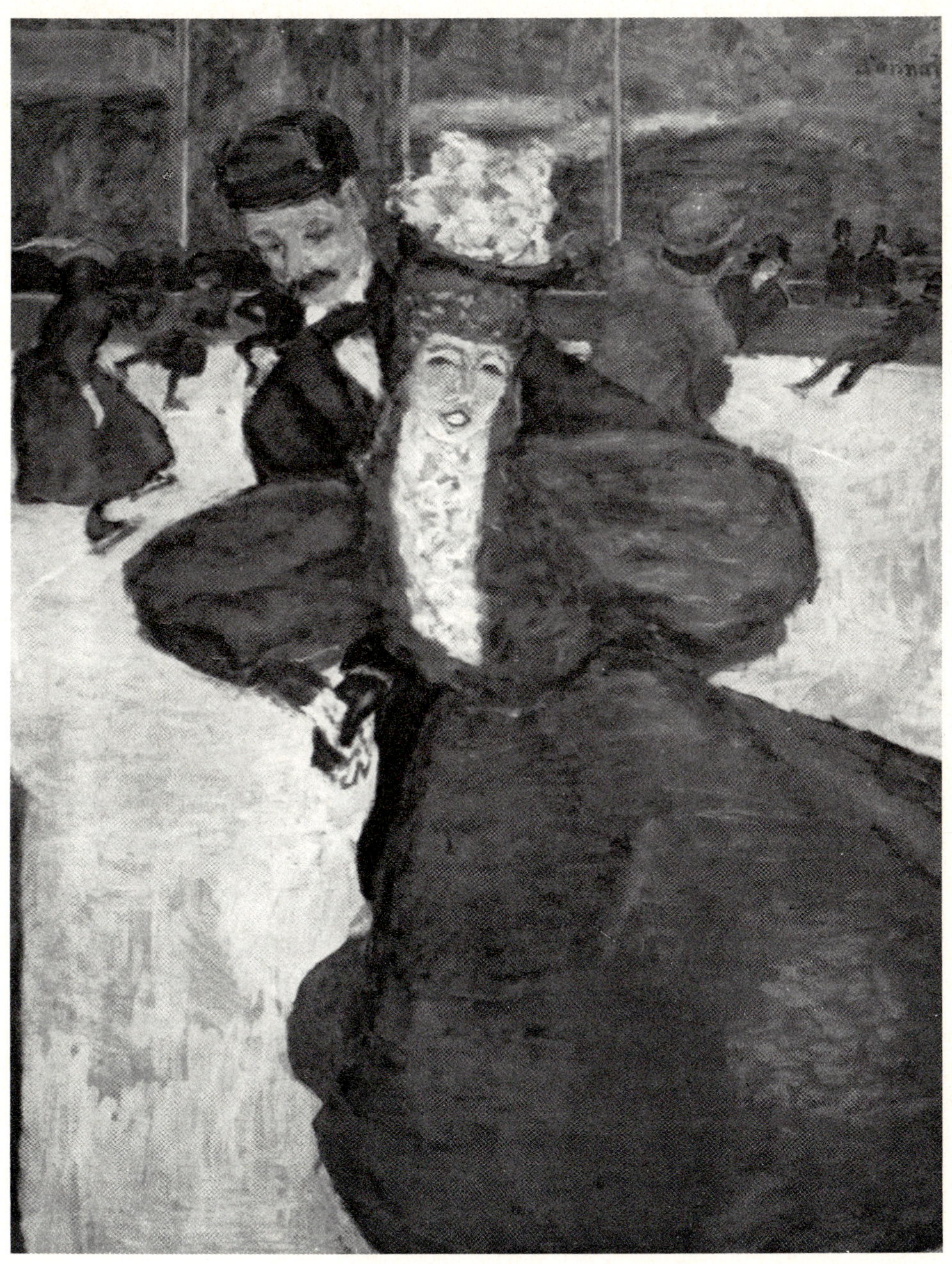

PIERRE BONNARD *The Ice Palace*, 1898

of vine and stem; it expressed the fugitive, the flexibility of the plant, the mobility of liquid; it tried to seize the fragility of transitory being, transmuting it into solid matter.

It is true that the school of Nancy gives us only examples of sinuous forms, like those described above, that the grillwork of the Paris Métro

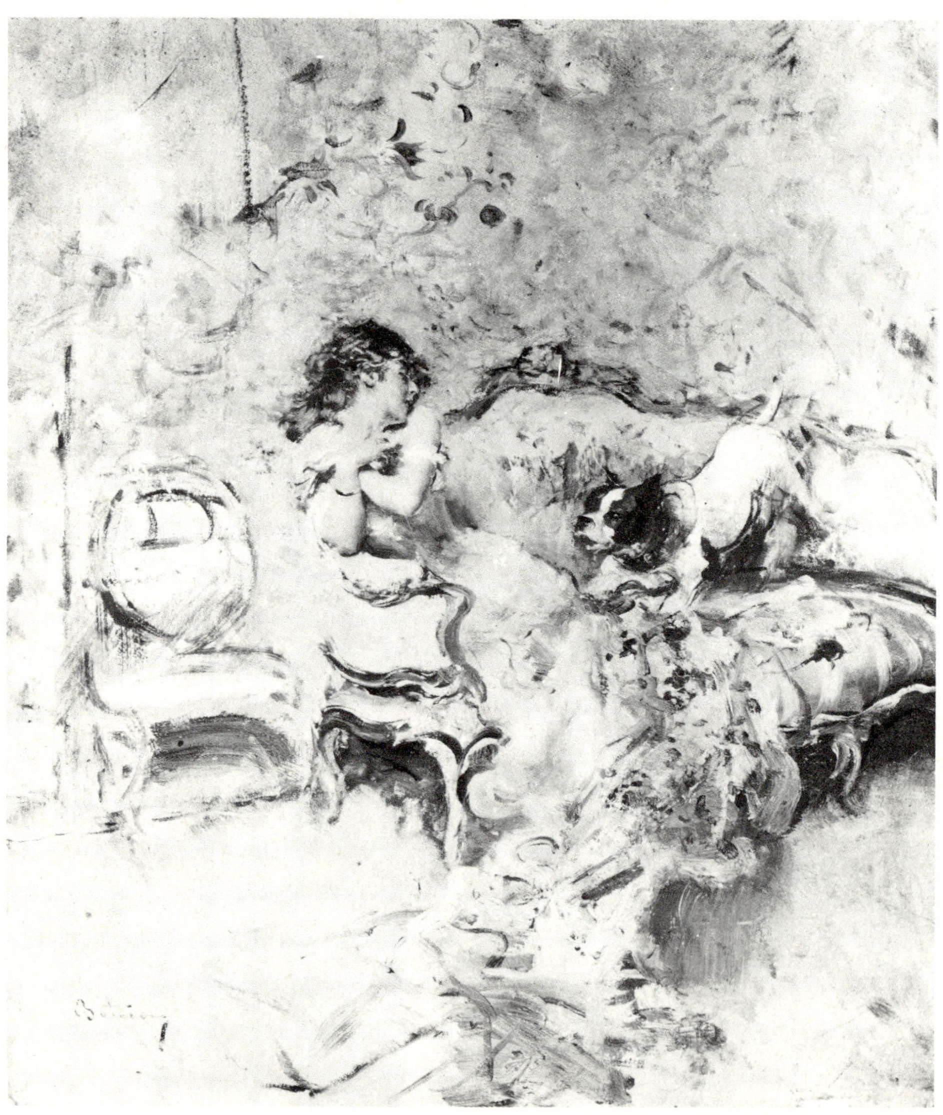

GIOVANNI BOLDINI   *Lady with a Dog*

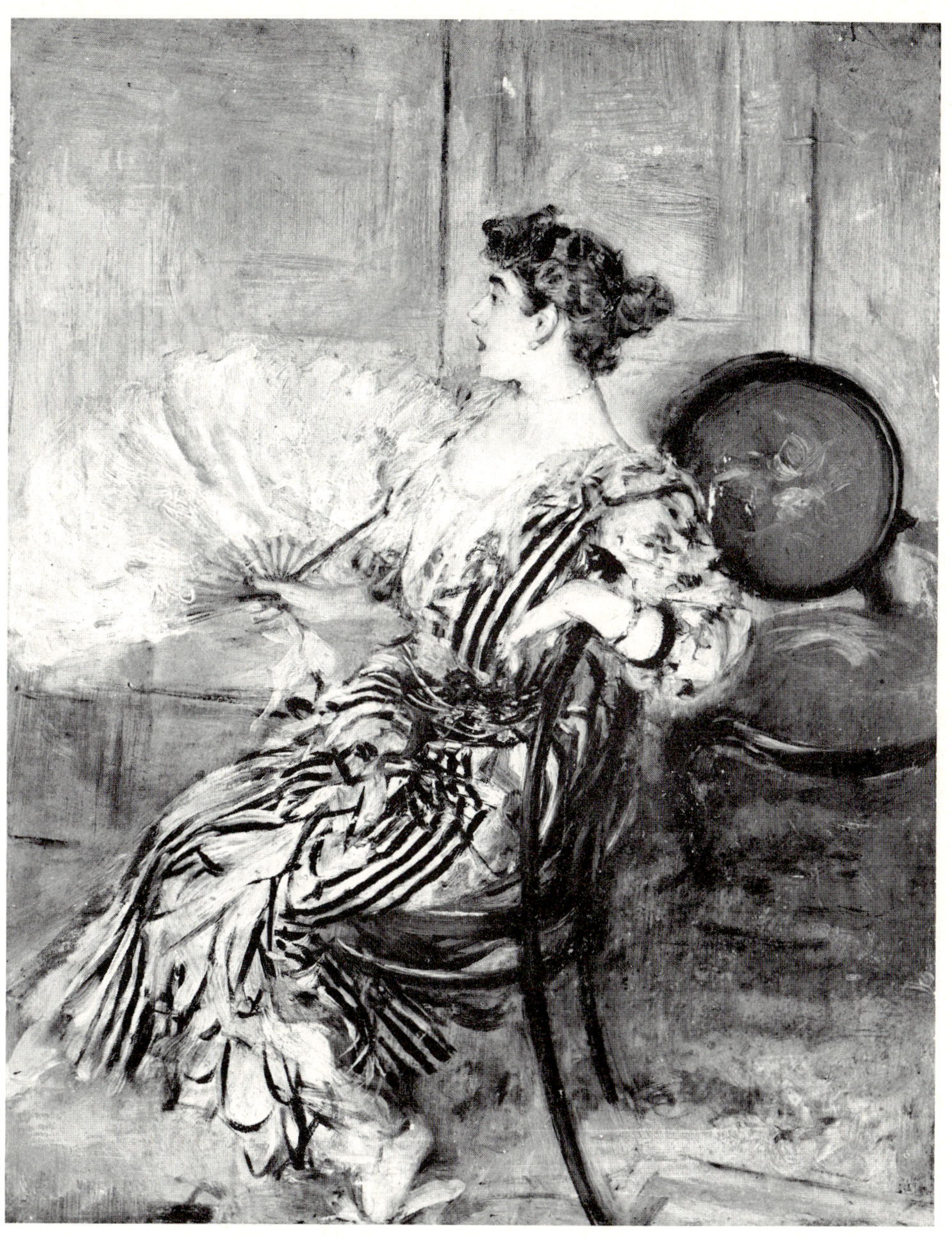

GIOVANNI BOLDINI   *Portrait of Madame Torre*

entrances made people laugh because they seemed serpentine. It is true that Gaudí was an enemy of the straight line, and that, in every country, the graphic arts multiplied the curve with stubborn insistence. The examples we shall soon discuss nonetheless reveal a coexistence between lines and other highly diverse forms, even when they derived from the same source and adhered to the same principles of design.

How then to define the central idea of art nouveau? It is safer not to seek criteria based upon appearances or upon exclusively visual evidence. Art nouveau is, above all, a response to a state of mind. It refuses to be imprisoned within any one definition, but, as we follow its course, we begin to discover its identifying characteristics. It has been said that the word *nouveau*, the *new* of its qualifying adjective, remains vague. After all, every art form was new at the time.

But, this truth notwithstanding, art nouveau still deserves its name. First, it must not be forgotten that generations of visionary artists had tried in vain to emerge from stagnation. The word *nouveau* is perfectly explained by the fact that, with this generation, they succeeded.

belgian architects and decorators

Belgium was receptive to new intellectual movements. Flemish or Walloon, poets like Max Elscamp, Van Lerberghe, Edmond Picard, Verhaeren, and Maeterlinck were steeped in symbolist literature and active in the search for new forms. They all contributed to *L'Art Moderne,* whose impassioned editor was Octave Maus, *La Jeune Belgique, La Wallonie,* as well as to the *Mercure de France* and *La Revue Blanche. Art Nouveau* was the name of a newspaper published in Brussels in 1884, which inaugurated a campaign to create museums of industrial art. The Belgians were about to redeem the original meaning of the words *art nouveau;* these writers were close to the symbolist painters; one of their most eloquent spokesmen was Khnopff, but they all sought escape from realism, and from the banality of the everyday. Groups of Belgian painters invited French artists to exhibit with them. Cézanne, Rodin, Monet, Redon, and Seurat, among others, were welcomed more warmly in Brussels than they had ever been elsewhere. Groups like the Cercle des XX and *Libre Esthétique* were avid for anything avant-garde.

Brussels had become a city of rich bourgeois who yearned to display the proof of their prosperity. Their opulent mansions, like the new public buildings, were distinguished largely by heavy-handed pastiche and lamentable poverty of invention.

victor horta, inventor

In this urban setting, Victor Horta (1861-1947) designed a town house for a Professor Tassel — a house whose simple and dignified structure had the added virtue, despite its originality, of harmonizing with its neighbors. The Tassel House can be considered the first example of art nouveau architecture (1882).

Until then, architects who designed houses for the bourgeoisie were not required to exert their creative imagination; each floor repeated the same simple-minded plan. Rooms were distributed along a dark corridor: narrow windows broke up the facade. But with Horta's first villa, the conventional plan was turned completely upside-down. The facade clearly articulated, in perfectly balanced design, an interior disposition planned in terms of its inhabitants' way of life.

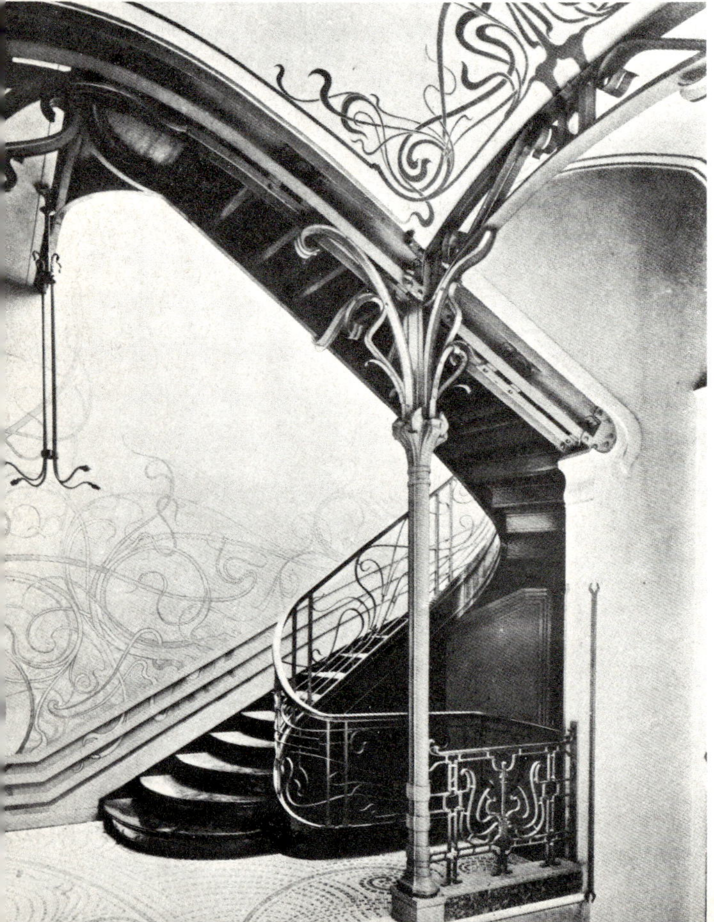

VICTOR HORTA
Staircase for Tassel House,
1892–1893

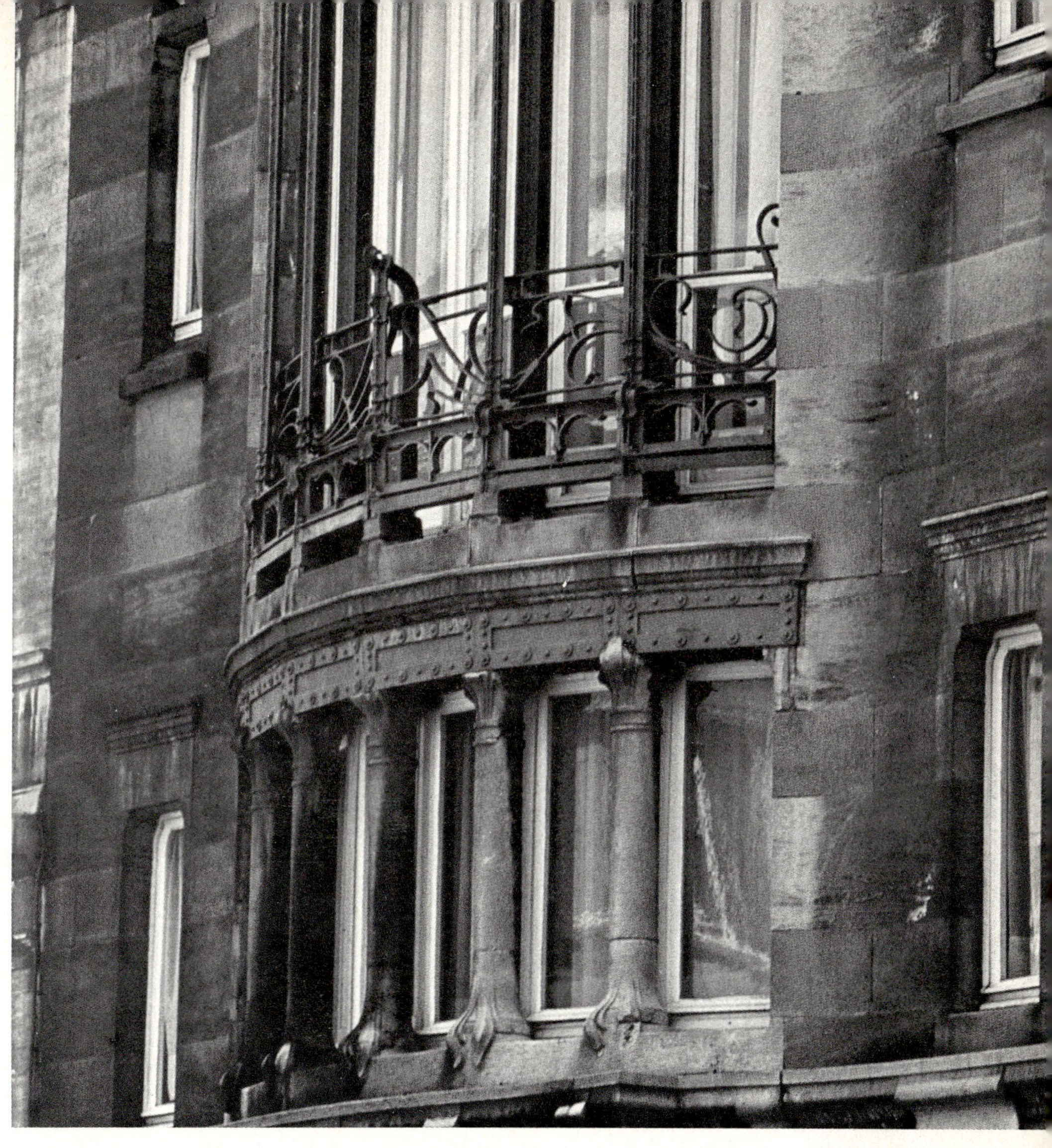

Victor Horta   Facade of Tassel House, 1892–1893

The Tassel House is not imposing (the facade measures 25 feet), but its design is characterized by a rhythmic fluidity which has a majesty of its own. The consoles flanking the entrance way support a corbeled loggia which links the ground and parlor floors. The completely glazed, curved bay window is supported by visible iron framework. The only ornamentation is the wrought-iron balustrade of the bay window. The story goes that Balat, the most eminent Brussels architect, a student of ancient Greece and Horta's teacher, burst into tears on seeing this facade. No one seems to know, however, whether he wept because his pupil repudiated his example, or because he was so moved by the sight of architecture of unquestionable distinction that owed so little to the past.

If the exterior was rigorous in its simplicity, the interior of the Tassel House was exuberant in its decor (a contrast which recalls the baroque churches of central Europe). The winter garden is supported by one iron beam. From an octagonal vestibule filled with natural light, a staircase sweeps upward. Sinuous iron lines wind around its balustrade and supporting beams, echoing more ironwork that climbs walls or twists along the floor, with all the luxuriance and freedom which, from now on, will characterize Modern Style. This was the beginning

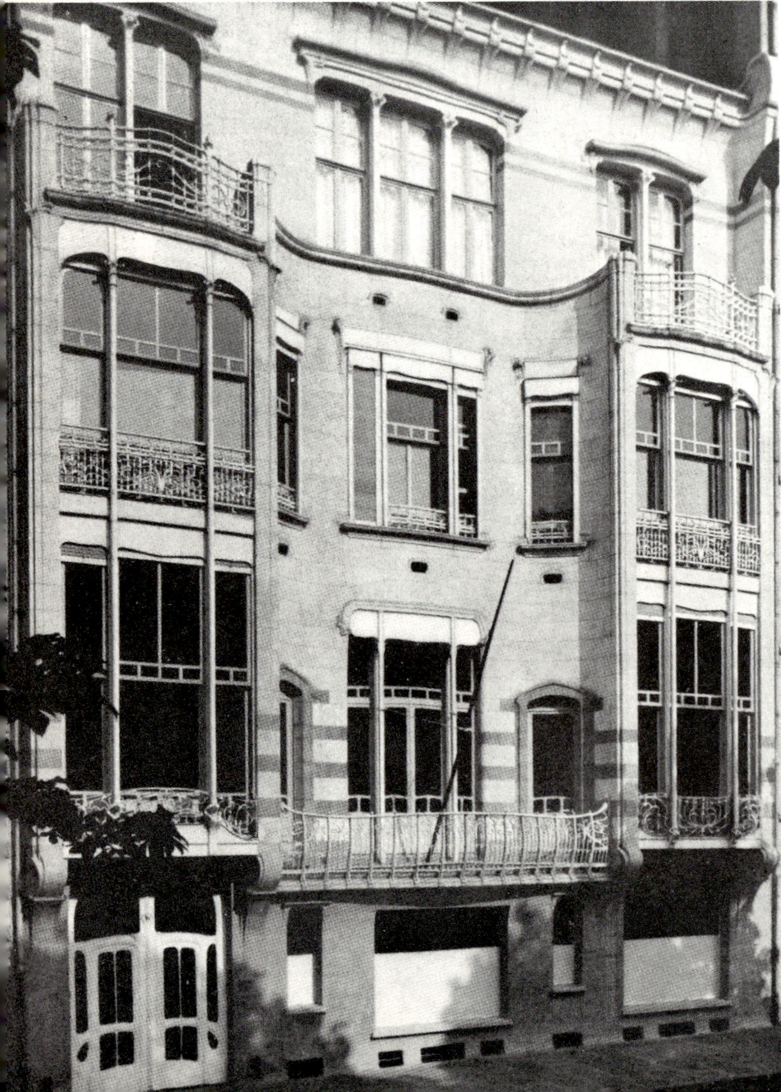

VICTOR HORTA
Facade of the Solvay House,
1895–1900

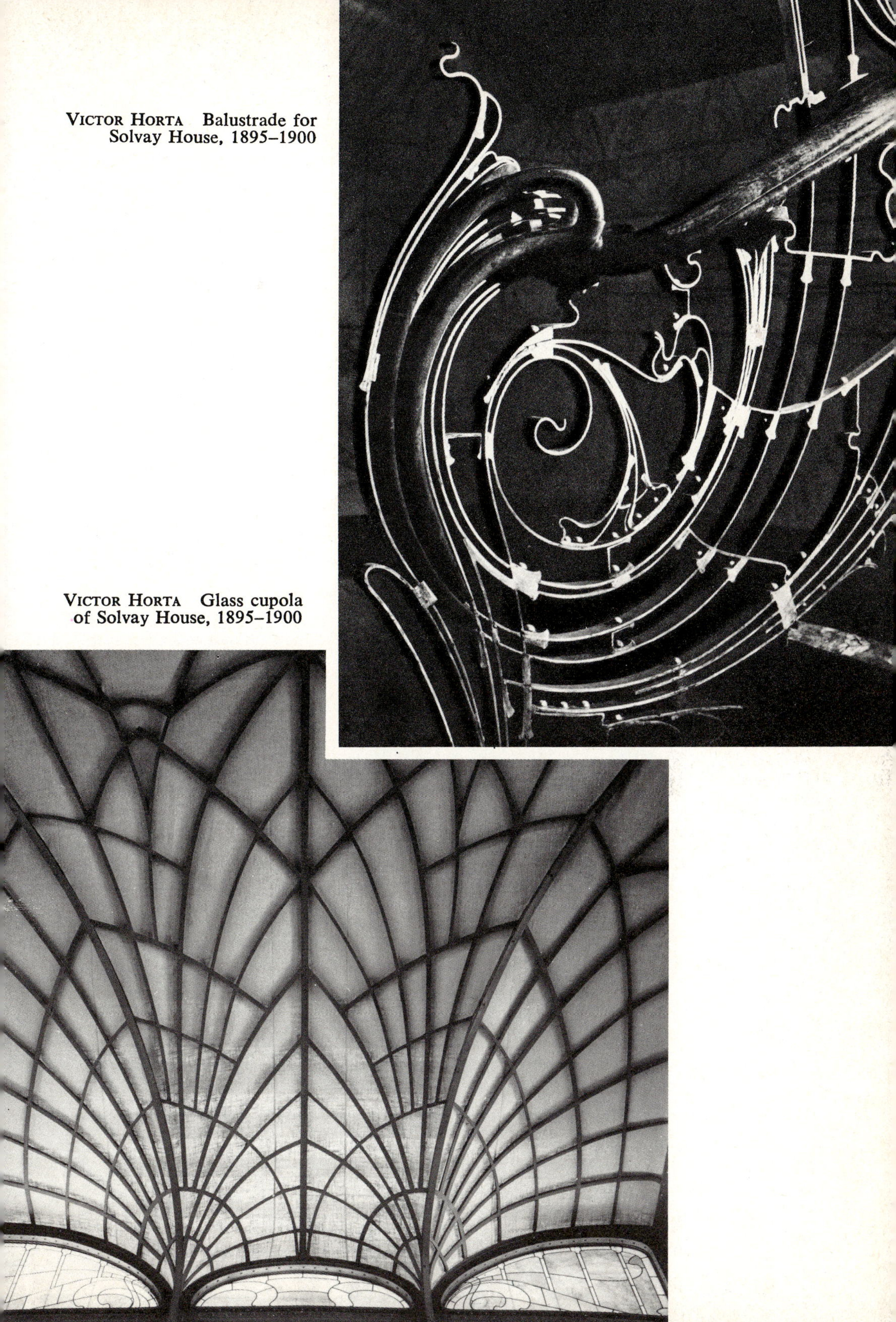

Victor Horta   Balustrade for
Solvay House, 1895–1900

Victor Horta   Glass cupola
of Solvay House, 1895–1900

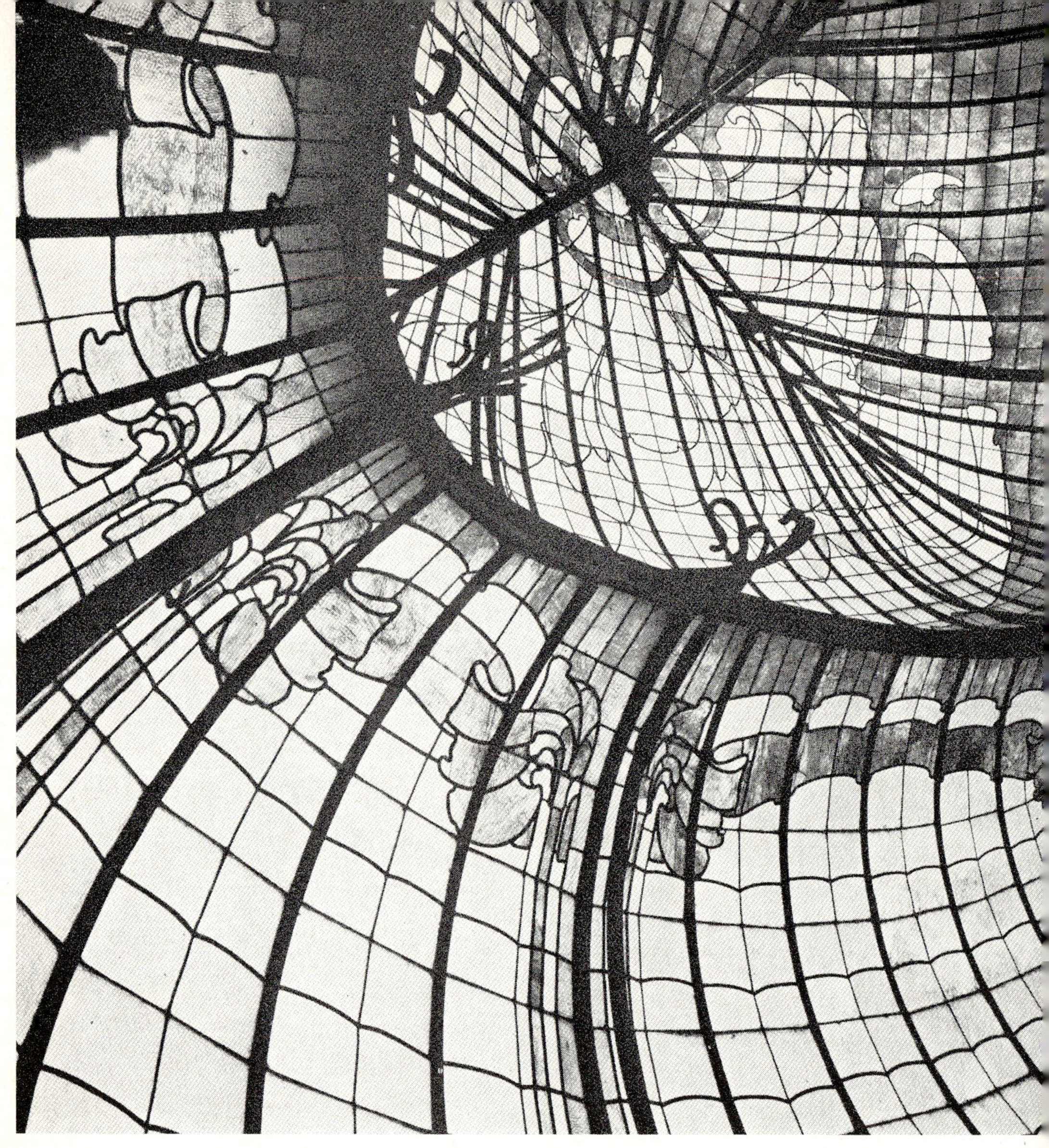

of what would come to be known as the *Horta line* or else, the *whiplash* style, a reference to its nervous vitality. Every element is decorative, but not a single one is gratuitous. Each is a response to an architectonic function, at the same time that it affords visual satisfaction. The real event was the visible use of iron and glass for solutions that were both logical and unexpected.

Horta's next commission was a town house on the avenue Louise

106

(1894), built for the industrial chemical tycoon, Armand Solvay. This project gave Horta the scope to carry out a very ambitious program for a client of almost limitless means. Solvay was also an architect's ideal, as he gave Horta a completely free hand. The Solvay House thus avoided the sacrosanct conventions of most bourgeois dwellings. The program consisted of the construction and decoration of apartments on four levels, with a drawing room 52 feet long, facing the front; a dining room of the same dimensions; bedrooms; bathrooms; basements; servants' quarters; and stables. The exciting facade reveals the disposition of the rooms which have moveable partitions for maximum flexibility. The atmosphere combines elegance and a new comfort — in itself avant-garde. The Solvay House belongs to the ranks of metal structures which allow bolts and rivets to show, in the interest of honesty. But, in a purely decorative vein, the balustrade of the grand staircase displays curves and countercurves of the most superbly wrought iron.

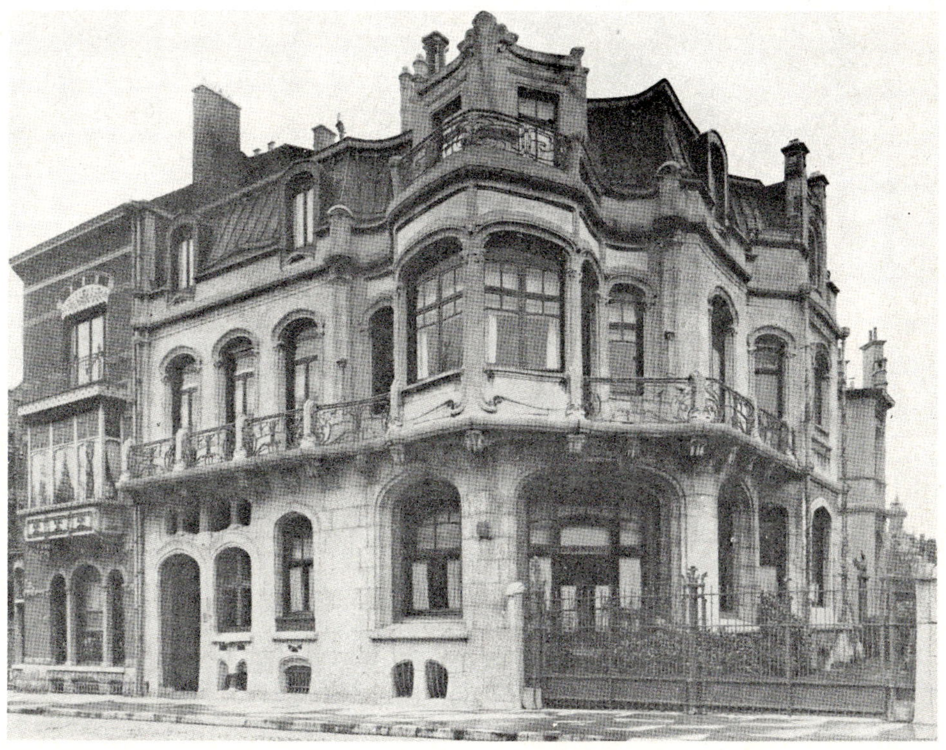

VICTOR HORTA   Facade of the Aubecq House, 1899

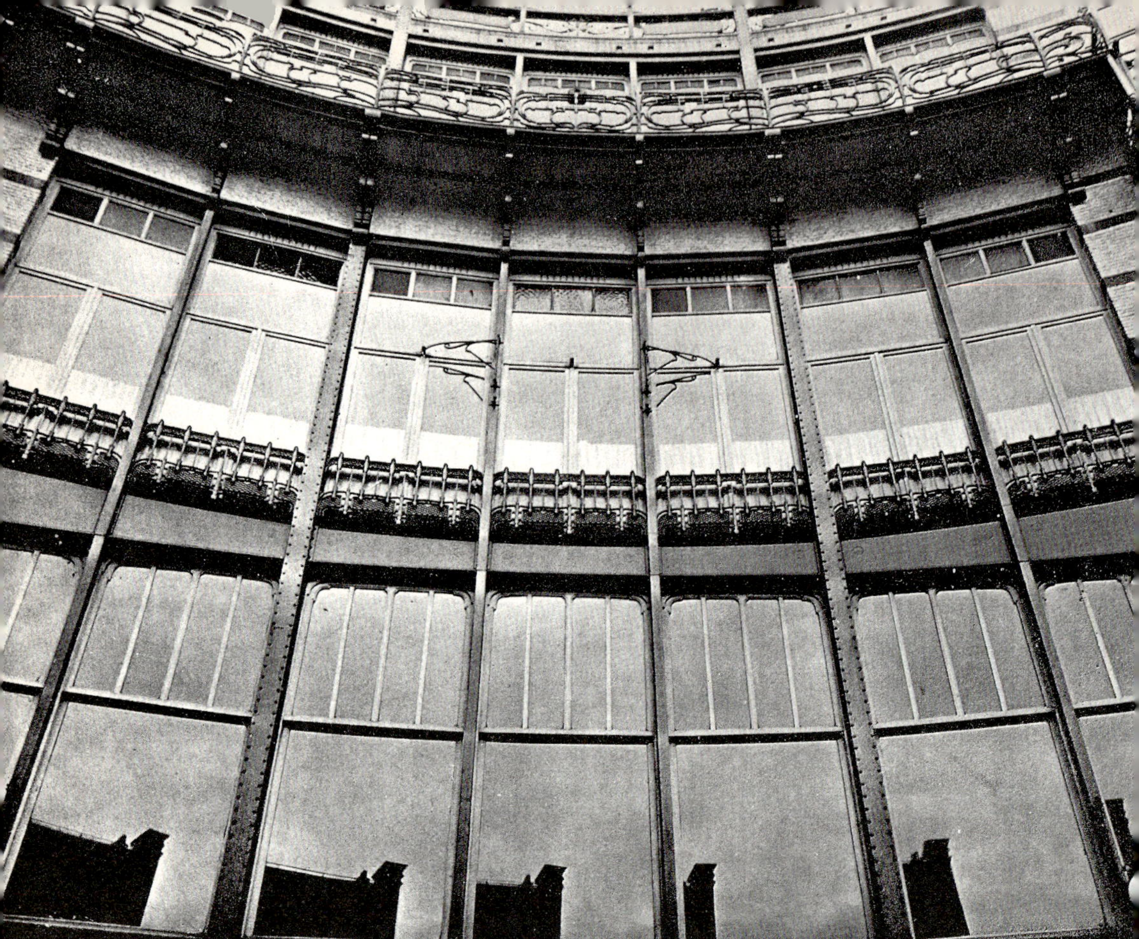

Victor Horta   Exterior of the Maison du Peuple, 1897–1899

Among the distinguished houses designed by Horta at the same period was the Aubecq House. Here the architect's extreme sensibility is revealed in every detail. The large glass dome, refaced with complex designs and supported by steel strips, was justly acclaimed a tour de force and a masterpiece of art nouveau. Other European architects, interested in learning what such bold disposition of luminous surface meant for the future, made the pilgrimage to Brussels. Among them was Hector Guimard.

At the same time, the famous Maison du Peuple, partially financed once again by Solvay, was going up — a prefiguration of contemporary architecture. The concave facade was almost entirely glass; a steel beam had replaced retaining walls which, despite the miracle of the Gothic nave, still had remained indispensable architectural elements since the beginning of civilization. Horta had already demonstrated his inventiveness in his domestic architecture, in which he ignored the rules of vertical superposition. Given the enormous size of this building, the liberty taken in the plan of each floor seems paradoxical, even when it corresponds to functional adaptations. In the vast auditorium, visible iron beams were part of the ornamentation, and were further emphasized by the irregular rhythm of the lateral balconies. The painting by Signac, which he titled *Au temps de l'harmonie (In the Time of Harmony)*, was both homage and definition. The Maison du Peuple may have seemed an unappealing scrap heap to a later generation. When it was conceived in 1896, it was futurism.

His wild inventiveness led Horta into occasional excess. He decorated the Max Hallet House, for example, with bow windows, topped by three cupolas in the shape of helmets joined together. The effect

VICTOR HORTA   Auditorium of the Maison du Peuple, 1897–1899

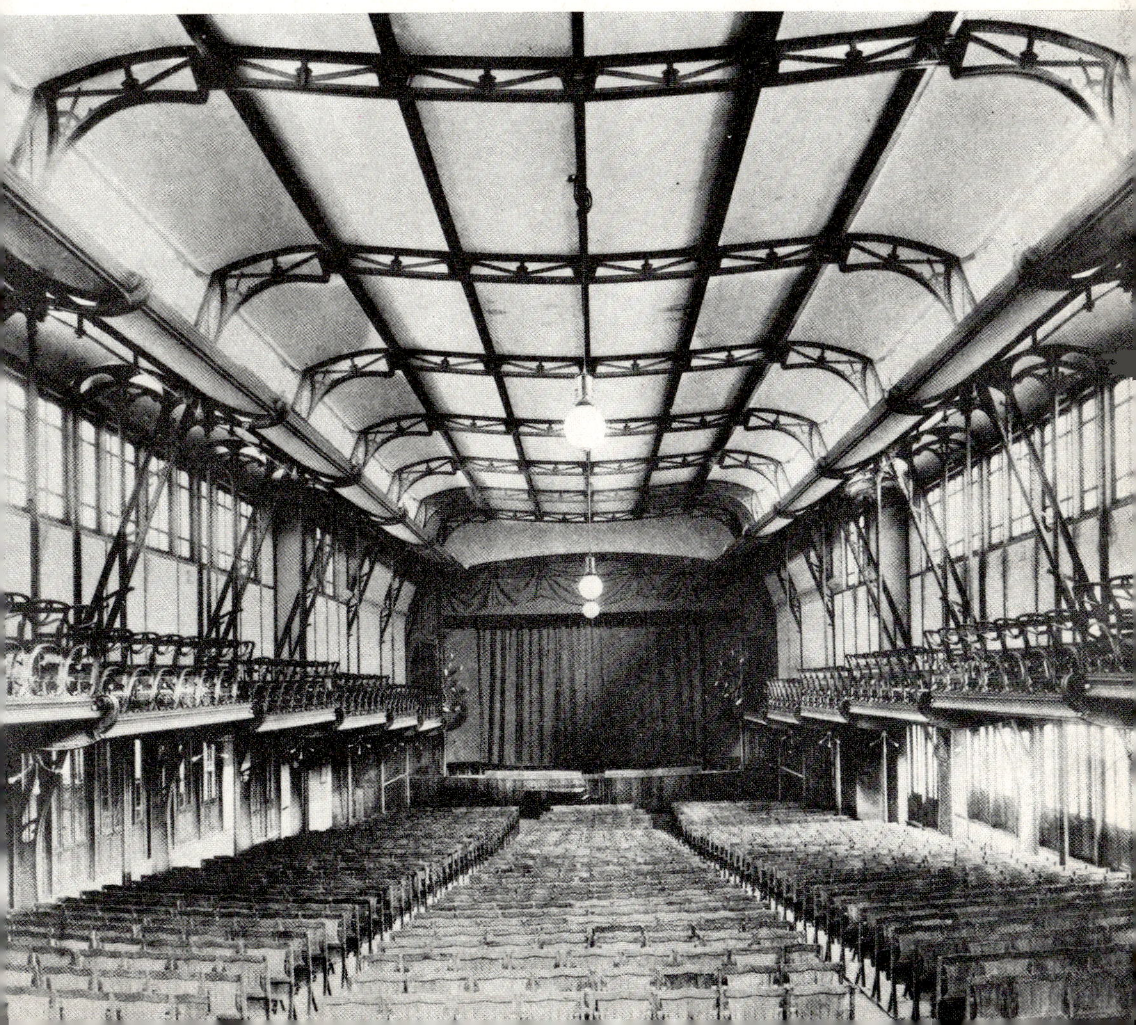

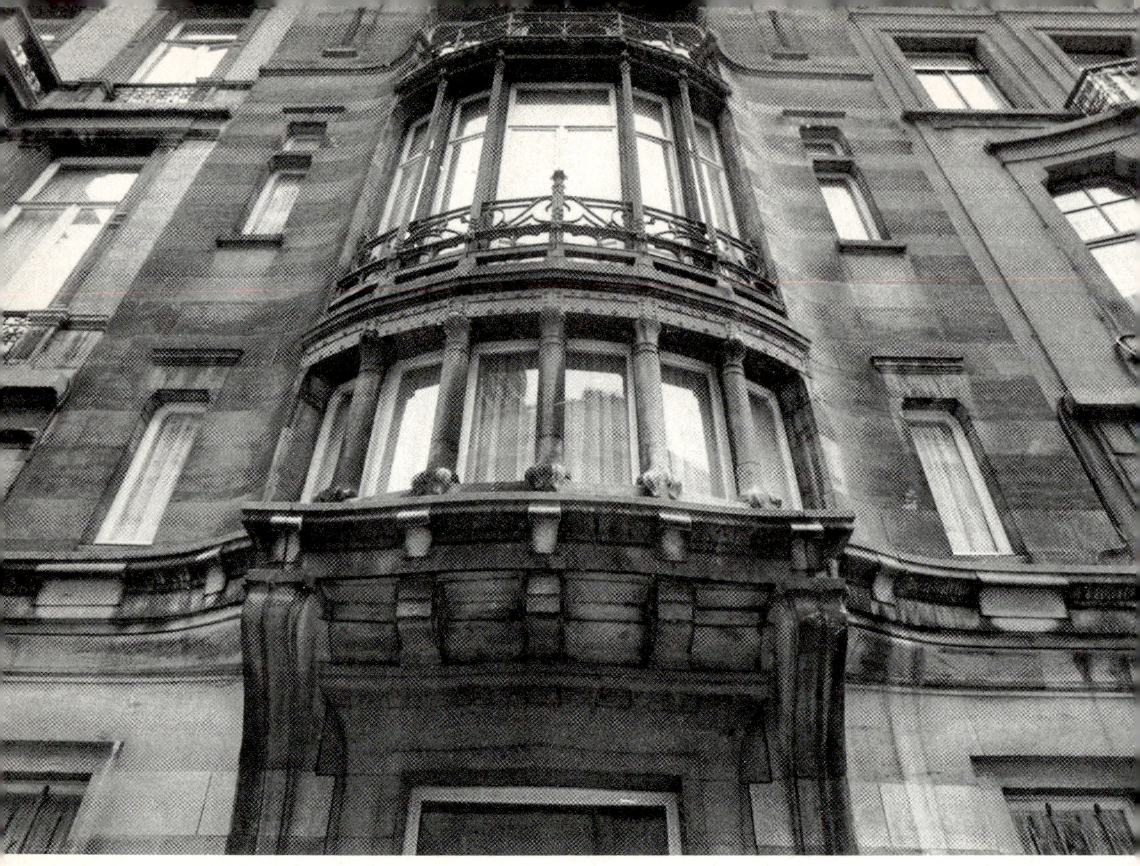

Victor Horta   Exterior of the Tassel House, 1892–1893

was of questionable taste. But such an adventurous and innovative mind should be allowed the occasional mistake. For, while he continued work on architectural projects, he was also designing furniture, textiles, and carpets, thus exemplifying the idea that the architect and artist should participate in one another's craft, in order to assure an environment for living, perfect in every detail.

Like many of the architects who have come to exemplify art nouveau, Horta soon abandoned, for a change in ideology, the very movement which he had led and which today is synonymous with his fame. But in fact, he had never really forgotten Balat's teachings; Horta finished his old teacher's work after the latter's death (1895). After he had designed so many Modern Style buildings — town houses, country villas, and commercial buildings like the famous department store A l'Innovation, built according to the same architectonic principles as the Maison du Peuple — Horta repudiated the style that he had invented and practiced with such brilliant results.

110

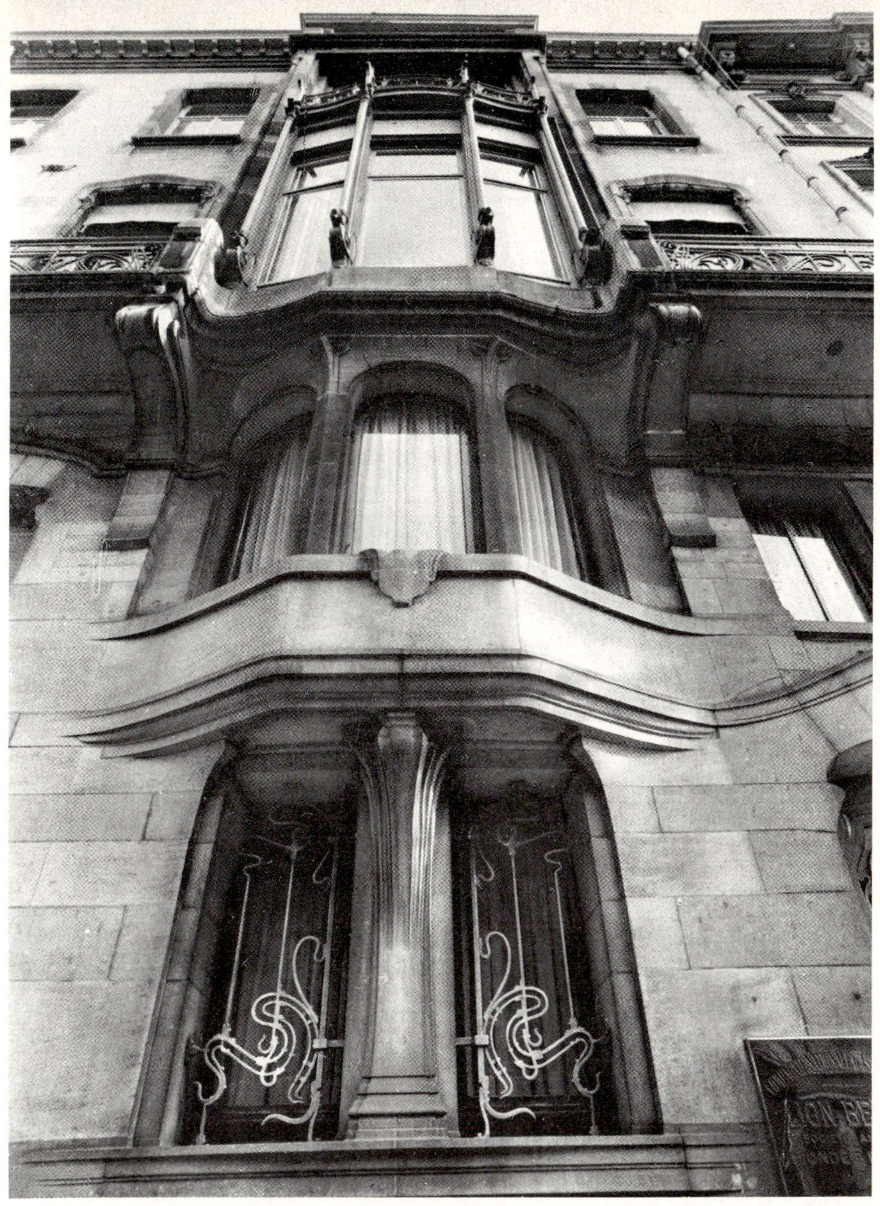

Victor Horta   Exterior of the Winssinger House, 1894

His stay in the United States after the invasion of Belgium in 1914 had an unexpected effect upon Horta's philosophy. He returned to classicism. Fame assured him the most lucrative official commissions, like the Musée de Tournai and the Musées Royaux des Beaux-Arts in Brussels. The Belgian Pavilion at the Exhibition of Decorative Arts in

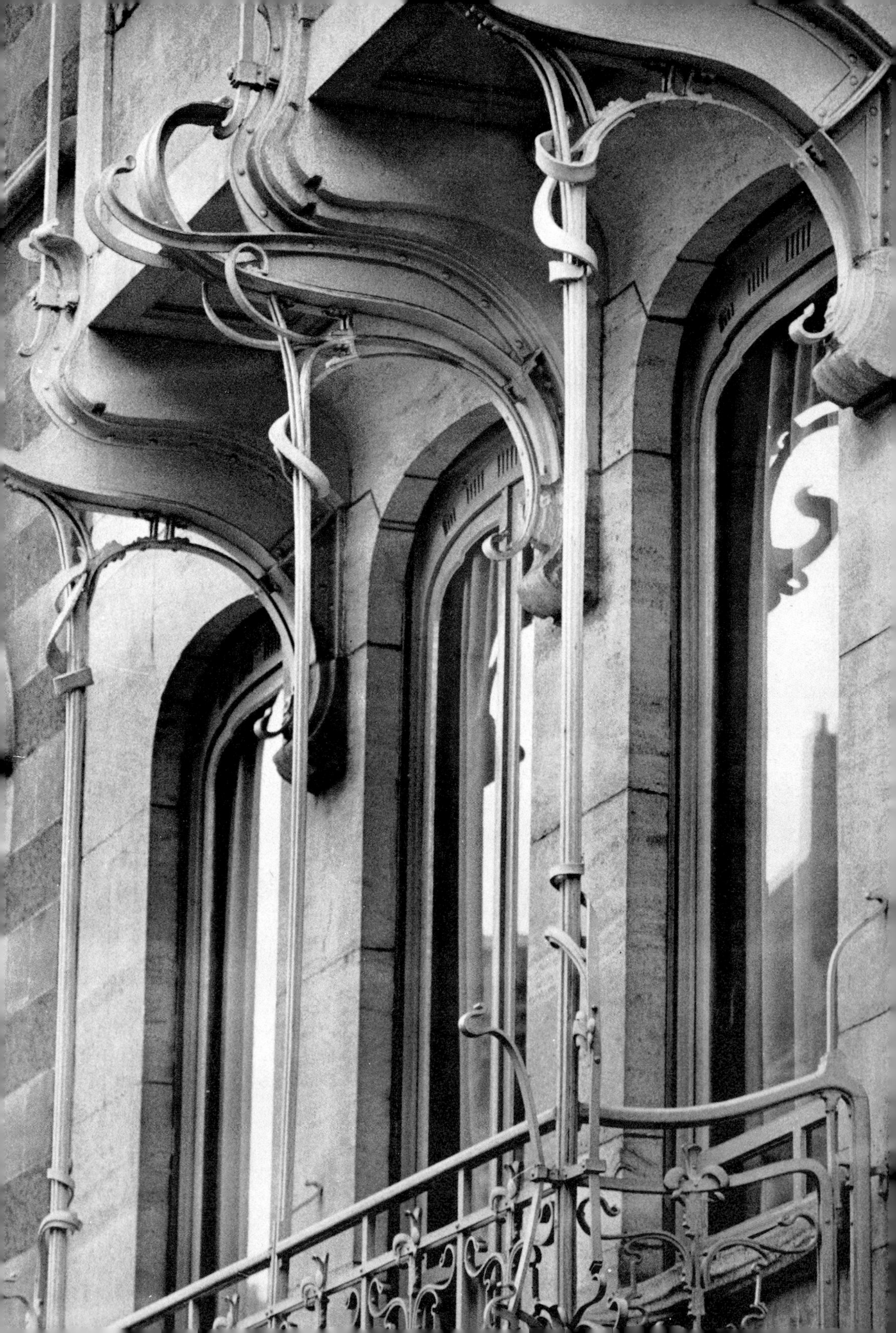

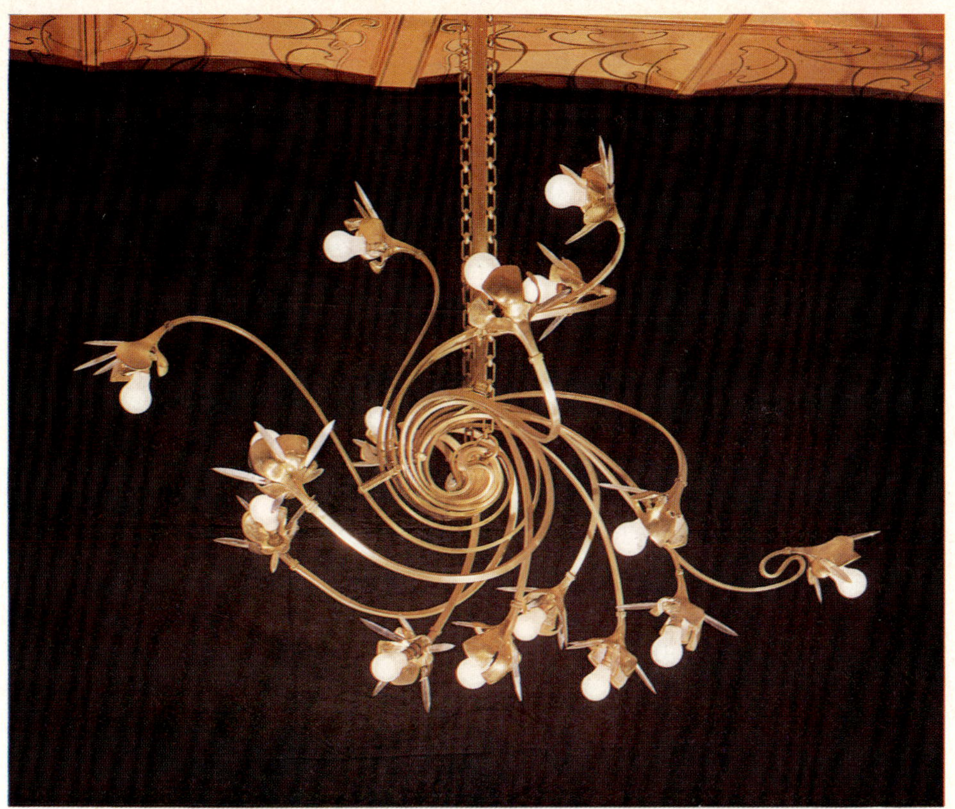

VICTOR HORTA   Chandelier for Solvay House, ca. 1900

1925 in Paris astonished those who were familiar with the innovative work of this architect — not that the building lacked harmony and simplicity, but it was another Horta that stood revealed.

A number of recent publications and exhibitions have been devoted to this pioneer of art nouveau, a happy circumstance, since many of his buildings can now be known only through photographs. The Aubecq House, one of Horta's most accomplished projects, and, in certain respects, his most interesting, was demolished in 1952 and replaced by an office building. In 1964, the Maison du Peuple, over the outraged protest of many architects and other concerned professionals throughout the world, suffered the same fate: it was replaced by an apartment tower. Although the Tassel House still stands, it was mutilated in 1958 by its new owners. And many others have shared this fate. As though ill-luck hovers over Horta's work, the two department stores he designed were consumed by fire: one in Frankfort was destroyed in the last war; the other, A l'Innovation, disappeared in a dramatic blaze in 1967.

113

VICTOR HORTA   Detail for windows of Horta House, 1898–1906

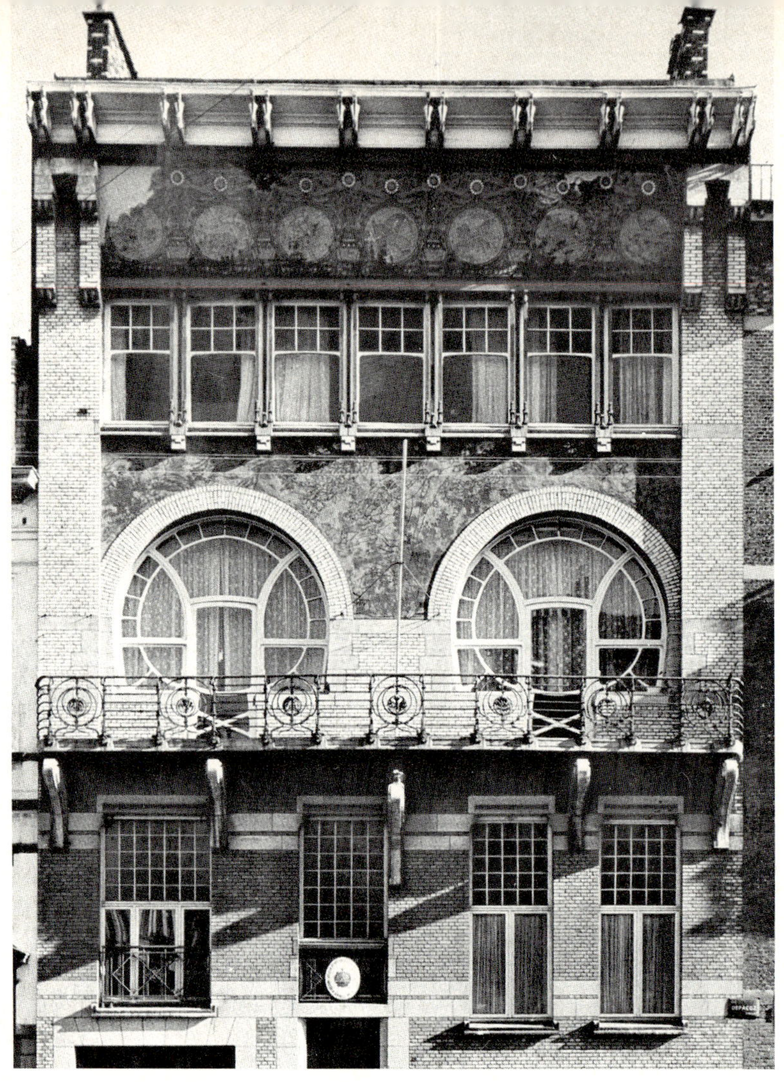

PAUL HANKAR   Private house, Brussels, 1896

The architect's own splendid house, built in 1889, would undoubtedly
have also been destroyed, had it not been bought by an architect-
admirer of Horta, who, besides living there, has made the house a
Horta museum.

Paul Hankar (1861–1901), an exact contemporary of Horta,
shared similar beliefs. Unhappily, he died when he was only forty,
without having had the time to make his mark. He began by designing
his own house, then various other houses in Brussels between 1890
and 1900 — all in the same spirit.

114

van de velde, the purist

A contemporary and compatriot of Victor Horta, and like him an adherent of art nouveau, Henry van de Velde (1863–1957) is usually discussed in the same context as Horta. However, the work and, in particular, the personalities of the two men were very different. Van de Velde was Flemish, born in Antwerp. Wanting to become a painter, he had enrolled in the Academy, following which he spent two years in Paris. There he gained entrée to the most fashionable society.

Like most artists of his generation, Van de Velde was a great admirer of Millet's paintings. His own pictorial *oeuvre* is solidly second-rate. He was too susceptible to others' influences. Following the academicism of his first period, Van de Velde saw the Seurat exhibition

HENRY VAN DE VELDE   Exterior of Bloemenwerf, 1895–1896

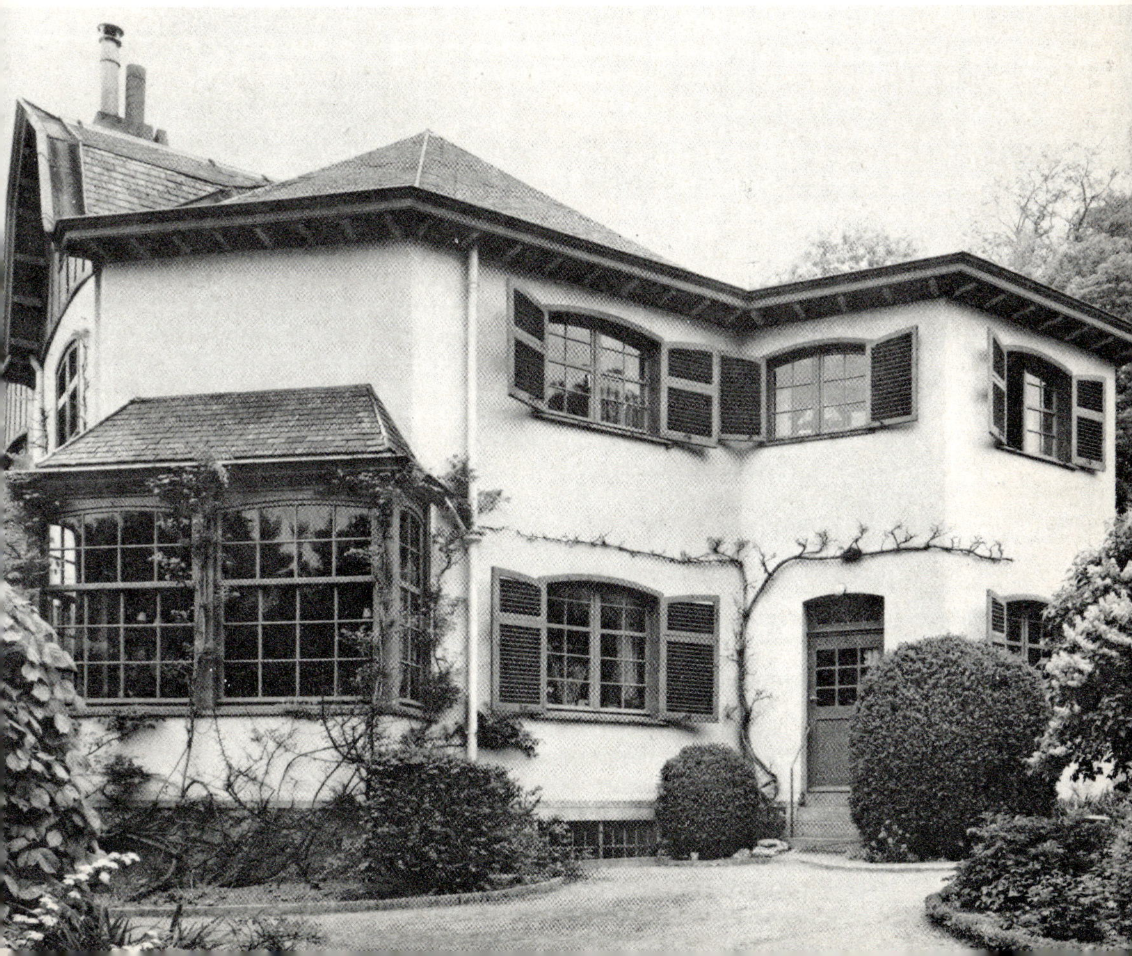

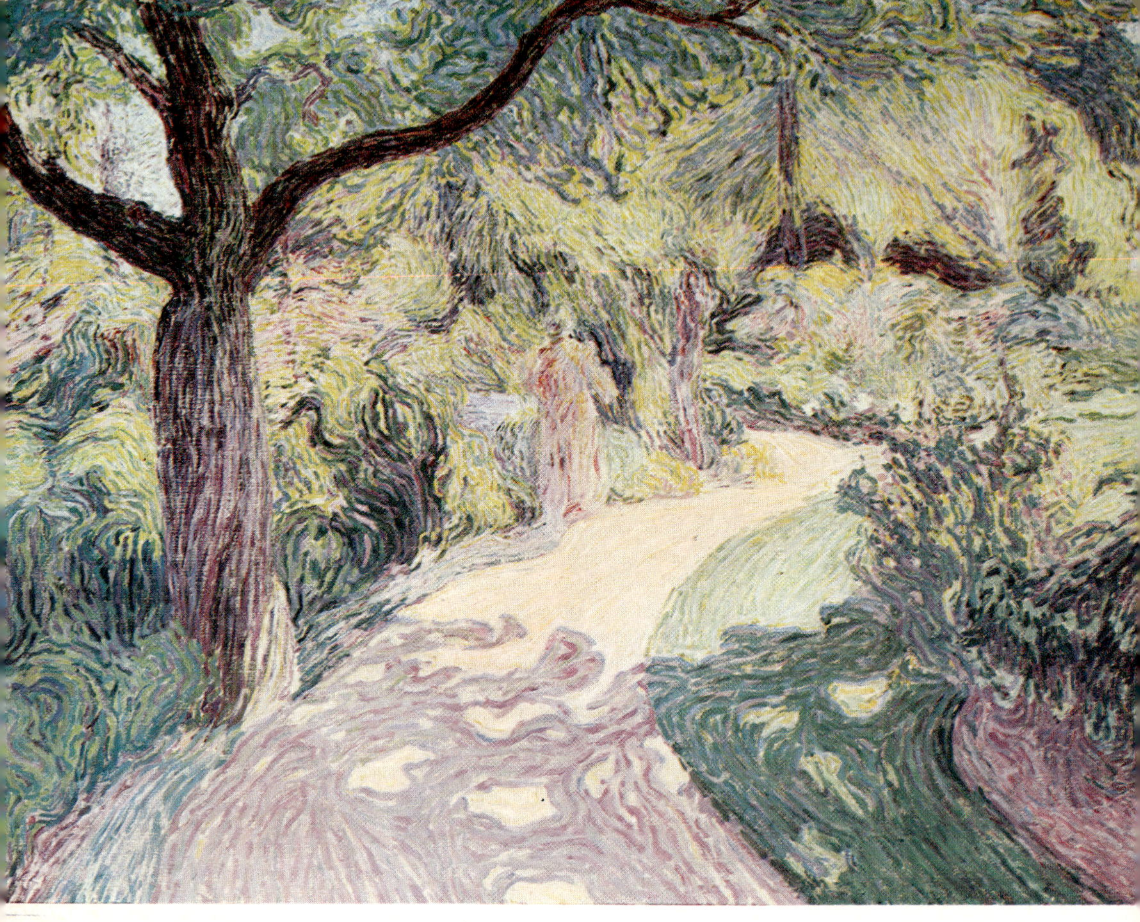

in Brussels (1888), which impressed him so deeply that he began to imitate the special technique of this master. Two years later, Van Gogh's paintings were exhibited in the Salon des XX and Van de Velde promptly began to imitate the slashes and swirls characteristic of the Dutch painter's brushwork, but to progressively more decorative effects.

A great admirer of William Morris, Van de Velde was involved in the founding of the Flemish review, *Van Nu en Straks,* selecting, with great distinction, the typography and design. He knew Mallarmé, at whose salon in the rue de Rome he was a regular visitor, and who seems to have had a formative influence on his ideas. It was at this time (1894) that Van de Velde abandoned painting to promulgate, instead, his philosophy of art, and to evolve a new style. His first writings bear revealing titles: *Clearing Ground of Art* and *First Sermon on Art.*

116

Van de Velde had no formal architectural training, nor had he pursued any studies or apprenticeship in the areas of decorating or cabinetmaking. He nonetheless became an ardent disciple of Morris, abandoning painting to start and manage a furniture factory. Why did he instinctively shift to architecture and design?

And how did even his visionary gifts manage to create the purified forms of the next century?

It all began with Van de Velde's visceral reaction to the things which had surrounded him since childhood. He explains it in his book *Formules d'une esthétique moderne*: "The public cannot imagine the conflict in our adolescence — the immense boredom of those houses where we grew up weighed heavily upon our childhood. Nothing seemed to hold out any possibilities, any of the virtues which enable things, just as much as people, to exude life-giving sympathy and confident affection . . . Instead, our childhood was crushed by the infinite ugliness of our classrooms, an ugliness as corrosive as evil to the heart, the mind, and the flesh: an ugliness as dirty as the filth of big cities, and which also sticks to the flesh, mind, and heart. And thus sullied, we started off in life . . . ."

HENRY VAN DE VELDE *Angels' Guard,* 1893

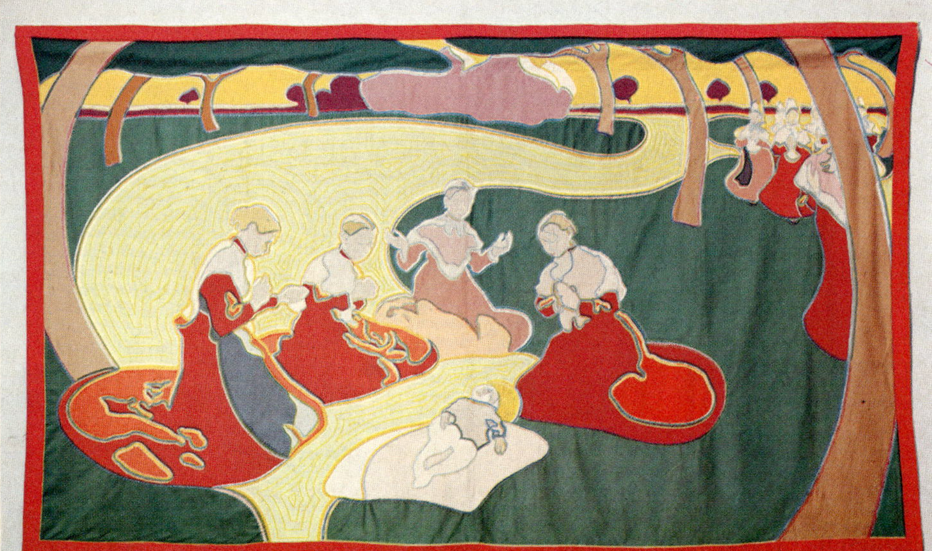

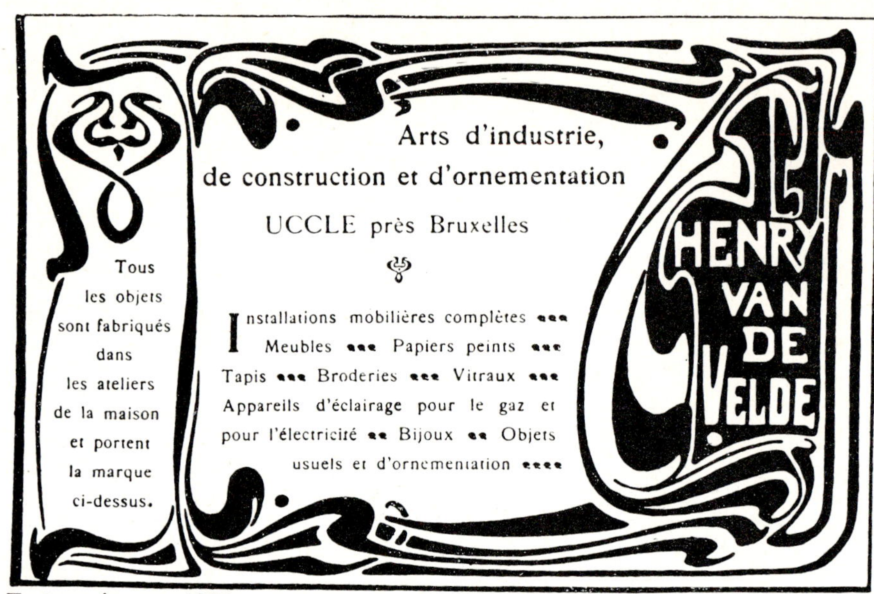

Factory sign, ca. 1897

The workshop and staff of Henry Van de Velde, ca. 1897

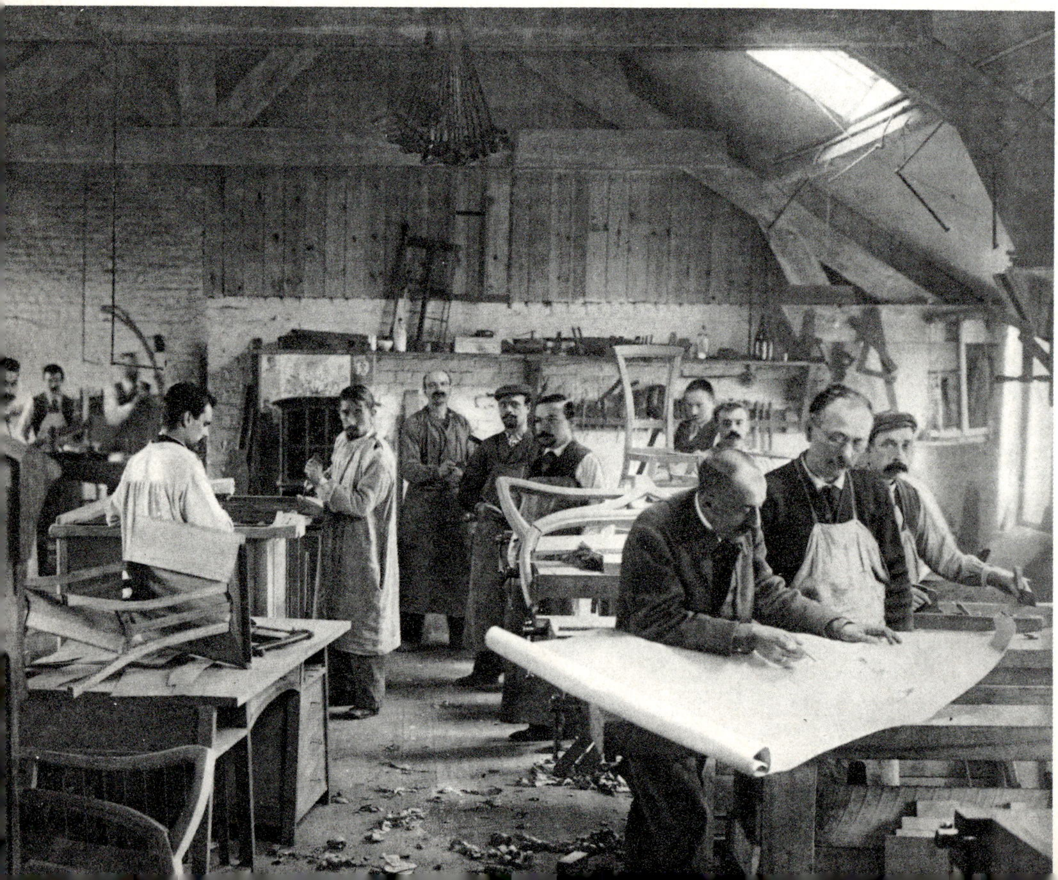

HENRY VAN DE VELDE
Armchair, 1898

HENRY VAN DE VELDE
Dining room, 1903

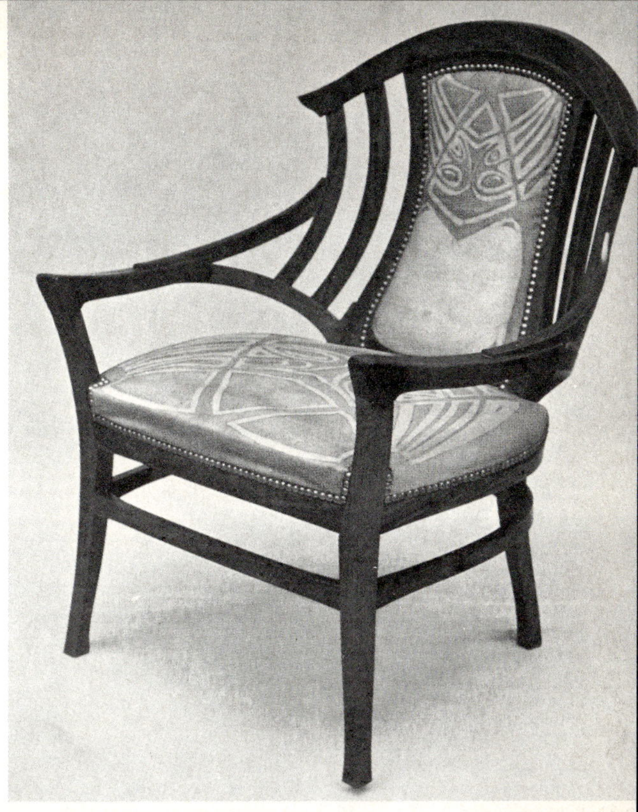

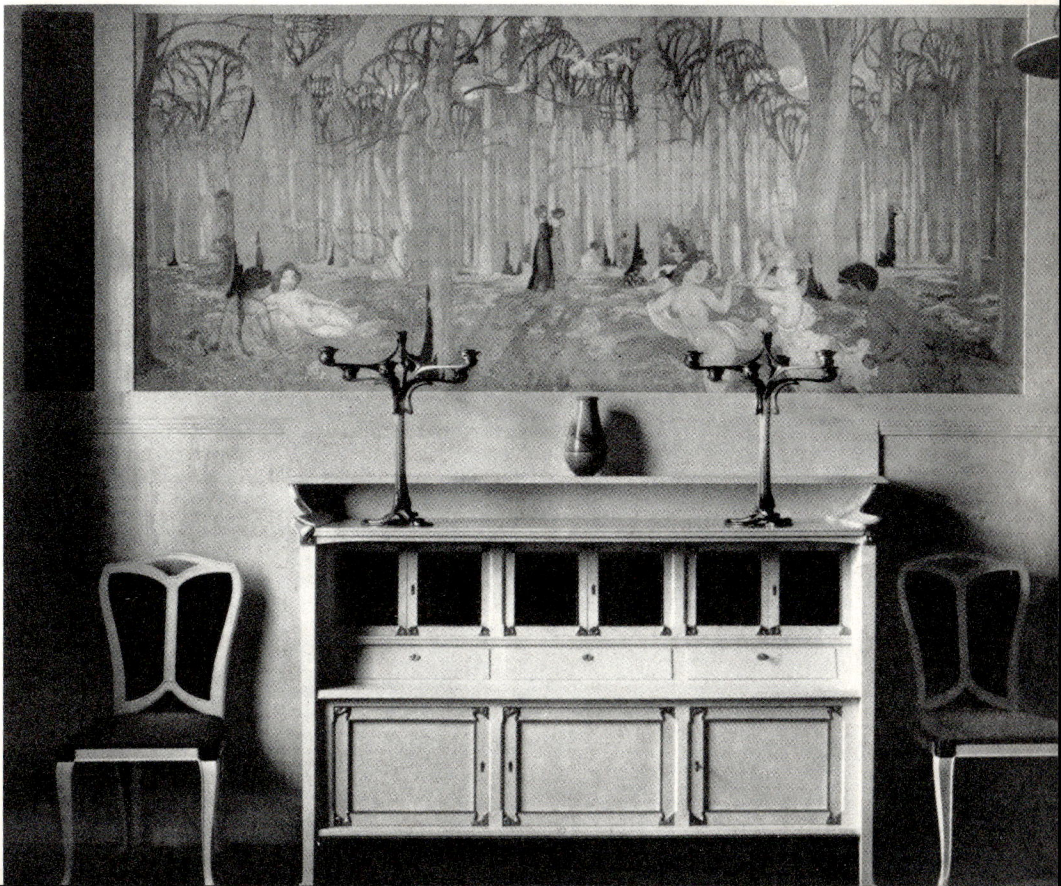

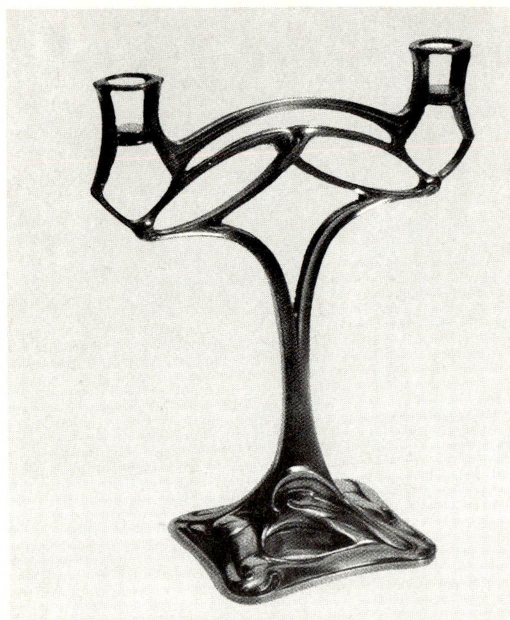

Henry Van de Velde   Samovar, 1903

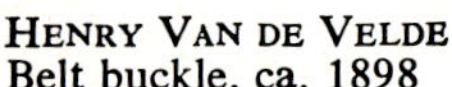

Henry Van de Velde
Belt buckle, ca. 1898

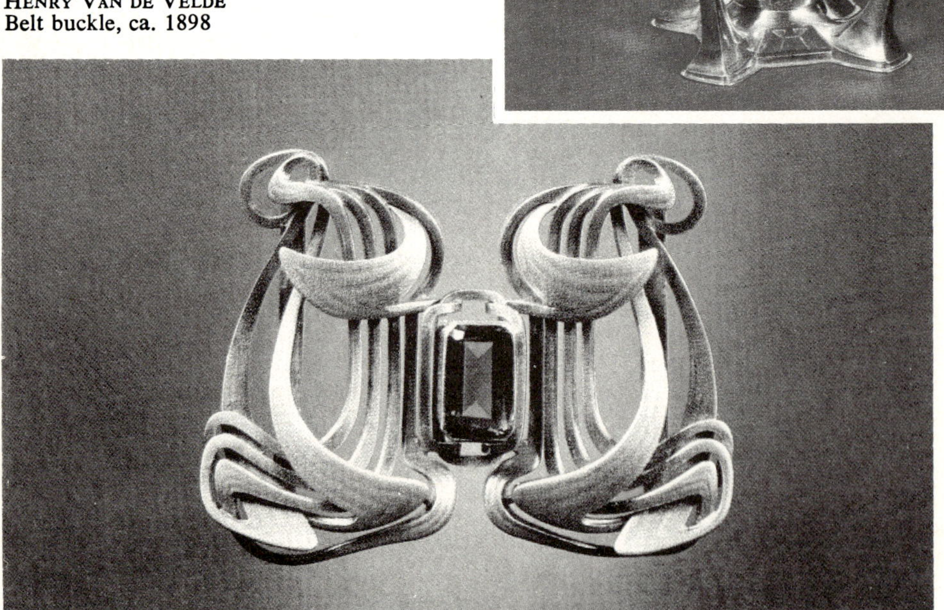

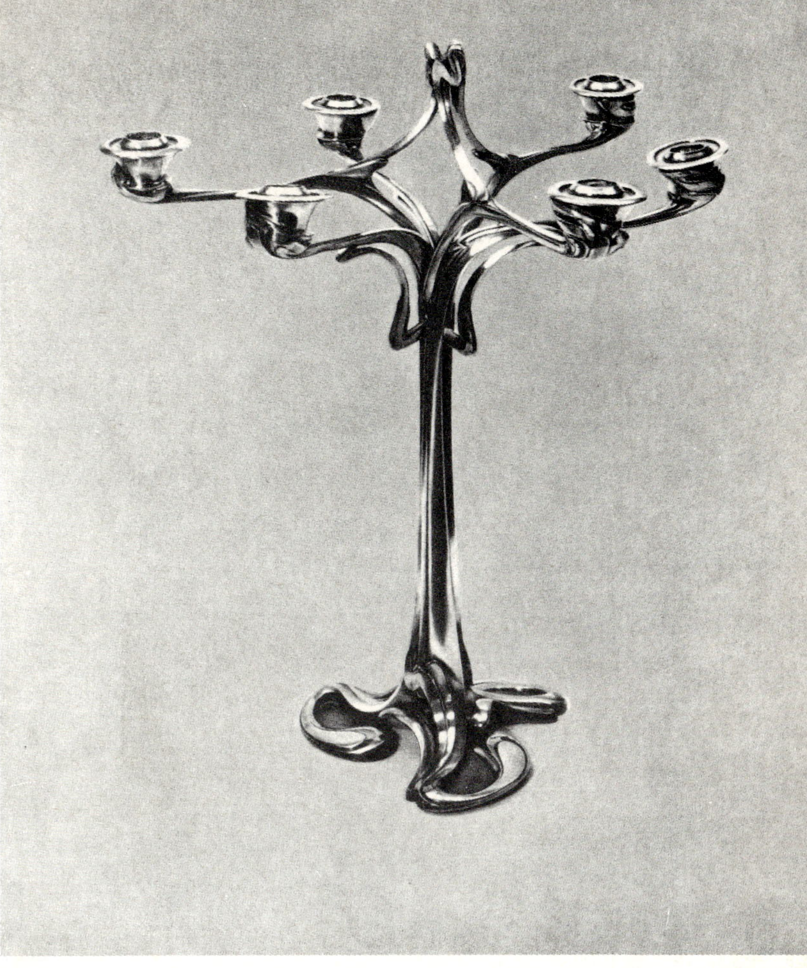

Perhaps Van de Velde abandoned easel painting when he realized that this was not a medium in which he would ever distinguish himself. Or again, he may have felt, convinced as he was of the social mission that it was his duty to engage in the more utilitarian areas of art. A hanging that he designed in 1891, consisting of fabric appliqués and embroidery, titled *Veillee des anges (Angels' Guard)*, and much influenced by Émile Bernard and Gauguin, is one of those examples of stylization so perfectly characteristic of art nouveau. The same spirit pervades his woodcuts, in which plant and landscape are suggested by a few wavy lines, and in which realism is eclipsed by decoration.

The only building that Van de Velde built before 1930 in Brussels was his own house in the suburb Uccle, Brussels (1896), which he

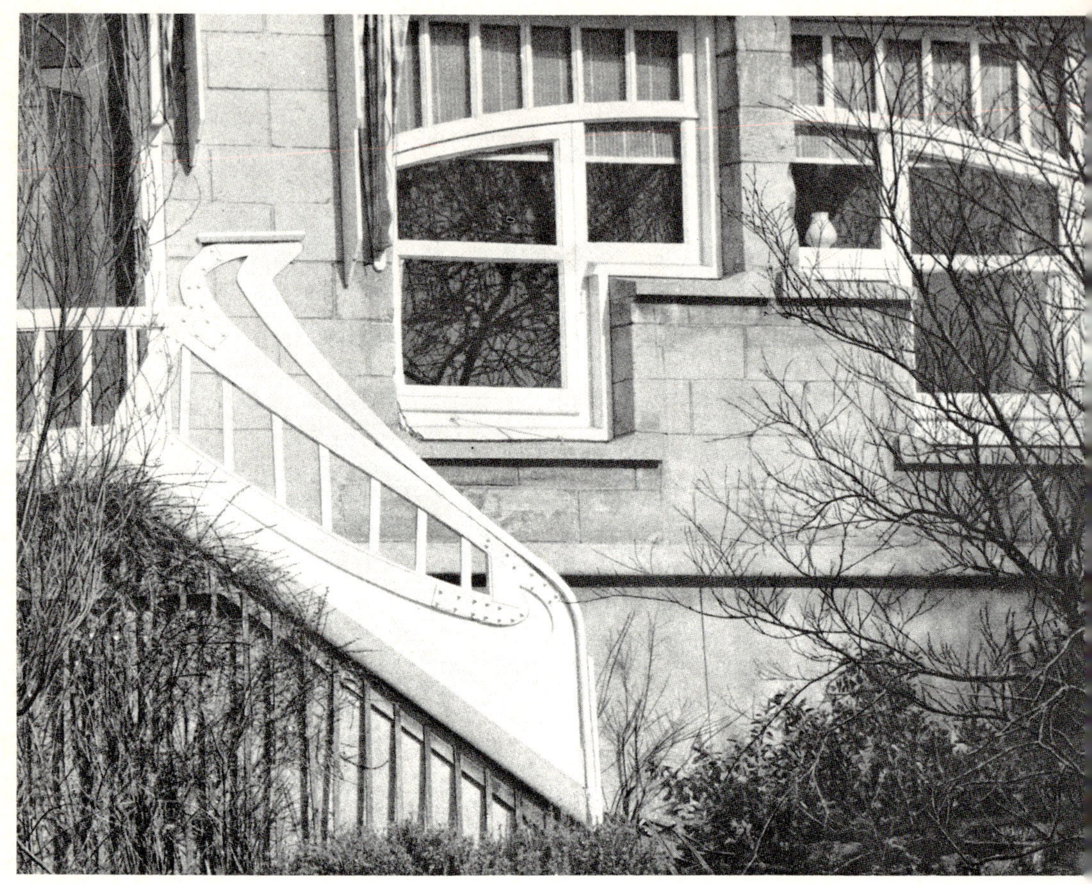

named *Bloemenwerf*. He wrote that previously "he had never been especially interested in architecture." But then he acquired a family. When he looked at houses, the examples all around him were "repulsive," to the point where he felt: "I must, at any cost, spare my wife and those who will be born from our union such horrors." And he drew up plans and elevations, designed carpets, hangings, heating units, lighting system, kitchen, and table services. To complete his desire for aesthetic harmony, he designed clothes in the same style for the lady of the house.

Bloemenwerf today looks to us like a large, simple, pleasant, and altogether unexceptional house. But this was not the impression it made on the other citizens of Brussels at the time. If we go by the

122

welcome given the new building, its only defenders were found in the meager ranks of the review *Libre Esthétique*. People criticized the large windows opening on the garden, the almost flat roof, the absence of cornices. But the worst offense was the complete absence — compared to other houses — of "historicism." The most felicitous element of the plan was the disposition of the studio and guest rooms. The furnishings were designed with their practical use in mind; devoid of ornament, they were in perfect harmony with the ensemble of the house. The total design was so far ahead of its time that it barely seems dated, even today. Most of the objects could have served as models of design for fifty years, despite successive changes in decorative styles. Purification of architecture. Purification of furnishings. This was the great clearing ground of art. The *form* of the furniture and household objects was *conceived* as decorative, needing no ornamentation. These furnishings illustrated twentieth-century formulas of clarity or functionalism: "The function creates the organ." These furnishings were already abstract volumes.

It was to be expected that Bing would ask Ven de Velde to become one of the exhibiting artists in his gallery, on the rue de Provence. The dealer found in the Fleming's work a purity akin to, although different from that of the Japanese. He invited Van de Velde to furnish completely four model rooms. They met with a disastrous reception. Mirabeau wrote a derisive and choleric article. And even Edmond de Goncourt spoke of Van de Velde's decor as the "yachting style."

van de velde in germany

Van de Velde acquired important patrons in Germany. Count Kessler, aesthete and cosmopolitan of wealth and distinction, promoted him energetically, introducing the Belgian to artistic circles in Berlin, introductions which led to commissions. With the financial backing of von Bodenhausen, Van de Velde founded his own company, bearing his name; given his level of support, the best publicity was assured and he opened a successful outlet in Berlin. Van de Velde was to realize his most important projects in Germany. He exhibited with the Sezession group in Munich, and was in charge of the layout and design of several important new stores. The decor of the Salon de Coiffure Impérial Haby, whose functionalism was total art nouveau, was the sensation of Berlin in 1901. Van de Velde gave an ever-increasing number of proselytizing lectures throughout Europe and the Austro-Hungarian Empire: he won over critics and detractors, becoming, in the process, a big star. Frau Foster, Nietzsche's sister, presented him to the Duke of Saxe-Weimar. The latter promptly appointed him Artistic Advisor for All Crafts and Industrial Products of that principality. We may question whether this was an appropriate role for an artist with the soul of an apostle. It can be argued that the hoped-for regeneration of the arts should start with the general public. But in fact, and ever more frequently, Van de Velde worked for captains of industry or on official buildings; i.e., a factory and an enormous villa in Hagen, the School of Applied Arts in Weimar.

He managed, however, to see one of his early dreams come true: the establishment of the Werkbund (1907), which gathered together artists, architects, and industrialists, and whose first meeting explored the relationship between Art and Industry. If we consider the time that elapsed between these first encounters and the international acceptance of industrial design, we can appreciate the importance of these early experiments.

HENRY VAN DE VELDE   Werkbund Theater, 1914

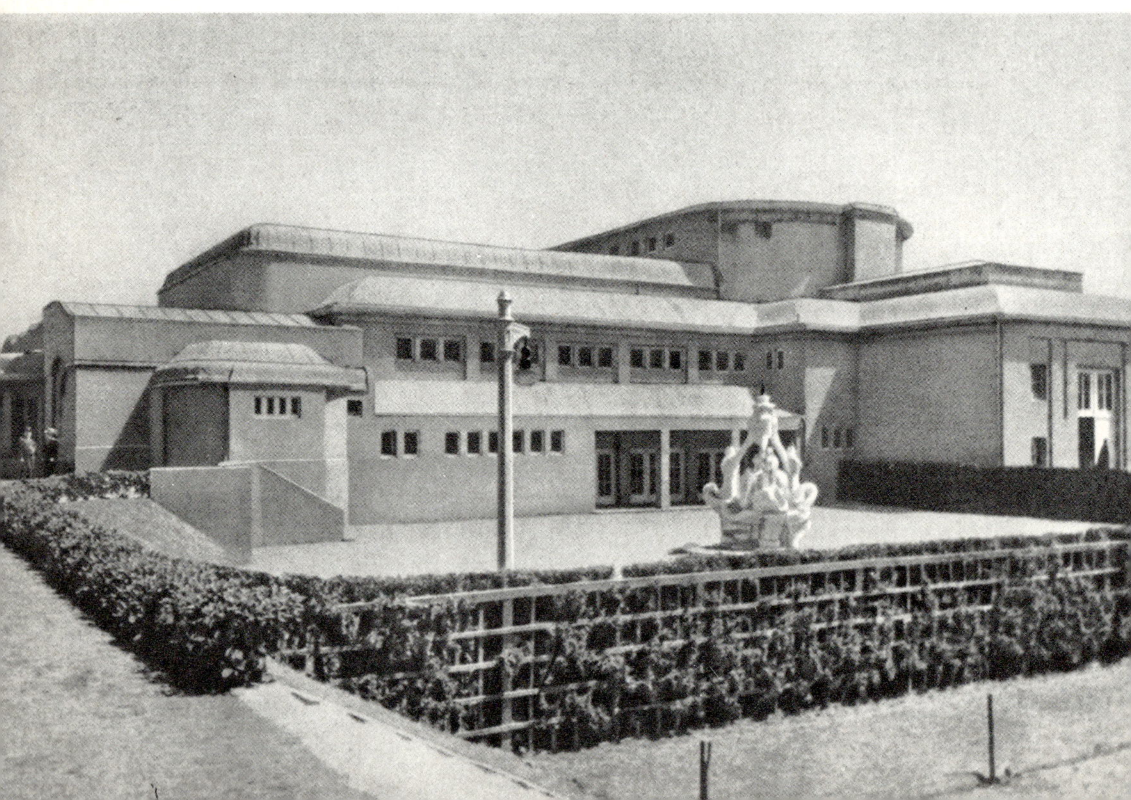

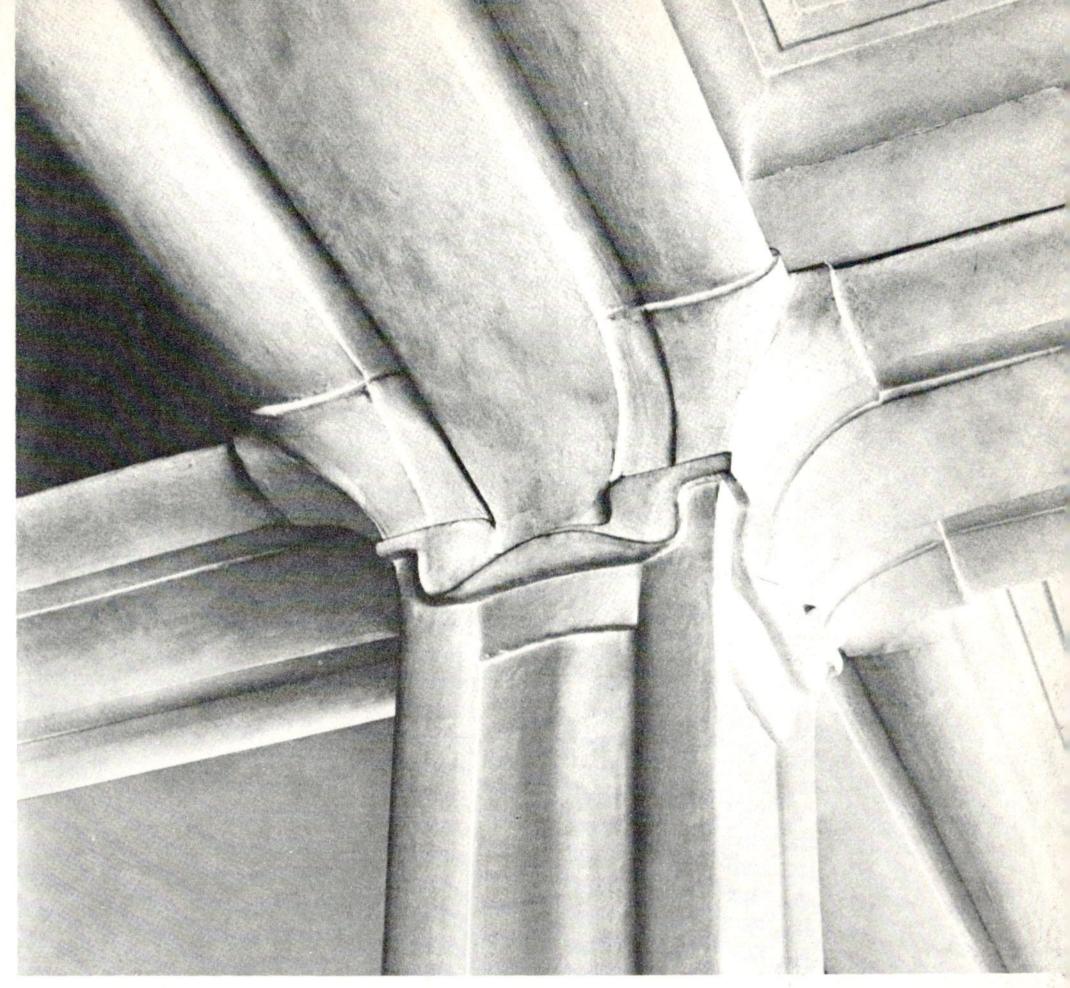

The crowning achievement of the Werkbund was the establishment of the Kunstschule (School of Applied Arts) in Weimer, whose organization and operation led eventually to all sorts of personality clashes. Here Van de Velde was able to use the pedagogical methods which became, in 1919, the basis of Gropius's teachings at the Bauhaus. Although his other aspirations, a Weimar Museum of Fine Arts and a national theater, were never realized, the building of the Kunstschule was the great work of Van de Velde's life. On the site of the monumental exhibition of the Deutsche Werkbund, which took place in Cologne on the eve of the First World War (and where, among the avant-garde works represented, were projects of Behrens, Obrist, En-

125

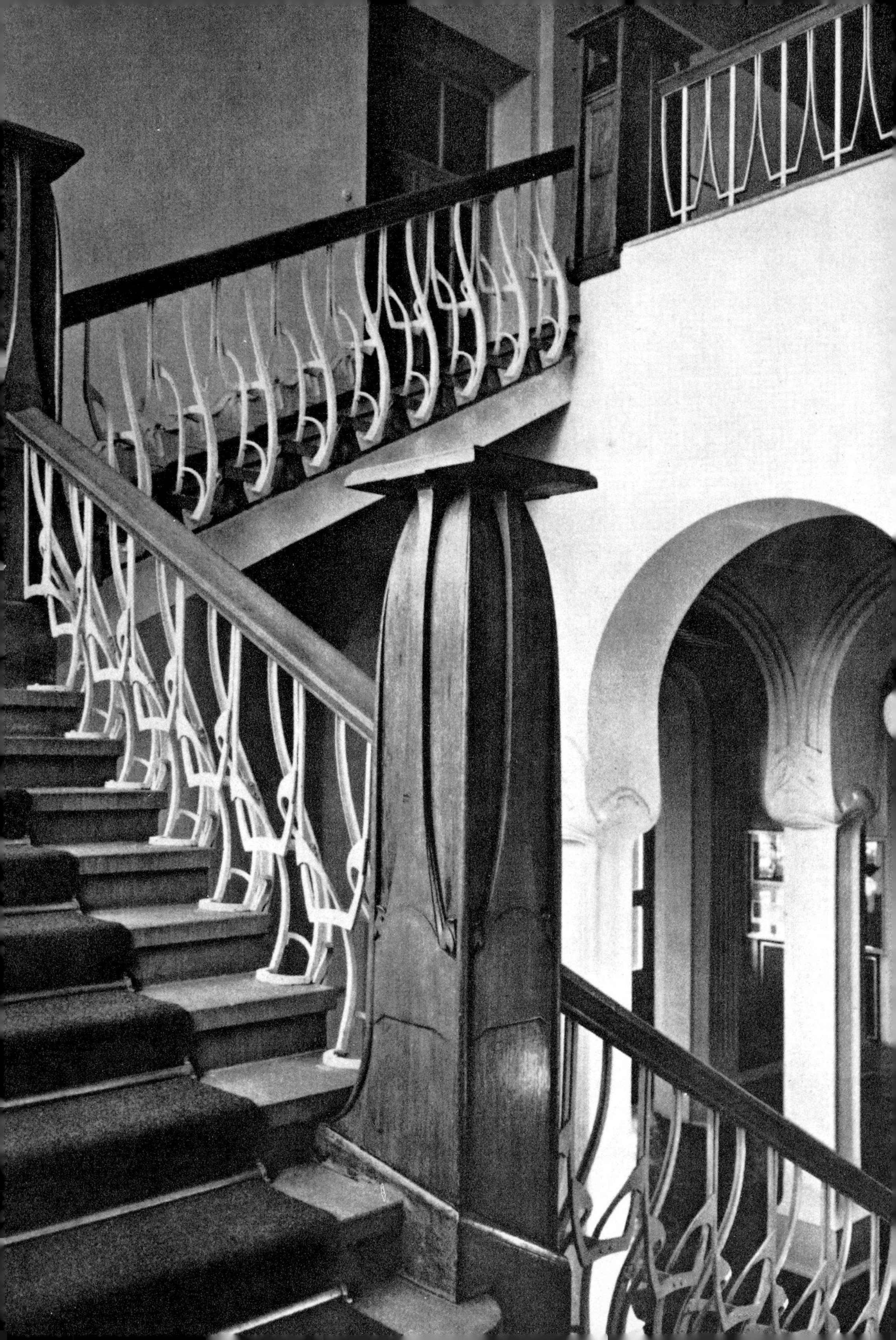

dell, and Gropius), Van de Velde designed the vast Werkbund theater (destroyed). Its rather complicated plan was a model of organic architecture, consisting of the play of bare forms, and revealing throughout the architect's goal of purity. The theater was dedicated on June 18, 1914. The most criticized element was the three-part stage design.

During the war, Van de Velde tried to leave Germany, but it was not until 1917 that he succeeded. He received a passport for Switzerland, with the condition that he organize some courses for German prisoners of war detained there. After the Armistice, Belgium refused to allow his return. He lived in Holland from 1921 to 1925, engaged as advisor to the Kröller-Müller family in the planning of their future museum. In 1926, Belgium welcomed him home; he was received by King Albert who asked him to give up his work in Holland, and named him director of the Institut Supérieur des Arts Décoratifs, housed in the former abbey of Cambre. There he taught until 1935 the revolutionary courses he had instituted at Weimar.

Van de Velde's architectural accomplishments were not all behind him. During the Belgian-Dutch period between the two wars, he designed villas and several public buildings, among them, the library of the University of Ghent. But instead of remaining a leader, he had become a follower, adapting to the mainstream of architecture, which had now begun to eliminate, just as he had done a quarter century earlier, any historical reference or ornament. His buildings no longer reflected the principles by which he earned his fame. Finally, there is not a suggestion of art nouveau in his last works.

In Germany, Van de Velde had encountered a movement, lively with argument and devoted participation, which acted upon him as a stimulus to creation. But that was all over. One masterpiece remains from his last period, however: the Kröller-Müller Museum, for which he had drawn the first plans in 1921, changing them many times in the intervening years. The one-story building, which reaches into the woods of the National Park in Otterlo, houses a prodigious collection of contemporary art; it is also an architectural triumph, both for the felicitous way in which its volumes fit into the landscape, and for its perfection as a museum building. Completed in 1954, the Kröller-Müller Museum had taken thirty-three years to finish.

Van de Velde retired in Switzerland in 1947, where he devoted his last years to the dictation of his interminable memoirs. He died ten years later, at the age of ninety-four.

HENRY VAN DE VELDE Balustrade of a staircase, 1902

social art

Van de Velde was not only an artist, but a theorist and man of action at the same time. Enthusiastic, belligerent, and persuasive, never hesitating to poke fun at whatever stood in his way, he was also, if his contemporaries are to be believed, a man of great charm, who must have been one of the best propagandists for art nouveau.

His idealism was well tempered by a sense of the realities. And his productivity is still awesome. He touched on every discipline which in any way related to his own, and in all of them he demanded a great deal of himself. In the course of his long life, he produced endless writings, whose style reflects the author's prolixity. "Van de Velde has written so much," Robert Delevoy said, "that it would take ages to complete a bibliography of his publications, and still longer to establish definitive texts. He produced so much, that a catalogue of his multitudinous and polymorphous work is still far from complete."

We can recognize in Van de Velde someone whose very existence was devoted to convincing others. He was the idealist who must convert society to his definition of truth. Van de Velde had always been involved with social issues. In his youth, he had read widely in Tolstoy, Bakunin, and Kropotkin. He was in touch with militant socialists, becoming early on, through revolt against his childhood milieu, an intellectual on the side of revolution and anarchy. This was one of the factors which led him to give up painting, which he called egotistical, to devote his life to the decorative arts, available to everyone and thus, a social art.

The alliance of the social and the aesthetic was the contradiction of art nouveau. Van de Velde turned toward politics, inspired to provide the poorest classes of society with beautiful objects created in a new spirit: their new possessions would be adapted to their way of life and would aim at improving their material circumstances and their minds at the same time. Here Van de Velde was echoing William Morris. The reason antique peasant furniture delights the modern eye is because these simple, sturdy objects have a vitality of style which makes them direct descendants of furniture made for nobility. And where Morris had failed — undoubtedly because he had put too much

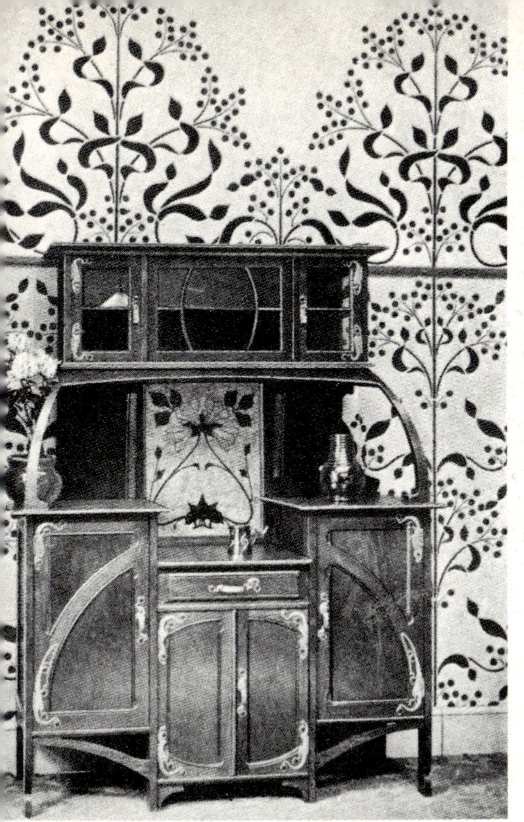

faith in the virtues of handicrafts — the masters of art nouveau would succeed. The latter, to be sure, only worked for the nobility of their own day — the financiers and captains of industry; they never really reached the people. Serrurier-Bovy was a cabinetmaker and decorator from Liege, a talented craftsman and fanatical exponent of art nouveau. Some of his productions were of questionable taste: he exhibited a "workingman's bedroom" in Brussels, which was a resounding failure. Horta was considered "the most expensive architect in the city," which, when we think about it, was to be expected, originality being inevitably more expensive than mass production.

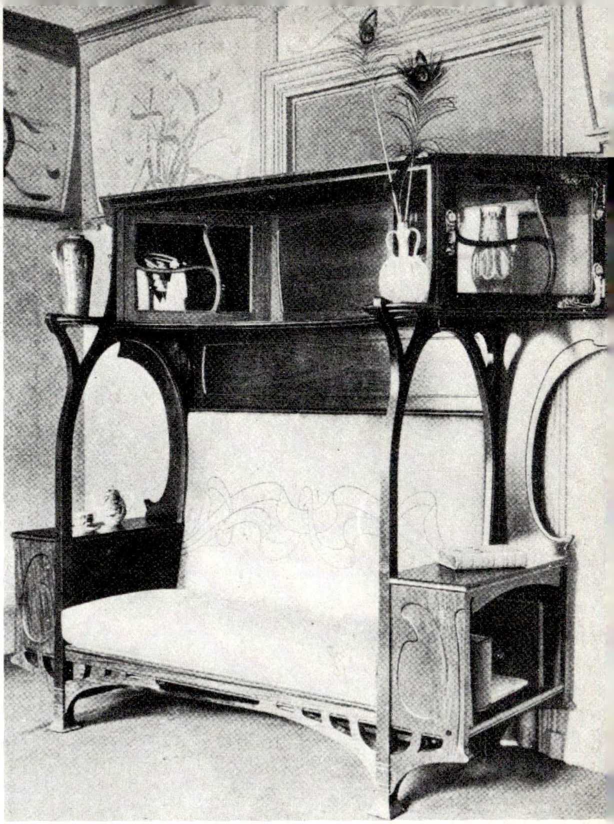

When the Belgian Worker's Party was founded in 1885, Van de Velde was named president. This elegant man of the world, who frequented the most glittering salons of the day, seemed to have no trouble reconciling his conflicting social and political allegiances. One might think, however, that he would have had more difficulty accommodating his theoretical anarchism with the belief in order and organization which was the basis of his artistic production. He maintained close relationships with some of his richest contemporaries — the only ones, in all fairness, who understood him and who throughout his career supported him unwaveringly, making it possible for 'him to create. The originality of this art, with its new forms, was in no way thought to be reserved for the pleasure of aesthetes; the hope was, depending upon the social concerns and degree of optimism of the artist, that art nouveau would contribute to a general improvement of the quality of life.

In their generous desire to disseminate a socially valuable art, these artists, the foremost practitioners of art nouveau, like the forerunners of the movement, met with complete failure in every country. Not only did the working class reject it — aside from any considerations of

JAN TH. TOOROP *Fatalism, 1893*

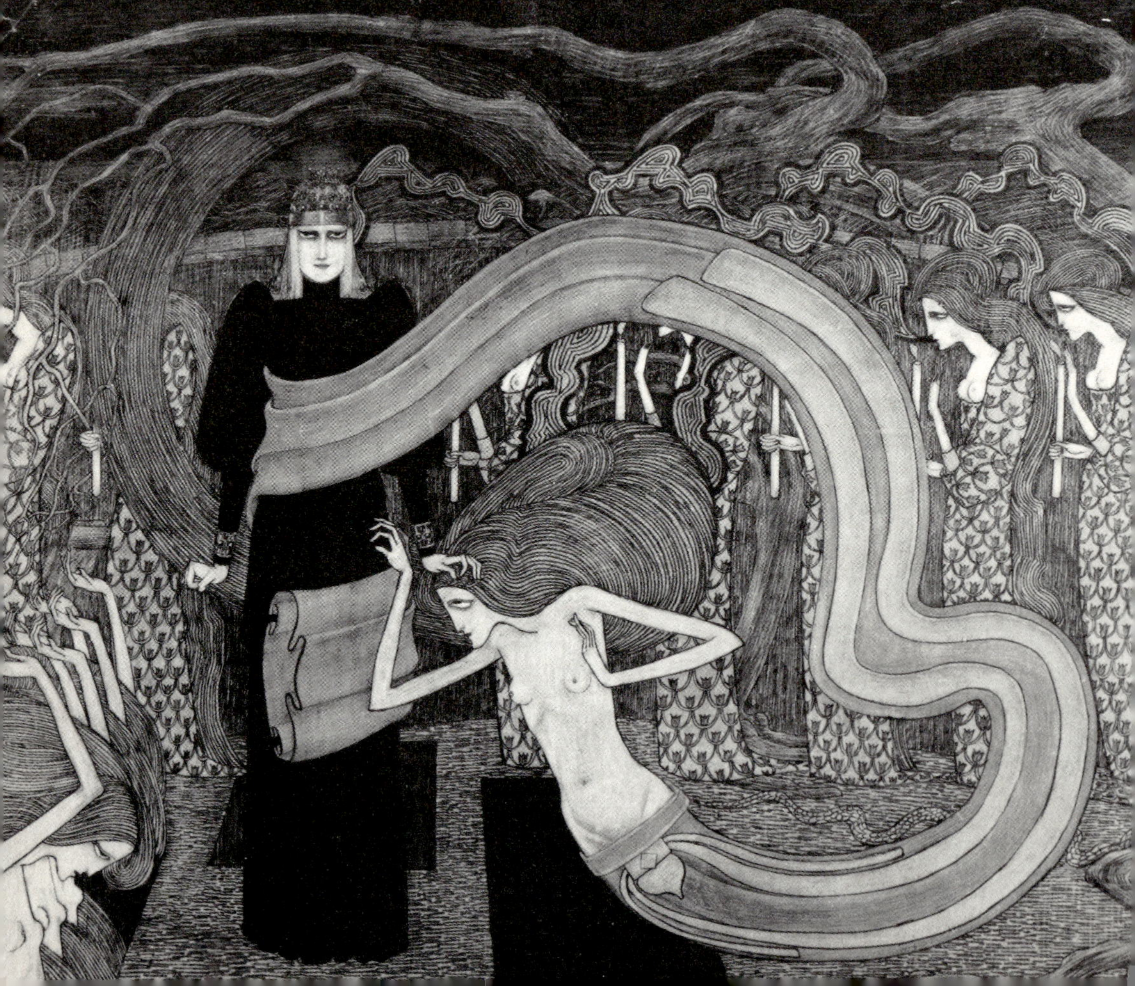

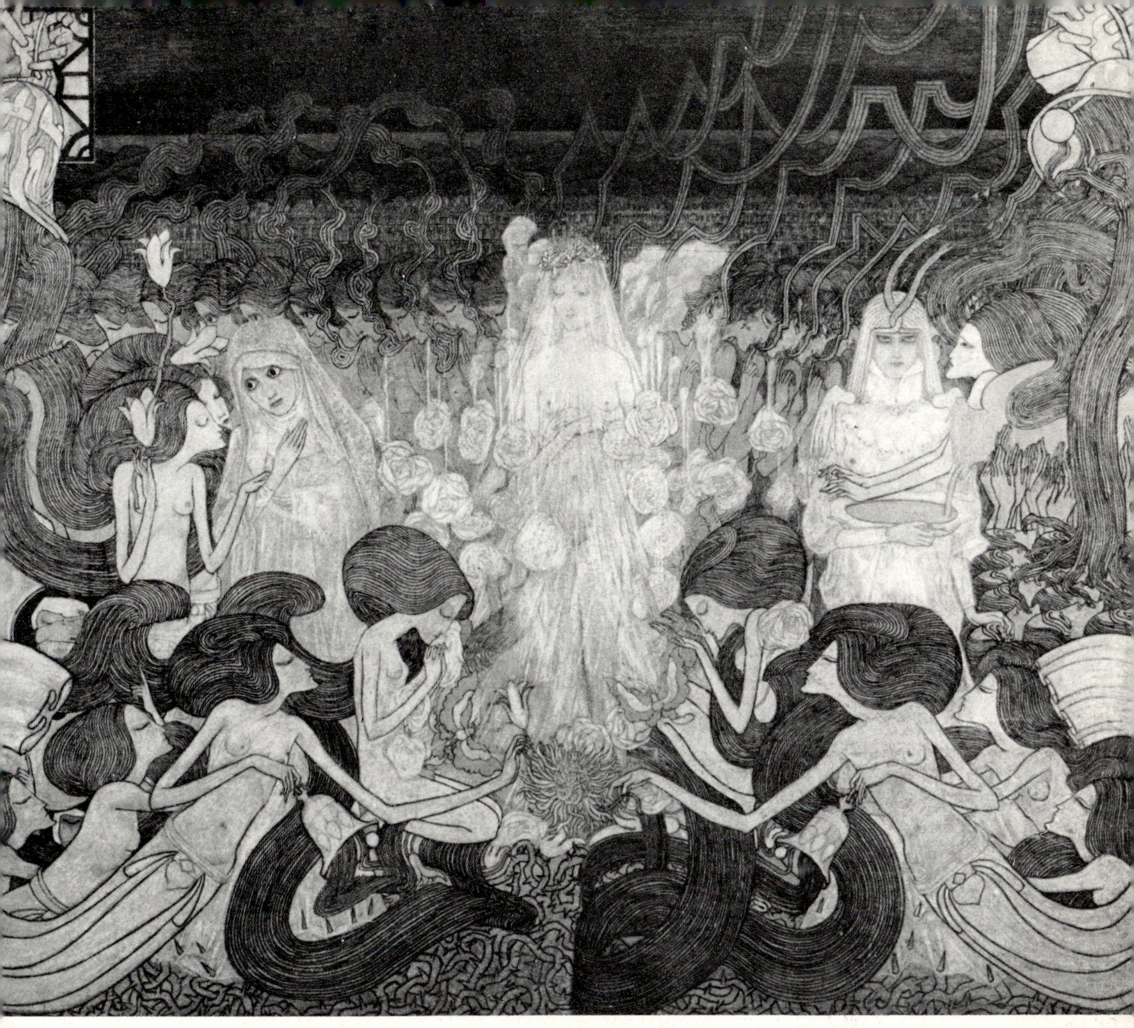

Jan Th. Toorop   *The Three Brides*, 1893

availability and price — it never made the slightest dent in mass taste. The modern aesthetic, for which these artists sought unanimous acceptance, remained individualized; this was a secret only whispered in the most rarified circles. It would not, moreover, have excited much interest elsewhere.

Here we should mention several Dutch painters of quite astonishing originality. During the period 1890–1900, these artists produced compositions in a style very deliberately situated at the farthest possible point of art nouveau. Jan Toorop (1858–1928) was born in Java of Dutch parents. Beginning his career as a vaguely impressionist painter, he went to England. There, he was overwhelmed by his discovery of Blake and the Pre-Raphaelites. Moving to Brussels, he became a friend of Verhaeren and Maeterlinck, who converted him to symbolism. Toorop was a gifted and brillian artist. Contemporary accounts describe him as able to play twenty-seven musical instruments with equal virtuousity, and to speak assorted foreign languages, each as though it were his native tongue. But these gifts of assimilation had their disadvantages. He could — and did — paint in the style of all the great painters, from Manet to Renoir. The art nouveau manner was an important discovery for him since it gave him the opportunity to invent fantastic forms in a transcendant decorative spirit *(Les Trois Mariées, La Jeune Fille aux Cygnes)*. Here again, his astounding virtuosity and highly mannered style, mixed with literary allusions, made a sophisticated combination. He capitalized on his talents by designing posters which enjoyed great success, even spawning imitations which retained his own personal accent. Toorop was, however, tormented

Henry Van de Velde   Executive suite, 1908

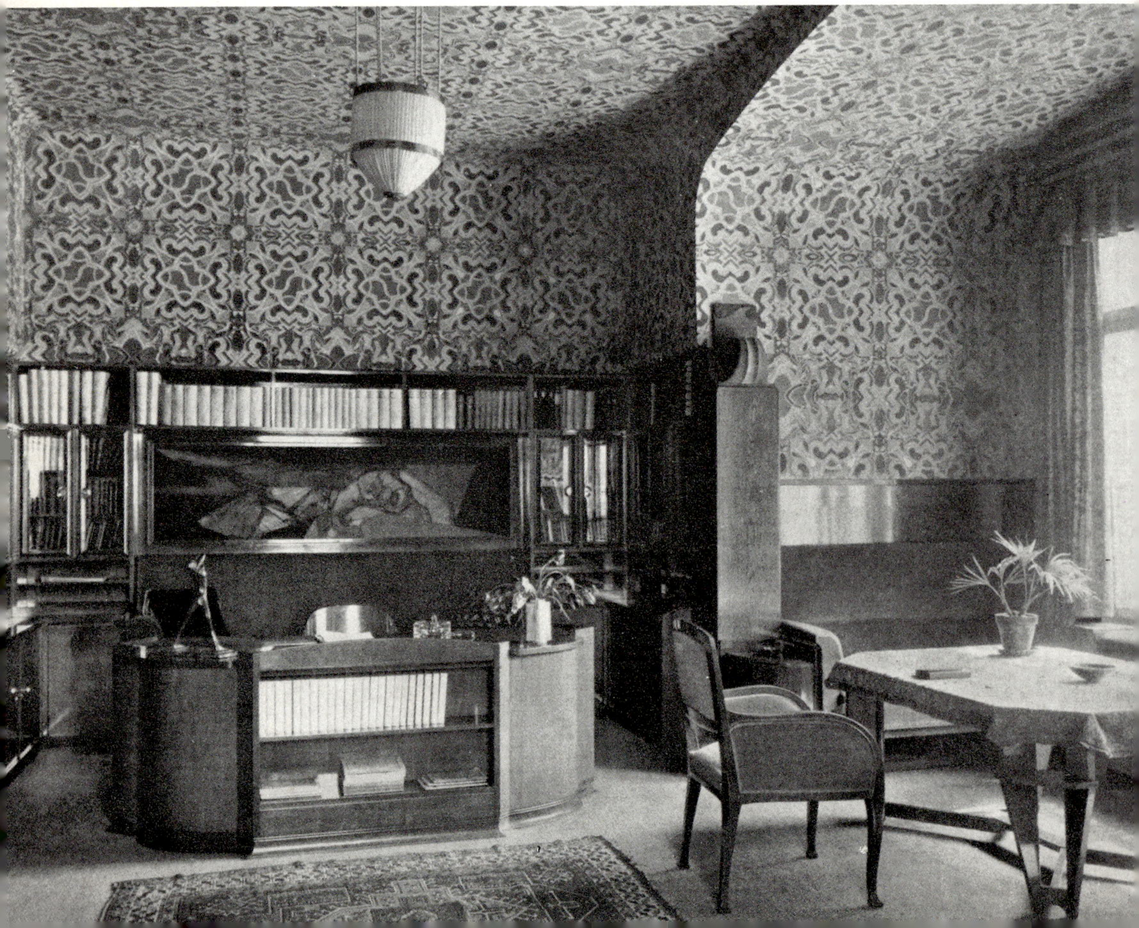

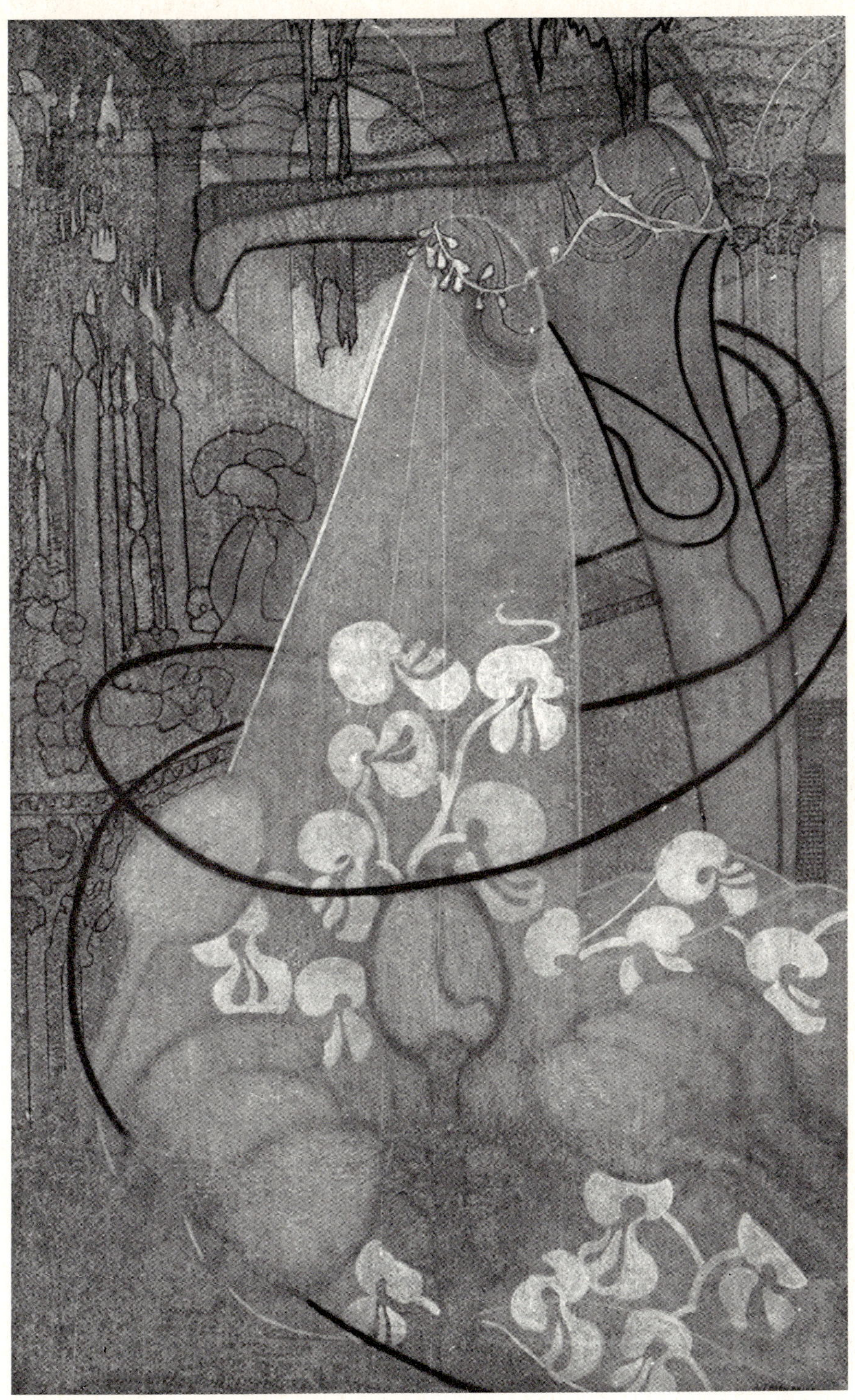

JOHAN THORN-PRIKKER *The Bride*, 1893

with religious anxieties; he finally found peace by converting to Catholicism in 1905. This also proved an artistic turnabout for the artist. There is scarcely a trace of his earlier work in the devotional pictures to which he subsequently consecrated his art.

His friend Johan Thorn-Prikker (1868–1932) was similar to Toorop in many respects. He, too, contributed to the review *Van Nu en Straks*. In the aesthetic spectrum, this artist was about halfway between symbolism and irrealism, ultimately moving toward an austerity close to abstraction. Van de Velde guided him toward the decorative arts, and he began to produce some quite interesting batik. Thorn-Prikker was also extremely devout; increasingly influenced by Maurice Denis, he, too, turned to religious art. He finally became completely absorbed by commissions for churches; these consisted of paintings characterized by a classicism steeped in art nouveau.

With Van de Velde defecting to Germany for the most creative part of his career, Belgium ceased to play the seminal role in the decorative arts for which it had held center stage in the last decade of the century. The artists who had been part of *Libre Esthétique* now looked toward Paris. Decorative abstraction made its appearance in the form of woodcuts, in which a lush landscape was reduced to a few lines, or where the oft-repeated theme of a woman with long flowing hair — hair which was then transposed into linear decoration of similarly wavy lines — filled the entire surface of the page. The subjects, even narrative ones, treated in this manner are too numerous to count.

jugendstil

In 1896, the first issue of the review *Jugend* was published in Munich. Symbolist in spirit, it welcomed all new experiments in art. The new periodical soon became so influential that it baptized a new style. Jugendstil was the branch of art nouveau that spread through central Europe. The curiosity of certain German intellectual circles for new forms in art manifested itself the following year by the publication of another periodical, one still more oriented toward the avant-garde for its own sake: this was the opulent review *Pan,* published in Berlin, whose founding contributors included the art critic Meier-Graefe, a friend of Bing, and Van de Velde. Besides engravings by Munch, Beardsley, and Vallotton, and lithographs by Toulouse-Lautrec, *Pan* also published works by Verlaine, Mallarmé, and the best German writers, as well as reproducing rare examples of the new architecture. The quality and inventiveness of the engravings, design, and vignettes all contributed to its distinguished format.

Young Austrian and German architects played a major role in the development of Jugendstil. Their luxuriant architectural style recalled the baroque and rococo. They were enthusiastic participants in a movement which swept them along in its irresistible flight from the traditional arts.

These same young architects who now threw themselves into Jugendstil with such abandon would turn away, just as resolutely, a few years later; they would then become champions of rigid volumes, bare surfaces, in short, of rational architecture, becoming its most intransigent and doctrinaire theorists.

For most of these innovators, Jugendstil was the first phase of an evolution in which old ideas were successively rejected in the aim of achieving purity of form. We shall find the same cast of characters associated with the important architectural movement, the Deutsche Werkbund, which we discussed in reference to Van de Velde. The invention of new techniques, and changes which affected people's way

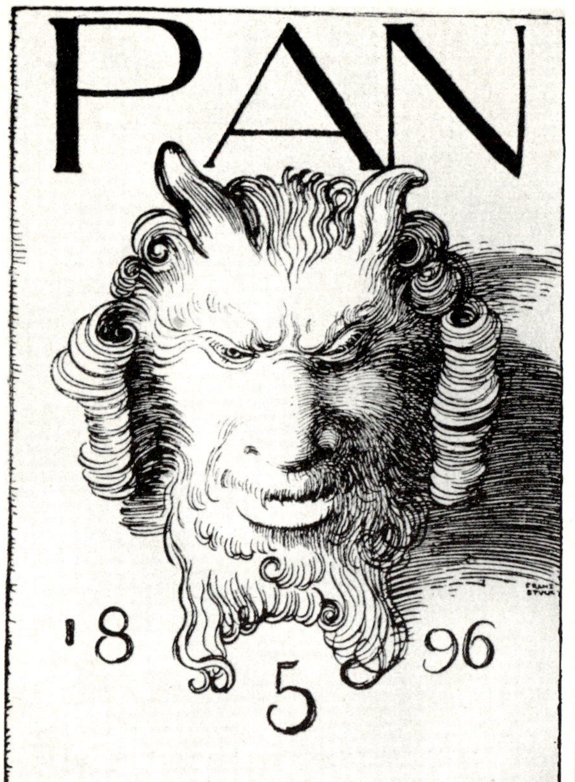

Cover of the review *Pan*, number 5, 1896

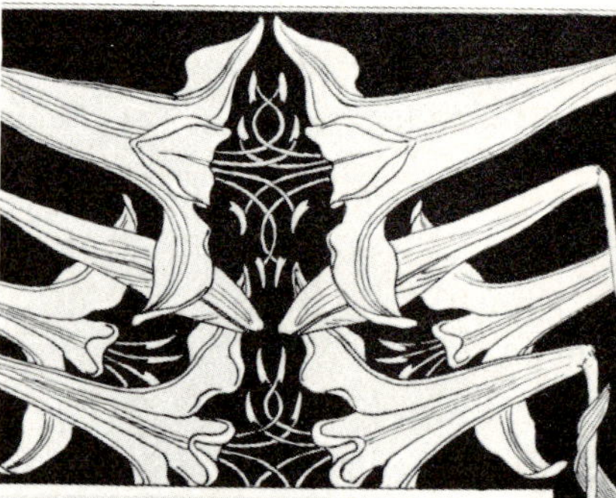

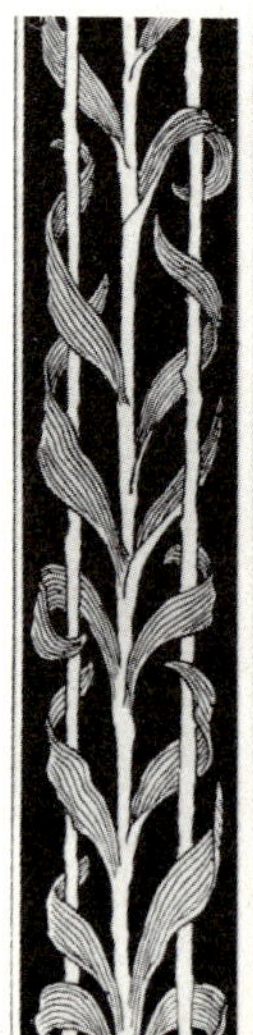

Das letzte Lied

Die Sonne schläft, der Sommer geht zur Ruh.
Schon schwätzt der Kieselbach, die Räder rauschen;
Die Sehnsucht schliesst die grossen Augen zu,
Schläft lächelnd ein .. Dort, wo die Wälder lauschen,
  Zittert ein Sensenlied, zittert und stirbt.

       *   *   *

Im bleichen Lichte krümmt sich die Chaussee
So müde zwischen weissen Meilensteinen,
In Pappelkronen flüstert Winterweh,
Und bei dem Teiche, wo die Weiden weinen.
  Zittert ein Sensenlied, zittert und stirbt.

                    Anton Lindner

       *   *   *

Page from the review *Pan*, number 5, 1896

of life and tastes, quite naturally moved these architects toward a new concept of architectural structures. The same evolution took place everywhere, but it was accelerated in the German-speaking countries because at this historical moment a nucleus of activist architects was there: an even more active group was based in imperial Vienna, worldly and elegant, but at the same time highly receptive to new ideas.

the vienna sezession

Otto Wagner (1841–1918) was the beginning. He was one of the first to foresee the evolution of modern architecture and decoration. Wagner perceived that it was logical construction that must define architectural organization; that instead of shamefacedly disguising the material, whatever its nature, it should be a visible contribution to the aesthetic of the building. His book *Moderne Architektur* (1895) is a breviary of the new ideas. The French aesthetician Paul Souriau, in his work *La Beauté rationnelle,* synthesized these ideas in the famous formula: "An object is beautiful when the form is the clear expression of its function." Otto Wagner put it more simply: "Only the practical can be beautiful." He said this, moreover, thirty years before the Bauhaus would popularize his ideas. In Vienna, Wagner had the good luck to find a clientele — private citizens and public agencies — which allowed complete freedom of expression (Länderbank, Magasin Neumann, suburban railway stations, Hofpavillon Hietzing). In the Ankerhaus (1894) Wagner hung mirrors in front of supporting pilons, creating the first wall curtain.

Wagner welcomed Jugendstil from its first beginnings, and the style soon appeared in decorative form on those parts of his buildings which could absorb it without destroying the architectural lines (ceramics and ironwork, for example). But even though the use of these decorative elements seems to reflect a certain aspect of art nouveau, the totally rational rigor of the construction is altogether different.

The social concerns of Otto Wagner assume an especially interesting form in one of his buildings, an apartment house, constructed in Vienna in 1910. The facade of Majolika House is very simple, austere, and completely devoid of ornamental sculpture; instead, it is completely faced with ceramic tiles decorated in a floral design of muted colors.

The sweeping line of the wrought iron balustrade is continued laterally by the curved railings of the repeated balconies. Rigor is joined to fantasy — a decorative fantasy intended to bring a touch of gaiety to the lives of the tenants.

Wagner was the master of the generation of architects who would later join the pictorial theorists to become the group calling themselves the Vienna Sezession. It was officially founded in 1897 by Josef Olbrich, Josef Hoffmann, and the painter Klimt, who was the animating spirit behind the group and its first president.

Gustav Klimt (1862–1918) was the most original talent of the Sezession. He was a regular contributor to the pages of their review *Ver Sacrum*; other notable collaborators were Hugo von Hofmannsthal and Rainer Maria Rilke. Illustrations were by the Swiss painter Ferdinand Hodler. Klimt borrowed some rather ill-digested elements from symbolism, but he then used them in a highly personal manner.

Thomas Theodor Heine   Illustration for the review *Simplicissimus,* 1892

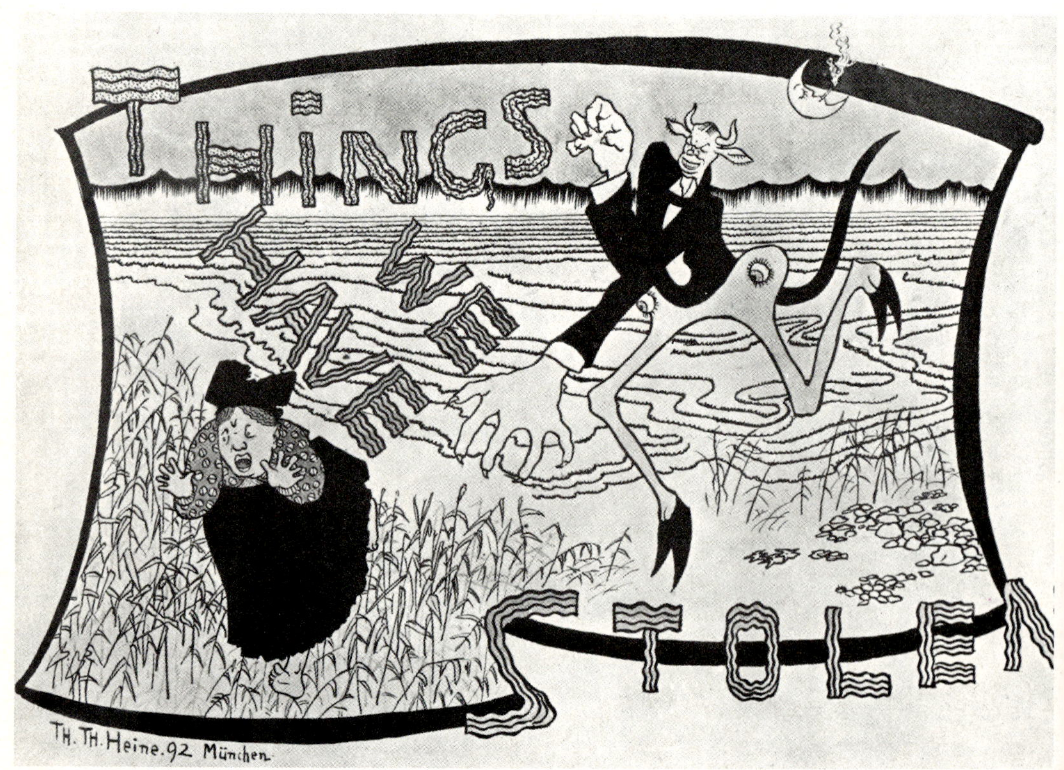

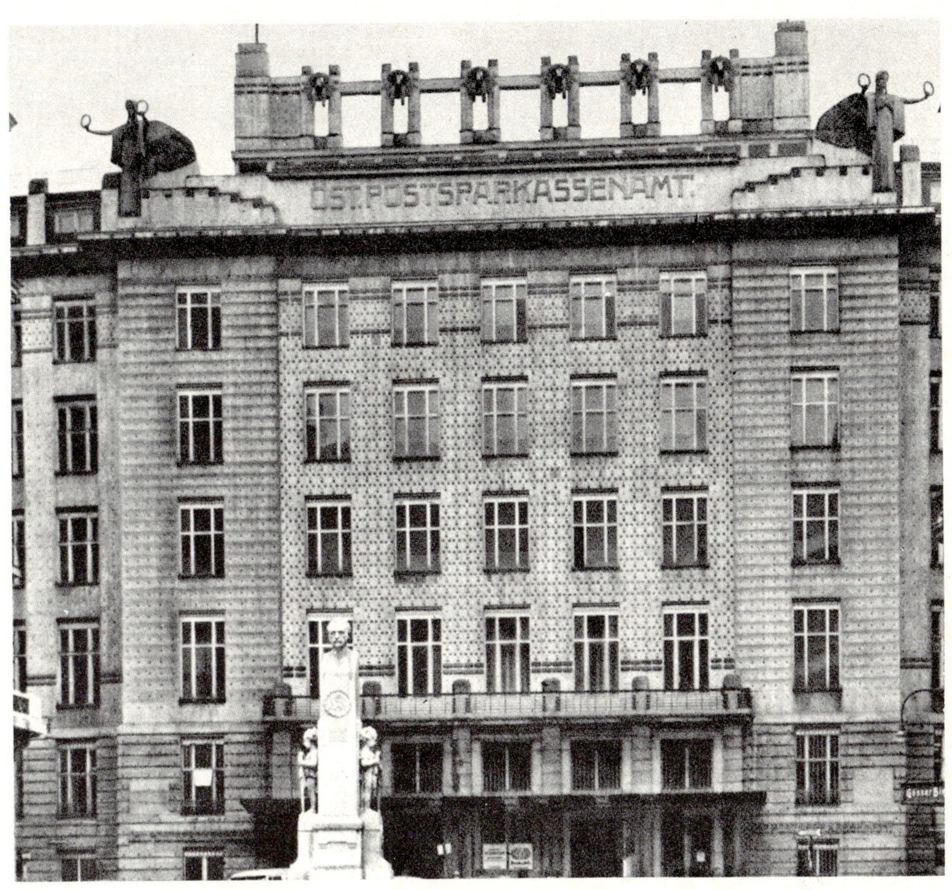

OTTO WAGNER   The Postal Savings Bank, 1904–1908

The darling of Viennese society ladies, women were the theme of his
strange pictures, a theme constantly repeated and always reworked:
the silhouette emerges from a pile of ornaments, in brightly colored
contrast to one another, an idea drawn from stylized Egyptian proto-
types and Byzantine mosaics. Klimt used no modeling in his flat colors.
They remained shimmering tesserae in which he freely used gold and
silver pigment; above this mantle of rigid composition, a face, or sometimes only half a face, was drawn, like a portrait marked by a voluptuous morbid intoxication. There is an excessive and overly mannered
side of Klimt which would be almost strident, if not restrained by his
unfailing taste. His paintings seemed to owe nothing to his immediate

139

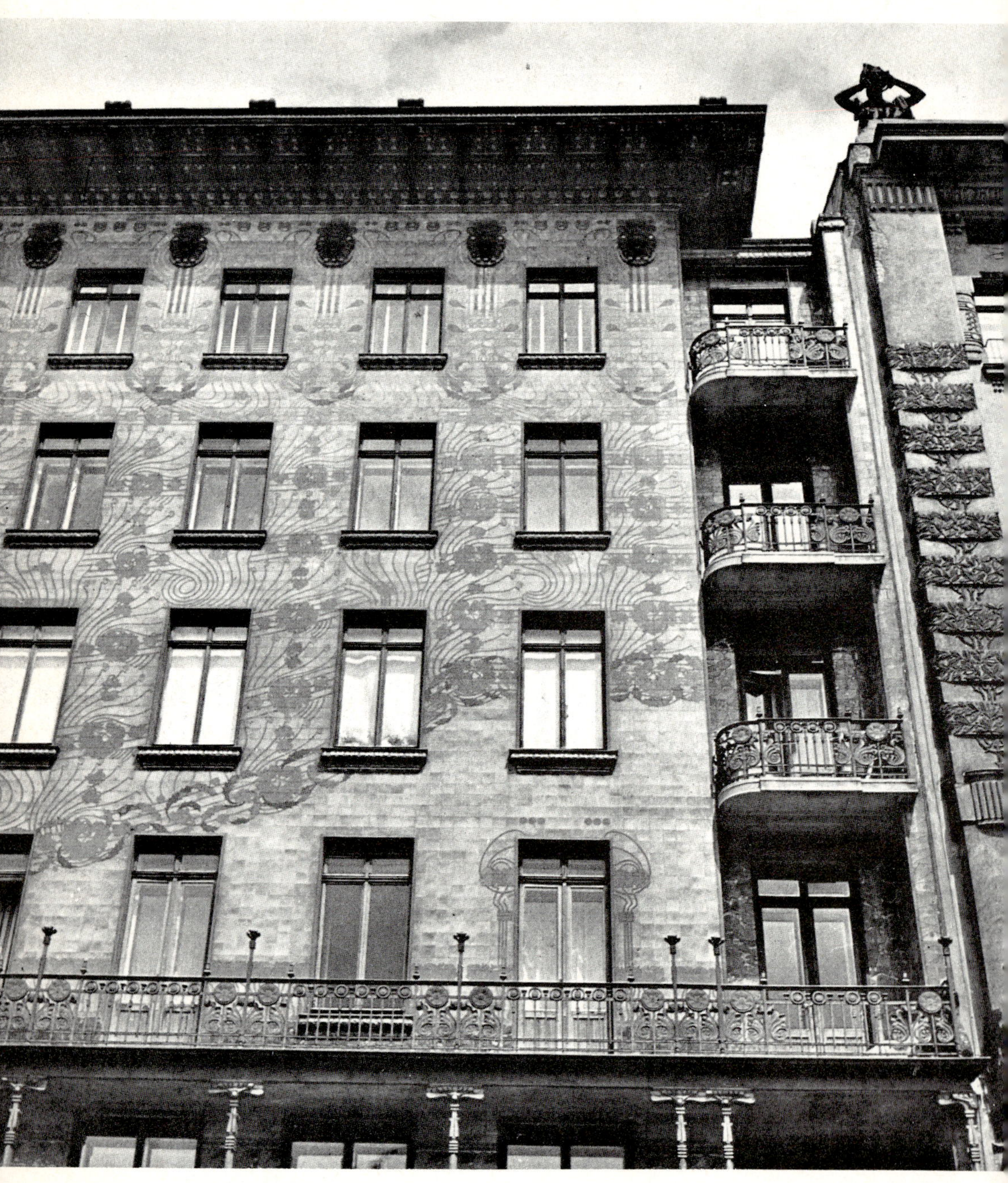

Otto Wagner   Majolika House, 1910

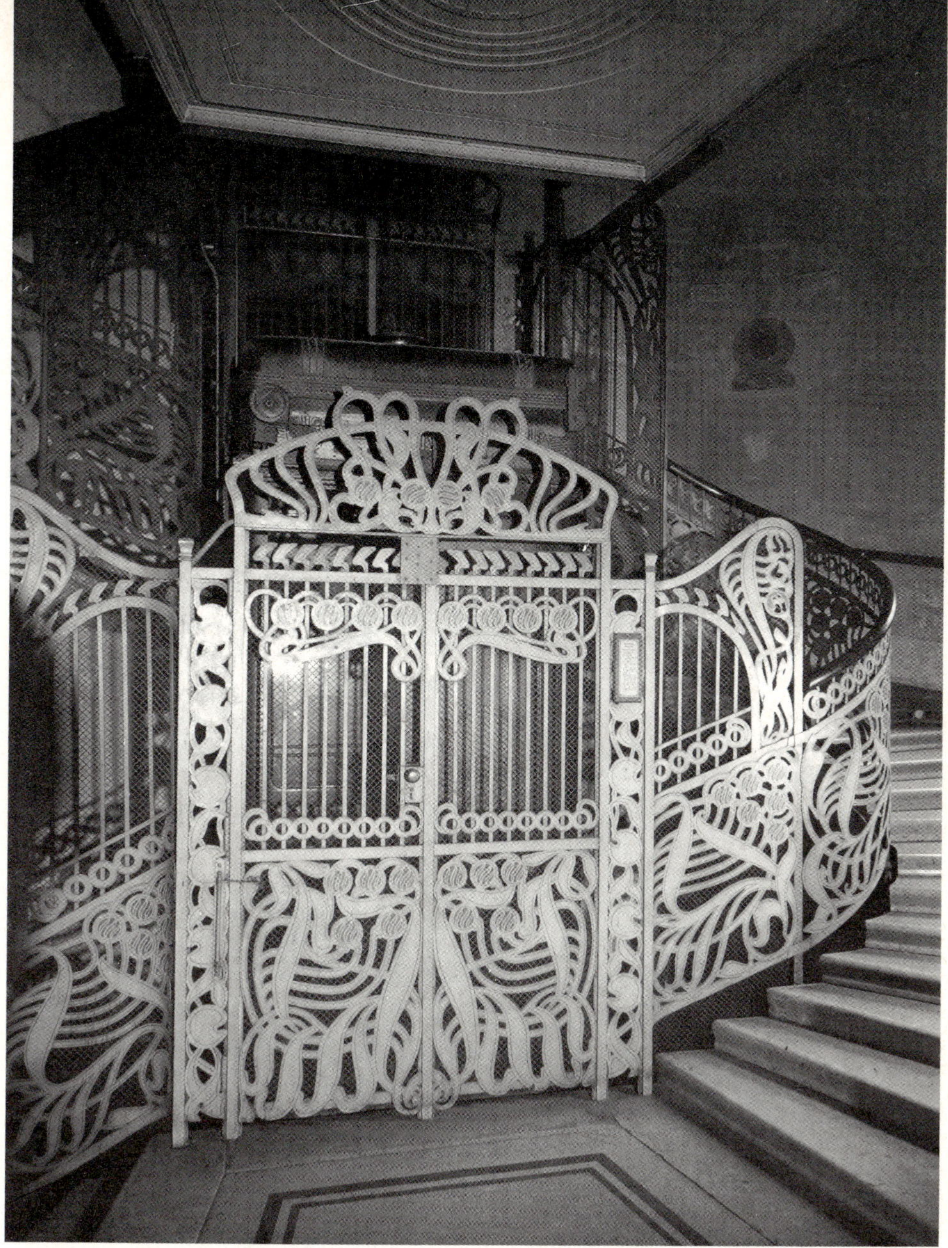

OTTO WAGNER   Elevator gates for the Majolika House, 1910

elders and they enjoyed enormous success, especially among the young;
their success reflected upon the Sezession movement as a whole. Klimt's
vision would seem to have inspired the pavilion designed by Olbrich
in 1899 for the Sezession Haus, a *petit palais* whose heavy parallele-
piped structure was crowned by a cupola consisting of foliage woven

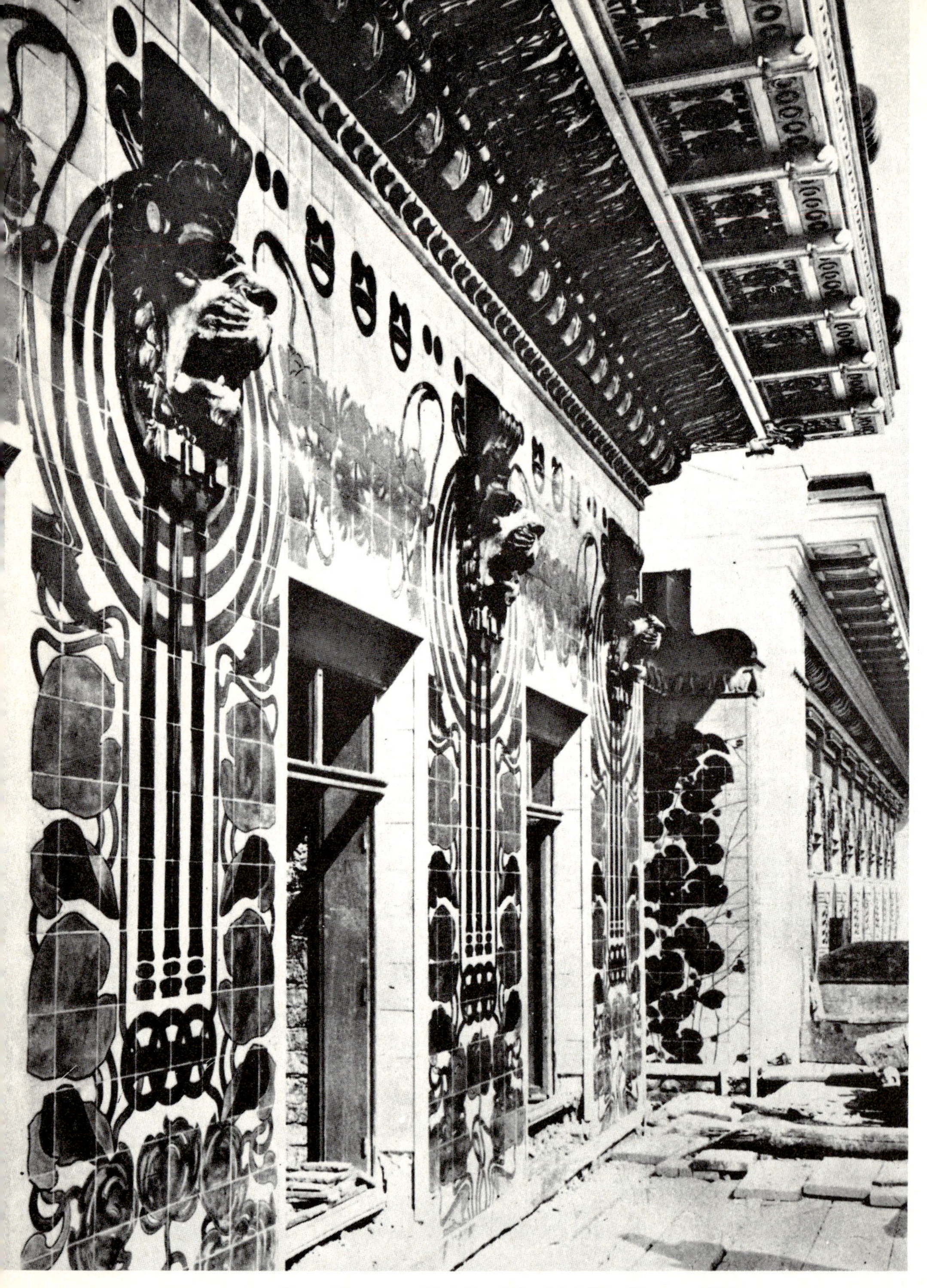

OTTO WAGNER   Detail of the Majolika House, 1910

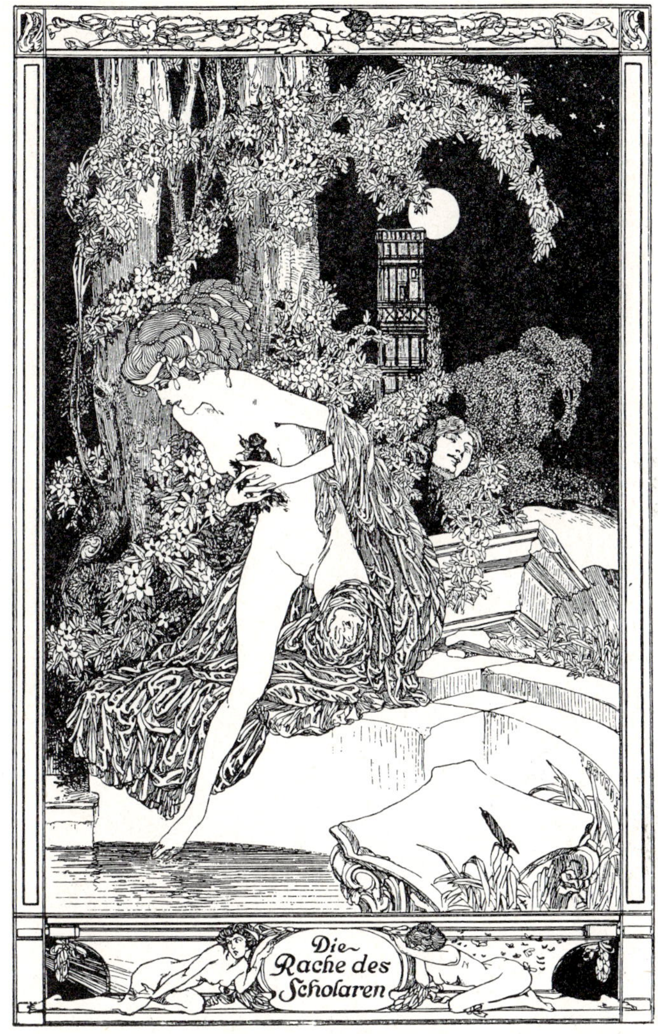

FRANZ VON BAYROS   *The Student's Revenge*, 1911

of gilt metal. Upon this strange monument, nicknamed by the Viennese "the gilded cabbage," there was an inscription chiseled in stone, which defined the Sezession doctrine succinctly: "To each century its art, to art its freedom."

Klimt was commissioned to do a ceiling (now destroyed) for the University of Vienna (1902), but the finished work created a scandal. He then became interested in the applied arts, working with the Wiener Werkstätte (decorating workshops created by Hoffmann based on

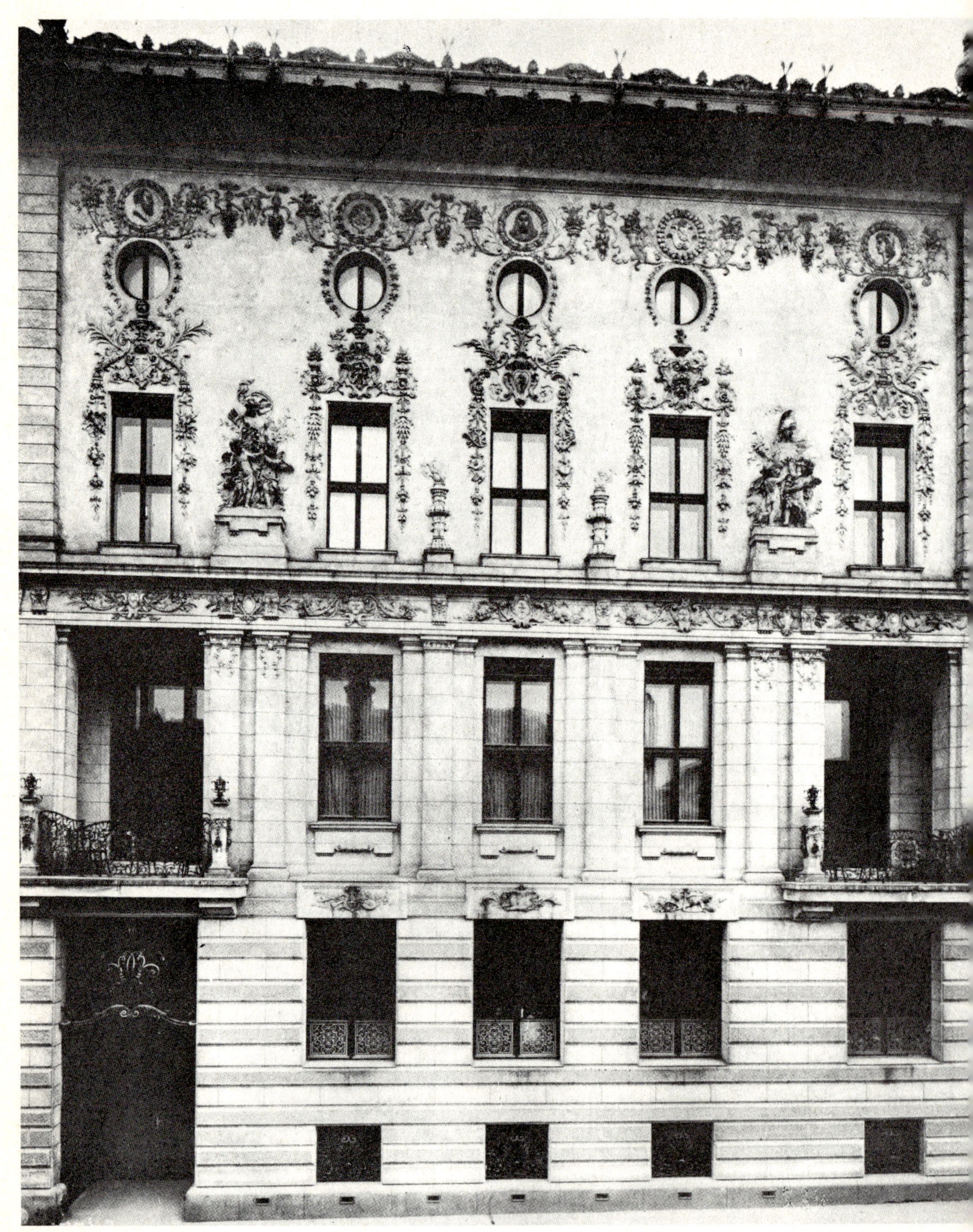

OTTO WAGNER Palais Wagner, 1890–1891

Morris's principles) — the formation of teams of architects and decorators who jointly tried to arrange commissions from patrons. In the plastic domain, Klimt's expressionism was soon abandoned, stripped of its Jugendstil language by Schiele and Kokoschka. Adolf Loos (1870–1933), another disciple of Otto Wagner and a regular of the Viennese group, could not quite accept Jugendstil. He had published an incendiary article with the title "Ornamentation and Crime." All ornament was, for him, a sign of decadence. And when he built the Steiner house in Vienna in the form of a cube, with sharp angles, no roof, and horizontal windows flush with the outer wall, it was obviously a manifesto. Many years would pass before construction of such pure geometric rigor would be seen again. Today, historians of architecture

ADOLF LOOS   Street facade of the Tristan Tzara residence, 1926

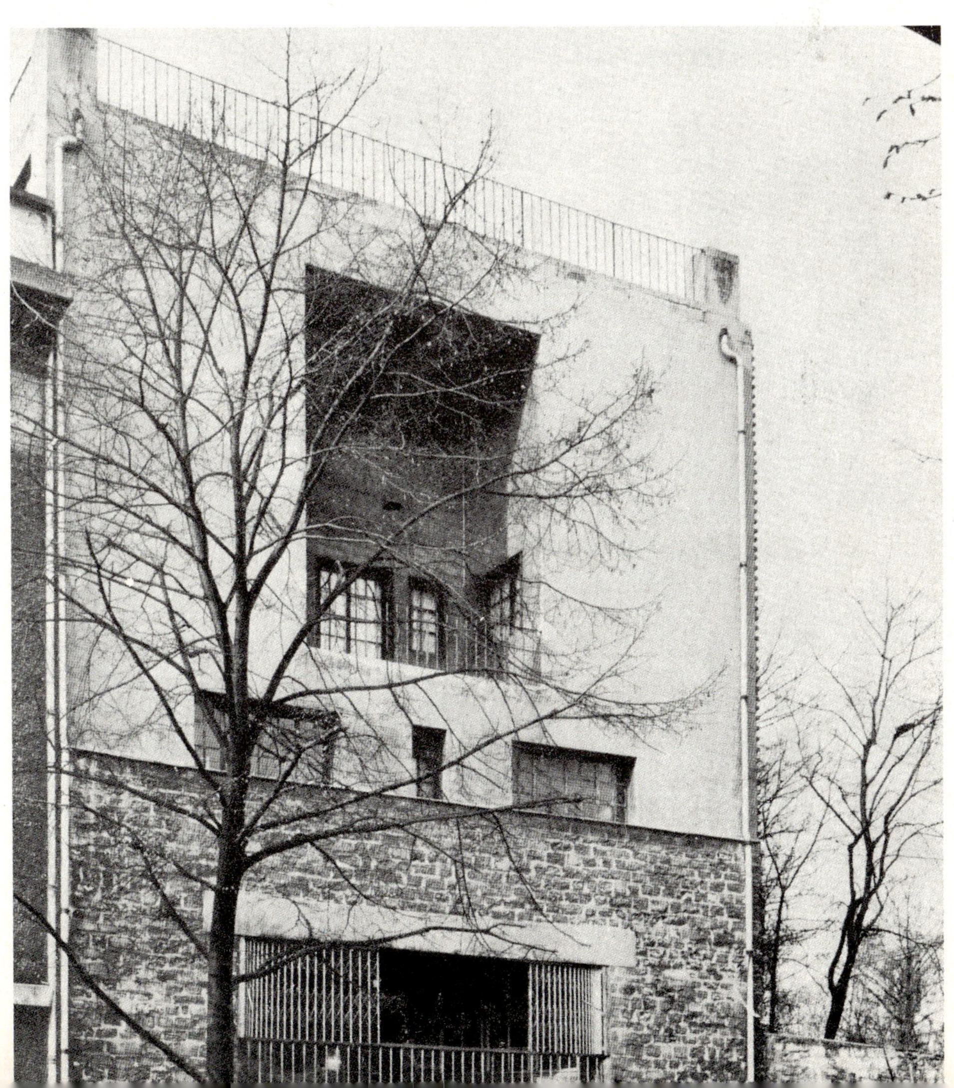

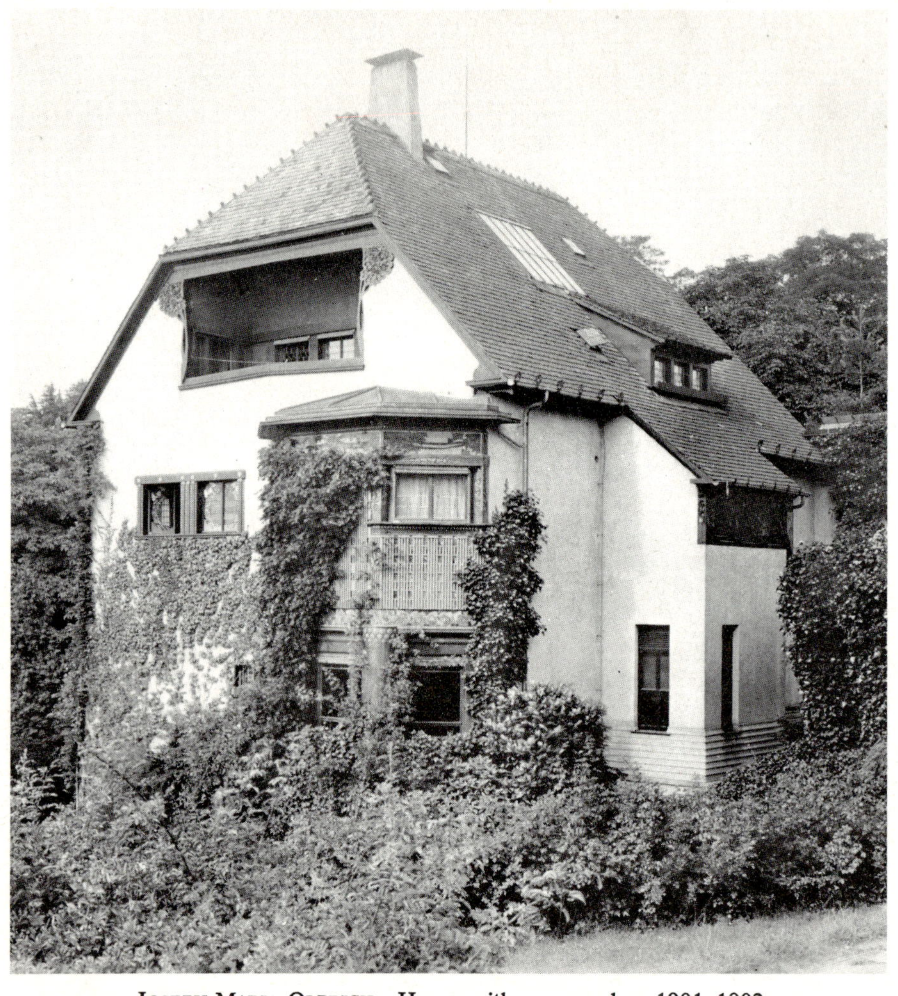

agree that Loos was the flying wedge of modern international style.

Josef Olbrich (1867–1908) was the architect who remained most faithful to the Sezession. The Grand Duke Ernst-Ludwig of Hesse, interested in the movement, invited Olbrich to create, on the Mathildenhöhe, near Darmstadt, a community to house artists of proven talent, in the hopes of encouraging artistic life in his state (1901). Olbrich designed a total plan resonant with subtle symbolic meaning. Seven houses (one of which Behrens had built for himself) were grouped around a large richly decorated central building which housed meeting

146

rooms and studios. A mini-skyscraper, the Tower of Marriage, completed the ensemble; its roof was covered in weathered bronze, and the rounded summit terminated in elongated elements which stood symbolically for the five fingers of the hand. The architect died before this monument to creativity could be finished.

Olbrich was also interested in furnishing and interior design. But the desire to break with the past is not enough to engender new forms. Jugendstil had the virtue of nonconformity, and a spirit of experimentation in the details, but, conversely, the furnishings themselves lack harmony. Indeed, they seem to have been too disparate in style to bear issue.

The case of Joseph Hoffmann (1870–1956) is a perfect example. Two years after he had founded the Sezession, and received the commission for the sanitorium of Purkersdorf (1902), his projects and

Joseph-Maria Olbrich   Tower of Marriage, 1901–1902

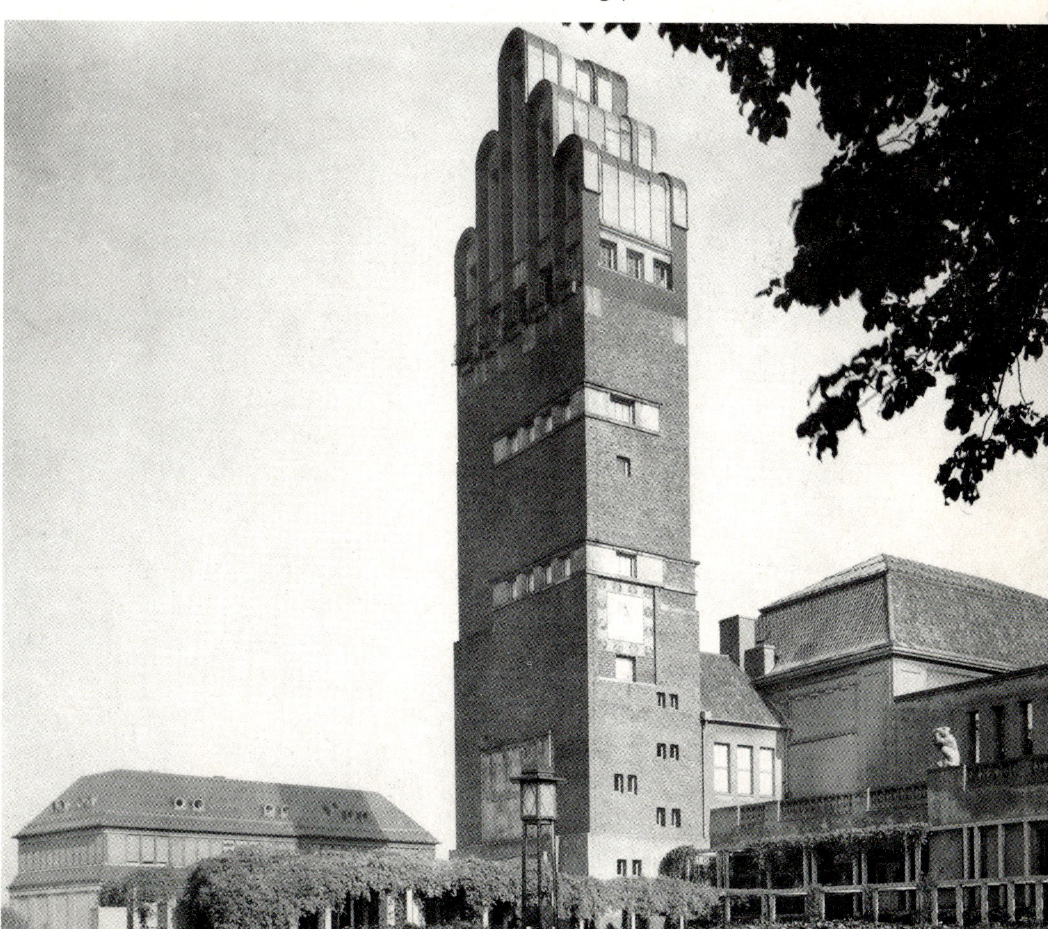

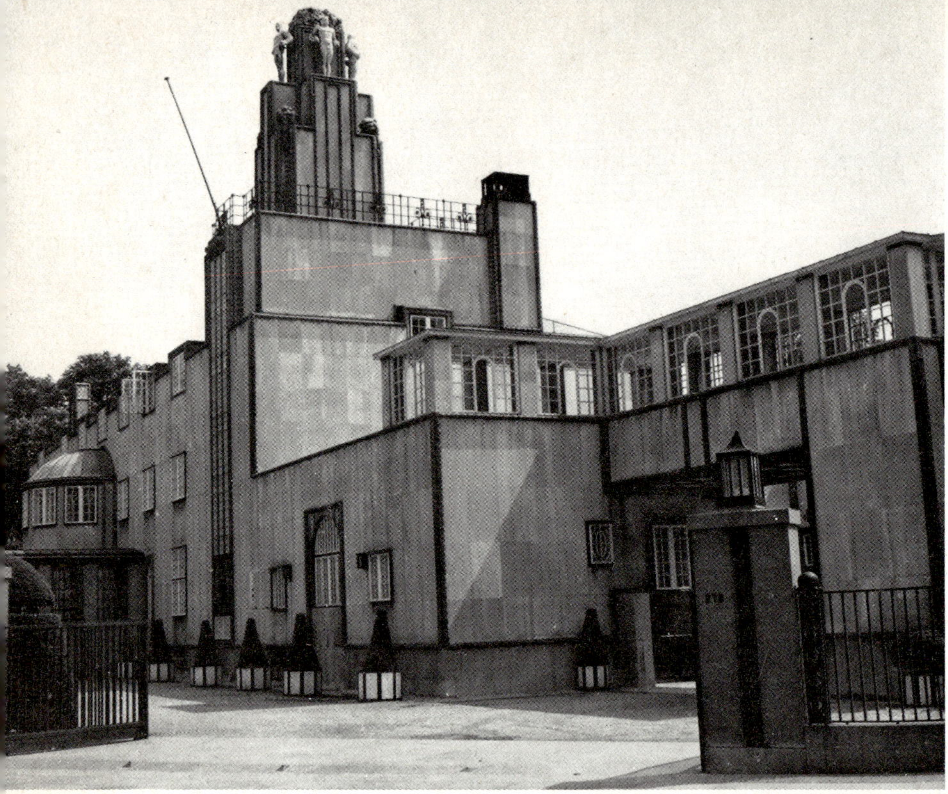

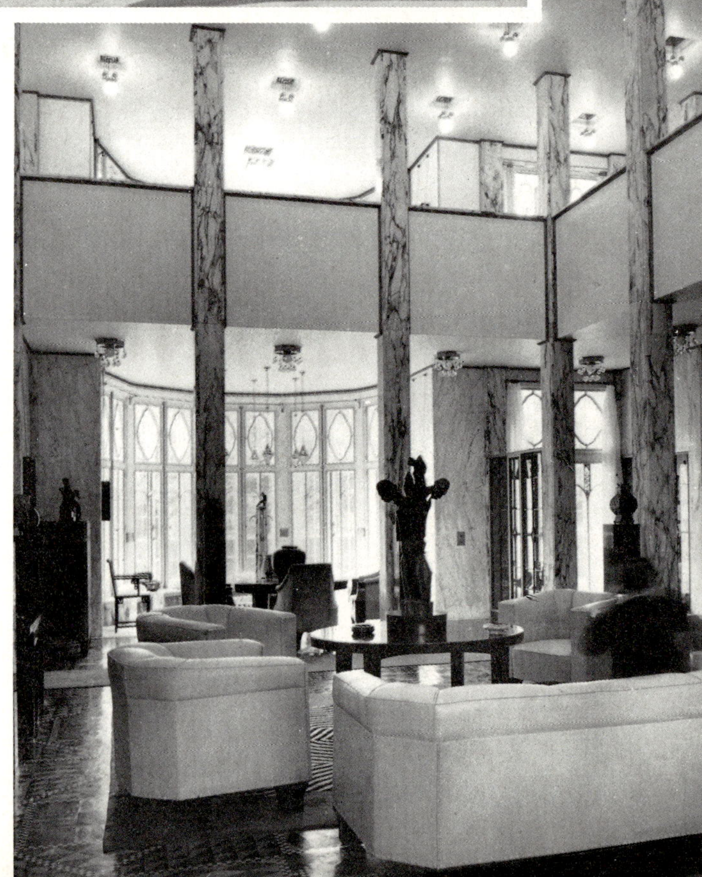

JOSEF HOFFMANN
Exterior of the
Palais Stoclet, 1905

JOSEF HOFFMANN
Interior of the
Palais Stoclet, 1905

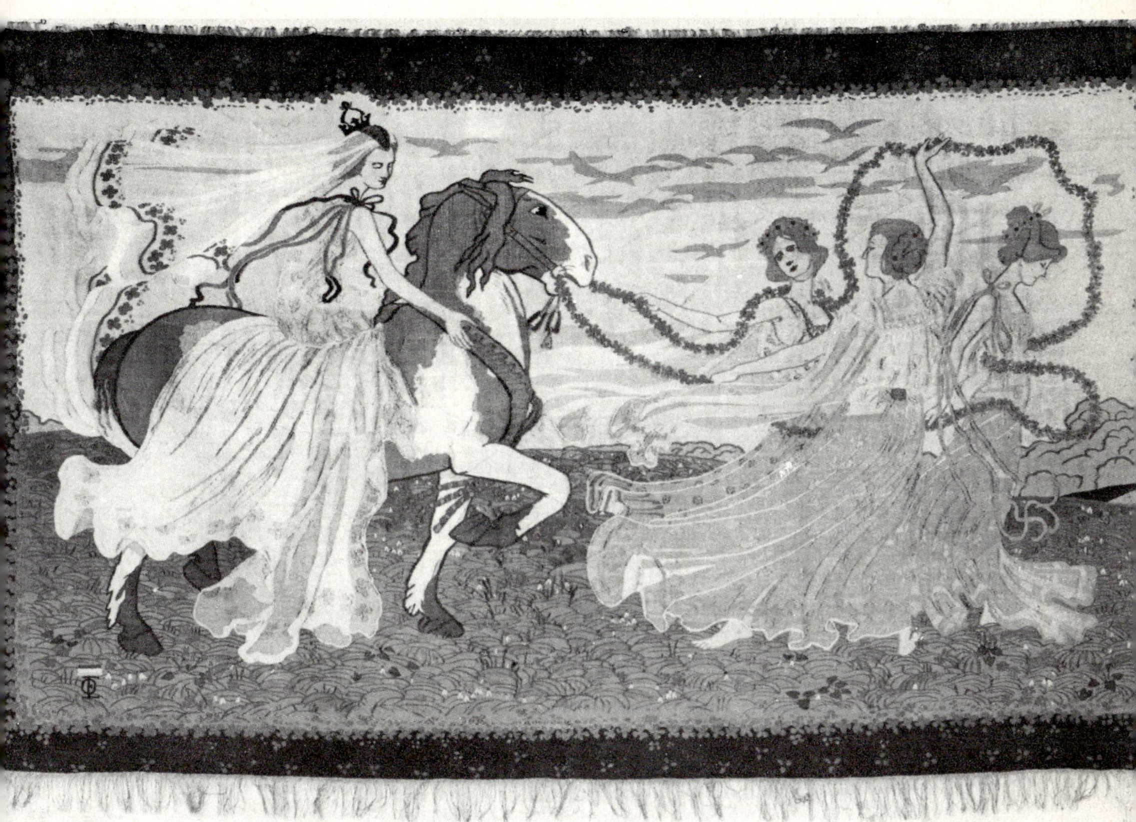

Otto Eckmann Tapestry, ca. 1900

designs were those of a stripped-down, functional architecture, far in advance of its time. When the architect met the financier Adolf Stoclet in Vienna in 1904, the latter invited Hoffmann to design his Brussels mansion, to be called the Palais Stoclet, for which he would provide an appropriately lavish budget. Hoffmann decided that the ornamental Jugendstil was unsuitable for this project. Instead, he created a very sober, precise architecture where geometric volumes, primarily circles and squares, were articulated with elegant precision. Faced with white marble, the outlines and ribs were delineated with chiseled bronze trim; the roof was covered in copper. On the interior, pastel colors alternated with silver, emphasizing the mosaics by Klimt. The very top of the building was a prism, circled by four athletes, sculpted by Metzner, silhouetted against the sky. The Palais Stoclet, taken as a whole, is

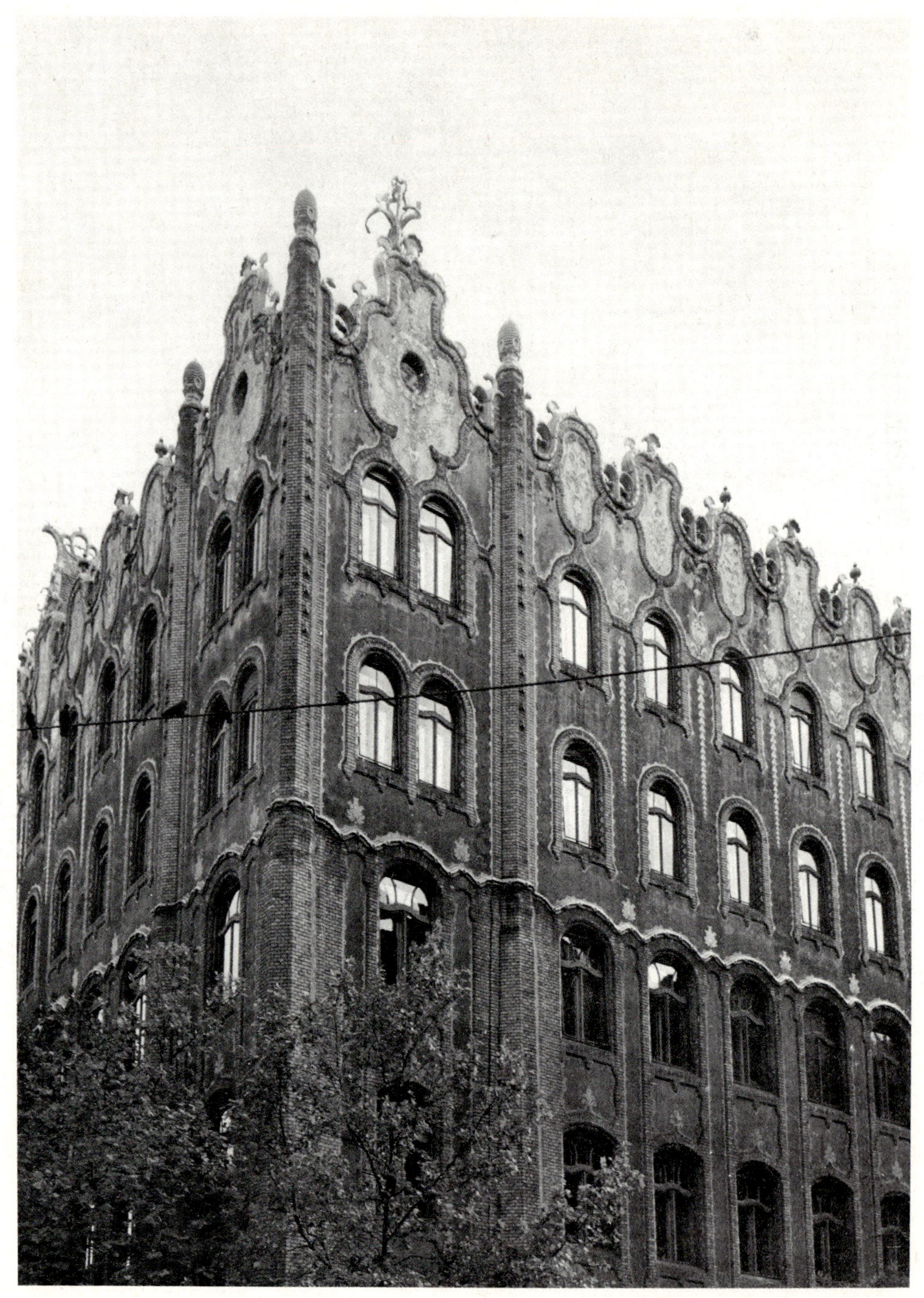

Odön Lechner   Exterior of the Postal Savings Bank, 1899–1902

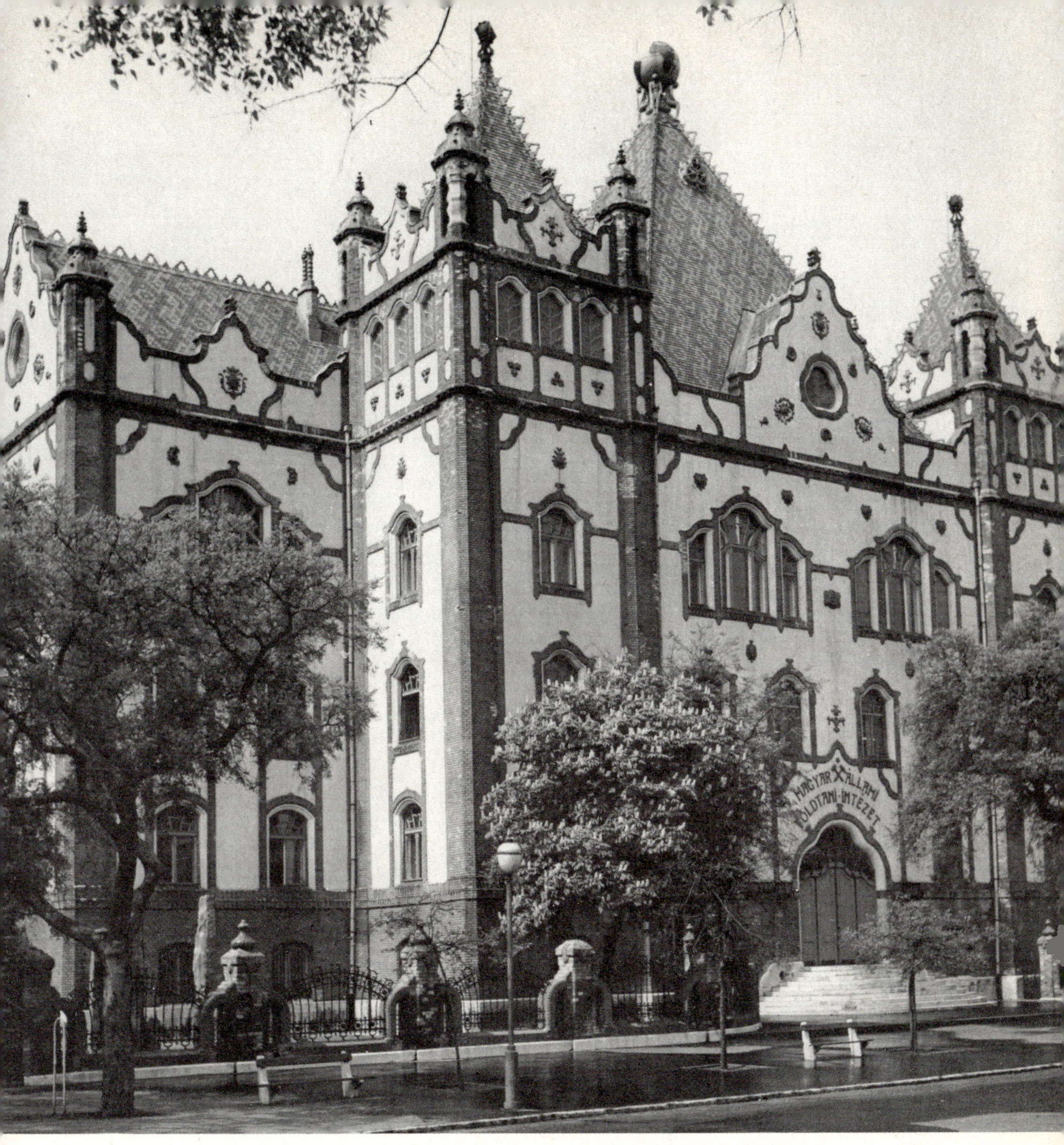

ODÖN LECHNER   Exterior of the Geological Institute, 1904

closer to the art deco style of the Paris Exhibition of 1925 than it is
to Jugendstil.

Even though Jugendstil could never seem to transcend its attach-
ment to the banal and the mediocre, it spread, nonetheless, far beyond
the confines of Vienna. Cities and buildings — scattered examples, to
be sure — can claim their relationship to the Sezession. Among the

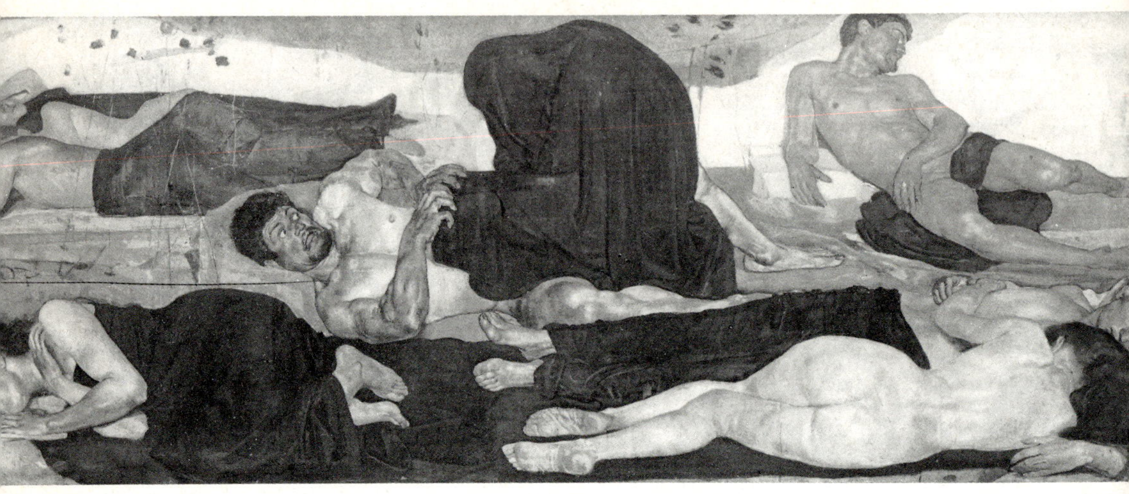

Ferdinand Hodler   *Night,* 1890

most important is the Savings Bank of Budapest (1901) by Odön Lechner, resolutely modernist in its wavy lines and tortured reliefs, which, by the way, are highly reminiscent of German baroque.

the munich sezession and its expansion in germany

The Sezessionists were, strictly speaking, living evidence of a rupture with the academies: the Sezession itself, however, was largely supported by princes of the oldest German families, either for diversion, or through a family tradition of patronage. We have already noted that Van de Velde spent his peak period of creativity at the court of the Grand Duke of Weimar.

Munich was a particularly active center of German art nouveau. The Munich branch of the movement began in 1892 — even earlier than the Vienna group — but Munich was established essentially as a gathering of painters. The group gravitated around Uhde, Trübner, and von Stuck, who remained under the admiring influence of Böcklin. It was only in 1896, with the founding of the review *Jugend,* that the Sezession established an independent identity. Munch had already exhibited in Berlin, where his paintings had outraged the public.

While art nouveau elsewhere mattered only to artists and dilet-

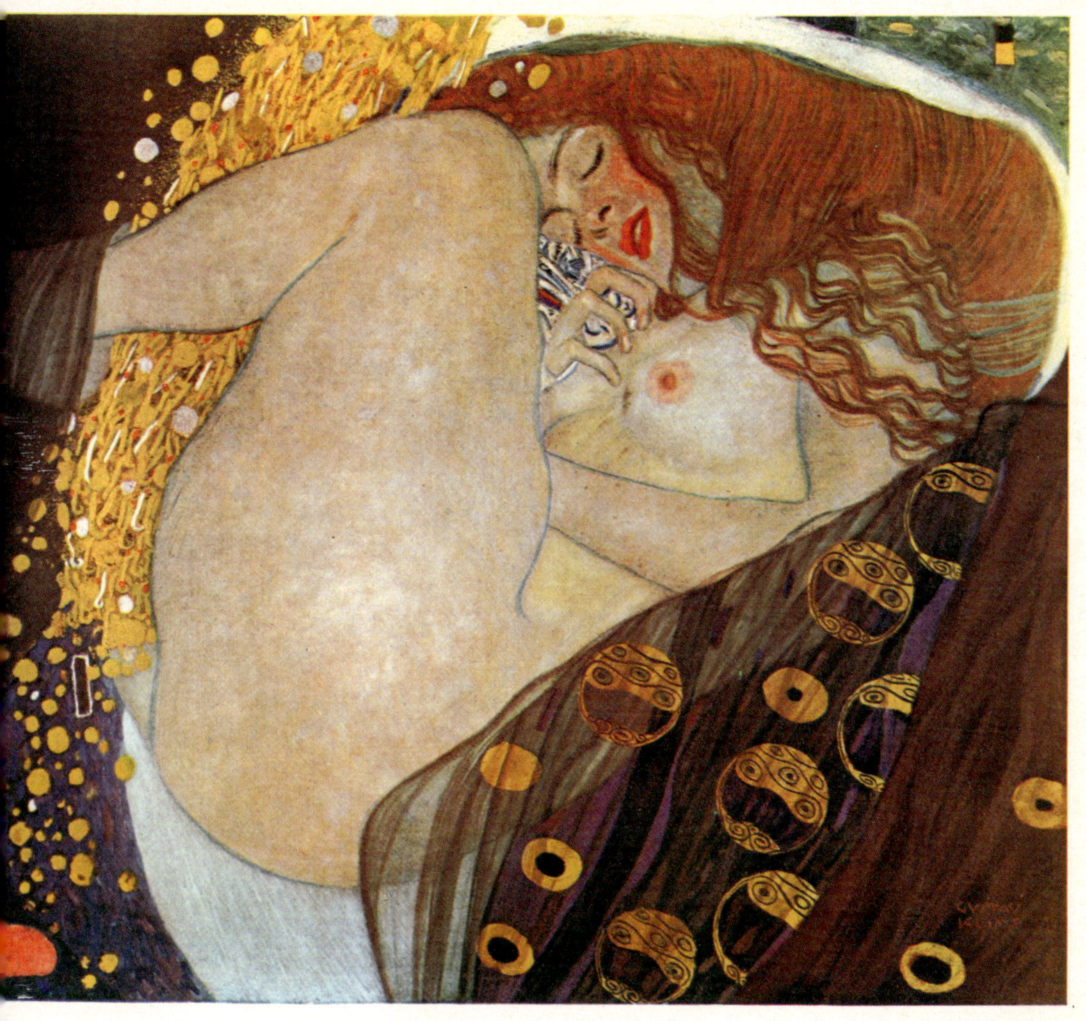

Gustav Klimt   Danaé, ca. 1907

tantes, in Munich it attracted the interest of a wide public who responded enthusiastically to *Jugend* and to the movement it represented. The International Exhibition in Munich in 1897, which featured an important section of decorative art, was dazzling affirmation of the new trends, and marked the coming of age of Jugendstil.

While the Viennese Sezession took its point of departure from a decorative symbolism, it was the tumultuous violence of expressionism which was to be the hallmark of the Munich painters. Vienna is characterized by a certain elegance in tonality; Munich, followed by Berlin, expressed a destructive violence which was unafraid of vulgarity. Next to the cyclones of color exploded from Munch palettes, Klimt seems a delicate gem-setter. In the one group, we find feminine languor in an overwrought decor; in the other, haunted faces crudely drawn. Both, however were attracted to arresting forms of expression. Jugendstil had so impressed its vision upon all these artists that even the virulent emotions of Munch were expressed — especially in the background of his compositions — by wavy, parallel lines which inevitably recall the decorative complexities of art nouveau. This kind of composition would be even more evident in the style of wood-cut which spread, as though by osmosis, through Germany, England, France, and Belgium. The technique itself imposes a simplification which favored Jugendstil's ornamental style. While he was living in Paris (1896–1898). Munich exhibited at Bing's gallery l'Art Nouveau, where his works were introduced by the Swedish writer Strindberg. The group Die Scholle (Clod of Earth), founded by Putz and Erler in 1899, is a sort of offspring of Jugendstil. It still had sufficient vitality to attract Kandinsky to Munich. Art nouveau is flagrantly apparent as an influence in Kandinsky's first period, as well as in the early works of Franz Marc, who later founded Der blaue Reiter (the Blue Cavalier) movement.

Born in Zurich, Hermann Obrist (1863–1921) studied botany and geology and subsequently enrolled in the School of Applied Arts in Karlsruhe. He became a sculptor in Paris, then an embroiderer in Florence, finally transporting his workshop to Munich, where he founded the Workshops of Arts and Crafts. The son of a Swiss doctor and a Scots noblewoman, Obrist himself possessed an intellectual subtlety which made him one of the most original and creative minds in art nouveau.

His brilliant boldness was apparent from the very first, when he exhibited an embroidered panel with the *whiplash* motif (1895). The abstraction of the design, done in yellow-gold thread on a turquoise background, is characterized by an extraordinary dynamism. Cyclamen are the ostensible subject, but they disappear in the movement of the composition. The stems emerge from a tangle of roots, describing their complex, exquisite parabolas in space. Nothing could be more allusive than such elegant freedom.

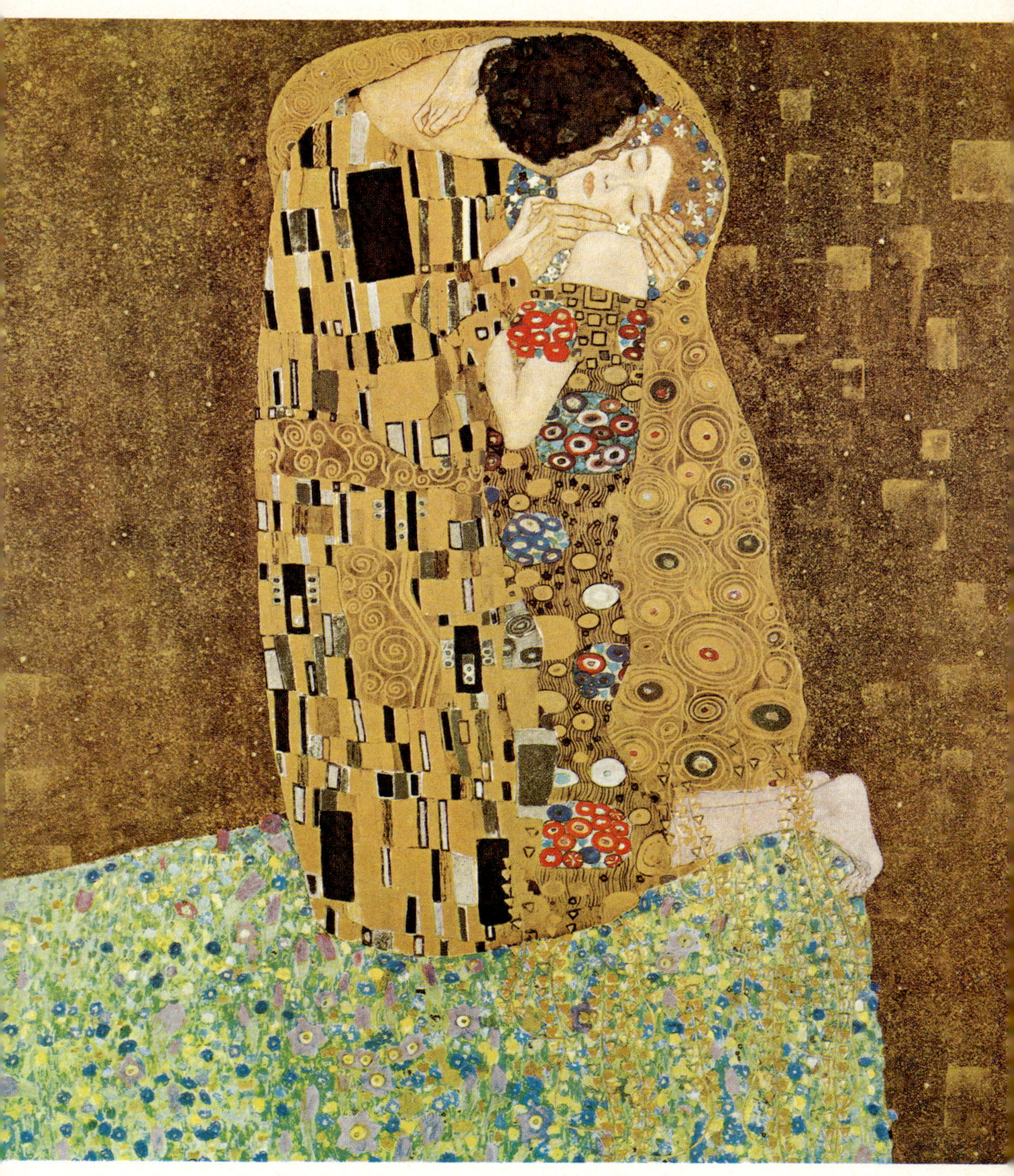

GUSTAV KLIMT *The Kiss*, 1911

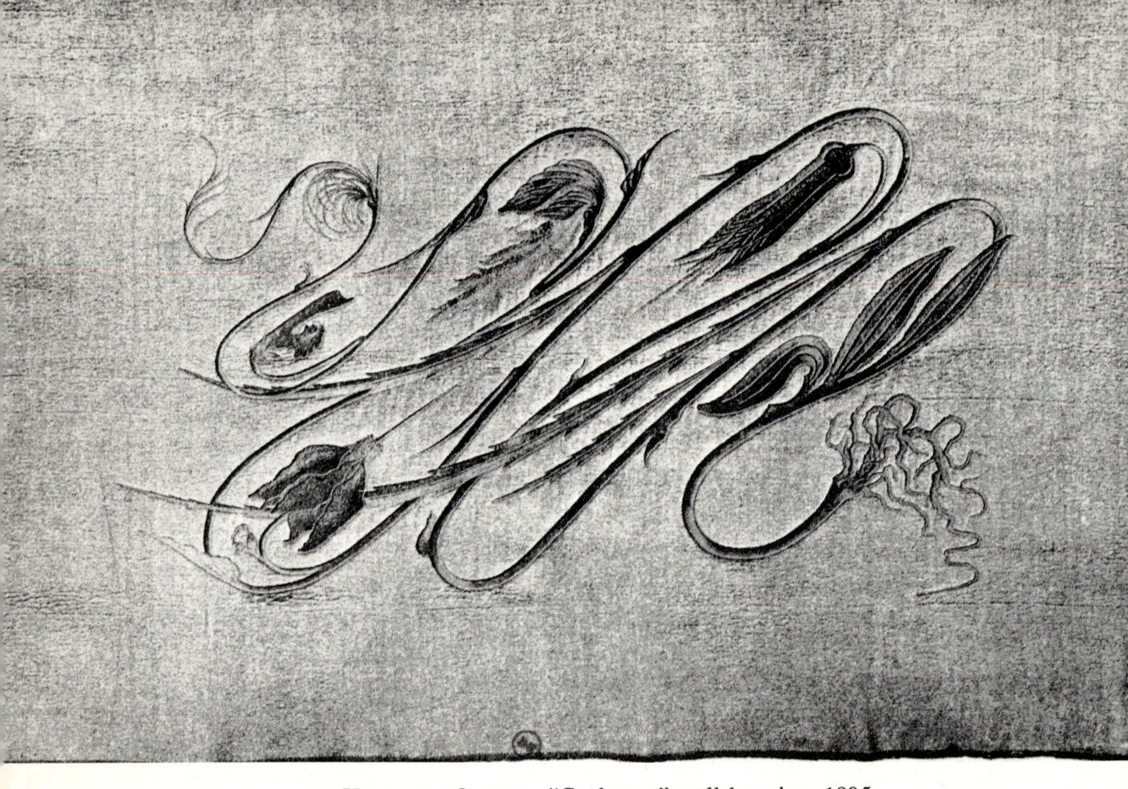

The *whiplash* line acted as a stimulus upon Jugendstil and Modern Style. Obrist became especially interested in decorative sculpture which served a very specific function. The forms that he thrust into space became more and more abstract. If the point of departure was the analytic description of a particular plant, by a process of successive syntheses he would end up with forms which no longer bore the slightest resemblance to the original model. An example is the fountain commissioned by the Krupp von Bohlen family in Essen, with its volumes and empty spaces, basins and complicated surfaces, which seem there only to conduct the sparkling play of water. A gigantic iris has lost its flower identity, only to be transformed into living sculpture. Obrist, moreover, believed that ornament was acceptable only if it was not subordinated to any reality, even an organic one; in order to be intrinsically decorative, it must be abstract. He made models of monuments characterized by their rejection of any reference to flower and plant forms, a rejection, that is, of the entire premise of art nouveau, while he remained one of its most important artists.

156

The name of his friend August Endell (1871–1925), an amateur architect, is associated with Elvira House in Munich, now destroyed. It was a photographer's studio; different-sized doors and windows were cut out of the ground floor, while the blind remainder of the facade is almost entirely faced with a relief of abstract motif, which suggests some sort of gaint winged monster. There are also the volutes dear to Obrist. This building lacks the architect's wild yet controlled organization, as well as his refined use of color and materials. The decoration, moreover, completely ignores the architectural lines. It is more reminiscent of Gaudí's extravagances, although, in the final

HERMANN OBRIST   Krupp von Bohlen fountain, 1913

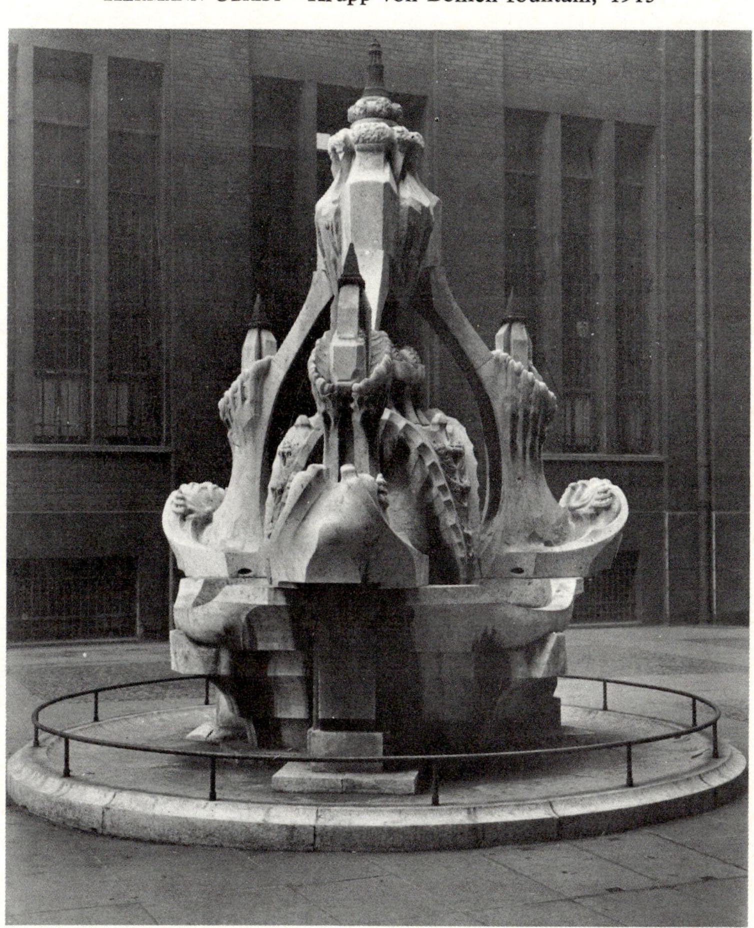

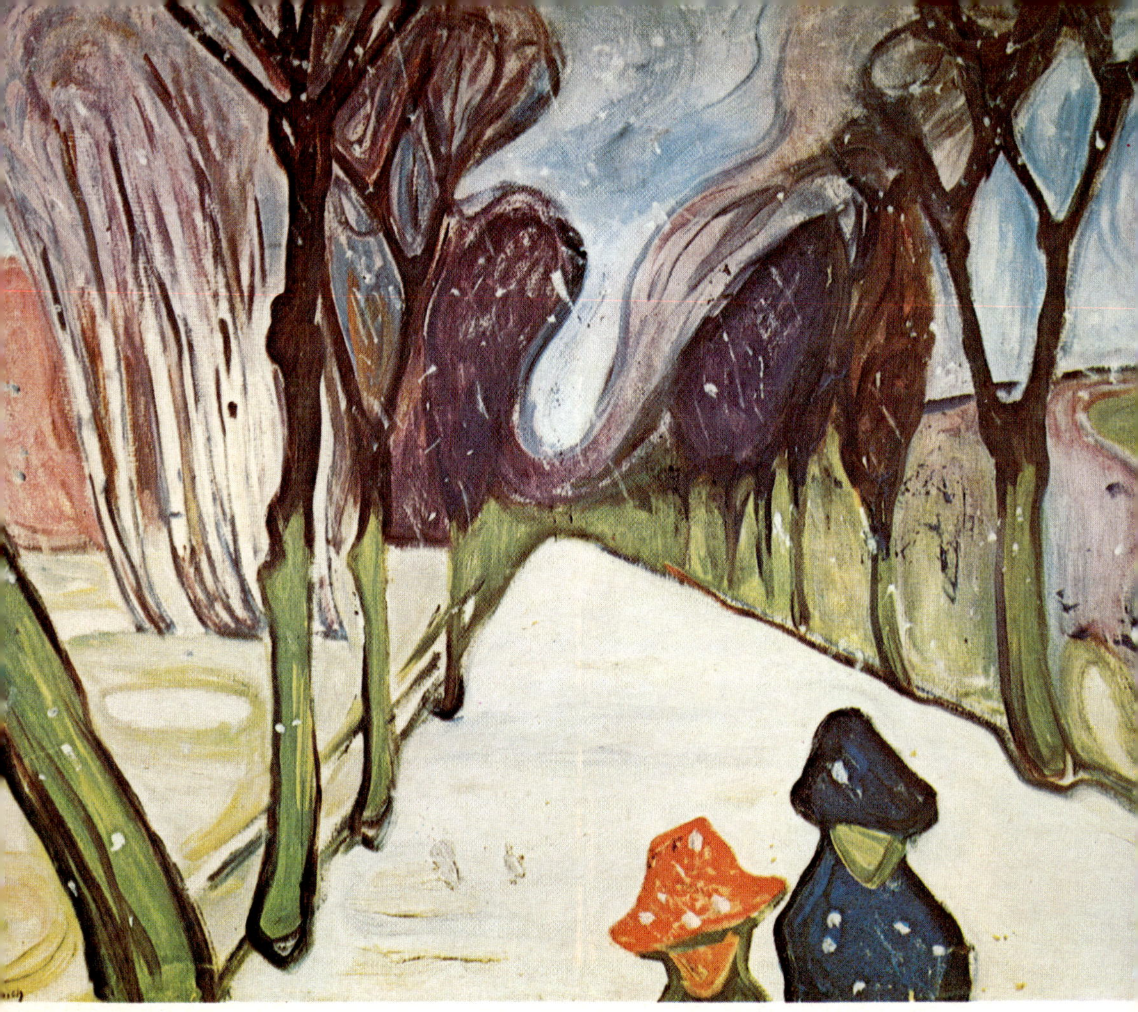

EDVARD MUNCH *Path through the Snow,* 1906

analysis, Elvira House has none of Gaudí's characteristic freshness, spontaneity, or harmony.

Max Klinger (1857–1920) is considered by many critics to be a precursor of Jugendstil. A painter and sculptor, he was a prodigious worker and world traveler. Educated in Karlsruhe, he lived at various times in Paris, Rome, and Berlin, before settling in Leipzig, where he also taught, from 1893 on. His huge sculptures and paintings are more notable for their ambition than for their plastic values. Klinger aspired to a total art, and, in this spirit, he designed numerous ornaments which can be viewed as a herald of Jugendstil. His best works are probably his engravings.

In Germany, art nouveau at first tended to the exclusively floral.

158

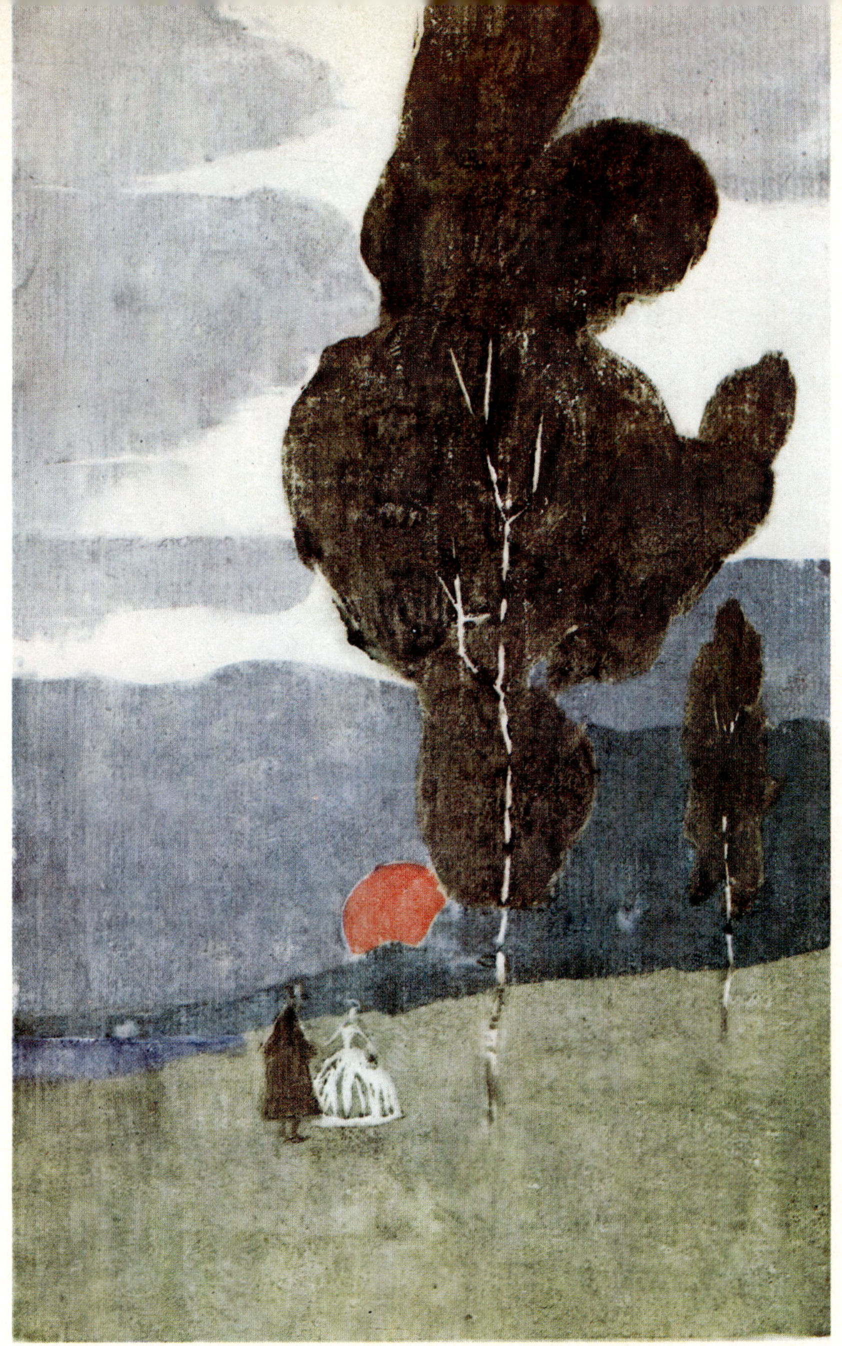

WASSILY KANDINSKY *Moonrise, 1902–1903*

From 1900 on, this idiom moved toward decorative abstraction; the two currents, however, really flowed in and out of one another. The principal sources of German art nouveau were in England, Holland,

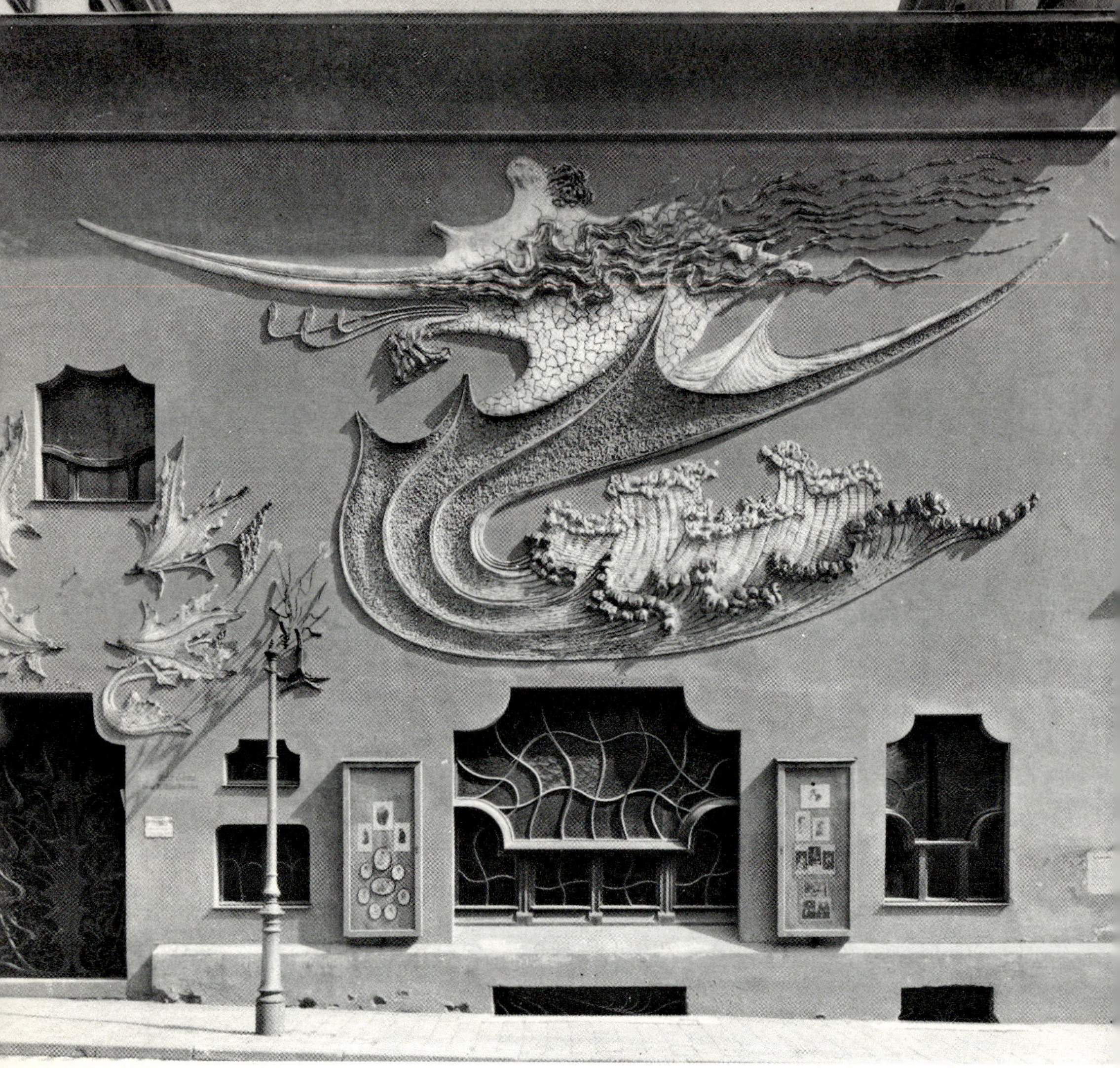

August Endell   Facade of Elvira Photographic Studio, 1897–1898

and Belgium: although the first German works were contemporary to those being done in Nancy and in Paris, there was no contact, it appears, between artists in the two countries.

Bruno Paul, Riemerschmid, and Pankok were the chief figures of art nouveau in Germany. Furniture designers, they were adept at getting the prestigious jobs which assured them not only commissions but status. Even though the emperor personally preferred the hunting-lodge style to Jugendstil, they received from time to time imperial commissions as well.

Otto Eckmann (1865–1902), whose name we associate with Jugend-

stil, was its most sensitive practitioner. He worked in Hamburg and
Berlin, becoming one of the first contributors to the review *Pan,* then
in Munich, where commissions were heaped upon him (he had also
been a contributor to the review *Jugend*). He designed wallpapers and
textiles, illustrated books, and designed type faces. He created furniture and well-proportioned household utensils — rare objects at the
time. But it is as an engraver and draftsman, and, we would add,
calligrapher, that Eckmann achieved greatest distinction, with a sense
of linear values that was absolutely exceptional. He drew ideas from

Augustus Endell   Vestibule and staircase of the Elvira Photographic Studio, 1897–1898

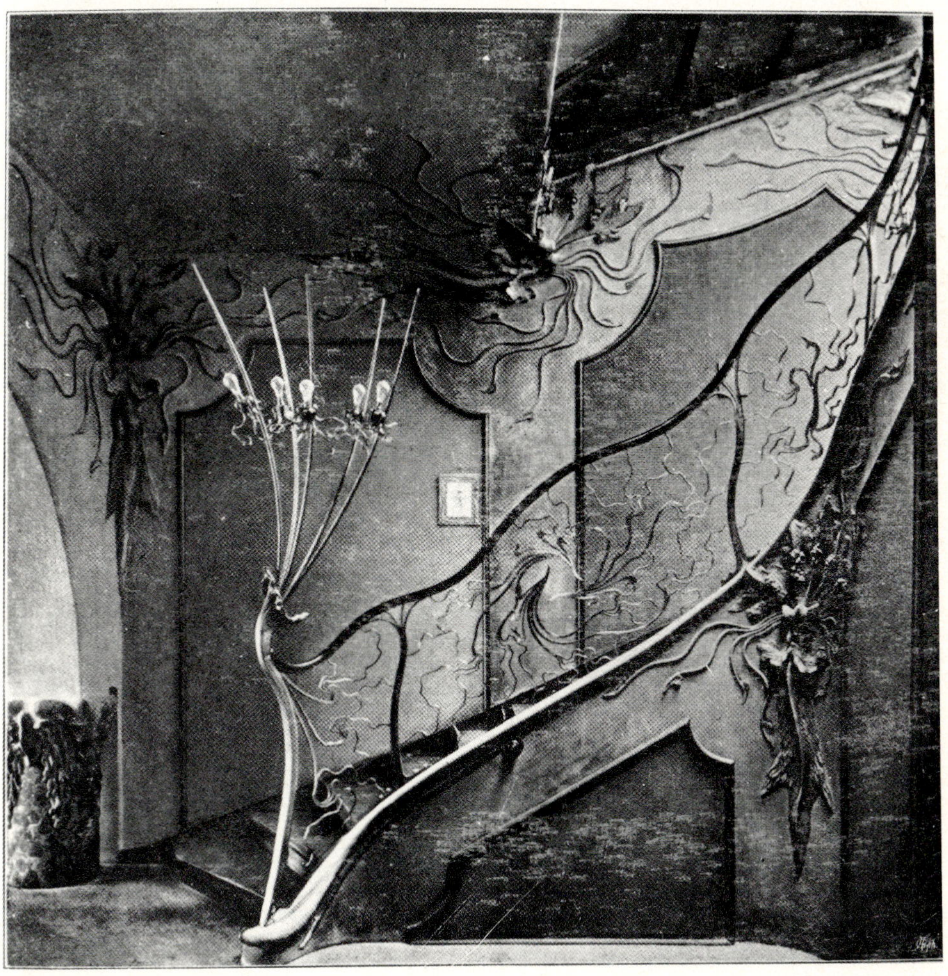

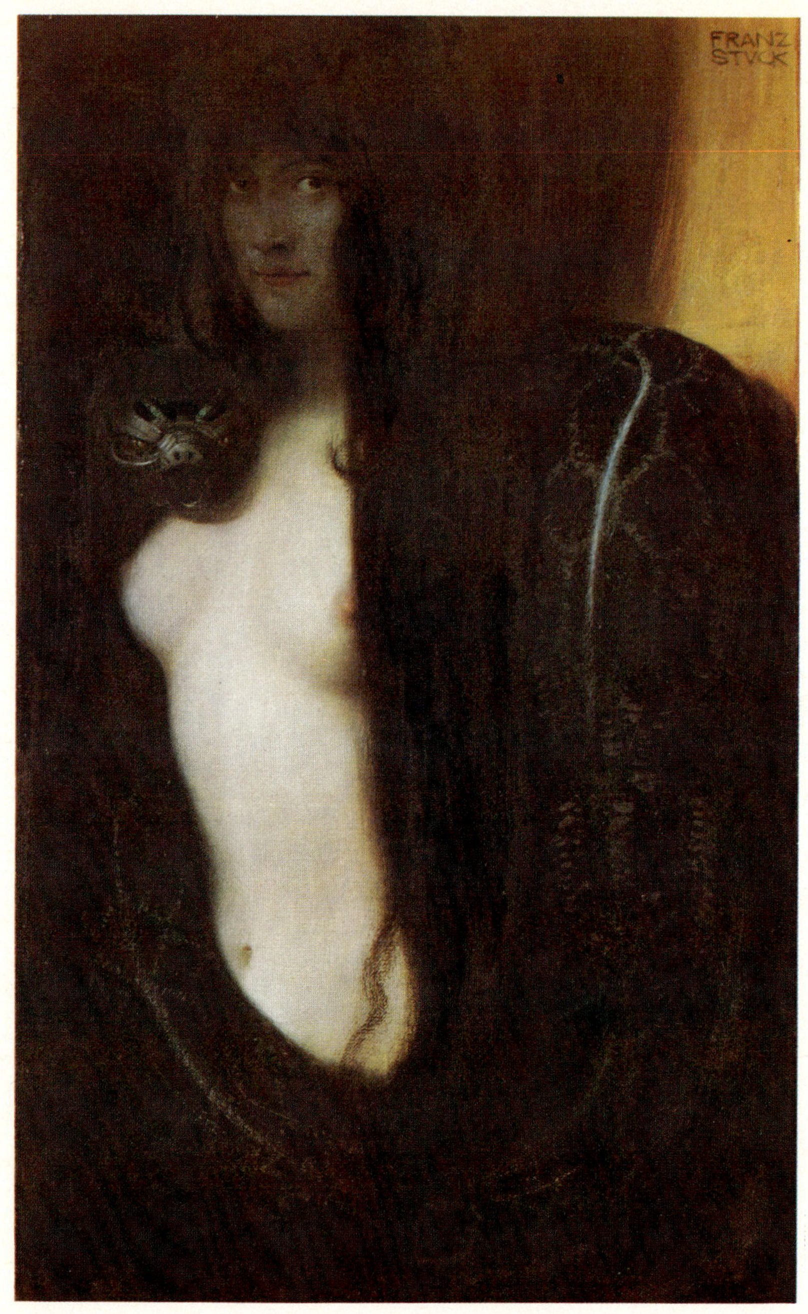

FRANZ VON STUCK *Sin, 1890*

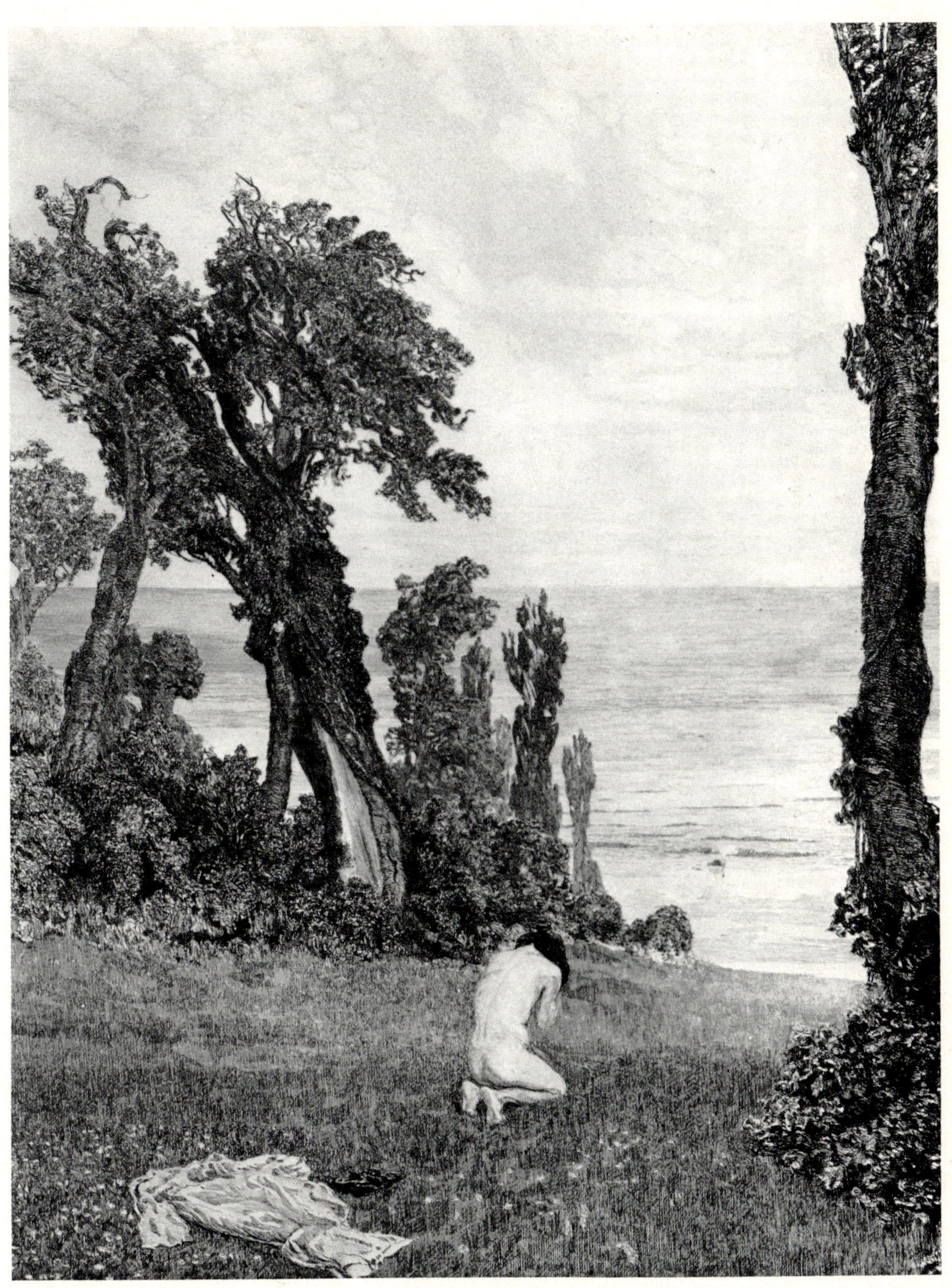

MAX KLINGER *To Beauty, 1890–1893*

plants to transform these into totally unrealistic simplifications whose purified linear form, although drawn from the organic world, determined abstract forms.

The aim of German artists of this period, and one shared by most of the artists associated with art nouveau, was to create objects for everyday use. They had started out believing that ornamental beauty should be prized above all else, including the functional. But the influence of Van de Velde during his Weimar period produced the reverse effect upon his German colleagues — a reaction particularly obvious in home furnishings, which adopted simple and spare forms.

Jugendstil dissipated rapidly. Its painters defected to expressionism and its modernist architects turned toward the Werkbund (founded in 1907); that is, toward an aesthetic determined by the use of new materials and the organization of functional structures which, one and all, repudiated ornament. The industrial aesthetic was about to devour the handicrafts experiment with which the revolutionaries of art nouveau had hoped to enrich the lives of their contemporaries.

ÉMILE GALLÉ (left) Small trilobed vase, 1895–1904; (right) Bellied vase with trilobed lip, 1895–1904

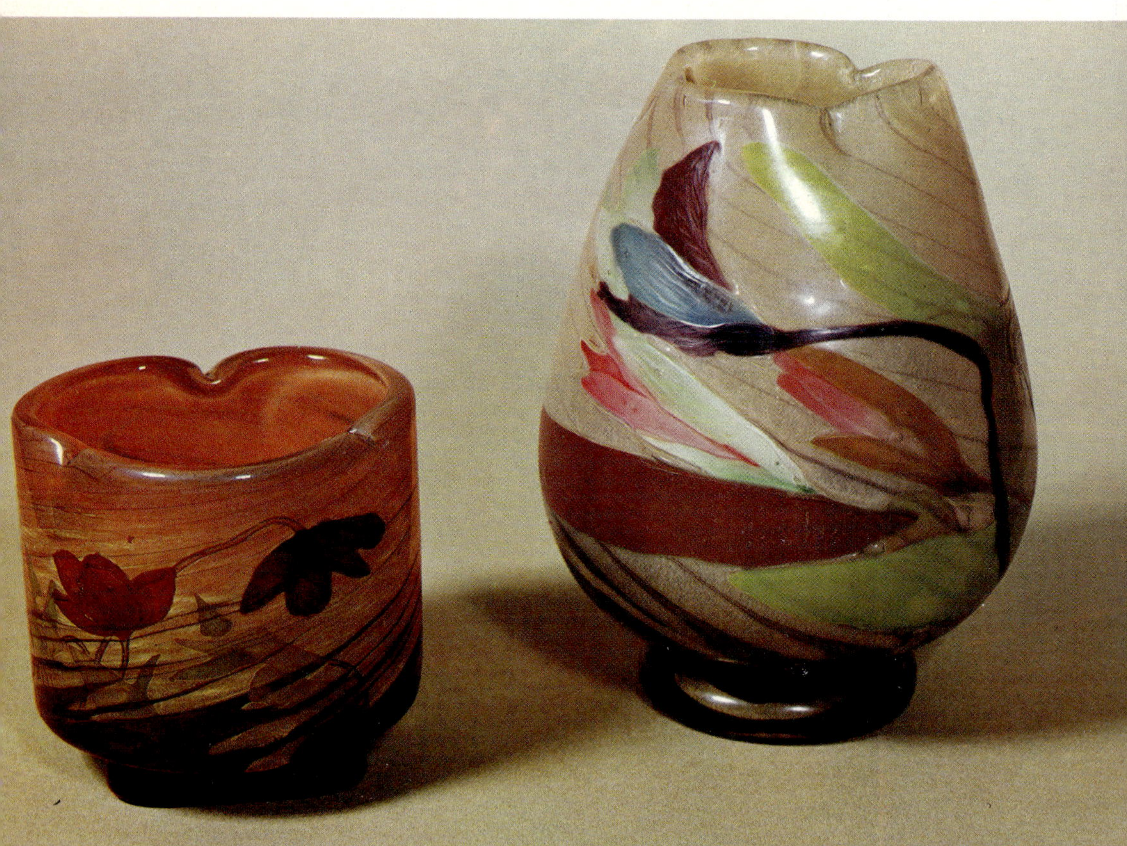

the school of nancy

For the first time in France since the Renaissance, a provincial center was able to generate and nurture a movement of artistic creativity that was completely independent of the capital. This movement was not an evolution of earlier forms, but a determined innovation in art and technique. The term *School of Nancy,* used to designate the works and the artists who labored with such original and stunning creativity to write this key chapter of art nouveau, corresponds perfectly to reality. When we speak of a "School of Fontainebleau" or a "School of Pont-Aven," we are really referring to the meeting ground — often brief — of painters who shared both ideas and friendship. In Nancy, the situation was quite different. Artists from different disciplines came together spontaneously to work in a similar direction; they defined a common program and officially established a school; more important still, these artists spent their entire lives — and labors — in their native city.

gallé, botanist-poet

Émile Gallé (1846–1904) was, by virtue of his rich intellectual resources, the precursor, instigator, and founder of the School of Nancy. He had not sought the role; it had fallen to him largely because of his generous-hearted, enthusiatic personality. He captivated everyone who met him. To say of an artist that he drew inspiration from nature is not only a cliché, but a vague one. With Gallé, however, we have to take these words in their literal sense. He was a naturalist and botanist who had maintained an herbarium since adolescence. The Horticultural Society of Lorraine invited him to serve on their board, and he contributed to all of their projects. Gallé always had a scientific interest in plants: this interest became more and more intense, stimulating his inexhaustibly fertile creativity. The more he studied the internal structure of the flower, the more fascinated he became.

The feeling for nature, common to most poets and artists since the romantic period, had a very special sense for Gallé. It was not a nature which gave rise to exalted spiritual states or to nostalgia, but a nature selected in the details of its fleeting bloom, details that were analyzed transposed, then captured in glass for eternity. Gallé had begun with scientific studies; he then worked in his father's ceramic and glass factories, becoming a designer. He started by drawing beribboned flowers in the eighteenth-century manner, which was also the commercial style of the period. After 1870, however, Gallé began experimenting with new forms, painting flowers in their natural state. At the World's

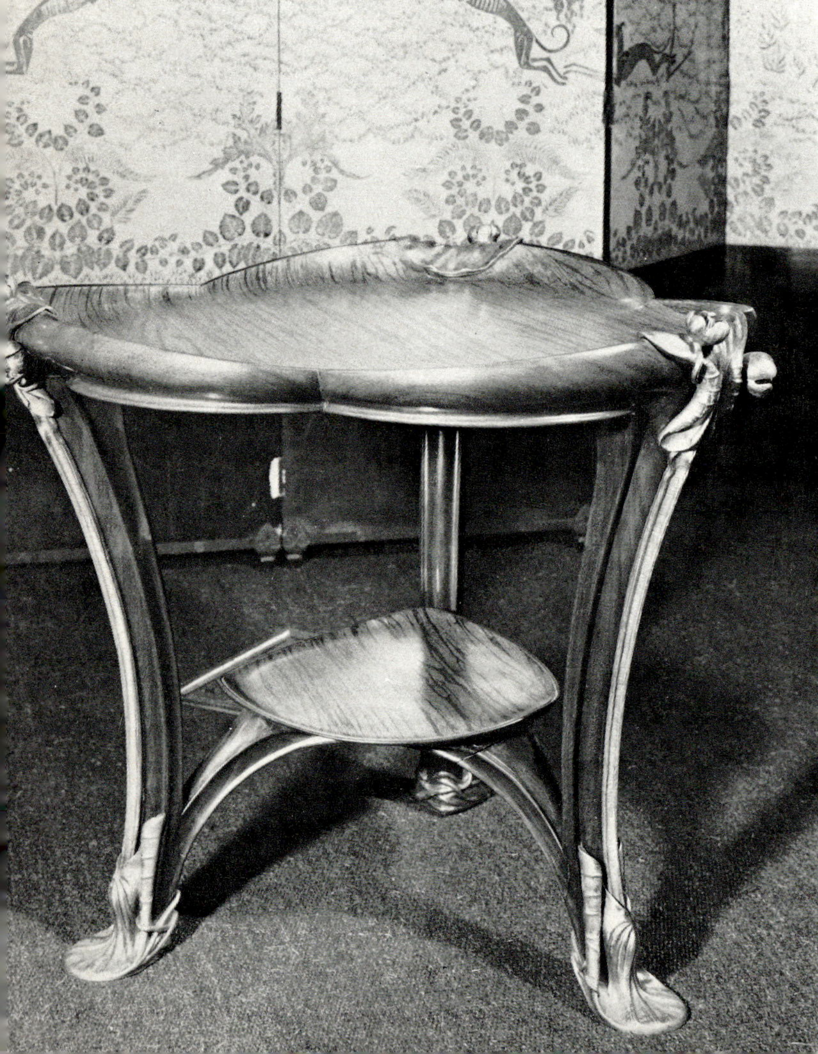

LOUIS MAJORELLE
Tiered table, 1902

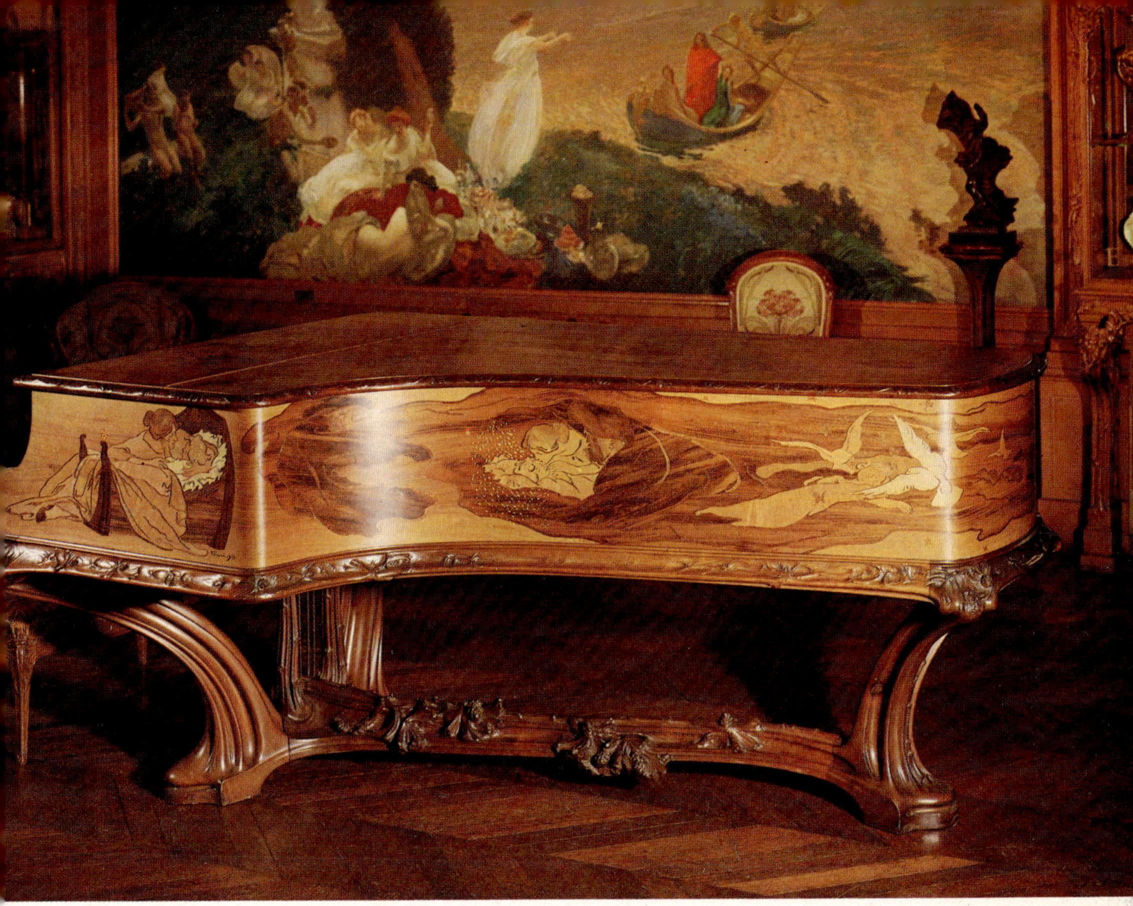

LOUIS MAJORELLE   Piano, 1903

Fair of 1878, he exhibited a vase which he called *la Nuit,* revealing his early symbolist aspirations. After much experiment, through which he gained the technical skills which made it possible to realize his decorative ideas, Gallé began to affirm his artistic identity. "Insofar as I can, I try to impose," he wrote, "on fluid, changing matter the qualities I want it to have, bending coloration and disposition to my dreams and my design." He would always write in this same tone of naïve openness. But his technique of a master craftsman in glass was that of a virtuoso.

It has been repeated far and wide that Gallé objects were made of glass paste. But, in fact, Gallé never made anything from this material. He used a much more delicate technique, which consisted of superimposing layers of glass of different thicknesses one on top of another. The pieces were then blown and reworked in a molten state. The enamel powders were next interspersed or disposed upon the sur-

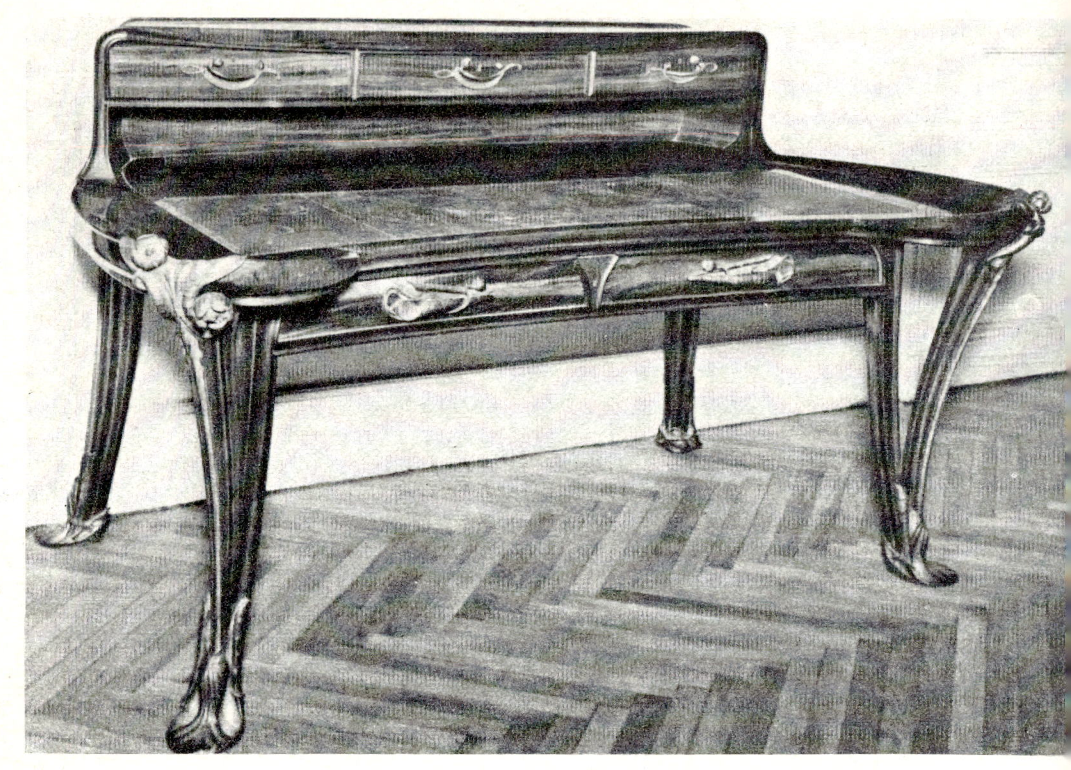

LOUIS MAJORELLE   Writing desk with "waterlily" design, 1902

face. Vitrification in the furnace produced the chemical reactions which created different shadings of color, forming a material which was then decorated with designs etched in acid. The artist had infinitely varied means at his disposal, allowing him free play within a whole symphony of transparent, opalescent, iridescent, sparkling, or matte tones, to which might be added a choice of engraved, carved, inlaid, enameled, or intaglio designs. For example, Daum used the same techniques, while giving particular importance to etching with a roulette. He too eschewed paste, that is, molded glass, except for the reproduction of statuettes.

Japanese, and especially Chinese, artists had excited Gallé passionate curiosity. But, in fact, he borrowed only technique from these masters. It was nature and nature alone which, revealing its ever-renewed treasures, constantly quickened his imagination. Gallé would set off for the countryside, herbalist kit in a knapsack, sketchbook in

168

Émile Gallé   Buffet, 1900

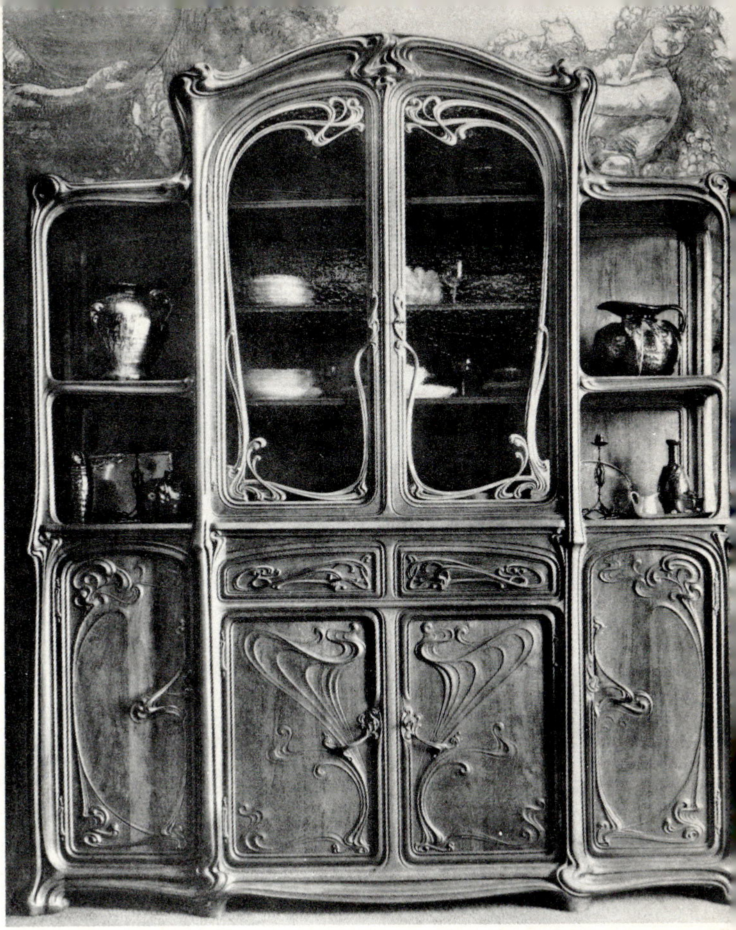

Émile Gallé
Bed with "dawn and
dusk" design, 1904

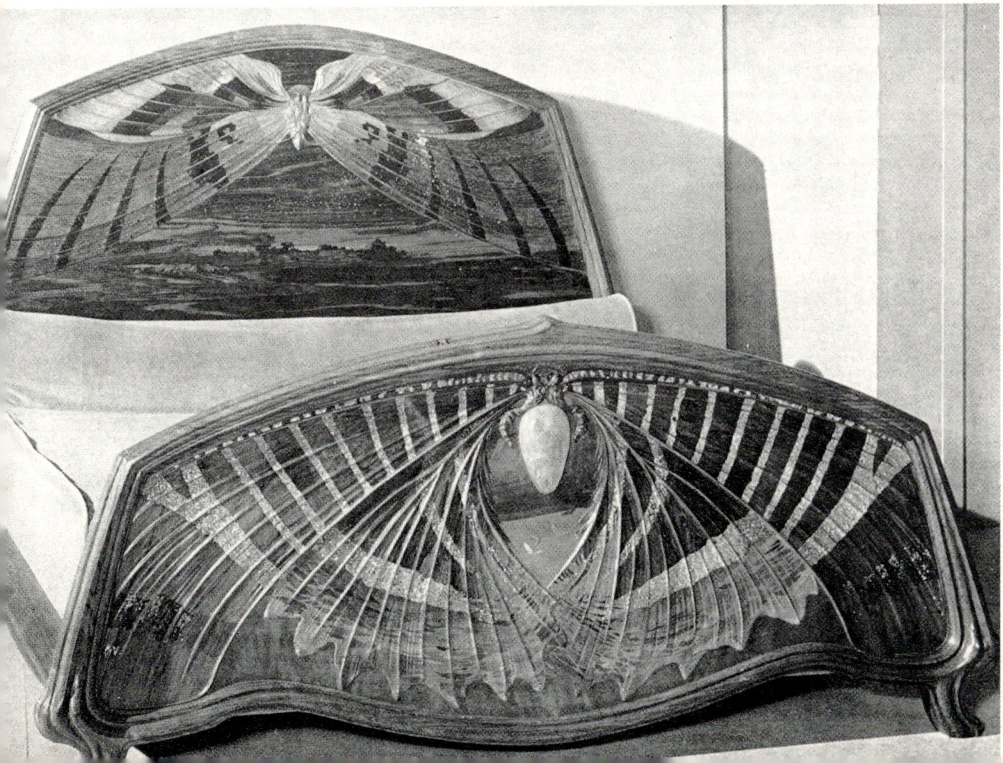

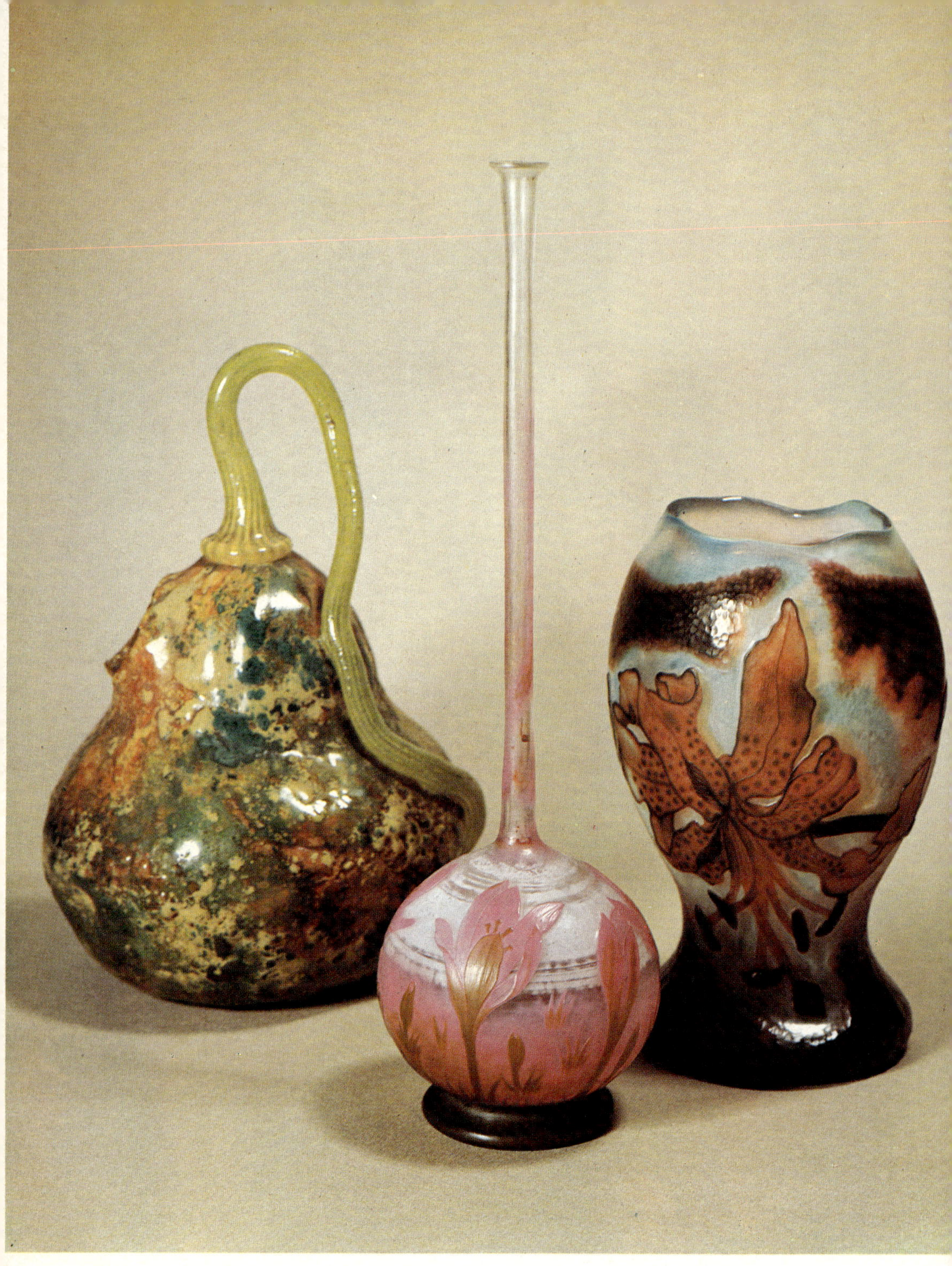

Auguste and Antonin Daum   (left to right) *Colocynth,* 1910–1915;
Bud vase, 1902; Vase, 1900–1905

AUGUSTE AND ANTONIN DAUM   Vase

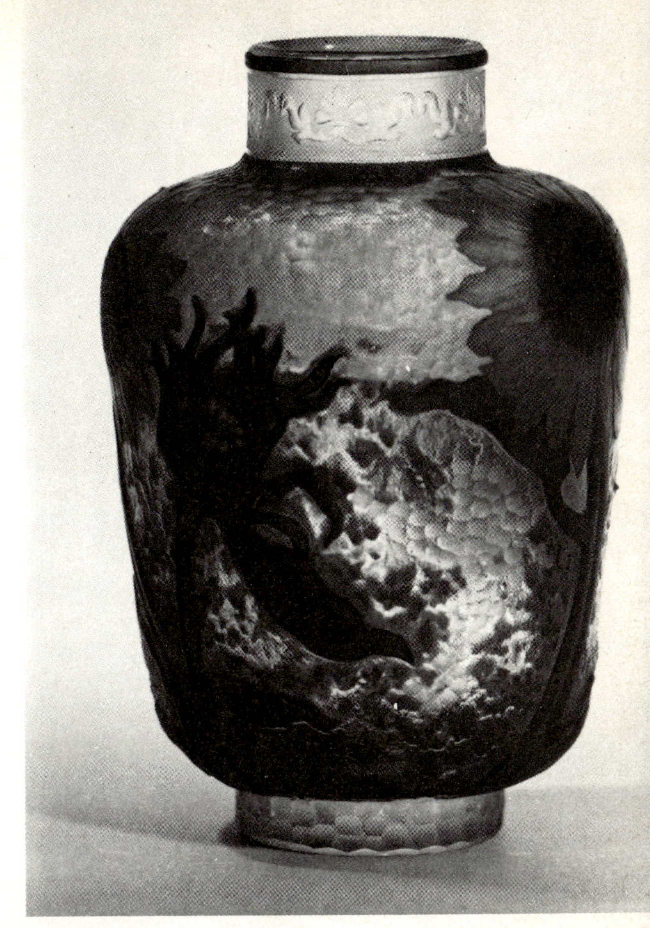

AUGUSTE AND ANTONIN DAUM   Vase

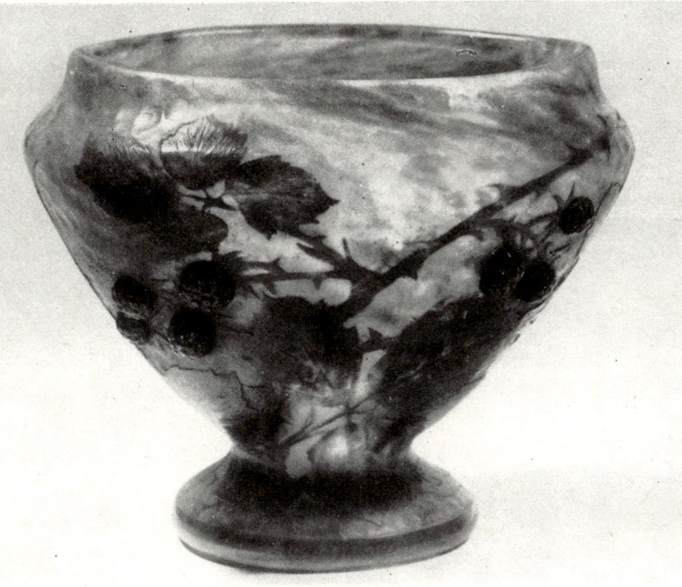

hand, and he always managed to find, in a flowering tree or a blade of grass, one subject — or a thousand — to inspire him. Over the doors of his studio he hung the motto: "My roots are in the heart of the woods, beneath the mosses, close to the springs."

From 1884 on, he converted public taste to his vases with their strange forms, which express the full flowering of art nouveau in colors ever more subtle in their refinement. Gallé was so skilled at exploiting his material that he even invented ways to exploit its flaws. He inscribed Biblical quotations or verses from his favorite poets on the sides of his vases; Verlaine, Rimbaud, Marceline Desbordes-Valmore, Sully Prudhomme, Mallarmé, Rollinat, or Maeterlinck. He evoked dream landscapes. Always close to symbolist literature. Gallé's bucolic fantasies sometimes take surprising form, such as the red lily transformed into a goblet, whose distortions and exaggerated curves are treated like sculpture.

Eugène Vallin   Dining room, 1903–1906

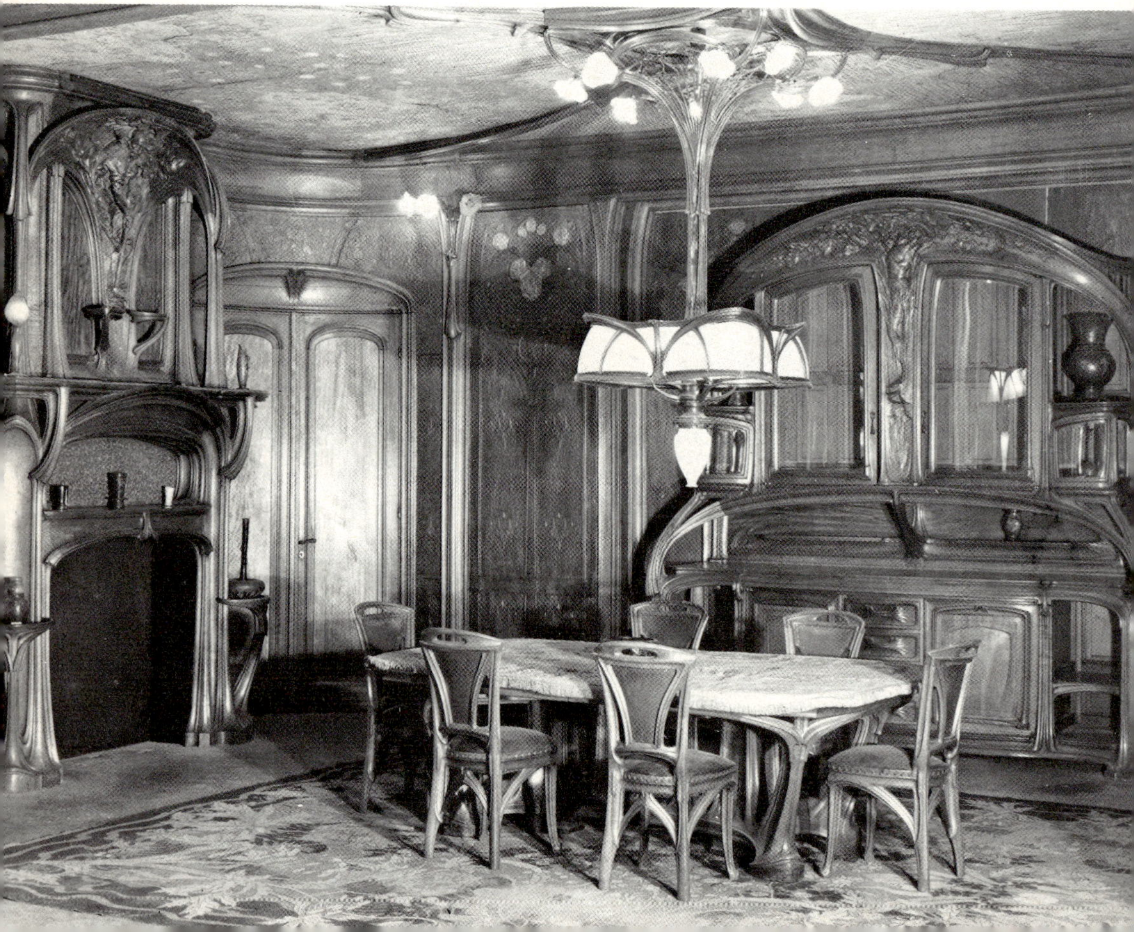

Success came suddenly to Gallé. His work received a great deal of attention, if not always appreciated, at the exhibition "Art in Clay and Glass" (1884), organized by the Union Centrale des Arts Décoratifs. He received First Prize at the World's Fair of 1889. Gallé's influence, already enormous in Nancy, soon spread throughout France and ultimately abroad. But he never stopped growing — or inventing.

In the last years of the century, Gallé moved toward heavier, more opaque designs, whose parts were no longer translucent. Commissions poured in, and he succumbed to creating a mass-production workshop where his designs, needless to say, lost their pure handcrafted character. He was pushed into this by the desire, shared by many creators of art nouveau, to popularize his products. He simplified the forms and designs to make them available at more accessible prices. But as these objects were never intended for everyday use, mass production simply loosed upon the market artistic knickknacks at bargain prices.

Gallé also designed furniture, often rather dubious in form and decorated with inlay, in the same spirit as his vases. Flowers, leaves, and branches proliferated freely, frequently accompanied by poetic mottoes. This would have been charming almost anywhere but on a piece of furniture.

Stricken with leukemia, Gallé was forced to give up all activity in the last years of his life; the products of his studios were fatally stricken with him.

the beginnings of the school of nancy

Three years before his death in 1901, Gallé gathered together the Nancy artists who had been his disciples, and each in his own area set forth to proselytize the message of art nouveau. Calling their group the School of Nancy, they started a society which proposed to "develop in Lorraine the prosperity of those industries using handicrafts." They planned an institution of professional training, where the highest quality of art could be exhibited. The bylaws indicate that the teachers, workers, and apprentices would receive no fees.

The School of Nancy claimed to "possess and put into practice certain carefully formulated principles." But the society generally left its members "absolute independence in their specific applications." The

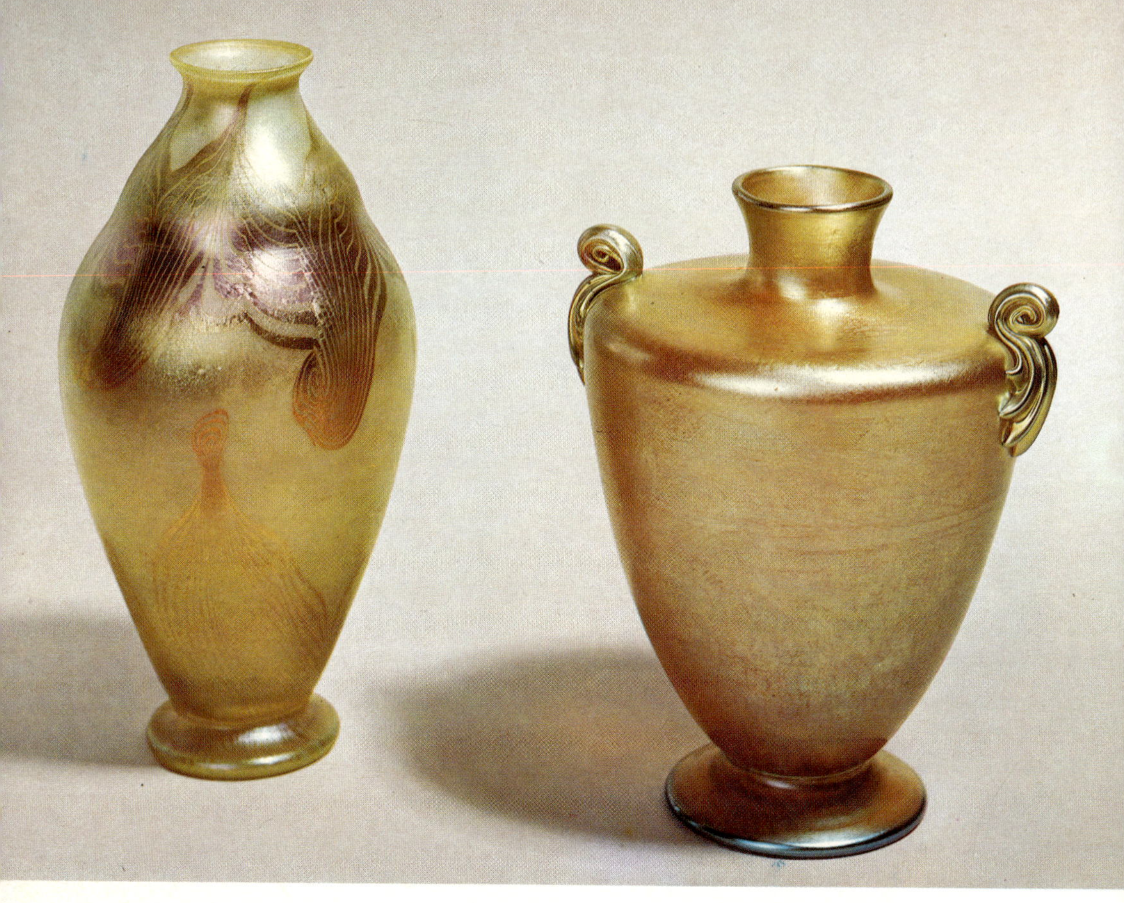

statutes affirmed that "we all adhere to a strongly held and definite Aesthetic, practiced in Nancy, and proven, with considerable success." Émile Gallé was named president. His administration consisted of the glassmaker Antonin Daum, and master cabinetmakers Majorelle and Vallin. On the death of Gallé, Victor Prouvé became the director.

If the School of Nancy was only now officially dedicated, it had already existed in fact. The example of the Daum brothers, Auguste and Antonin, is significant in this respect. Their father, who had chosen to live in France when his area of Lorraine became German, found himself, through an unsolicited combination of circumstances, proprietor of a wine glass factory, which manufactured a type of glass then in wide use. The business was declining when in 1887 his sons took over its management. It was Antonin, a brilliant businessman, whose sensibilities had been formed by art nouveau and by his fervent admiration for Gallé, who converted the factory to the production of art glass

174

in 1891. He chose a staff of talented artists, like Jacques Grüber, who later turned to stained glass windows. Antonin himself was an engineer. And he took pride in giving every piece signed "Daum" the benefit of the most advanced techniques — like superimposed layers of glass. These pieces were then etched in acid; with the use of a chemical process similar to the one employed by Gallé, the transparent shimmer and soft color harmonies were conveyed with rare delicacy. Moving from naturalist themes realized with virtuosity — plants in their natural state, forest landscapes, effects suggesting snow and storm — Daum turned to more stylized design, but he always maintained the same standard of technical perfection, allied to a constant search for new ideas and forms.

Daum always managed to resist stagnation. Today the same company, owned by the same family, works with artists like César and Salvador Dali.

The principle of unity in art was fundamental to the School of Nancy. Through this precept, the constellation of artists who were responsible for both its genesis and activity practiced, even while they maintained their essential individuality, the professional disciplines which were required for interior decoration. Most of these artists studied the crafts involved in these allied arts from the first step to the finished products so that they could create a total décor.

Louis Majorelle (1859–1926) was primarily a master cabinetmaker, but he also worked in wrought iron and designed textiles. He, too, was inspired by nature, that same nature, devoid of straight lines. His furniture is constructed with the combination of fluidity and sturdiness, characteristic of a tree. Majorelle worked his furniture as though it were sculpture, preparing clay models for the pieces. The wood retained the honesty of the material; even when he sometimes added bronze appliqués, the ornament was never strident, unless other artists had collaborated on a work. Majorelle "rethought" completely the question of style in furniture, finally evolving forms that were natural and new, full of both tension and dignity, while yielding nothing in their character and authority. His mastery was rewarded: whatever doubts may have been elicited by the unfamiliar shapes of his work, the quality of his furniture gained it entry into the most traditional and conservative houses.

Eugène Vallin was an architect and master cabinetmaker whose

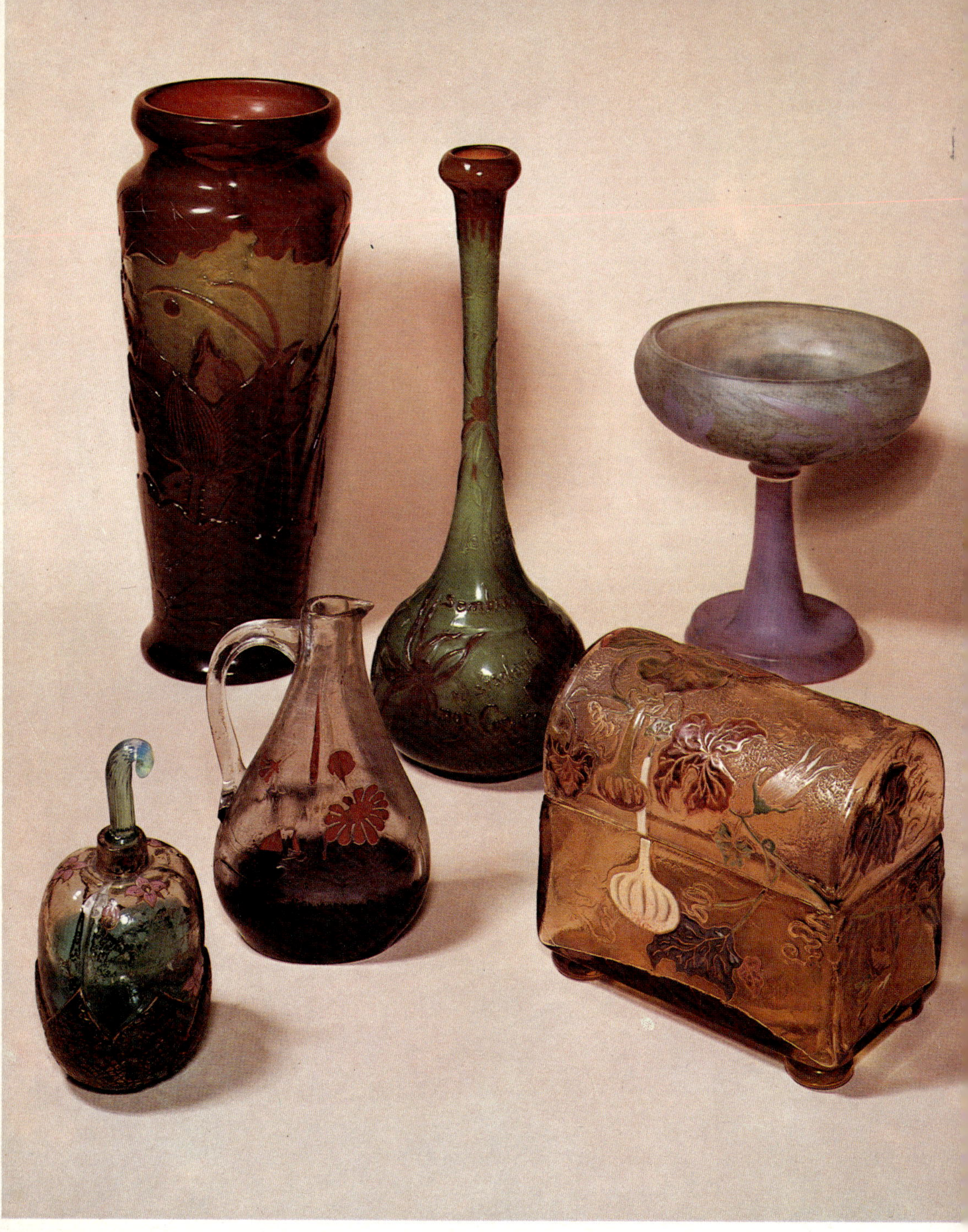

ÉMILÉ GALLE   (left to right) Tall vase, 1895–1904;
Bud vase, 1890–1895; Footed cup, 1895–1900; Individual salt cellar,
1890–1895; Cruet, 1890–1895; Coffer, 1878–1882

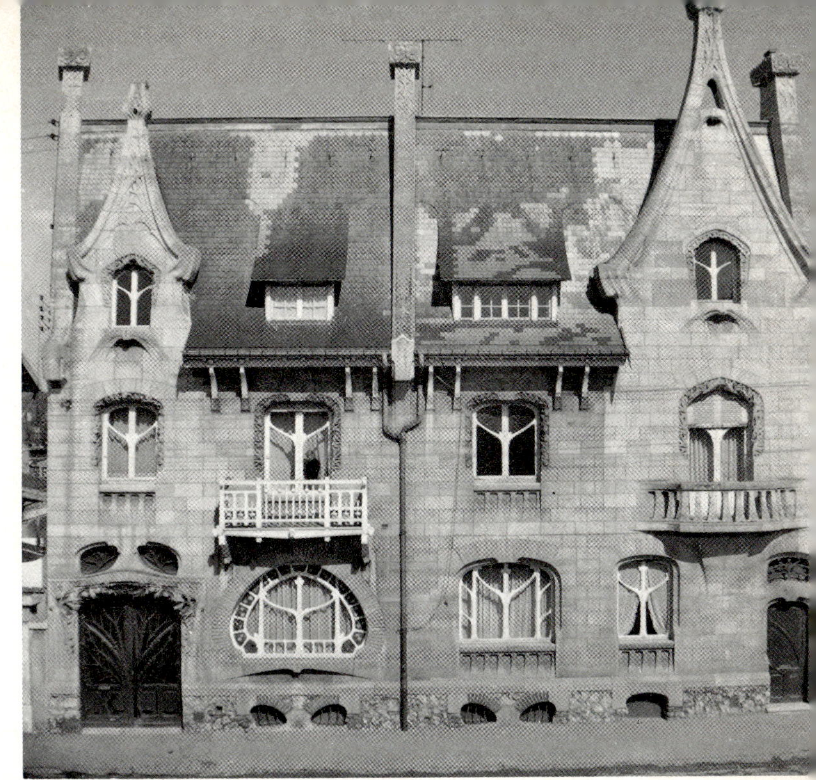

ÉMILE ANDRÉ   The Huot House, 1903

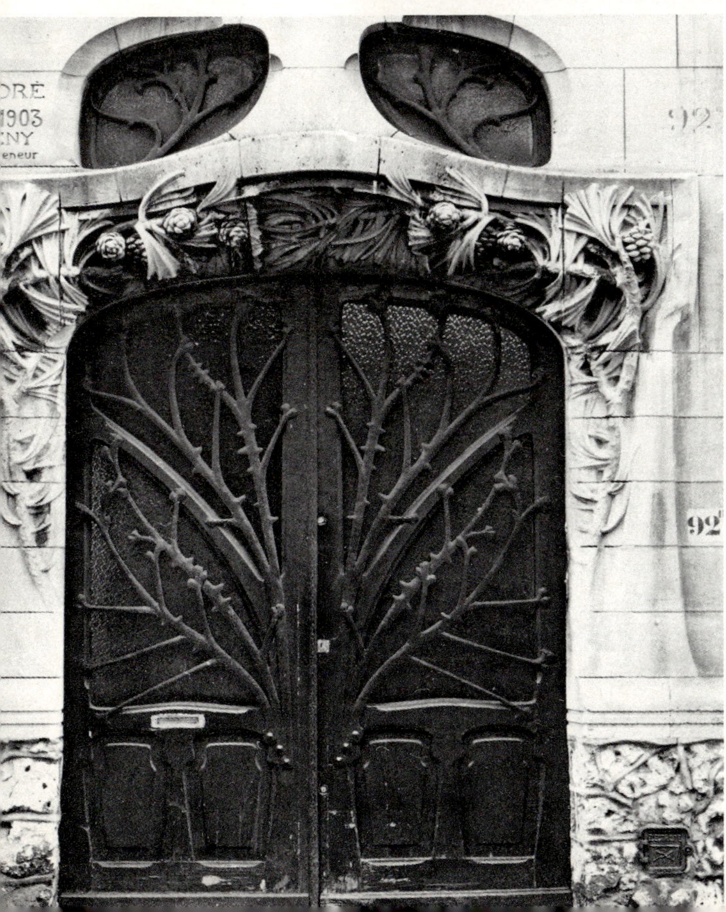

ÉMILE ANDRÉ   Entrance door of Huot House, 1903

talent was equaled only by his modesty. He continued to refer to himself as a carpenter, when, in fact, he was one of the most distinguished artists of the School of Nancy. Although he occasionally produced pieces which emphasized too insistently the character of the wood, the art nouveau aspect of his work reflected subliminally the power and logic of Gothic construction which he had carefully studied. The large dining room, with wood paneling, built for the J. B. E. Corbin house, is total design of real distinction. But the limitations of one room seem too restrictive for this grand-scale designer. And, indeed, he later received more congenial commissions, becoming a decorator of palaces.

Known primarily for his stained glass windows, Jacques Grüber (1870–1936) was also an engraver and furniture designer (his designs were actually built by Vallin). Floral designs played an important role in his furniture, notwithstanding his attraction to the historical imagery of the great windows that he loved.

RENÉ WIENER   Binding for the notes of *L'Estampe Originale,* 1894

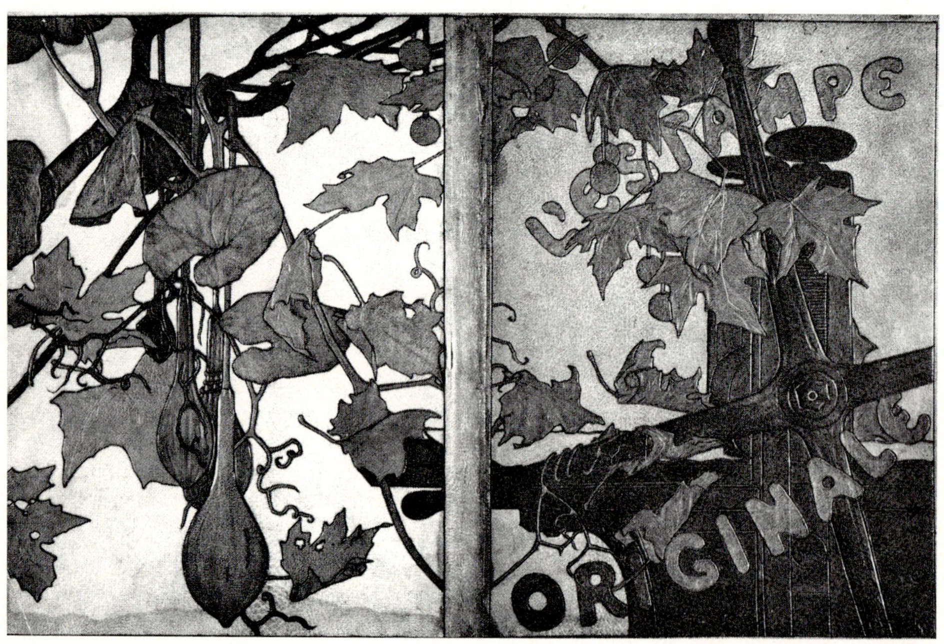

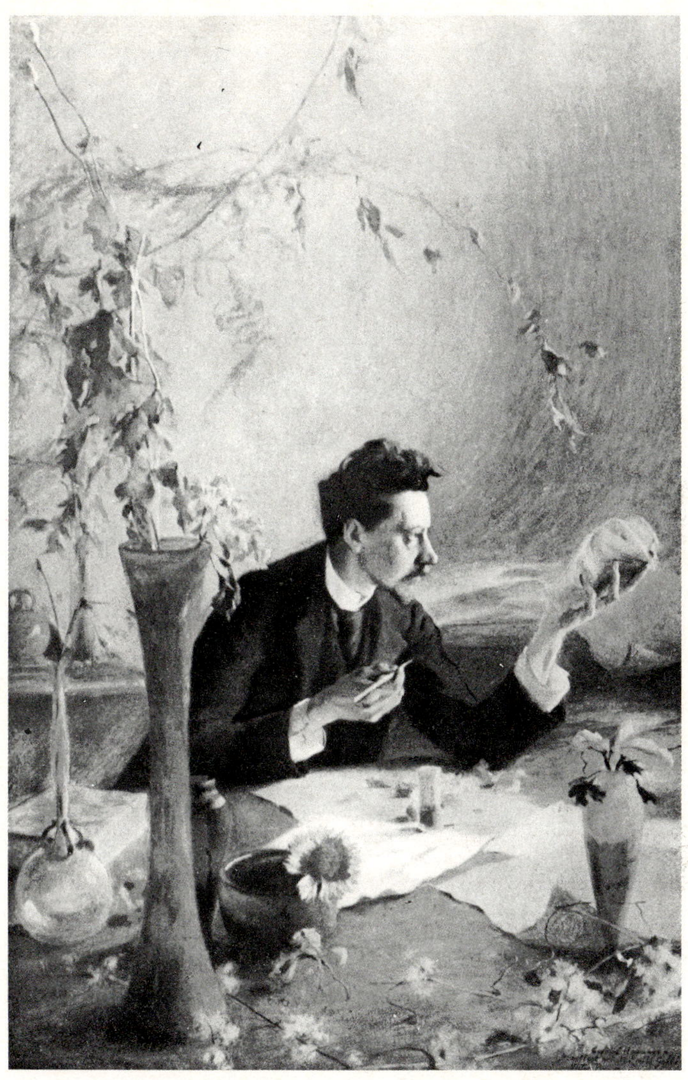

VICTOR PROUVÉ *Portrait of Émile Gallé*

We should also mention an associate of the Nancy group, René Wiener, a designer of luxury leather goods. Always in search of the original, Wiener decorated handbags and bookbindings with works by artists who would later be famous. He even went so far as to exhibit, from 1890 on, in his shop window, located in the most elegant street

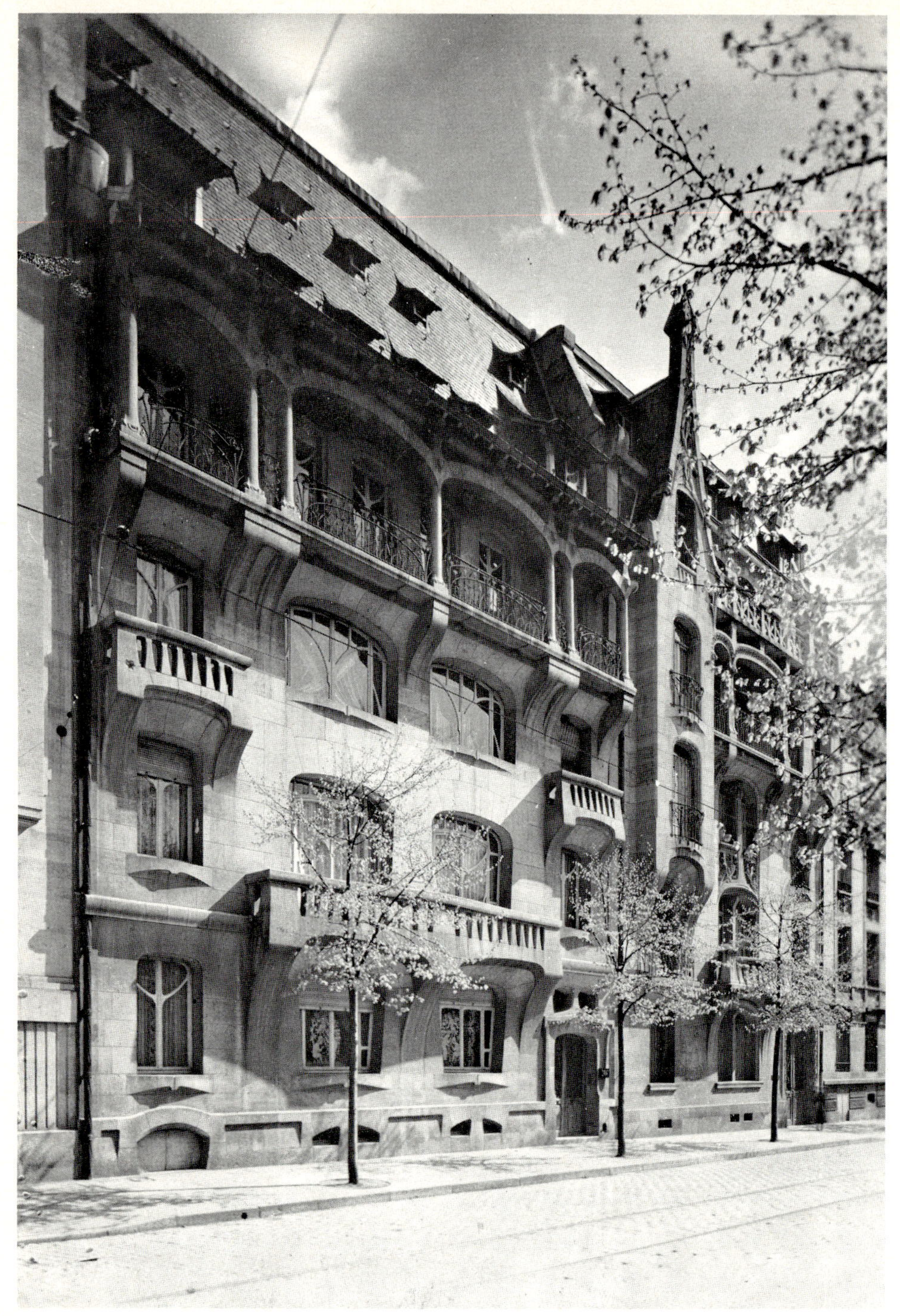

ÉMILE ANDRÉ House, Nancy

in Nancy, paintings by an unknown artist, Paul Cézanne. With Wiener, art nouveau rediscovered the refined charm of tooled leather.

The dynamic creativity of Victor Prouvé (1856–1943) deserves an entire chapter. Draftsman, painter, engraver, sculptor, decorator, jeweler: his enthusiasm and warmth were always at the disposal of fellow-artists, and he gave every encouragement to their experiments. He played an active and needed role in maintaining the exceptional cohesiveness of the School of Nancy, assuring the group its unequaled homogeneity. Prouvé was habitually self-effacing before others' talent. When he was appointed director of the École des Beaux-Arts, he was known for his encouragement of students who gave evidence of a distinct style, even when they chose directions other than his own. Among them were Paul Colin and Jean Lurçat.

The artistic climate of Nancy could hardly help but influence the architecture. One merely had to stroll through those new sections of the city then in the process of development. Even though most of the facades might still harken back, as they had earlier, to remote historical fantasies, others reveal distinctly modern forms, a direct outgrowth of the School of Nancy. A group of architects had emerged who sometimes worked together. The most talented were Gutton, Weissenburger, and Émile André (1871–1933), who came from a family of architects and was the most outstanding among them. In collaboration with Vallin, he designed the revolutionary facade of the Vaxelaire Store in downtown Nancy (now destroyed). The Maison Huot, 32, quai Claude-de-Lorrain (1902), the house of the painter Armand Lejeune, 37, rue de Sergent-Blandan (1903) — these too bear witness to his interest in innovation. Like the artists in the movement who advocated decorative unity, André did not design plans just for a house but for the balconies and wrought-iron grills as well; if the client was agreeable, he designed the furniture too.

art nouveau in lorraine

Art nouveau in Lorraine owed nothing to the outside world. It lived on its own resources and inventions. The floral repertory was chosen from plants which grew in the local woods and meadows. By creating a style, these artists had avoided outside influence. It has been said that Gallé determined upon his vocation by his discovery of the

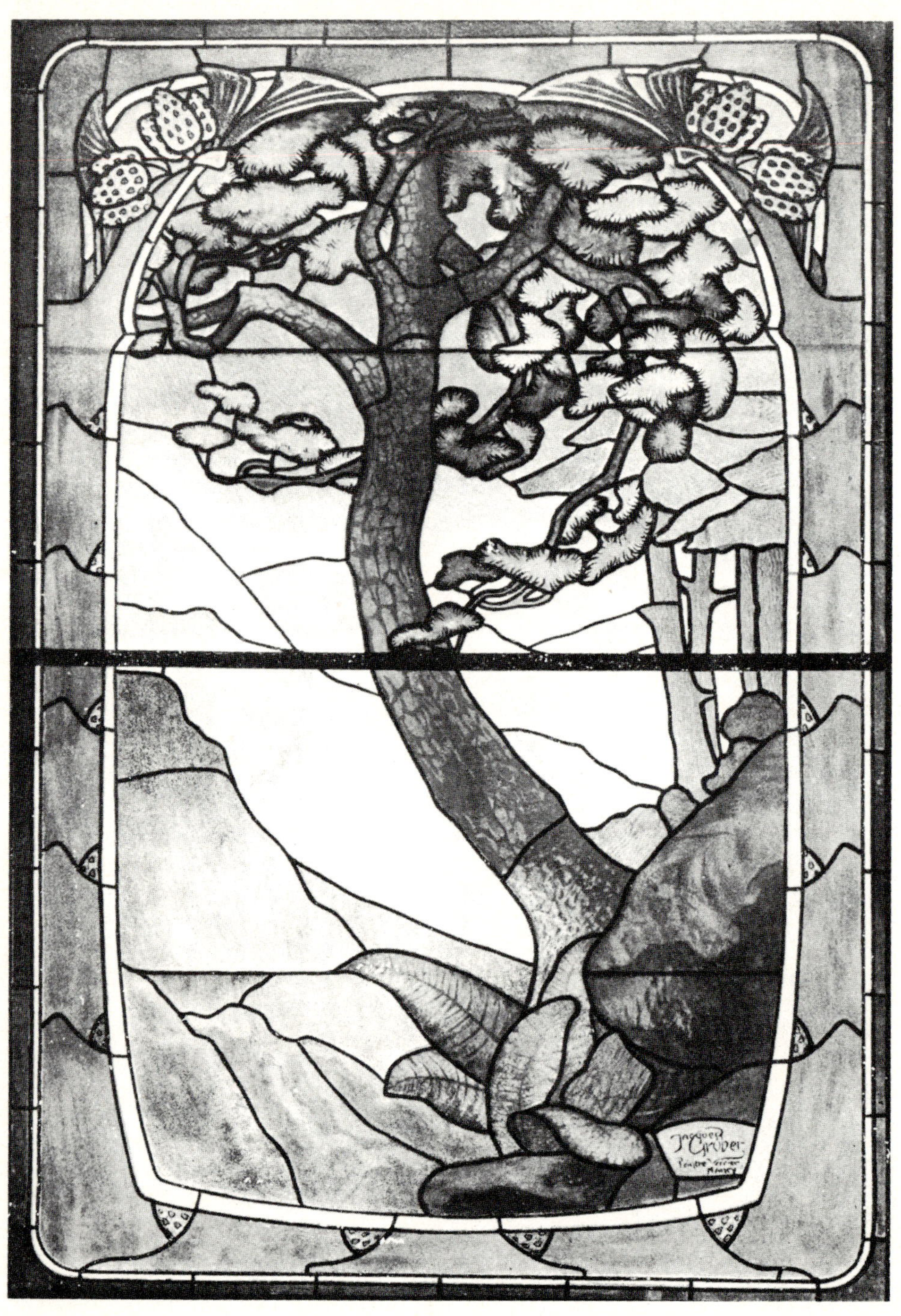

JACQUES GRÜBER   Stained glass with the design "Paysage des Vosges," 1909

Pre-Raphaelites. In fact, he not only owed nothing to the Brotherhood, but, from studying his correspondence, Mme. Therese Charpentier discovered that, as late as 1890, he had never even heard of William Morris. To Gallé, art nouveau really was brand new: a highly personal creation and a great adventure.

The Nancy artists had very little contact with other art circles. Their entire professional lives were spent in their native city. The Lorrainese had strong regional feeling and a deeply rooted love for their native province. They joined regionalism to a patriotism that was all the more ardent since, as a frontier province, they suffered from seeing their region amputated by annexation to Germany.

This was one of the reasons that art nouveau won a relatively huge public in Nancy. The Lorrainese were proud of what they saw as a local style: it became a symbol to them of their small native land. The thistle and cross of Lorraine abound on the glassware. The School of Nancy had an important regional market. Until this point there had not been an entire region claimed by art nouveau, only certain artistic subcultures. These products of Lorraine were found in local households. Furniture designed by Majorelle became the vogue, and a status symbol for elegant young couples. Fashionable ladies took up embroidering iris on silk cushions. The fad of pyrogravure provoked an invasion of waterlilies and pine cones burnt into wood. Jacques Grüber's stained glass illuminated hotels, safes, restaurants, and shops; he even decorated a banker's office with giant ferns, cast in bronze. Ferdinand Brunot, a professor at the Sorbonne, a famous historian of the French language, and a nature lover who also came from the Vosges region, used to relax by designing and carving with his own hands the furniture for his Paris apartment.

In the first years of the new century, the School of Nancy enjoyed real prosperity, supported by industrialists and by a sophisticated bourgeoisie. The members of the group worked in perfect independence and considered, with deserved pride, that they could claim the honor of having been the first to create an art nouveau of real quality. In the *Revue de la Société Industrielle de l'Est,* Antonin Daum wrote: "When history came to judge the attempts to create an art nouveau which, at the turn of the century, were going on everywhere, only the name of Nancy was remembered. Modern Style became an object of ridicule through its ignorance of the nature it claimed to imitate; in

Nancy and art was affirmed and prospered, which was conscious, vital, and based on living models, displaying a rare example of provincial taste and energy." Note that he places the art of the School of Nancy and art nouveau in opposition to Modern Style which he views as a Parisian extreme and "the object of ridicule." This was managing to forget Guimard, but there was some truth to the statement, nonethelsss. There was nothing in common between Parisian whimsy — which did indeed often fall into the category of the ridiculous — and the painstaking and serious work done in Nancy, concerned with reaching an entire population, and directly inspired by nature. Nor was the artistic production of Nancy a passing vogue. Art nouveau reigned supreme in Lorraine until the First World War.

Antonin Daum was well aware of the inevitable march toward mass production. Together with Victor Prouvé, he confronted the powerful industrialists and, in the name of maintaining French prestige, challenged them to produce "beauty and goodness," naming Lorrainese artists from among whom they should choose their designers. Through all this runs the obsession of acceptance by the working class, as proof that "the good, the true, and the beautiful" win out. At the Fair of Eastern France held in Nancy in 1909, the vast and durable pavilion of the School of Nancy, designed by Vallin, exhibited (next to those showpieces which always enjoy the same success) a great novelty — machine-made products over whose quality the artists had been given control, and for which they now assumed full responsibility.

But what happened to all of this is what happens everywhere. A style, especially in the twentieth century, does not last more than thirty years. And, as everywhere, handicrafts had to capitulate in the confrontation with industry, never known as the source of distinguished taste.

varieties of art nouveau in great britain

mackmurdo

With the publication of his book on Wren churches in London (1883), Arthur H. Mackmurdo (1851–1942) launched art nouveau in England. The frontispiece of the book, which, by the way, has nothing to do with the subject, is a floral design, of deliberate asymmetry, so highly stylized and synthesized that its subject disappears, buried under the extravagant flamboyance of pure ornament. It consists solely of thick lines, emphatically parallel, whose curves fill the space of the entire page. That same year, Mackmurdo designed textiles in the same spirit, printed in Manchester; these were vaguely organic compositions in which all the elements stretch upward like flames.

ARTHUR HEYGATE MACKMURDO Wallpaper, 1882

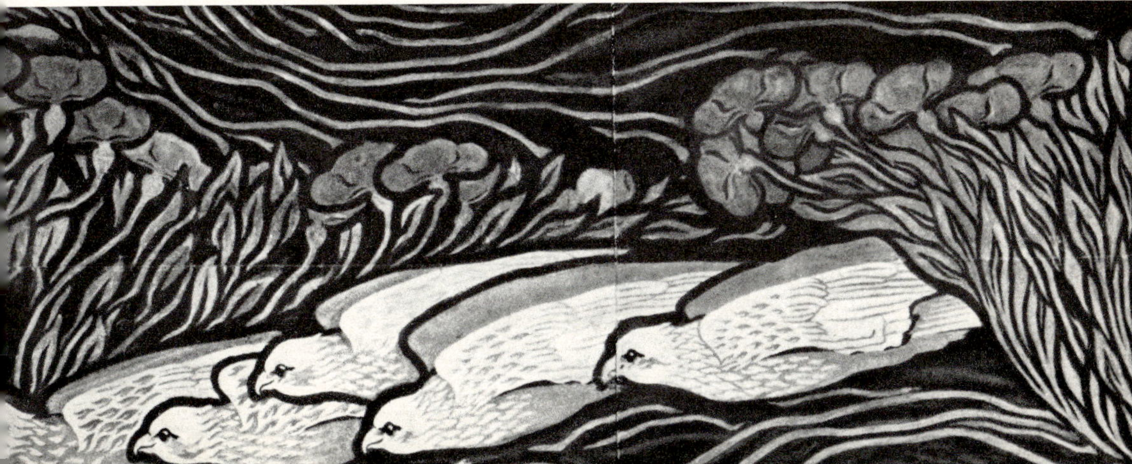

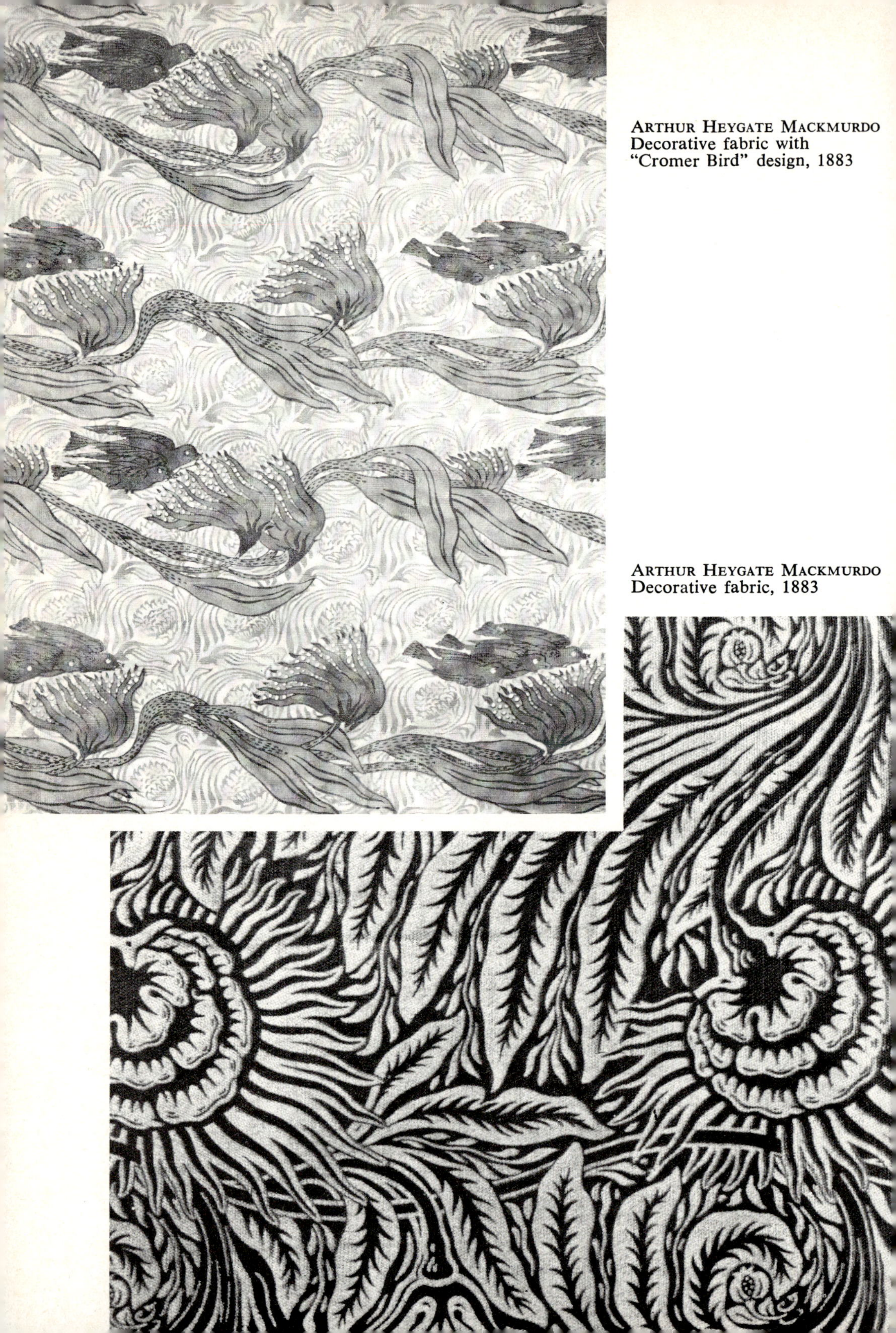

Arthur Heygate Mackmurdo
Decorative fabric with
"Cromer Bird" design, 1883

Arthur Heygate Mackmurdo
Decorative fabric, 1883

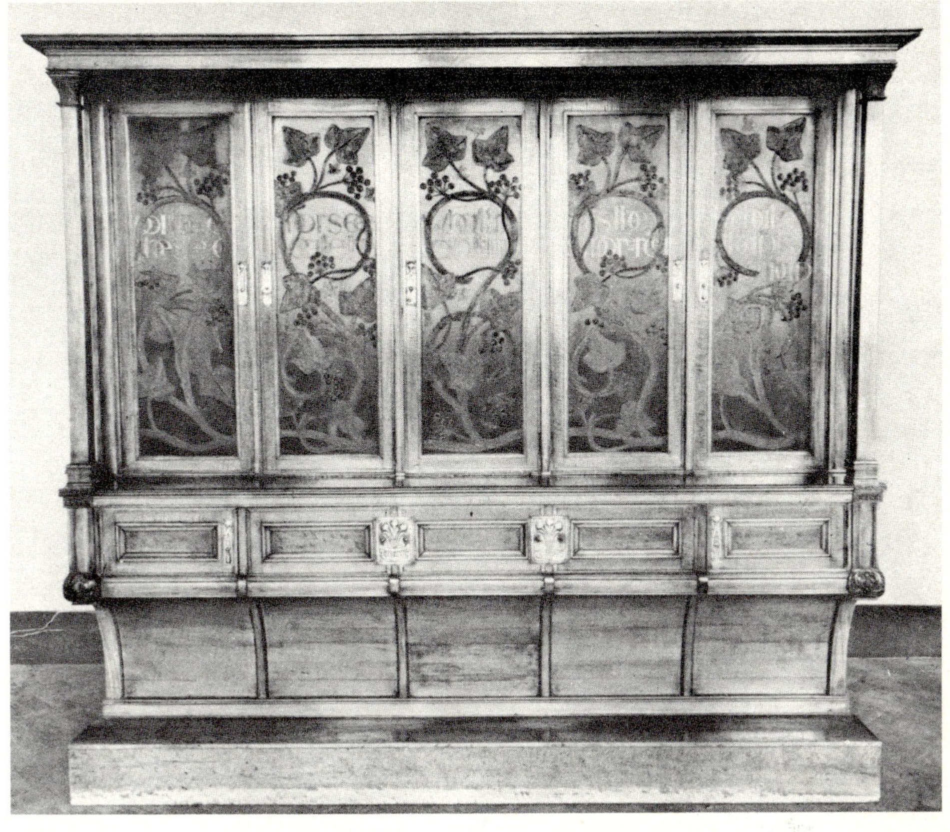

Mackmurdo had been trained as an architect. But he was a decorator by vocation, a vocation which he had acquired in part through Ruskin, his traveling companion in Italy, but above all from William Morris, who had been his friend. The tongues of fire in his designs recall Blake, and they keep recurring obsessively in Mackmurdo's work. Steeped in the doctrines of his teachers, Mackmurdo, a plastic artist, also wanted to design furniture. But this craft does not seem to have suited his talents. His furniture is cold, rectilinear, and burdened by ponderous classicism, as his designs and engravings exult in a swirling lyricism. In his sketches for textile designs, conversely, Mackmurdo's linear exuberance finds its happiest expression. The floral backgrounds luxuriate freely in their decorative framework. We can compare these designs by Mackmurdo to the bright and charming patterned wallpaper

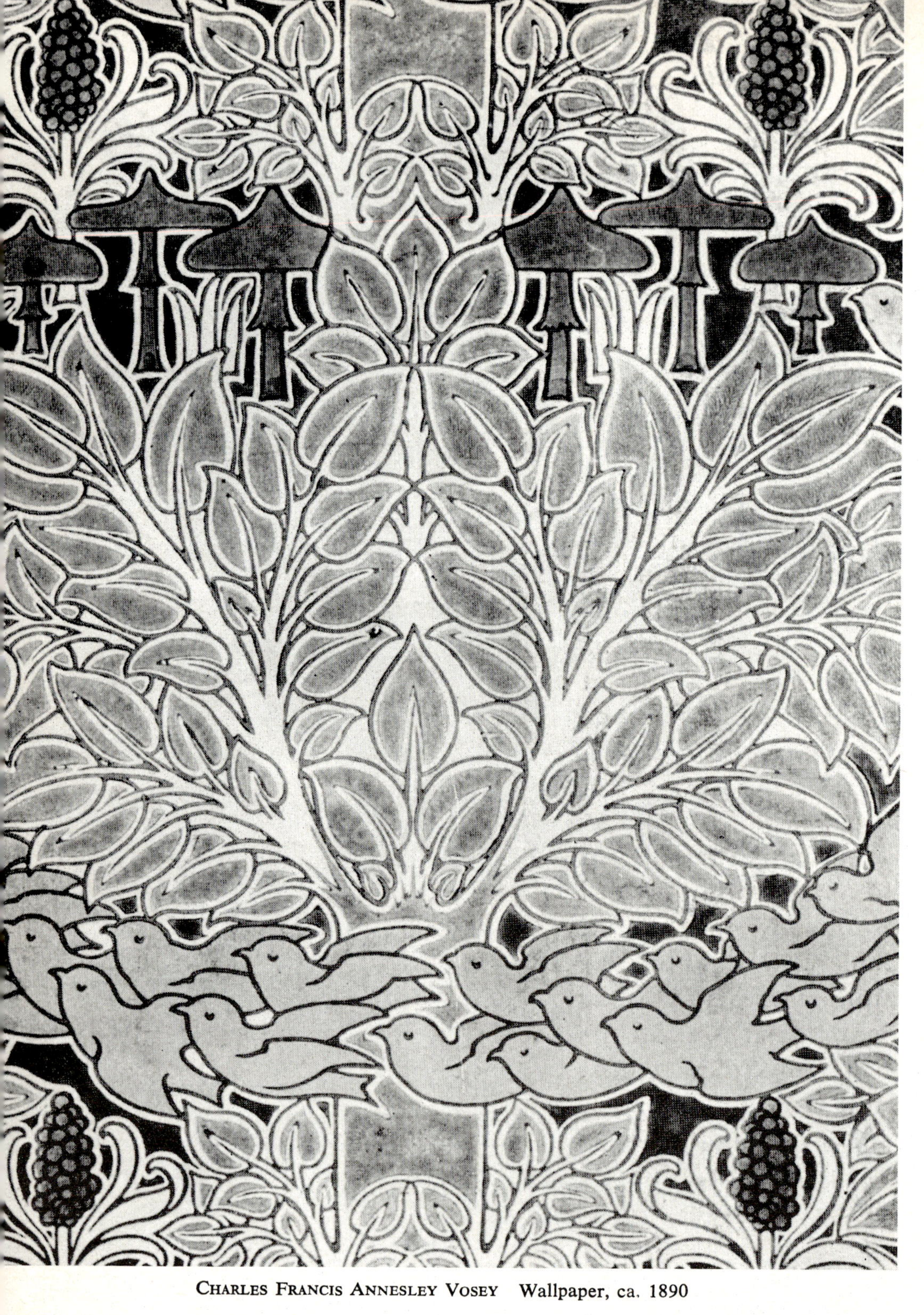

Charles Francis Annesley Vosey   Wallpaper, ca. 1890

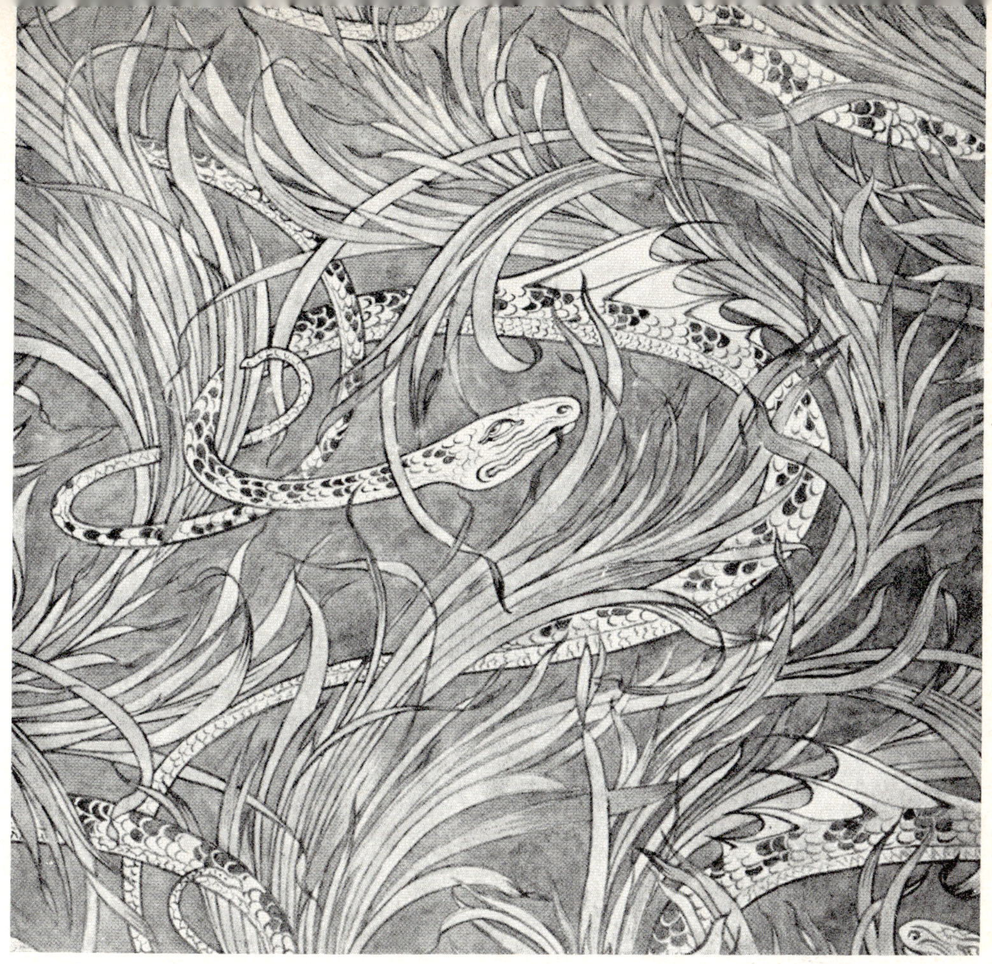

by Voysey, an artist skilled at giving a modern accent to traditional English motifs. Charles Francis Annesley Voysey (1857–1941) was also an architect. His houses exude a new warmth and feeling of intimacy. He took particular care with their interior design. If the arts and crafts movement generally went farther than he did in its spirit of inventiveness, he was probably the architect-decorator of the period best known for conveying a sensibility and human warmth to his houses. On the exterior, they are perfectly simple and rationally ordered, with bare walls, and windows devoid of moldings. But, unlike Van de Velde's house near Brussels, which also suggests the same sort of rustic simplicity, Voysey's interior is done in an entirely floral décor; a décor which has the singular virtue of being almost naturalistic and, at the same time, modern — so modern, in fact, that it has never gone out of style.

189

the mackintoshes

The most important event in British art nouveau happened in Scotland. Charles Rennie Mackintosh (1868–1928), his wife, Margaret MacDonald, and his sister-in-law Frances MacDonald, married to the architect MacNair, established a fervent little community in Glasgow, which worked toward the establishment of a new style in applied arts. This family cooperative made it possible to practice a "total art"; to the Mackintoshes, this was the key concept and imperative of art nouveau.

The Mackintoshes were not imbued with social theories like the Pre-Raphaelites, although the latter had once been part of their aesthetic universe. More interested in achieving perfection than in spreading the word, they worked for a limited clientele, surrounded by an indifferent or hostile public. Such patronage as they had sufficed them to develop a style whose instantly recognizable quality is an extreme originality.

The first Mackintosh works (1893) already showed an exceptional level of taste, but these were timid, compared to what they would later create. The Mackintoshes only became known to the public through their contributions to the Arts and Crafts Exhibition of 1896, but critical esteem from their fellow artists had continued to grow.

The major project of the Mackintoshes, in which they expressed themselves most freely, was the Glasgow School of Art, begun in 1897, and only completed twelve years later. It was to be their immortality. The general effect, seen from a short distance, is of a Scottish fortified castle, made of local stone, somewhat varied in color. But this impression is dissipated as we approach the facade, which articulates the basic aesthetic principles of the entire Mackintosh *oeuvre,* whether lamp or castle. The symmetry of the long verticals is broken up by asymmetries whose unexpected disposition gives a new expression to the building, without throwing it off balance. It is, moreover, in stark contrast to the preciousness of the interior design. Placed between immense studio windows, the majestic entrance way is off-center, but all the other architectonic elements are disposed to compensate skillfully for this ordering. In the upper stories, the structure is emphasized by delicately wrought iron and eccentric volumes of unconventional style. The interior facade is no less unusual. Tall, excessively narrow windows form oriels, which, in turn, become part of the corbeled walls which extend almost the entire height of the building, recalling the buttresses of medieval architecture. We find these same singularities everywhere, in the most traditional context. It required all the creative confidence of the Mackintoshes to carry off programs like this one. The interior is equally striking. The space is divided into simple volumes which reveal the play of perfectly homogeneous perspectives. In the library and main classrooms, slender wooden partitions designate the work spaces. The purity of these satisfying geometries seems inspired by the traditional Japanese house —

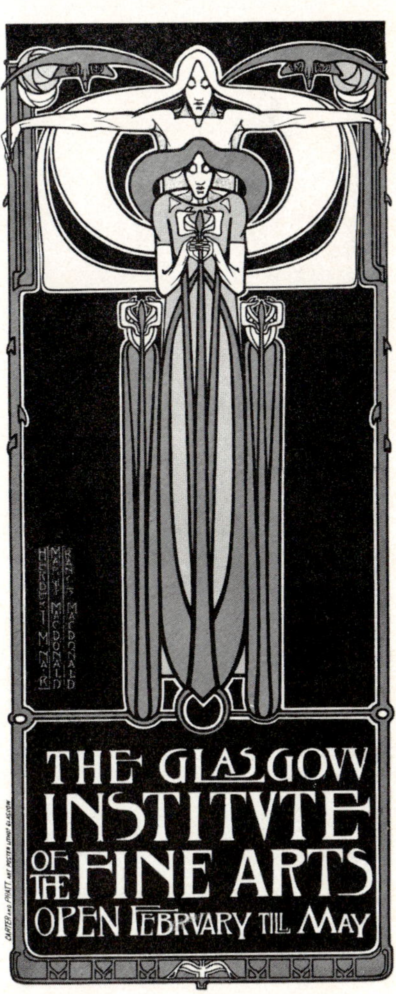

HERBERT MACNAIR, MARGARET MACDONALD, FRANCIS MACDONALD Poster for the Glasgow Institute of the Fine Arts, 1897

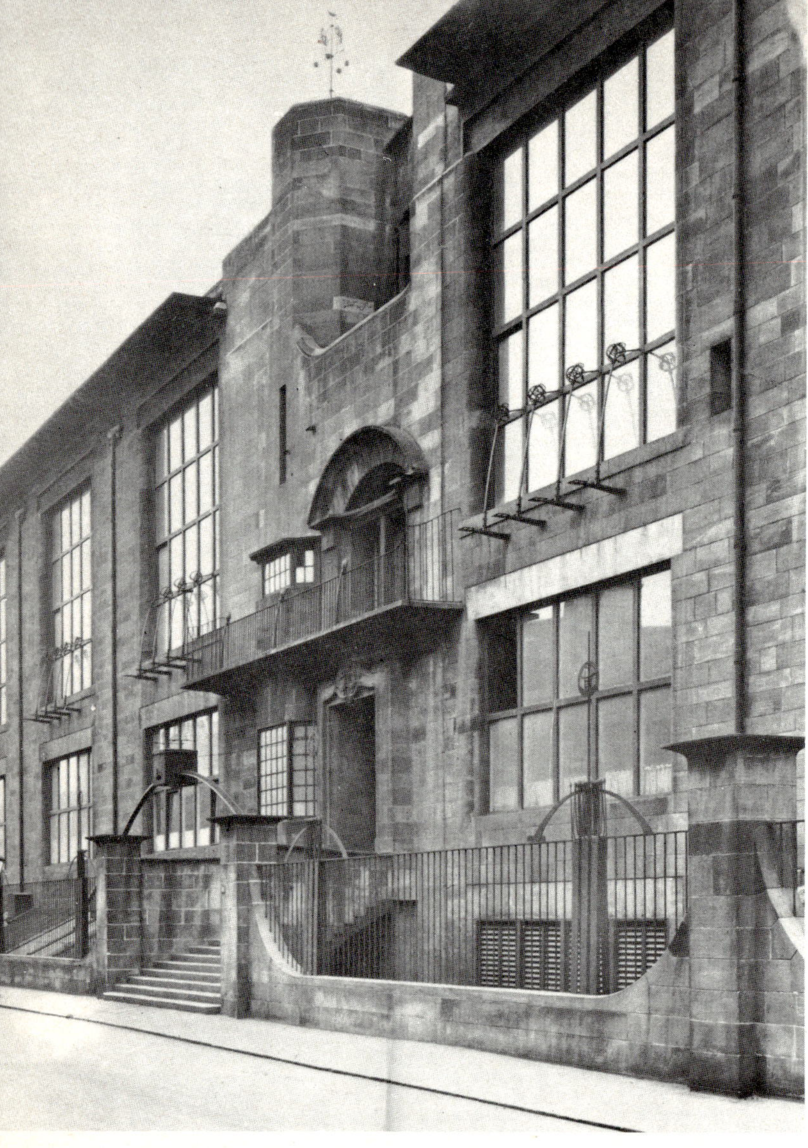

not that the Mackintoshes were incapable of producing every element from their own fertile imaginations.

The commission for the famous Willow Tea Room is dated 1904. Every element is dominated by consideration of the whole — a purely artistic concern — resulting in unprecedented forms, or rather in linear totalities which are very different from Modern Style or Jugendstil.

What the educated eye finds so enchanting today was then greeted with chilly reserve. Glasgow was a very tightly knit city. It could not be pried from the conservatism of its customs to confront works which expressed the taste, reasoning, and aspiration of artists who represented such a violent break with the past. The public came away from Mackintosh's work carrying an impression only of the bizarre. His fame was far greater on the continent than in Great Britain. "He was too art nouveau, and England, after a few years of its own unofficial art nouveau, had now turned away from everything which seemed too unconventional" (Nickolaus Pevsner). At the Vienna Crafts Exhibition of 1910, then at exhibitions in Germany and Turin, Mackintosh furnishings were admired by those whose taste was sufficiently developed

Charles Rennie Mackintosh   Library of the Glasgow School of Art, 1907–1909

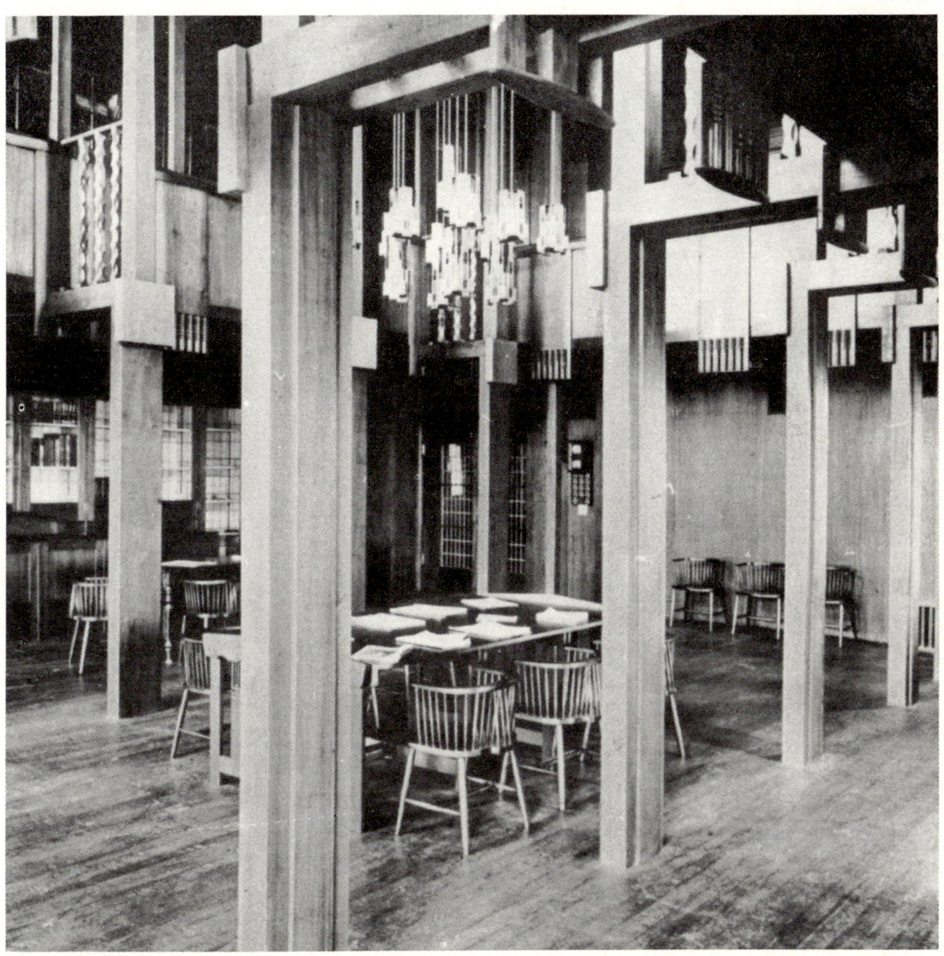

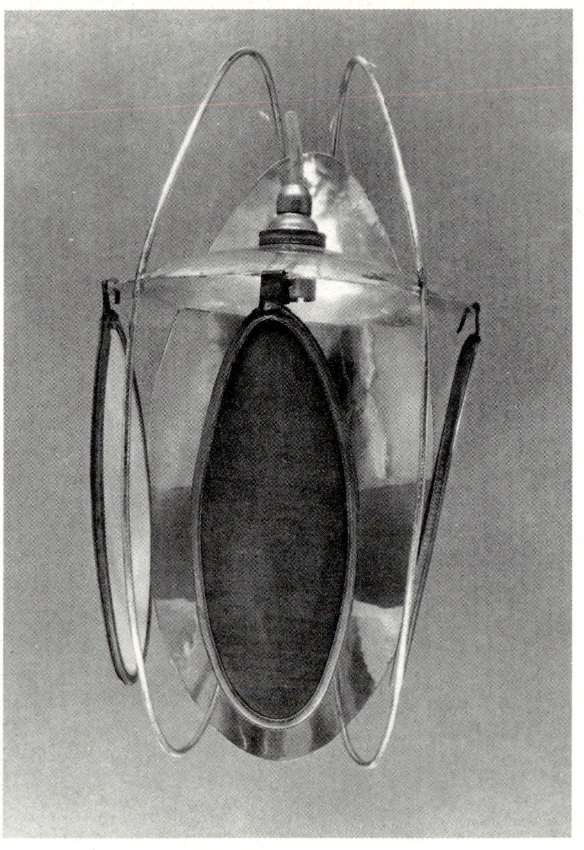

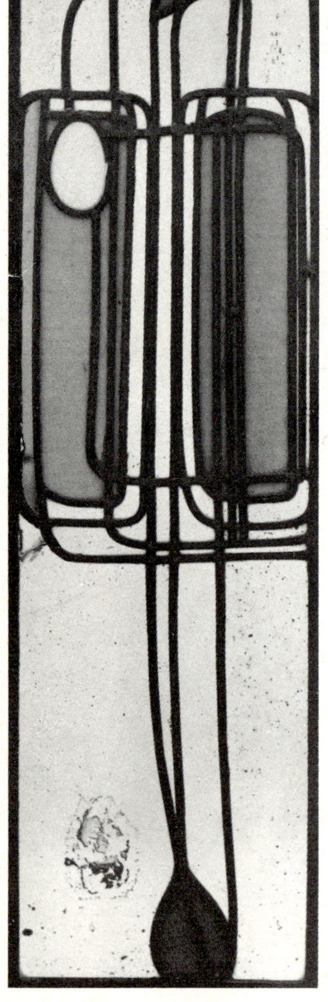

Charles Rennie Mackintosh   Mirror for
"Room De luxe," Willow Tea Room, 1904

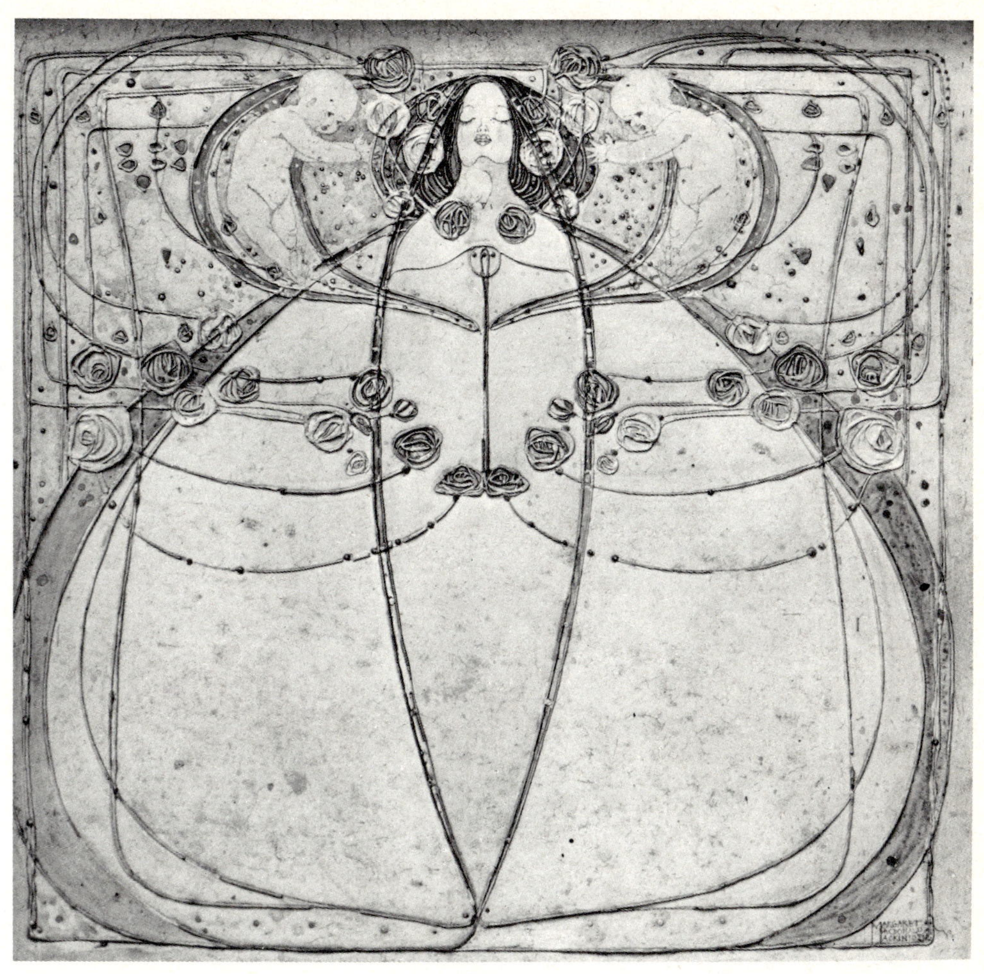

to accept them. In 1902, Mackintosh was asked to decorate a music room in Vienna, using motifs based upon *The Seven Princesses* of Maeterlinck. But England remained indifferent to his genius, and he spent the last years of his life almost completely without commissions.

Mackintosh, nevertheless, kept on creating furniture and décor of the most extraordinary quality. Obviously his chairs can be so extravagant in design as to seem to be straining for effect. In order to achieve his linear harmonies, he built some of the chairs entirely of right angles — inimical to comfort, however elegant — and did not

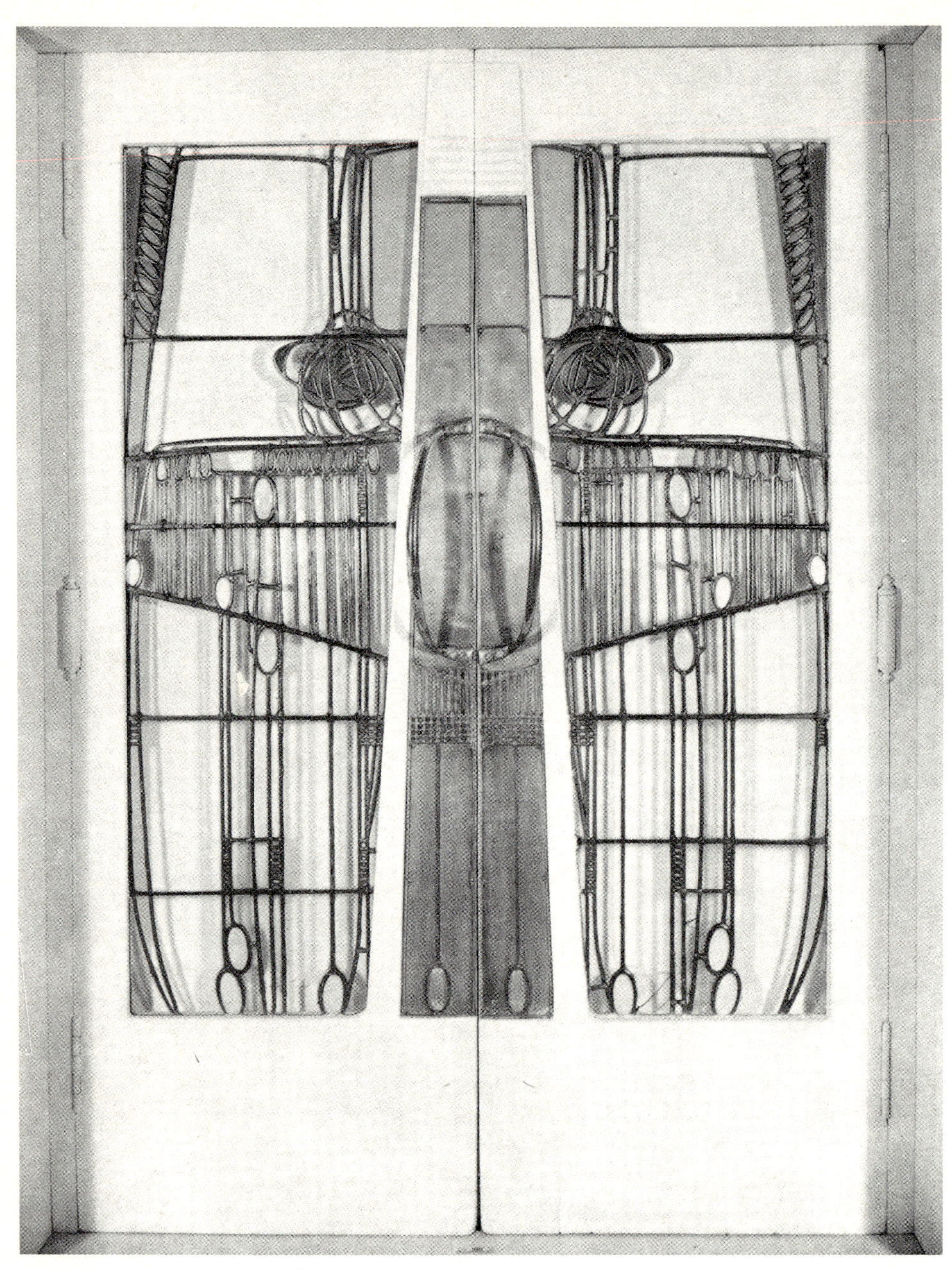

CHARLES RENNIE MACKINTOSH   Door to the "Room De luxe," Willow Tea Room, 1904

hesitate to make the back of a chair two or three times the height of a seated man. But, conversely, what subtleties he managed to incorporate in his designs! In the Willow Tea Room, Mackintosh used transparent doors, mirrors, appliqués, whose attenuated wrought iron work imposed long verticals, while the spaces left by the interlaces revealed unexpected figures, most often oval shapes, set with mother of pearl. To these background transparencies, he then added dull silver, mauve, and sea green designs.

The Mackintosh style, with its obsessive verticalism, is obviously very different from art nouveau as it evolved in other countries. Even within Great Britain, a Mackintosh, to take one example, had nothing in common with the floral style of a Voysey. The Scot's designs are abstract, with scarcely more than the barest allusion to organic form.

Between 1890 and 1910, Britain produced a number of talented architects who brought, especially to domestic architecture, a taste for purity of form, generally colored by nostalgia for the romantic. Cottages sprang up which, in certain respects, were related to Van de Velde's house near Brussels, although there was no direct influence between the two. But, unlike so many other architects who kept on stirring their historical pastiches, these houses reveal, in their intimate scale and relationship to the natural environment, a new concern for pleasure and comfort.

beardsley

Vincent Aubrey Beardsley (1872–1898) is the artist perhaps most representative of art nouveau, even to the point where he becomes the caricaturist of the movement. A child prodigy, his first efforts in the arts were guided by Burne-Jones and Puvis de Chavannes. As an adolescent, he was interested in music, drawing, and literature. When he was commissioned by an editor to illustrate a new edition of Mallory's *La Morte d'Arthur,* he was not even twenty. Beardsley made more than five hundred drawings for the book. Nostalgia for the Middle Ages was transposed by the young artist into an unexpected style. Creatures attenuated as spindle shanks, drawn in a deft, completely linear style, appear in a floral setting, in which everything was artificial: Beardsley made a fetish of his hatred for anything related to nature.

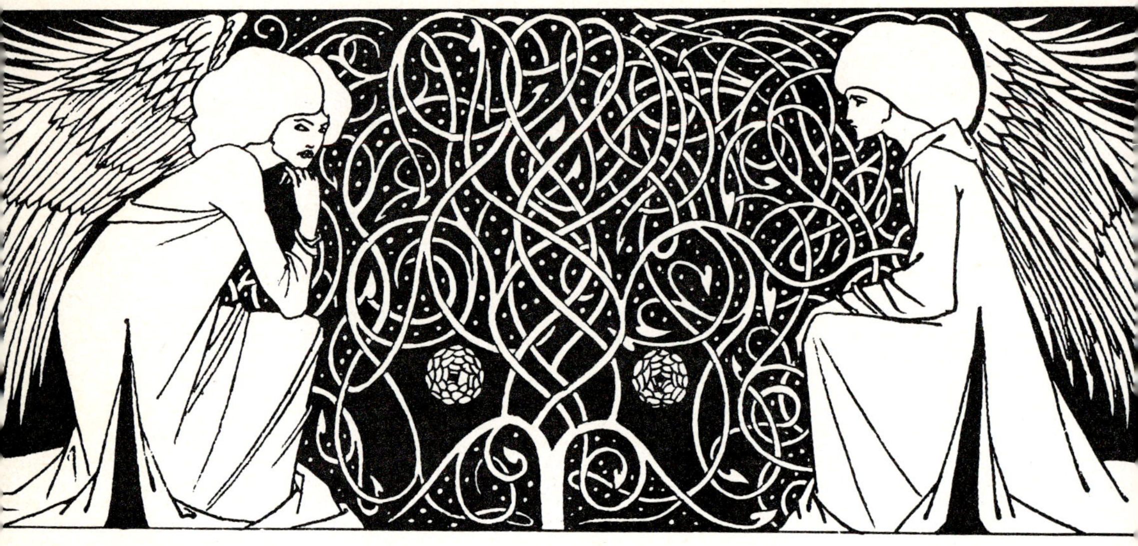

At the age of twenty-two, he became, with its first issue, art director of *The Yellow Book,* an implacable defender of art nouveau. His impossible temperament caused him to be relieved of his duties the following year. He then published caricatures in the *Savoy* magazine.

The prince of dandies, Beardsley combined social success with scandal. He had a study curtained in black, with sealed-off windows, and lit by candles, where he played the piano, a skeleton seated at his side. He made the Hedonists' Club famous, whose members wore a withered rose in their buttonholes. He practiced black magic and received his guests in a drawing room whose walls were covered with erotic Japanese prints, of which he made his own provocative, scabrous English versions. Naturally, he became a friend of Oscar Wilde, whose *Salome* he illustrated, while designing the binding for other Wilde books.

A born graphic artist, Beardsley could express himself in only two dimensions. Space interested him not at all. His posters have the same precious quality as his manuscript letters or his book designs. When on rare occasions he used color, it was limited to a few subtle tones, without modulation. He had obviously studied Japanese draftsmanship very carefully, but his figures are really closer to Greek vase painting. His style, nonetheless, remains highly personal. The facility and sheer number of his drawings are unbelieveable. His figures are drawn, with an absolute certainty of line, in firm and precise curves. Beardsley's style is unique. It is as though the sharpness and clarity of his writing highlights his perversity. The forbidden seems to bloom in broad daylight. In every image, there is underlying irony and it is difficult to discern a borderline between his serious work and caricature; the sardonic is always ready to surface. If his point of departure is an old Japanese woodcut, it is metamorphosed into a page unmistakably English in style, from which exudes the most fin de siècle atmophere imaginable.

Beardsley's linear art and his elegance had considerable influence, especially in Germany, on artists like Marcus Behmer or Thomas

AUBREY BEARDSLEY   Title page for *The Yellow Book,* 1894

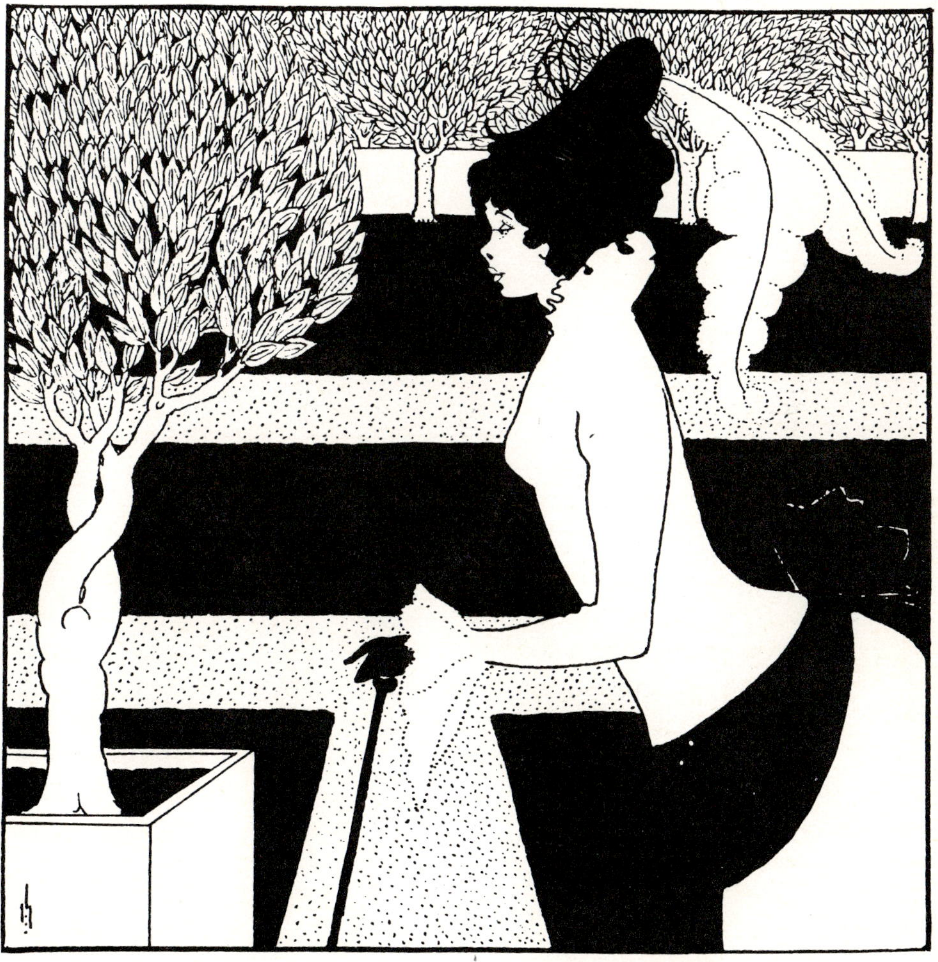

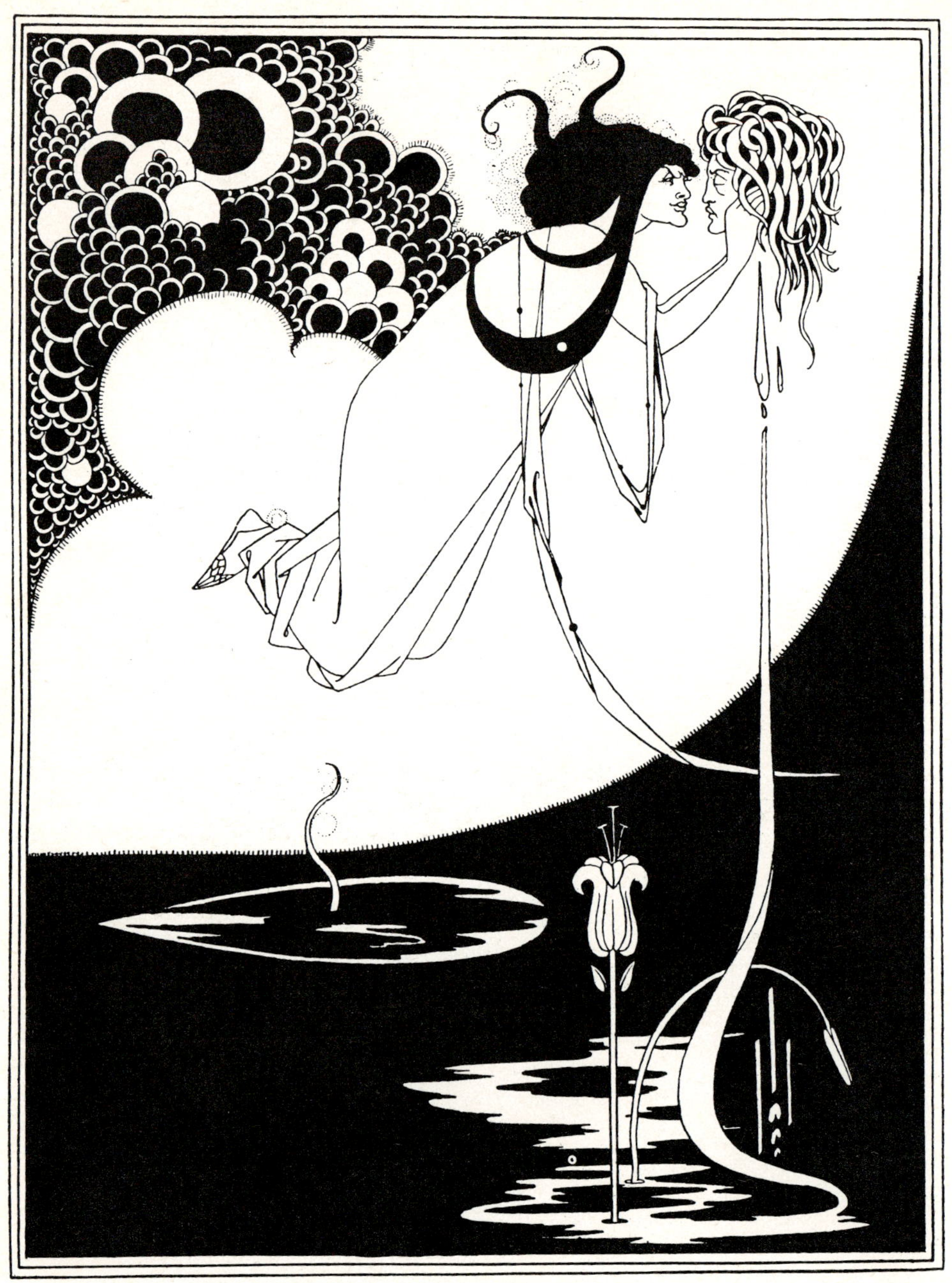

AUBREY BEARDSLEY   Illustration for *Salome*, 1894

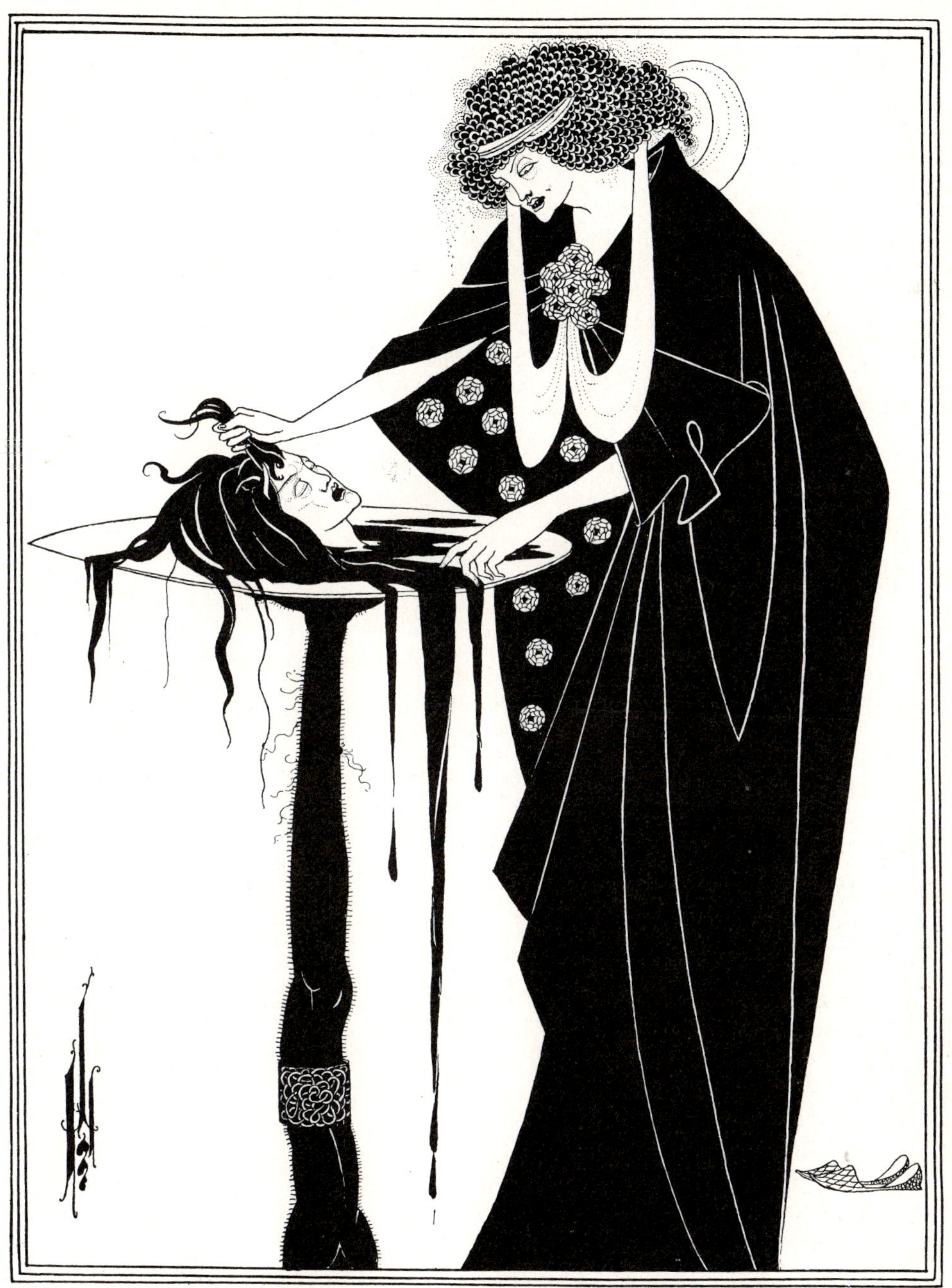

AUBREY BEARDSLEY *The Dancer's Payment;* illustration for *Salome,* 1894

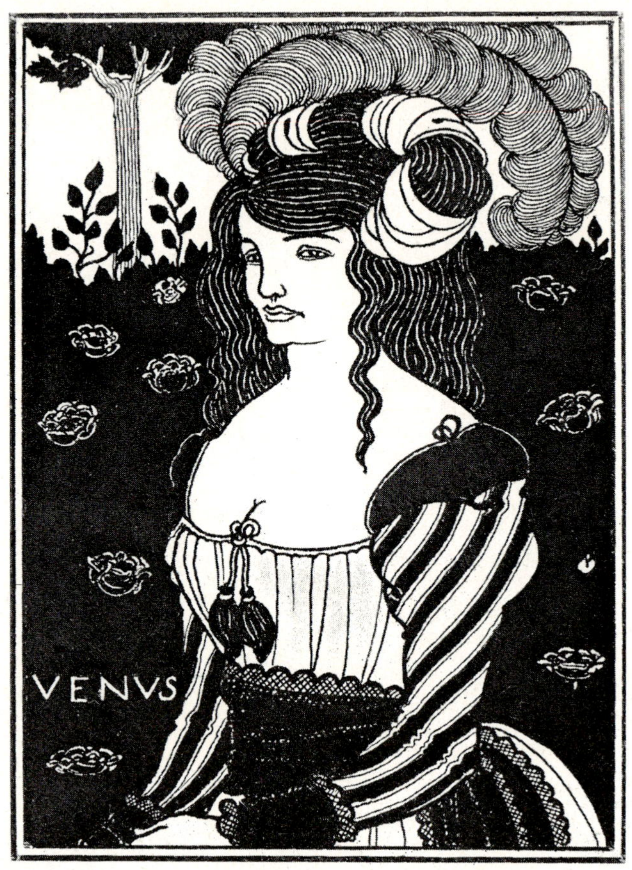

AUBREY BEARDSLEY   Cover design for *The Story of Venus and Tannhauser,* 1898

Theodor Heine, and upon the Viennese artist Franz von Bayros, notorious for his erotic book illustrations and bookplates. The Beardsley influence continued until the First World War; its accents reappear in St. Petersburg, in the art of Leon Bakst, and in Paris, in the work of the most fashionable designers, those with the most "snob appeal," even when the savor of art nouveau had disappeared. Never again would it reach the profundity of his aggressive, witty, and morbid intelligence.

Stricken with tuberculosis, Beardsley tried a cure in Menton, where he died in 1898, aged twenty-six. His illness in part explains his effervescence and febrile enthusiasm, which enabled him to complete such a prodigious amount of work in so short a lifetime.

202

paris 1900

The importance of the World's Fair, the number of foreign countries participating, the crowds that visited, all make it easier for us to measure the influence of art nouveau at the time. This experiment becomes all the more interesting as the movement could, in today's idiom, be

The Chateau d'Eau as seen through the base of the Eiffel Tower, 1900

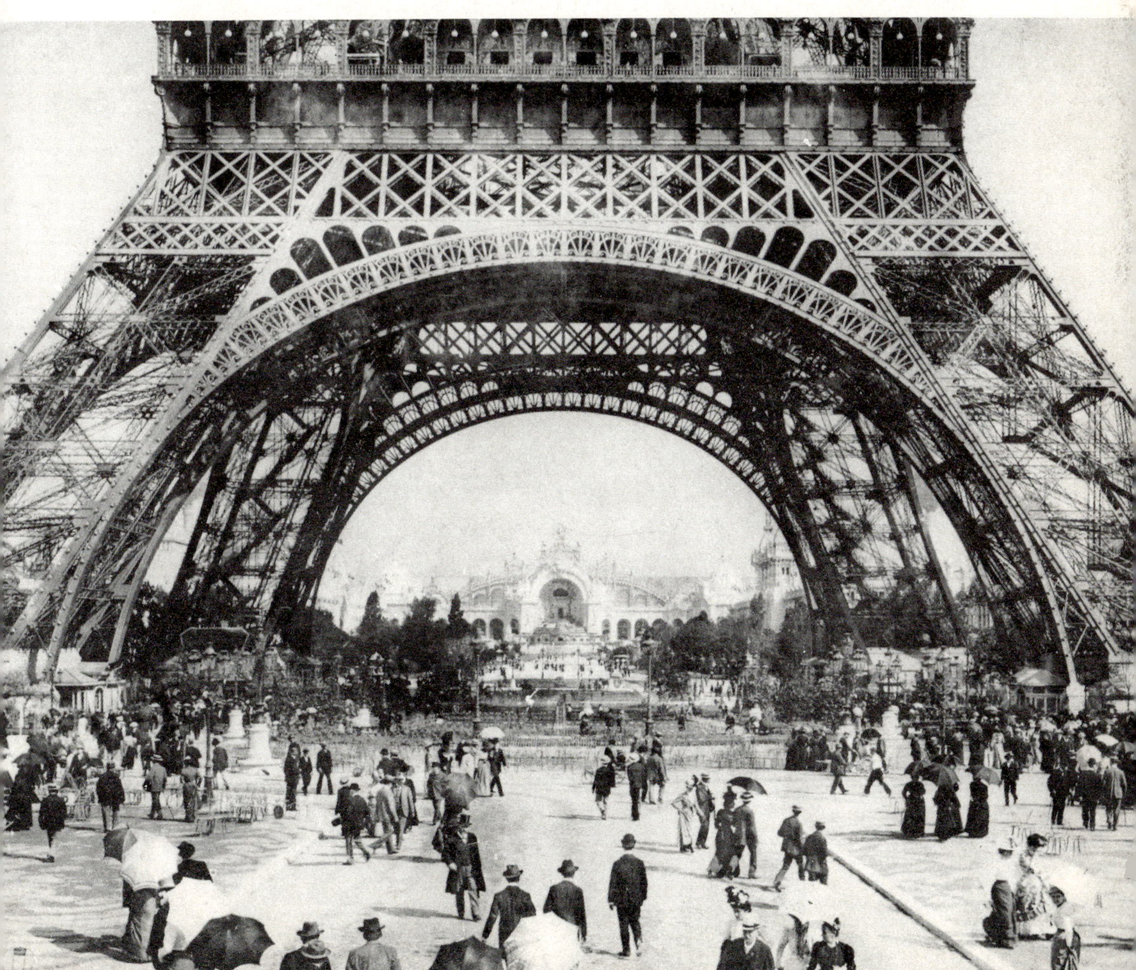

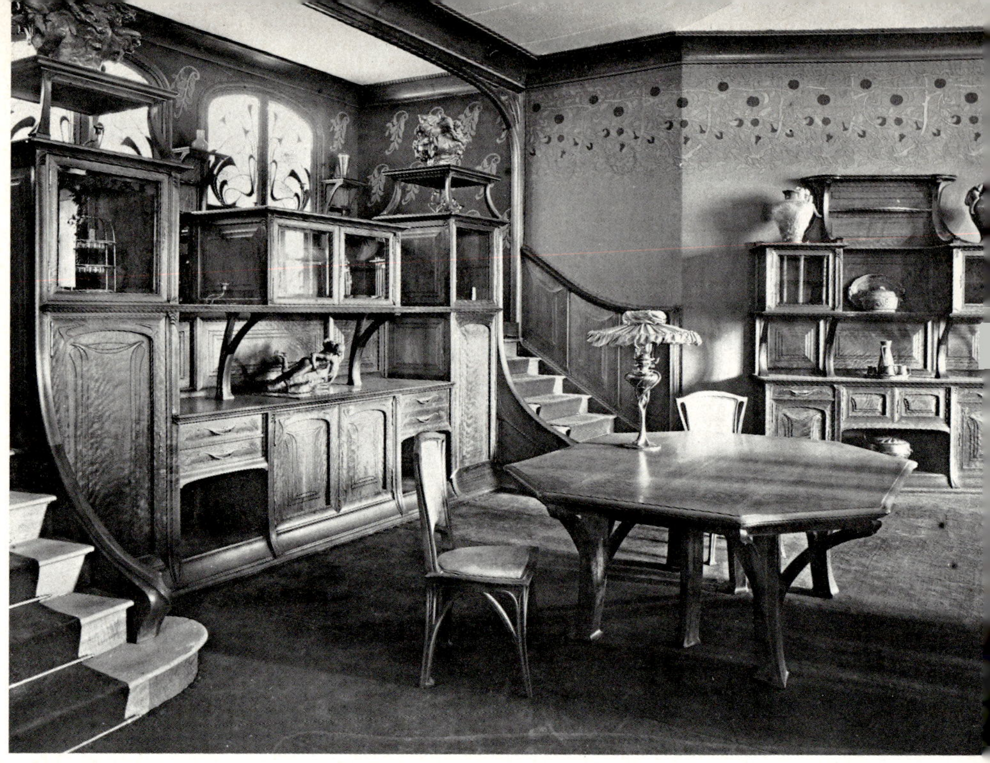

Display of a dining room at the Universal Exposition, Paris, 1900

said to have peaked at that particular time. And so closely was art nouveau linked, in the popular imagination, with the World's Fair, that it came to be known, derisively, as "1900 Art."

But, in fact, if we are thinking in quantitative terms, the results of the Fair are highly deceptive. The foreign pavilions strung out along the Left Bank of the Seine were satisfied with suggesting, in brick and stucco, the most glorious national monuments back home, while the main fairground of Chaillot was taken up with architectural samplings from all the European colonies.

It should come as no surprise that, in this incredible mishmash, historicism reigned supreme. A few of the ephemeral buildings, like the German pavilion, did manage to display, somewhat ponderously, certain "modernist" tendencies, but on the whole the general impression was one of fidelity to national ideals, affirmed through an eclecticism which ran the gamut of the whole nineteenth century.

One pavilion, however, had been organized by Bing under the banner of art nouveau. It consisted of a vast six-room apartment whose furnishings and décor had been designed by Eugène Colonna, Eugène

Gaillard, and Georges de Feure. Everything was based upon organic motifs and it was all unquestionably modern, but modern in a peaceful and simplified manner so as not to alienate the bourgeois visitor, as prospective customer. Remember that in 1895, Bing had opened a Salon de l'Art Nouveau on the Champs-Elysées, which, for most Parisians, was a revelation. There, side by side with Signac, Denis, Carrière, Gallé, Rodin, and Bourdelle, were works by Tiffany, Mackintosh, Bradley, and Beardsley.

The furnishings exhibited by Bing in 1900 lacked both the vitality and plastic quality of the School of Nancy; the exhibits reflected different tendencies, but the unifying spirit of the participant artists was the will to create new surroundings for a new social order. Gallé, unfortunately, was represented by naturalistically inspired designs applied to tea tables and whatnots of the most impoverished form. The various booths devoted to the decorative arts bear witness to the fact that the new ideas had taken root, but were superficially understood. Art nouveau decoration, tracery, and flowers were borrowed, then pasted onto forms rooted in fake Louis XV or XVI. Gaillard, in fact,

Display of a dining room at the Universal Exposition, Paris, 1900

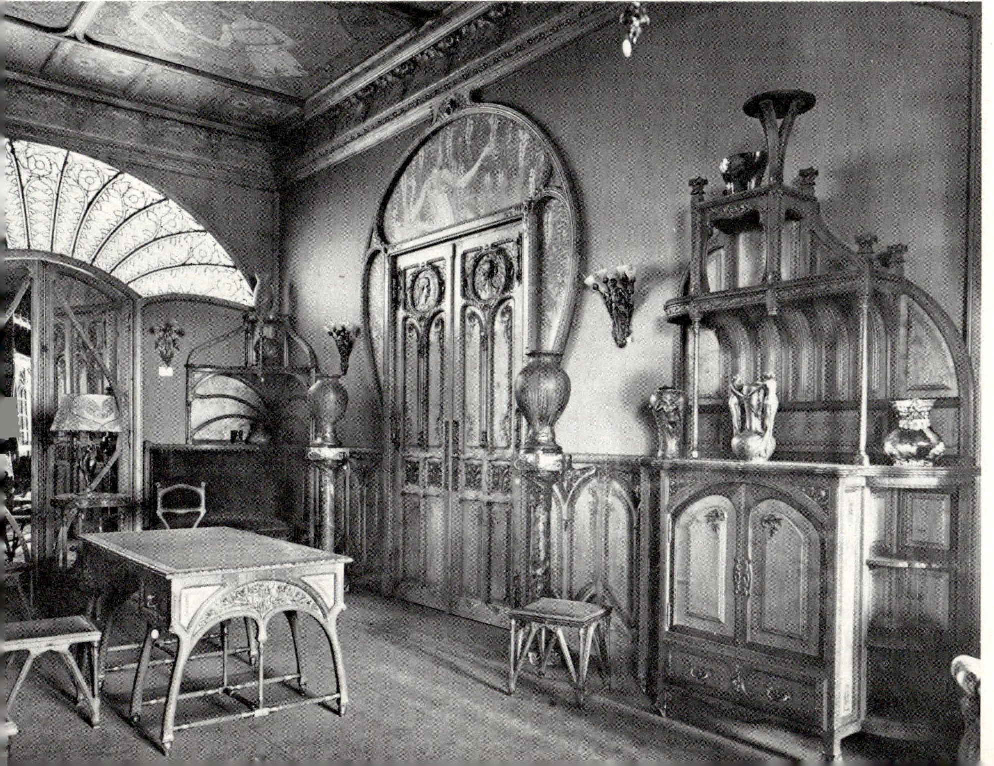

did design furniture which was more original in its ideas, and the architect Guimard had "architected" his study, producing curves and ribs, all designed to reveal the essence of art nouveau. Unfortunately, Guimard, who had just bestowed his first Métro entrance upon the city of Paris, was not a contributor to the Fair. In any case, he would have been largely out of place. For, truth to tell, visitors avid for a glimpse of art nouveau architecture would have found only two examples.

The first of these was Loïe Fuller's Theater. Each night, enthusiasm for this captivating performer was reborn. Undoubtedly, there was a large element of theatrical effect, as well as chance and accident, in the spirals of light and color which seem to emanate from her dances and veils; but the phantasmagorical impression that *she* illuminated a

PIERRE ROCHE   Loïe Fuller Theater, ca. 1900

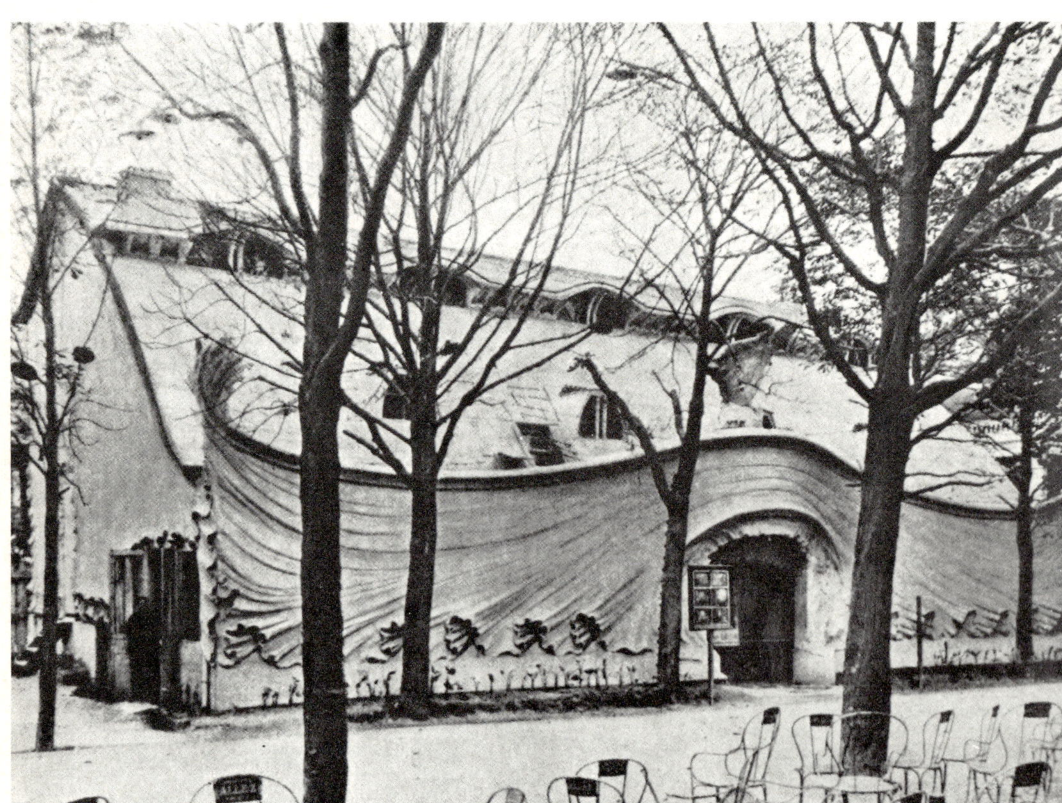

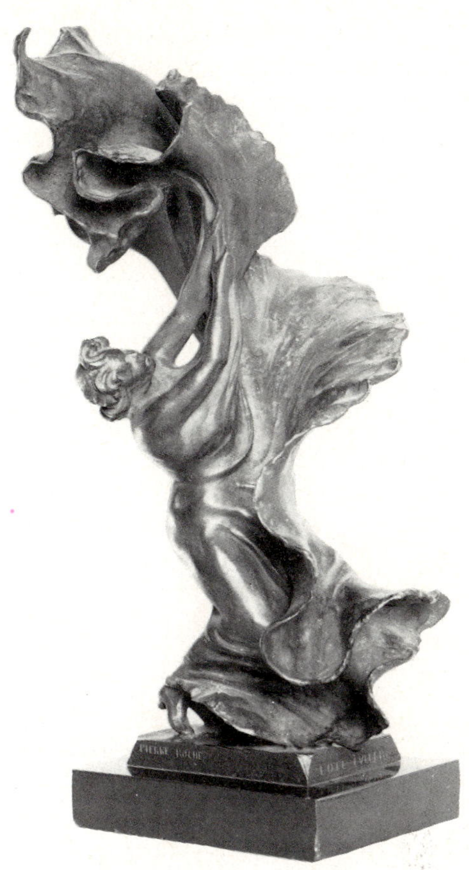

PIERRE ROCHE *Loïe-Fuller,* 1900

stage plunged into blackness was a fascinating work of art. Painters and sculptors from every country tried to seize and render her flaming whirlwinds; indeed, they had only to imitate the spectacle and the result was a perfect example of Modern Style. The American dancer attracted fellow artists from every European capital. Lautrec did marvelous impressions of her, while Rodin had a long relationship with "la Loïe." The Loïe Fuller Theater, strikingly original in concept, was designed by Pierre Roche; its facade, long and low, was entirely modeled to suggest the movement of Loïe's floating veils.

The other art nouveau presence was — and still is — to be found inside the Grand Palais. The pretentious Ionic colonnade which serves as peristyle was built to camouflage the vast space within, to make it appear less "industrial." Designed by Louvet, the 200-meter-long (650 feet) nave was built of iron and glass; iron was also used exclusively in the building of the grand double staircase at the back of the hall. The supports of the stairs terminate in ornamental forms, inspired by tree trunks and branches; their volutes intertwine with fluid vitality, making this staircase a masterwork of the new organic style.

If the Fair of 1900 exhibited only historical reconstructions or hybrid pavilions, it was because its organizers did not dare or were not ready to accept an innovative art. The Academy was getting old. And the new architecture, despite recent examples in Brussels, or perhaps because of them, was declared shapeless and denounced as sacrilege. Modern art had its natural enemies — the timeservers, the timid, the established — but it also had sincere detractors. A critic as independent as Gustave Geffroy voiced his reservations and even

Staircase of the Grand Palais, 1900

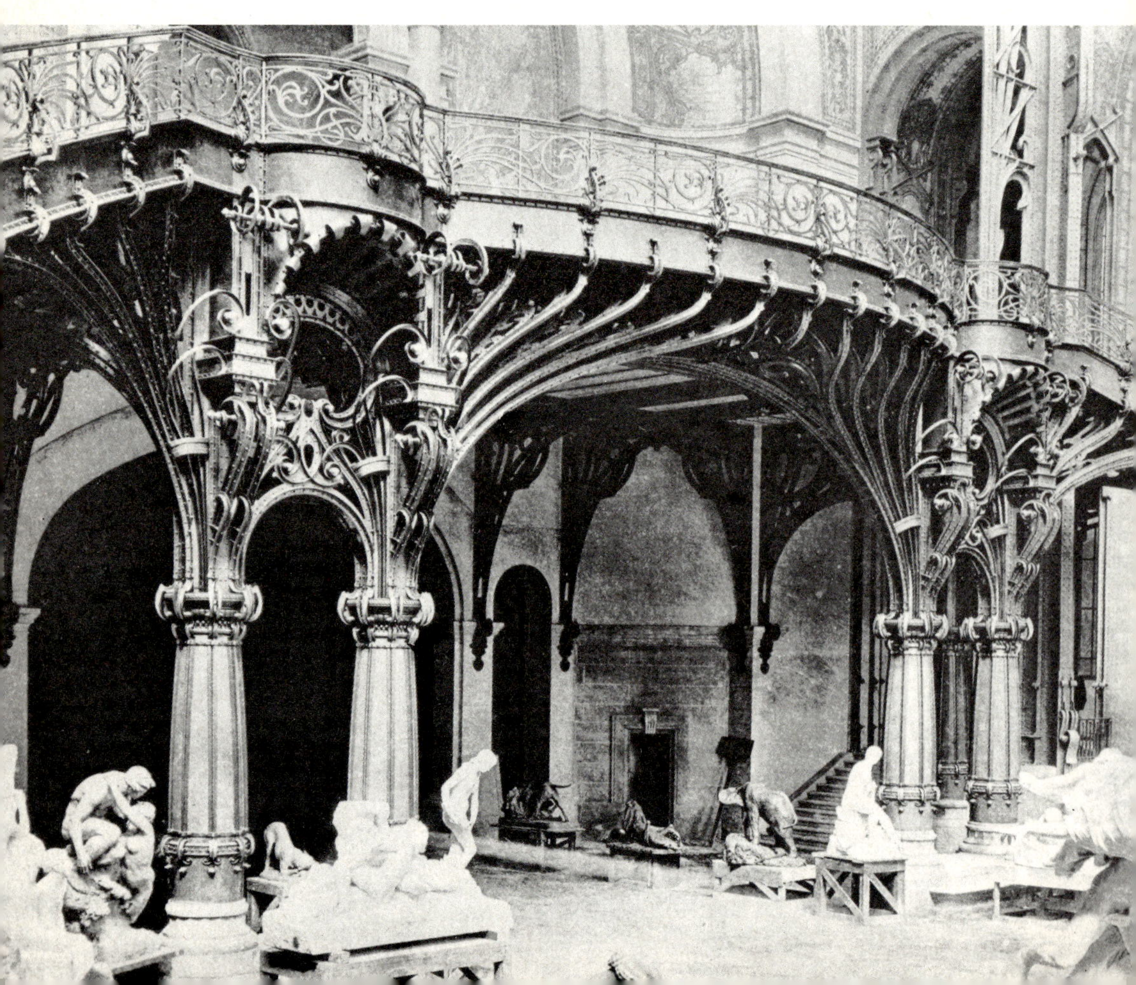

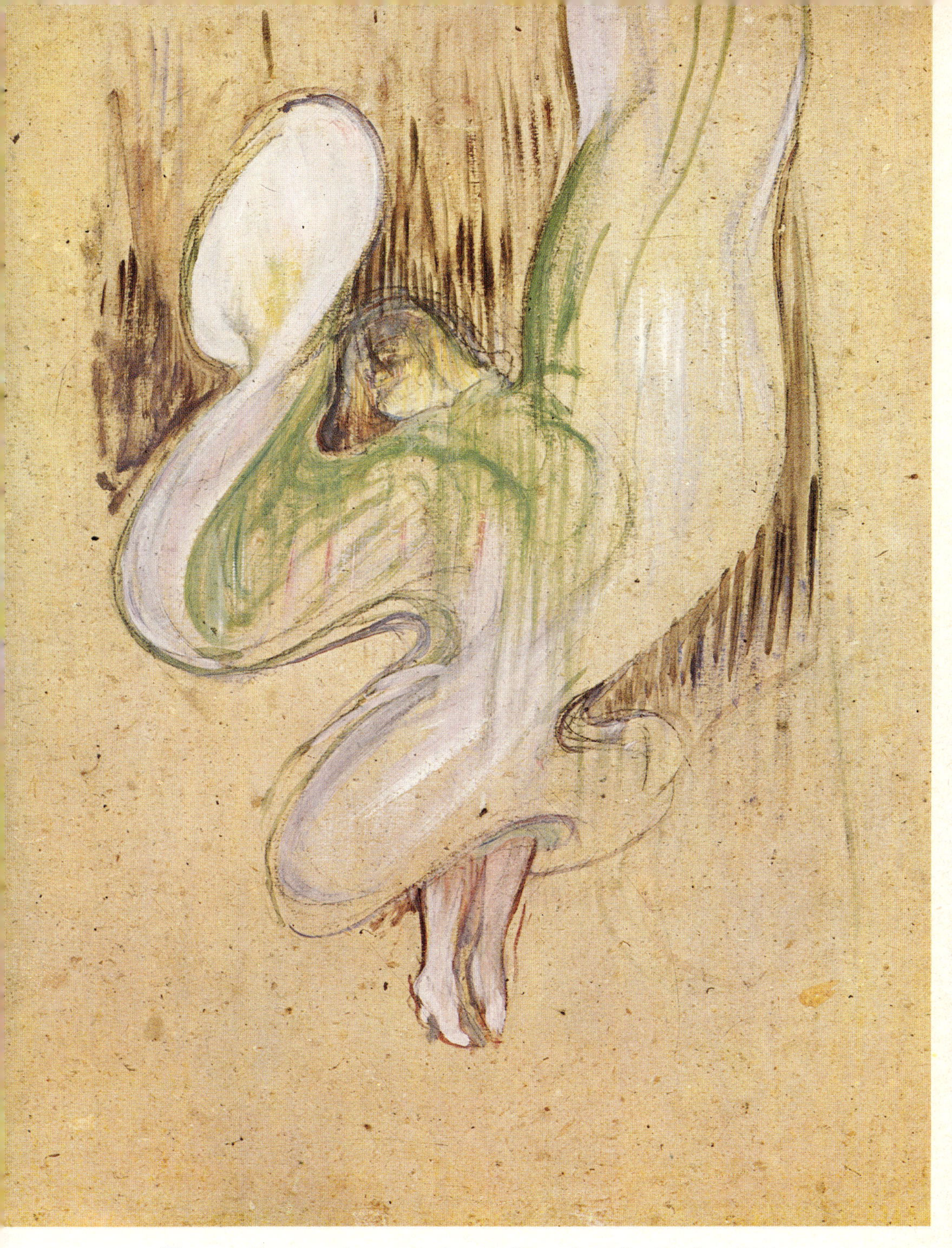

HENRI DE TOULOUSE-LAUTREC   *Loïe Fuller at the Folies Bergère*, 1893

antipathy toward art nouveau. About the World's Fair, he wrote, "Too many art nouveau whimsies, wood carved to look like ribbon or strings, hangings made of peacock feathers, with staring eyes, corselets of bull's-eyes and flames, the whole wall quivering. Too many faded colors; sick pink, aqueous green, wood painted mauve or covered with insipid scribbings, wood treated like metal, made to look cast, as though oak, chestnut, and ash had been melted in a crucible together. . . .

"This baroque style has spread all over Europe, and indeed it is a cosmopolitan style — everywhere and nowhere. Germany and Austria, following France and Belgium, have glutted themselves on this fad. But we will escape, thanks to those artists who have affirmed their belief that form is more important than all this so-called ornament." Appaled by a display of modern furnishings, he wrote: "Are the decorative arts going to follow the meanderings of art nouveau?"

hector guimard

Hector Guimard's architecture suffered the most from ostracism by the Academy, and it is not hard to see why. It was one thing to buy a knickknack or jewel whether for reasons of taste or fashion, but quite another to build a house in this elaborately decorated modern style. Building in a newborn style, and one whose rapid demise could be easily foreseen was taking too serious a risk. All the more so as architects, who tend to be perfectionists about detail, require costly handwork. Thus, although in this prosperous period there was a great deal of building in Paris, examples of art nouveau architecture are few and far between.

Hector Guimard (1867–1942) began his career early; he was barely twenty when he worked on the Pavilion of Electricity at the 1889 Fair. If he was conspicuously absent from the 1900 World's Fair, it was because he had moved, in the meantime, from a banal academic architecture to the style of the Castel Béranger, or, as his critics would have said, from good sense to anarchy. The Hôtel Jassedé, built in 1893, reveals Guimard's desire to break with tradition. Not only are the outer walls incrusted with colored ceramic tiles and enlivened with floral designs by the architect, but the interior also reflects his work.

In 1894, the widowed Mme. Fournier commissioned Guimard to build an apartment house of thirty-six units, which came to be known

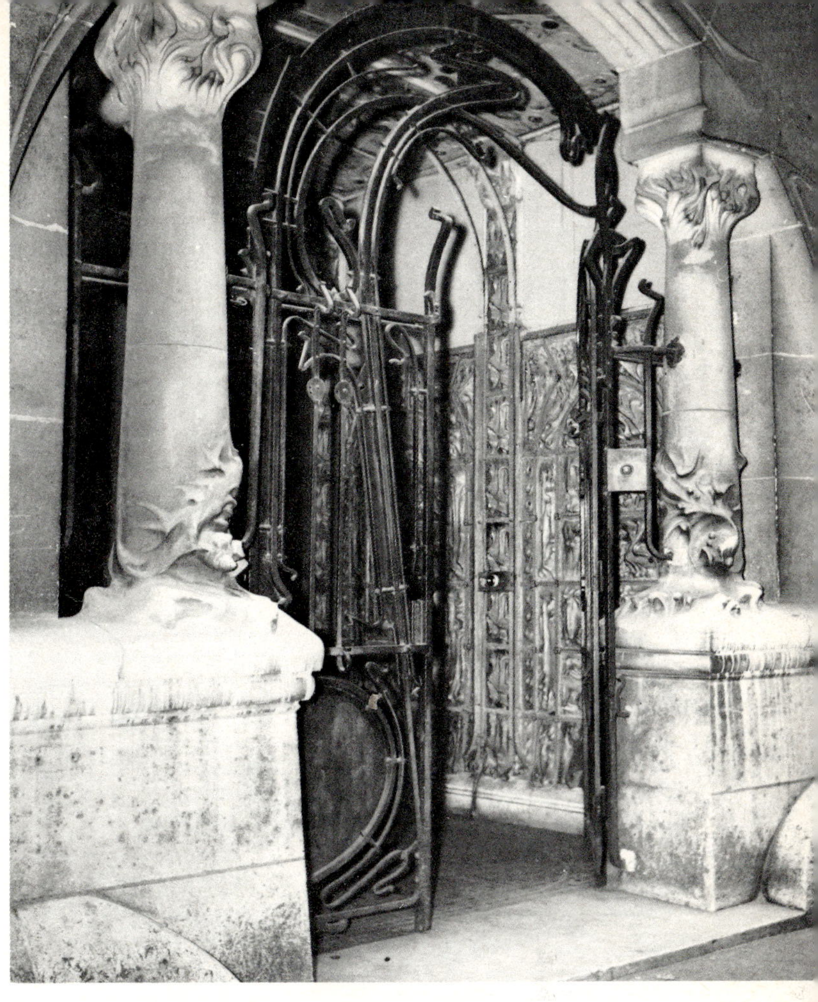

as the Castel Béranger (14, rue la Fontaine). The project has a fascinating history. The designs submitted by Guimard and accepted by the owner of the property were altogether unoriginal. The facade did not even have that hint of the dynamic which had characterized earlier Guimard buildings. But as the building went up, changes, modifications, and mutations appeared, which were apparent not only in the ornamentation but in the structure itself. Every detail was the subject of numerous drawings. Guimard was, moreover, a remarkable draftsman. One might well be surprised that continuous increases in the estimate, due to all these changes, were accepted by a client whose only interest was increased income. But such was the case. Because the lady found him so convincing, Guimard designed the most interesting art nouveau house in Paris.

By this time, Guimard had also visited Horta in Brussels, where he

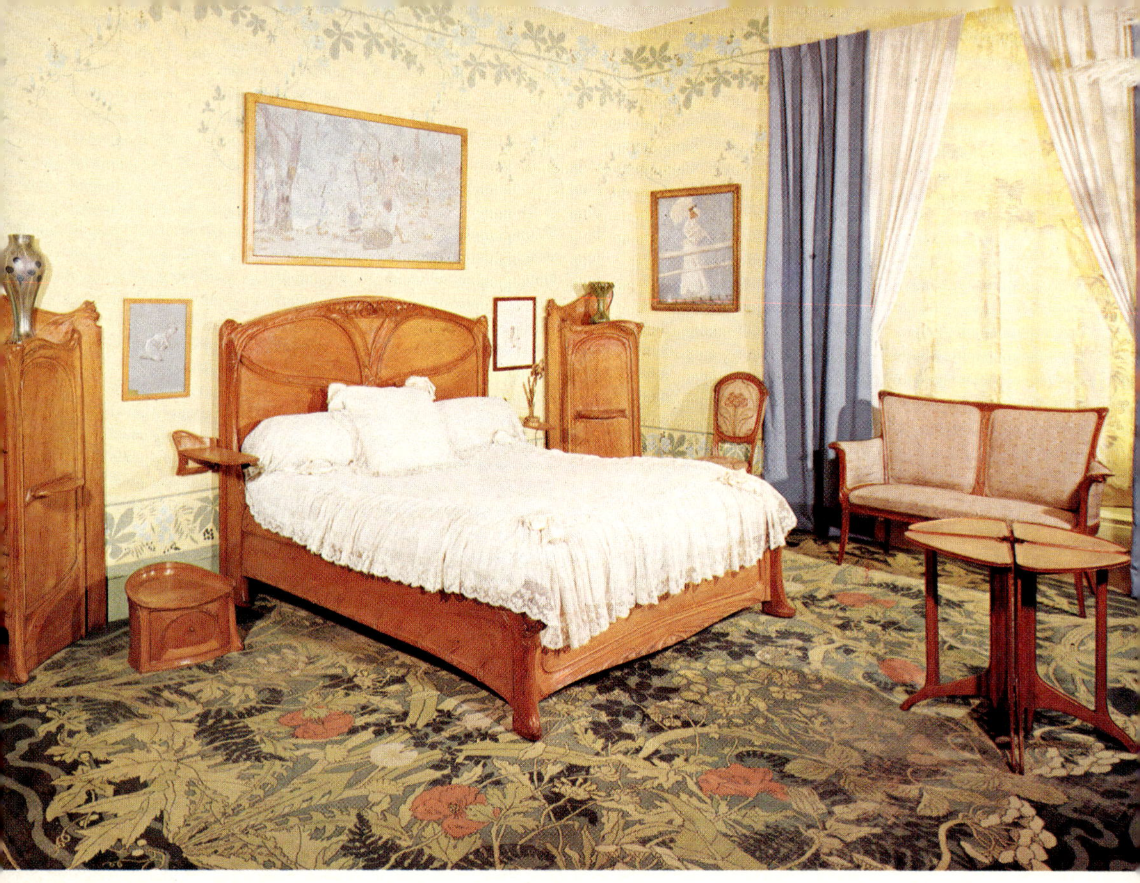

HECTOR GUIMARD   Bedroom, ca. 1900

had seen the Tassel House, just completed; he was so impressed that he decided to change his own preliminary design for the Castel Béranger. Nothing in the latter building, however, is the result of any borrowing from Horta. The rapport was intellectual and the ideas themselves were, to a certain extent, already in the air. The wrought-iron and copper entrance door of the Castel Béranger and the sculpting of the surrounding colonettes show a deliberate asymmetry and freedom of architectural expression. The exterior ornament is completely original but discreet: a delicate relief of broken spirals, *whiplash* lines. Nothing in the facade is inert: the patterned stonework and ironwork are so judiciously placed.

Guimard established his own firm on the ground floor, where from his office he was able to supervise the interior. He designed all the decorative elements himself, inventing many of them — like the interior wall made of rounded pieces of blown glass, providing light for the

212

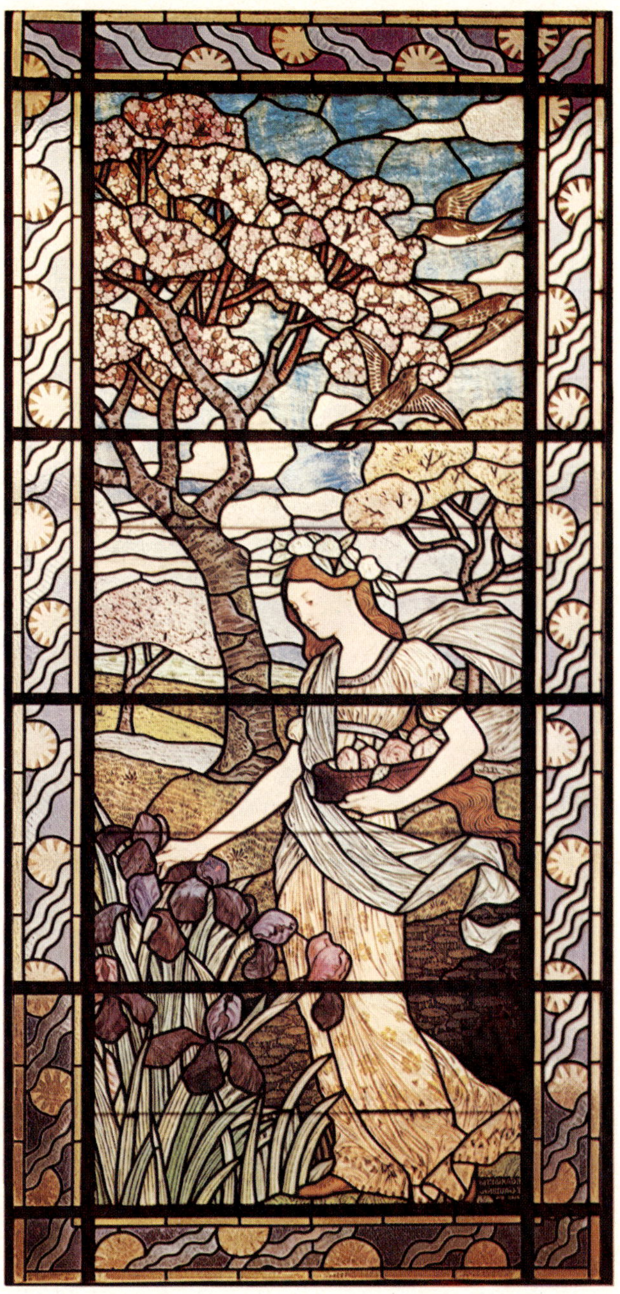

EugÈne Grasset   Stained glass window with the design "Spring," 1884

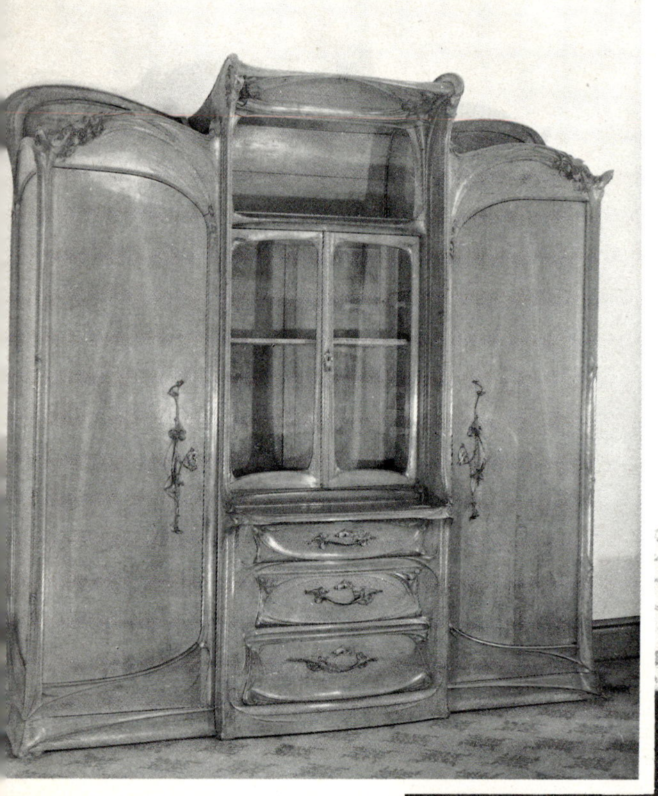

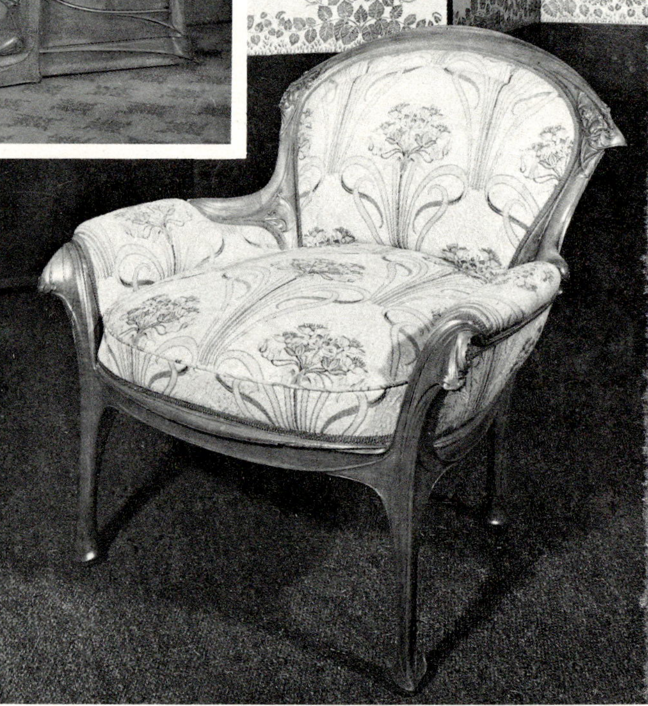

HECTOR GUIMARD
Armchair, ca. 1900

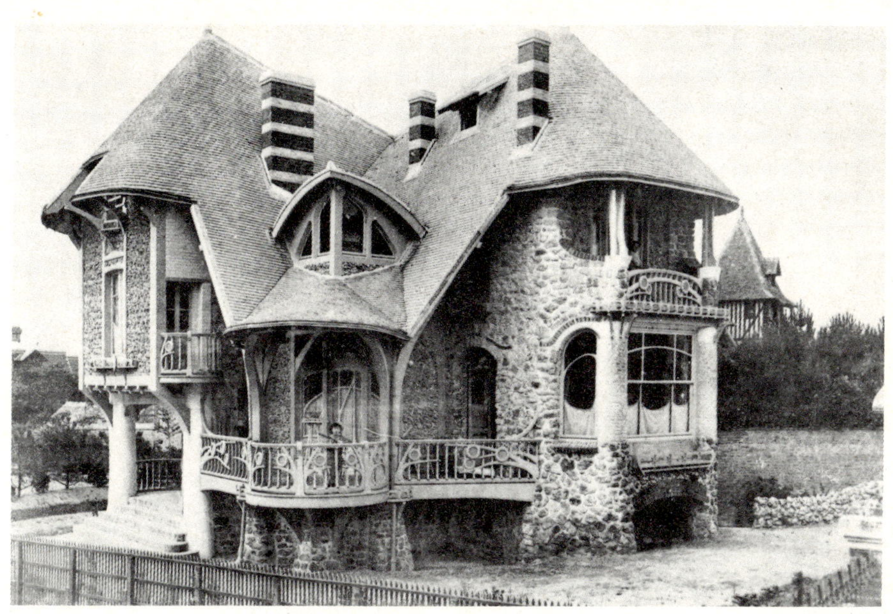

HECTOR GUIMARD   The Chalet Blanc

entrance, which was decorated with glazed earthenware. Staircases, walls and wall facings, ceilings, fireplaces, and lighting fixtures — everything was designed by Guimard. He even designed casement bolts for the windows, and doorknobs for the doors — a functionalist before the fact — after he had defined their form by grasping the wet clay. The Castel Béranger exemplifies all the precepts of unity and coherence preached earlier by William Morris, but expressed in a new style which, in France, was called Modern Style and which Guimard, with sovereign self-assurance, called Style Guimard.

Academic architects shrugged their shoulders: notwithstanding, the house was nominated for a prize awarded to facades, established by the city of Paris (1899). Guimard's innovations were now so widely admired by a certain sector of the public that the architect felt called upon to organize, in the reception rooms of *Le Figaro,* an exhibition of his drawings, watercolors, and models of the furniture and decor of the Castel Béranger. This also provided an occasion for him to expound on his ideas in lectures on the role of the architect in modern

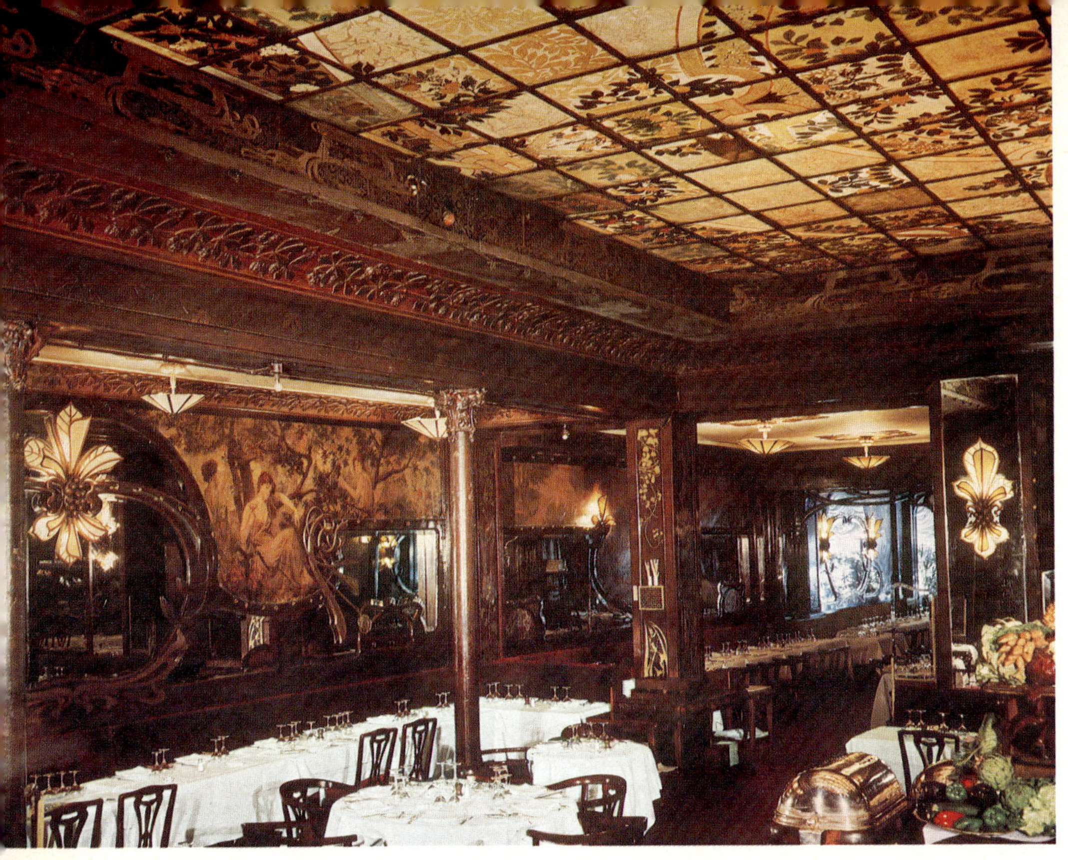

LÉON SONNIER AND LOUIS MARNEZ   Interior of the restaurant Maxim's, 1899

society. Architecture and decoration, he said, must be above all logical, but at the same time expressive. The architect must be an artist who can make use of the resources provided by modern industry. The same ideas would be taken up lated by the Bauhaus.

Guimard's ideas took form in the buildings he designed on commission. In 1897, he finished the vast Humbert de Romans concert hall, with its immense iron and glass nave and overhanging balconies, whose iron fittings described a curvilinear decorative element — somewhat reminiscent of the Maison du Peuple in Brussels. (This auditorium, accommodating fifteen hundred people, was unfortunately demolished a few years later.) The house built for Louis Coilliot, a ceramic manufacturer from Lille, is, along with some of Gaudí's structures, one of the strangest buildings of the period. Above the ground floor a large blind bay extends to the roof, which, in turn,

216

reveals the iron structure on the interior. All openings are curved and asymmetrical; ribbed molding is their only ornament.

Guimard was awarded the commission — which became his best-known work — to design the entrances of the first Parisian Métro line, whose opening was planned to coincide with the World's Fair of 1900. The commission was totally unexpected. A competition had been organized which Guimard had not even entered. But, purely by chance, the president of the Fair, Adrien Bénard, happened to be an admirer of art nouveau. Unaware of the competition, he invited Guimard to submit models of his now-famous cast-iron designs, whose baroque arabesques still scatter rare and precious notes of fantasy through the Parisian cityscape. They were greeted with hostility and criticized as attacks upon the standards of taste and dignity of the city of Paris. Then, of course, the public became so accustomed to them that the models remained in use until 1914; that is, for nine more Métro lines. Some of them were demolished, along with several Guimard stations, when they were found to take up too much space. But the ravishing screened entrance to the Métro station at the Port Dauphine is now a classified historical monument.

In the years just before the First World War, Guimard designed apartment buildings, town houses in the sixteenth *arrondissement*, and two villas in the suburbs of Paris. He always remained faithful to the Style Guimard. But the public did not, and it very quickly went

HECTOR GUIMARD   Detail of a Métro station grill, 1899–1904

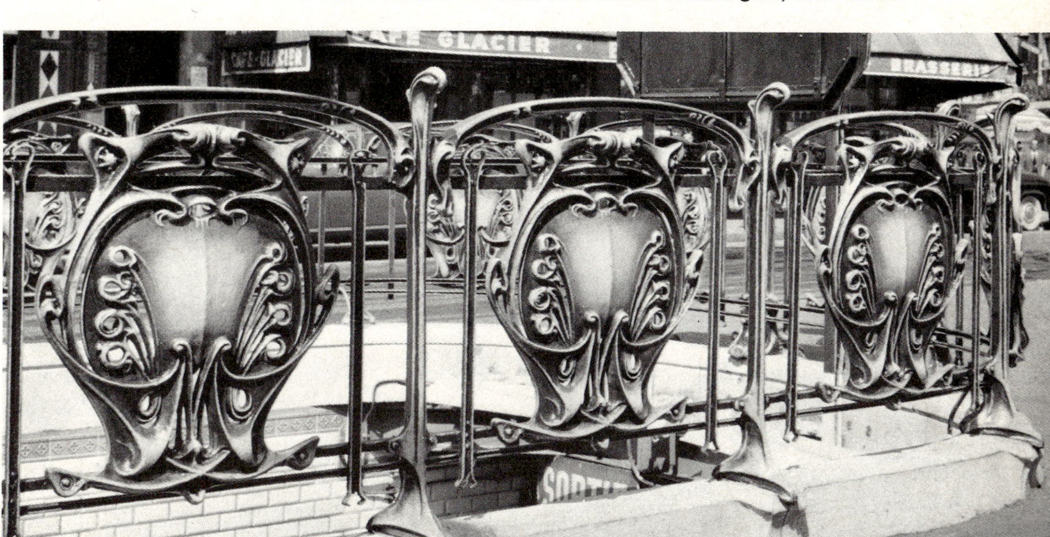

out of fashion. Completely forgotten, Guimard could not get a single commission. His death, in 1942, went unnoticed.

Guimard did not have the consolation of knowing that a mere twenty years later his work would be the subject of renewed interest on the part of younger French and American architects. His methods of construction, visible use of new materials, original concept of interior space, and highly personal experiments in emphasizing, with severity, the architecture itself place him squarely among the great structural artists of his period. But, even more importantly, he was a precursor of major significance to twentieth century architecture. A research team from the Museum of Modern Art in New York is preparing a catalogue of his complete works. Although his career spans a relatively short period, the documentation is vast, especially in the areas of furnishing and interior design. Guimard believed in the "total work" and its unity. Not a detail of ornament escaped him and he gave no less care and imagination to a doorbell than to a facade. We can only admire in everything he produced an elegance and distinction which

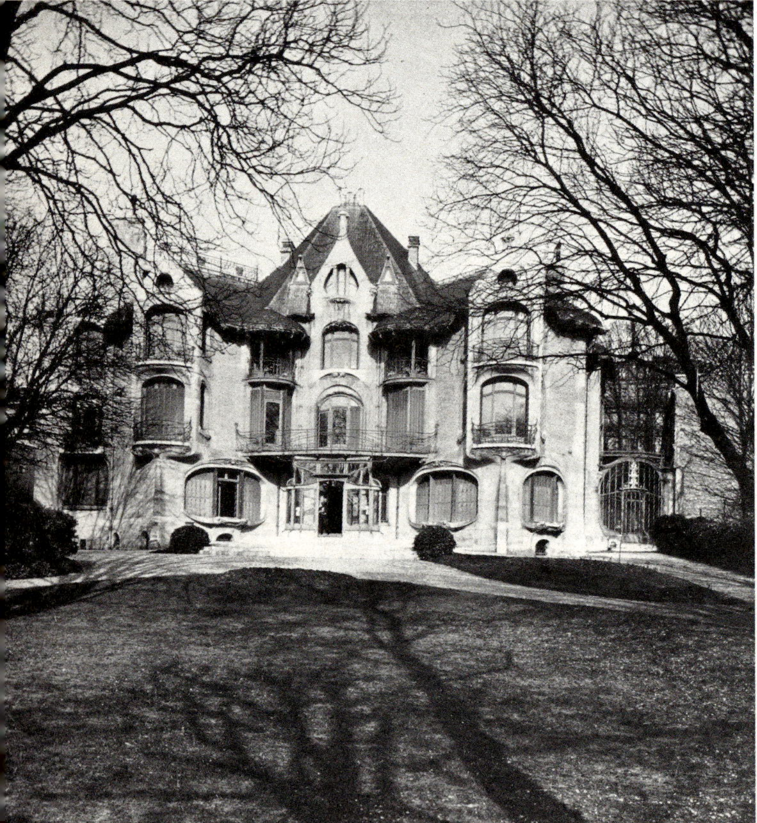

Hector Guimard
Hotel de Léon Nozal, 1902

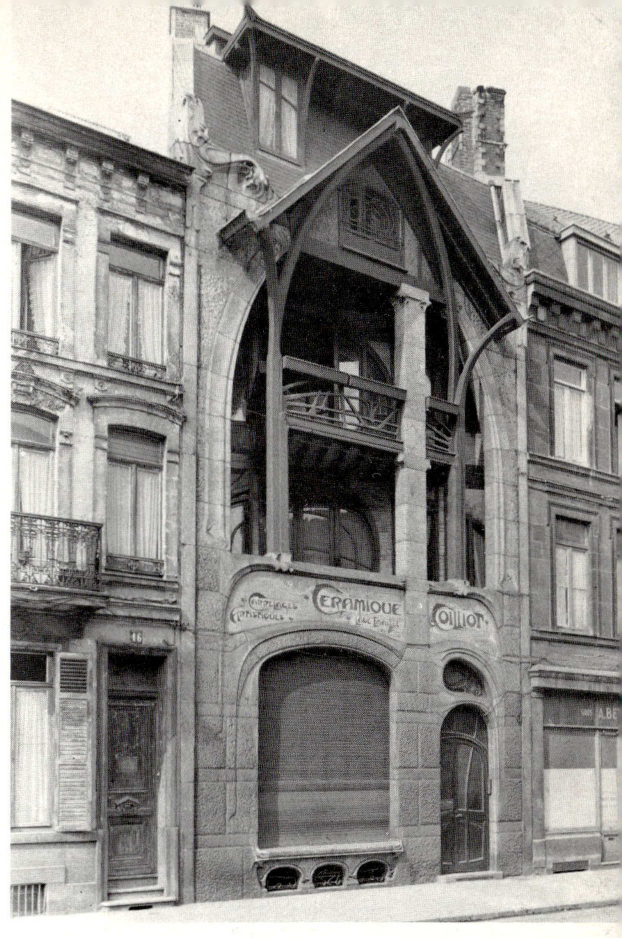

HECTOR GUIMARD
Louis Coilliot House, 1897

ranks this architect of the individual dwelling among the great plastic artists of his time.

Guimard had the ill luck to create a baroque style at a moment when the baroque was completely out of fashion and when individualized architecture was soon to give way to the double influences of cubism and mass production. The rhythms of curve and counter curve, of organic symbolism, of complex interlacings had gone completely out of style. But rehabilitation was not far in the future. When the Great Exhibition, *Sources of the Twentieth Century,* was organized by the Council of Europe in 1960 in Paris, arriving visitors passed under a Guimard Métro entrance transformed into an arch of triumph.

Guimard remained consciously sparing in his use of architectural ornament. There is some question whether his colleague Jules Lavirotte (1864–1924) was shaped by his influence, or whether he was spontaneously drawn to Modern Style — just beginning to surface in the

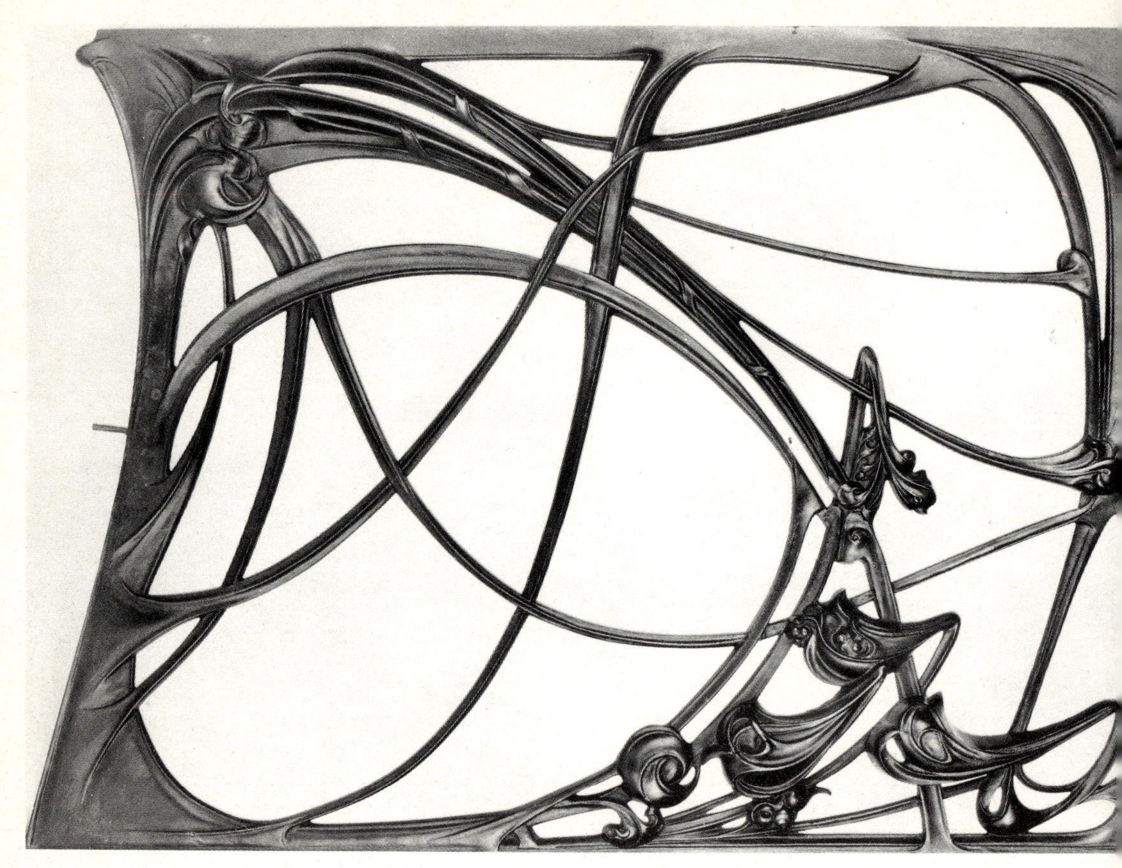

Hector Guimard   Balcony screen, 1898

realm of applied arts. In any case, the few buildings that Lavirotte designed in Paris display an exuberance, a decorative lyricism, which goes far beyond what Guimard, several years his junior, was able to achieve in this area. Unlike Guimard, Lavirotte was not preoccupied with habitability and interior space. His personality only emerges in the design of the facade. This was first evident in his apartment house on the Square Rapp (1899), then burst forth more confidently in No. 29, avenue Rapp (1901). The tumultuous abundance of this decoration, where foliage and fern intertwine with human figures, avoids confusion through its unusual sense of harmony. Lavirotte was primarily a decorator. He subsequently designed the Ceramic Hôtel, avenue de

220

Jules Lavirotte   Private house, Paris, 1901

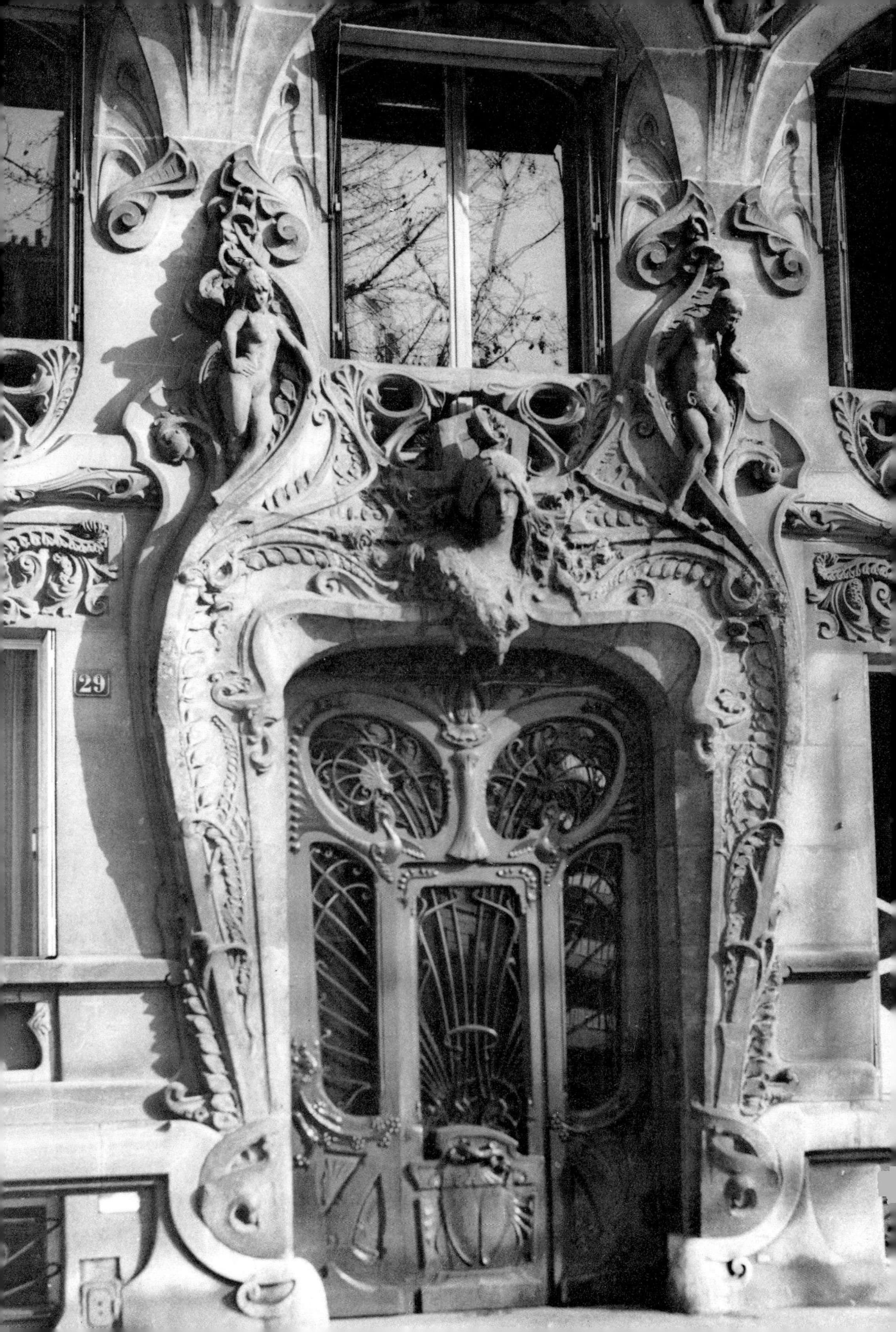

Wagram. As its name implies, it was faced with ceramic tiles, designed by Bigot.

Modern Style houses were very rare in their time in Paris, and are still more so today. Several have been destroyed which would have provided invaluable historical documentation. A real loss is a small town house, built for Yvette Guilbert by the architect Schoellkopf, in a style — and it was the only example in Paris— inspired by Gaudí.

Many smart places in which "to be seen" adapted Modern Style, such as cafés and restaurants; some of them have preserved the mirrored panels and painted tiles of the period. Among the most famous are the restaurants Voisin and, of course, Maxim's (1899), which remains the most evocative symbol of high living in *la Belle Epoque*.

The general term *1900 style* encourages all sorts of confusion. There were then, and still remained until 1914, intelligent and skilled craftsmen who, answering the requirements of luxury housing, translated the ideas of architects seeking to personalize their buildings. It

JULES TREZEL   Interior of the restaurant Julien's, ca. 1900

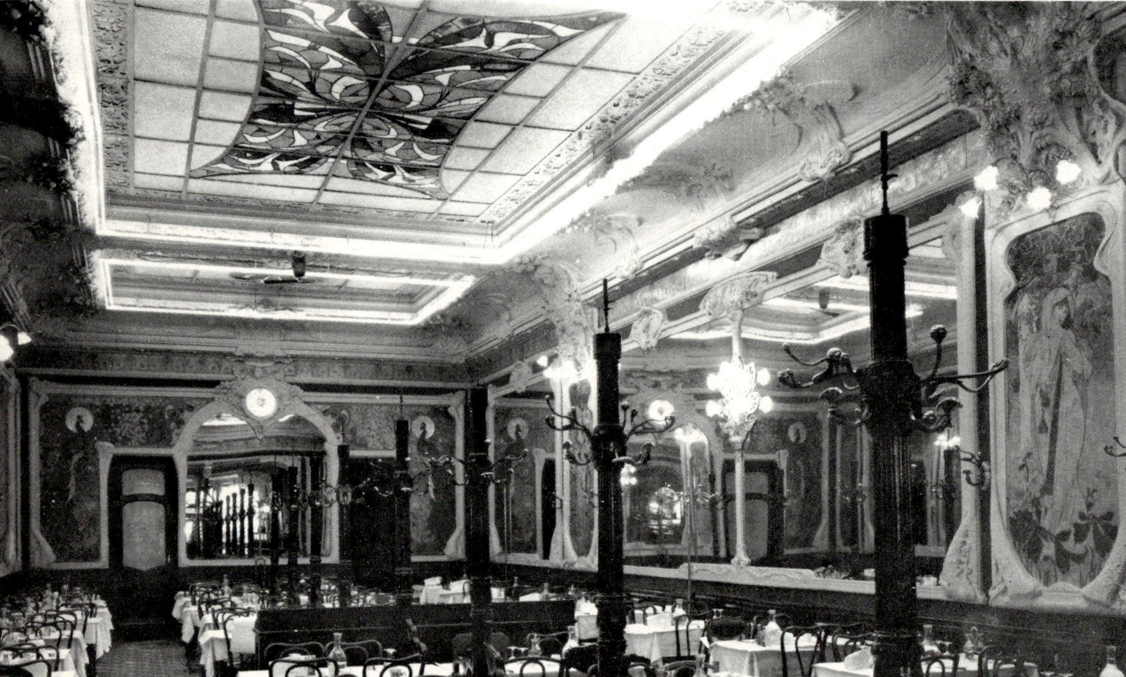

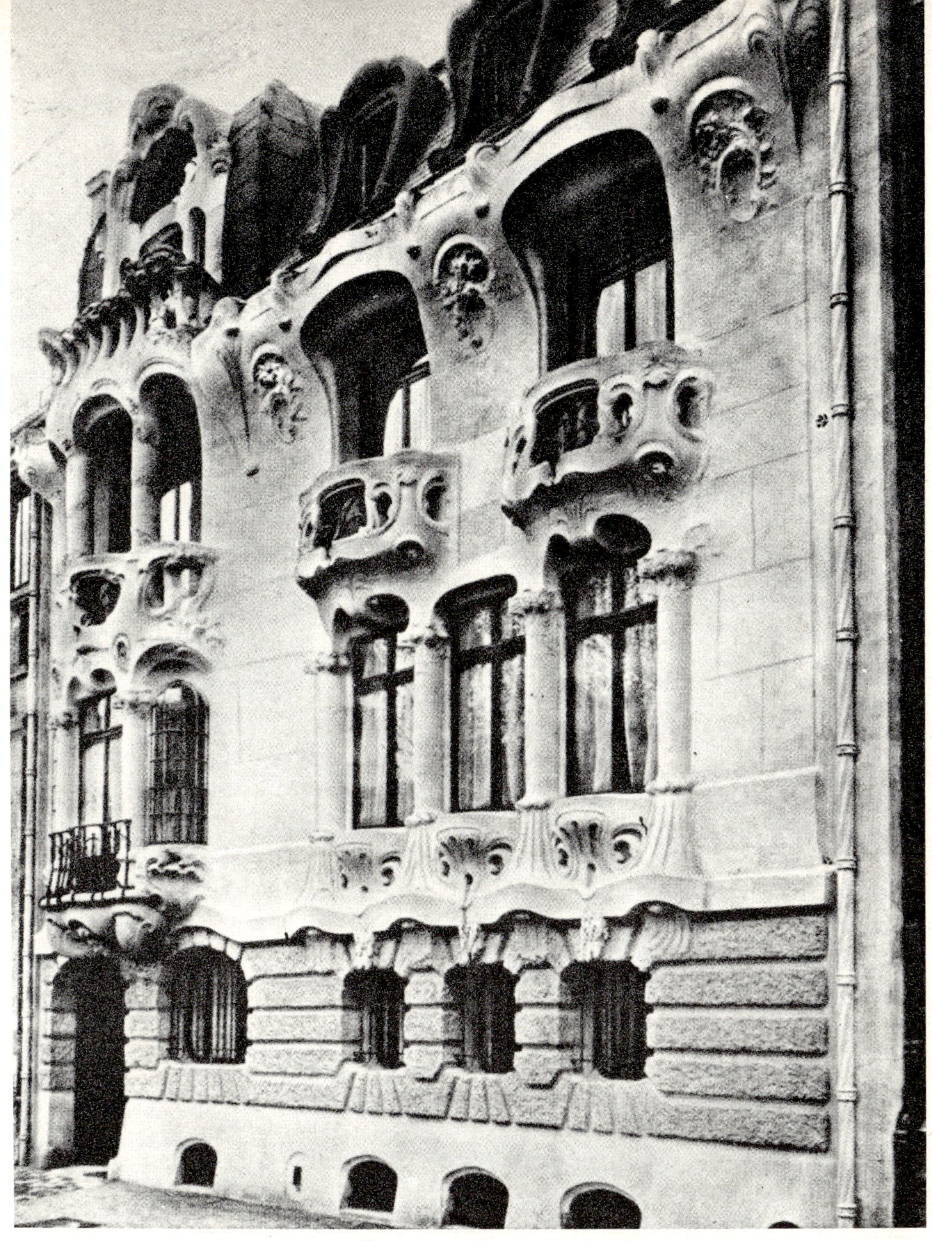

was not yet the age of conformity. But, although the facades were full of life and, to a greater or lesser degree, decorated — even showing evidence on occasion of Modern Style influence — these palaces did not come out of that aesthetic. It would have been impossible because art nouveau was intransigent and would have conflicted with decisions based on the profit motive.

the applied arts

The French vocation for decorative arts was constantly reaffirmed until the mid-nineteenth century, when the great decline took place. It is difficult to explain why, after producing such marvels, French design degenerated into imitation and shoddiness. And it is even more difficult to assign the blame for such a precipitous decline. We can, at any event, make an attempt at explanation. Furniture and art objects had formerly been the work of craftsmen. Master craftsmen signed their pieces. Others, sometimes village carpenters, worked conscientiously for ordinary people, and from their small workshops emerged that rustic or provincial style which has lost none of its robust charm. Things began to go wrong with the simultaneous emergence of the industrialist and dealer. It did not matter to either that the revival of period furniture means a conglomeration of fake styles. These offerings had no trouble finding buyers and even seemed to satisfy them. There was no reason to do better. Whether textile design or dining room chair, creating a new model meant taking a piece of tracing paper and a pattern book; the work would then be reproduced by the hundreds or thousands; at all costs, the unfamiliar must be avoided, and the same banalities repeated. The result was a pastiche of pastiches. It is not hard to understand why the decorative arts came to be known at this period as the minor arts. It was indeed a debased form of art that the artist, whether painter or sculptor, practiced only with distaste.

It would be unfair, however, if we neglected to mention the efforts made in France and elsewhere to counter this state of affairs. As industry expanded, there was established in 1864 the Union Centrale des Beaux-Arts Appliqués à l'Industrie, whose title was its definition. In 1882, merging with a society whose goal was to create a museum of decorative arts, the new group became the Union Centrale des Arts Décoratifs, which still exists. Its function is to protect and assure the growth of everything that pertains to decoration. Furthermore, the École Gratuite de Dessin, founded under Louis XVI, had been reorganized in 1877 to become the École Nationale des Arts Décoratifs.

Eugéne Grasset (1845–1917), born in Lausanne, and a naturalized Frenchman, lectured passionately on behalf of stylistic renovation and

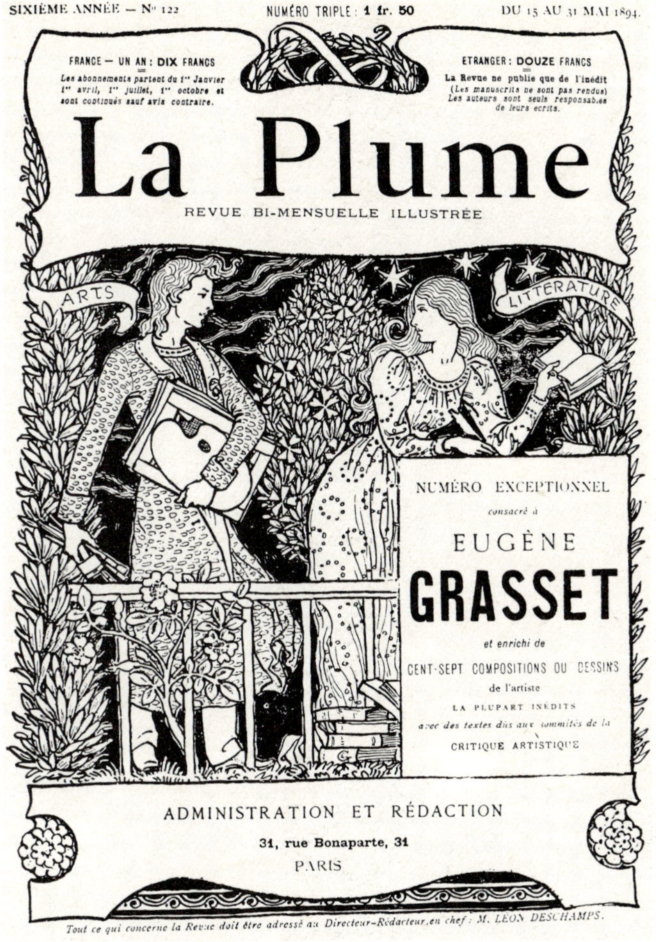

EUGÈNE GRASSET   Cover for the review *La Plume*, 1894

rebirth of crafts. He was a virtuoso who could move from book illustration to furniture models, from stained glass to typography. Fascination for the Middle Ages, common to most artists of this time, led Grasset to produce a large volume called *la Legende des quatre fils Aymon* (1883). At the same time, Grasset was much interested in the floral style. Similar in genre to Christopher Dresser's album of botanical motifs, *le Receuil d'Ornements* (1856), Grasset compiled *la Plante et ses applications ornementales*. In thirty years, style had evolved, and the transformation of the plant, by Grasset's pen or brush, was nourished

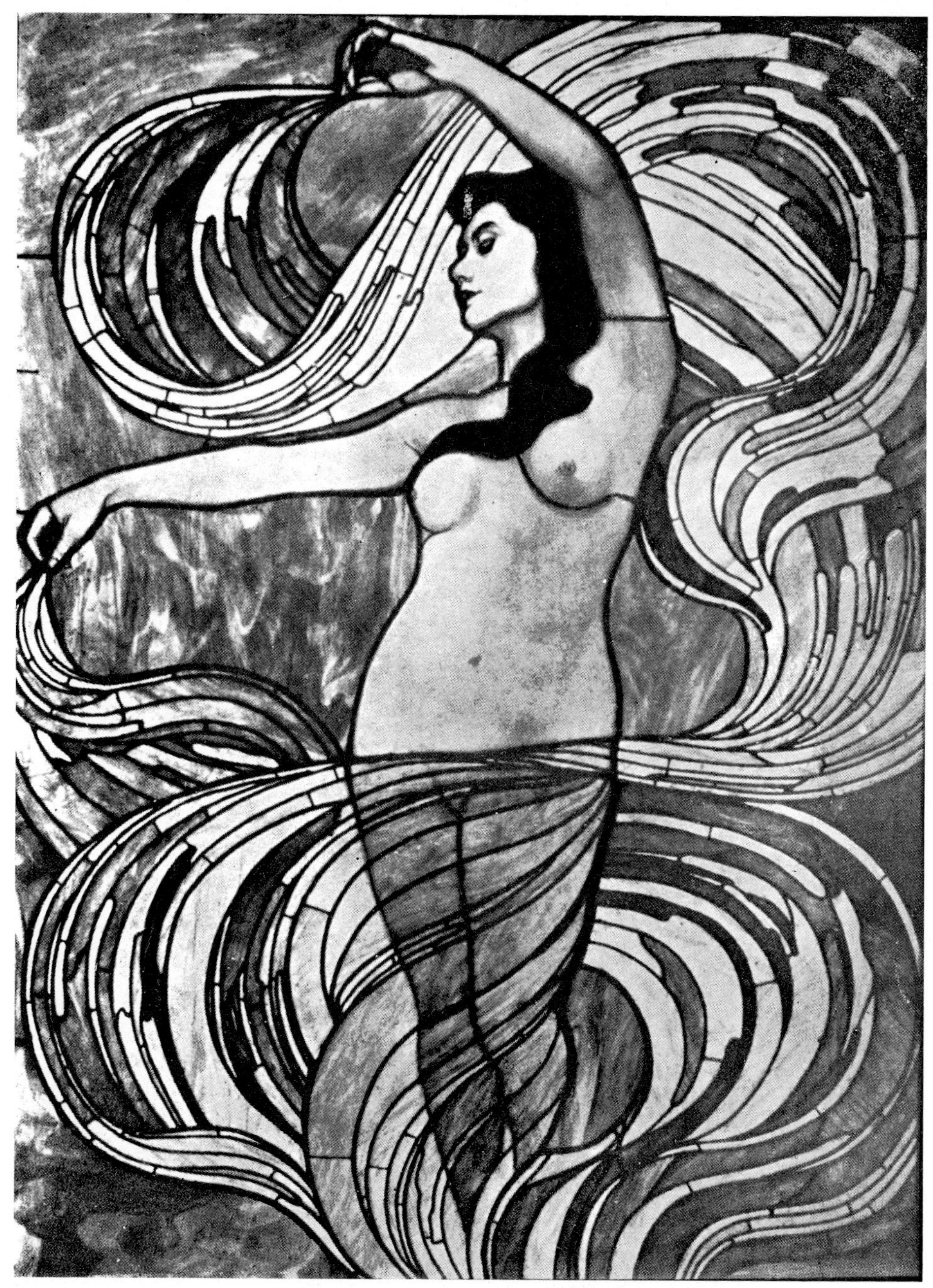

HANS UNGER   Stained glass picture of a ballerina

on art nouveau. While Gallé, whom Grasset admired, predicated unde-
viating fidelity to nature, considered as transcendant model, the plant
was, for Grasset, the basis of stylized design, the point of departure
for a new style expressive of the modern era.

One result of this nostalgic passion for the Medieval, which had
begun with eighteenth century pre-romanticism, was that stained glass,
primarily a liturgical art form, now found its way into Paris apartments. Its new avatar was, to be sure, a decadent version of past glory.
In 1890 Grasset began designing glass, executed by Gaudin; the principal motifs were women and flowers.

Grasset became more and more interested in the graphic arts,
or, more precisely, in posters, lettering, and design; since he was

LUCIEN MAGNE   Mosaics and high altar, 1900–1902

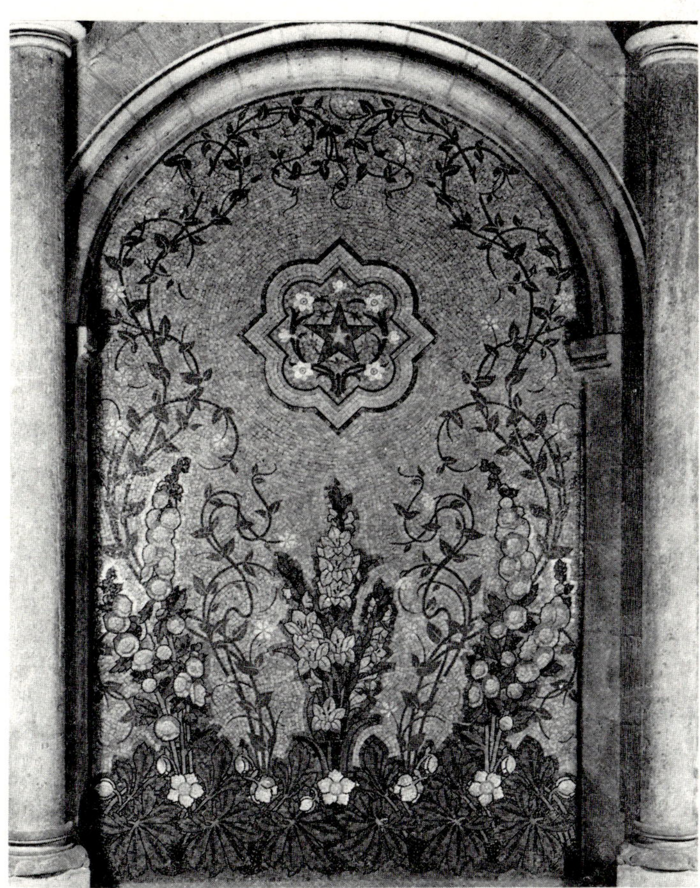

Émile Muller   Ceramic decoration for a house, 1903

extraordinarily productive, his work, thanks to new methods of color printing, was to be seen everywhere.

We can say that Grasset did more than most for the propagation of the new style. He became the principal graphic source of the modern art magazines whose covers he designed, and for the advertisements of the most fashinable products. He designed posters and logos, of which the best known is the motto "Je sème à tout vent" ("I sow to the four winds") of the publisher Larousse.

As was the case with Guimard, Van de Velde, and many others, the attraction of art nouveau did not stand in the way of Grasset's calling himself a functionalist. In contract to the English apostles of arts and crafts, however, Grasset realized that industry would eventually take over the world, and that, although he might think of himself as an artist, as a designer, he must accommodate himself to that fact of life. Although the phrase had not been invented yet, Grasset was really looking ahead to the collaboration of "industrial design."

228

Some disciplines eluded the conquest of the machine. Glass blowing, and the subsequent modeling of the form at the end of the pipe, is an antimachine gesture, and we have already seen to what advantage it was used by the glassmakers of Nancy. Ceramics enjoyed, at the end of the nineteenth century and beginning of the twentieth, a long overdue resurgence. Bracquemond was the first to give pottery new and exemplary forms. Experiments by the new masters of this forgotten art were concerned with form, design, and even the material with which they worked.

The origin of the pottery renaissance can be traced to the rediscovery of Chinese and Japanese objects. Next to these pieces, the products of Western manufacture look sad indeed, even when they followed traditional techniques. Porcelain was almost entirely abandoned by the designers of this period, who preferred austere-looking material, like clay, as more suitable to the sturdy objects they created. There emerged noble craftsmen of earth and fire, with names like Carriès, Chaplet, the master of fired clay, Delaherche, Deck, Dammouse. Decoration played a small part in their creations, but the forms they favored were based on the organic. Ceramic tile was also used as facing for exterior and interior architecture, and some ceramists became specialists in this area, like Georges Bigot, and, in a more commercial vein, Émile Muller; "Muller earthenware" became synonymous with quality ornament for buildings which were not always worthy of the honor. But all of these craftsmen shared the same goal: escape from convention.

jewelry

This was the period, *la Belle Epoque,* after all, when women were adorned like ex-votos. Jewels went along with homage like hand-kissing, deep bows, formulas of respect, and murmurs of adulation. If matching sets of jewels and glittering single gems found fitting company in art nouveau, it was because the new style so easily accommodated every fantasy and each new idea. The jewel has no other function than to embellish, and no other object than to satisfy vanity.

By tradition and vocation, Paris was the center for the most dazzling inventions and precious refinements of the jeweler's craft. To

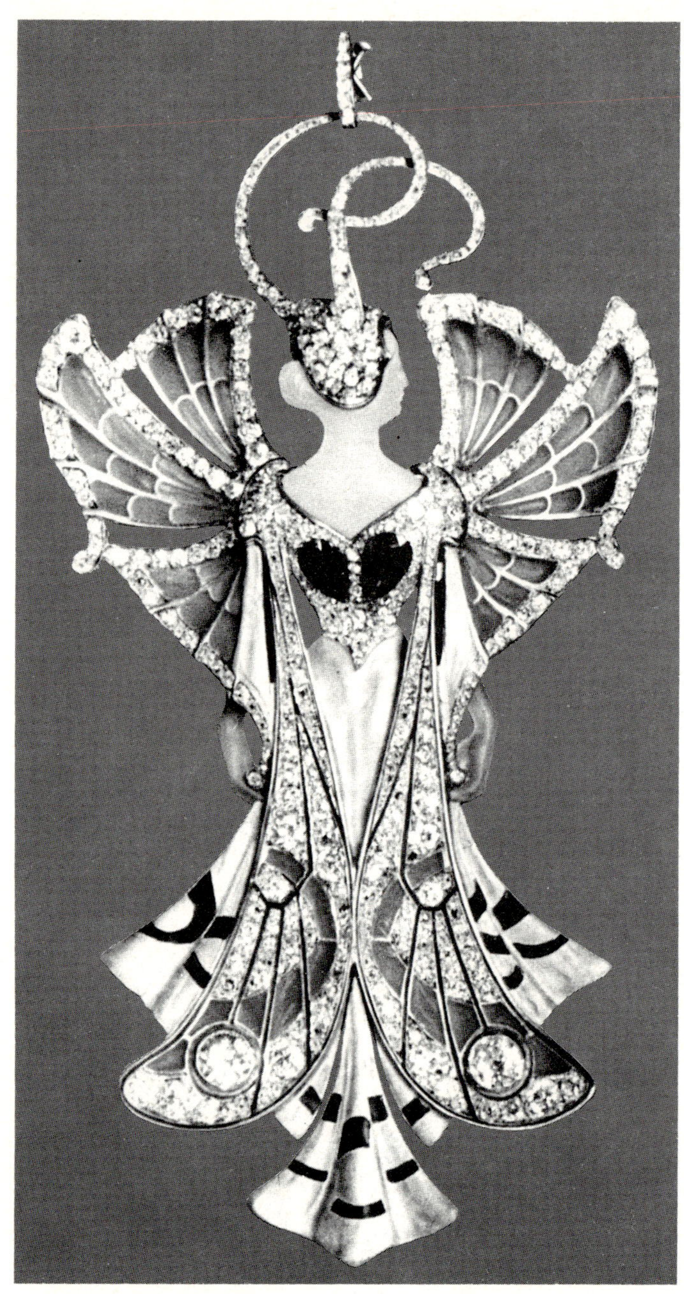

Henri Vever Pendant "Sylvia," 1900

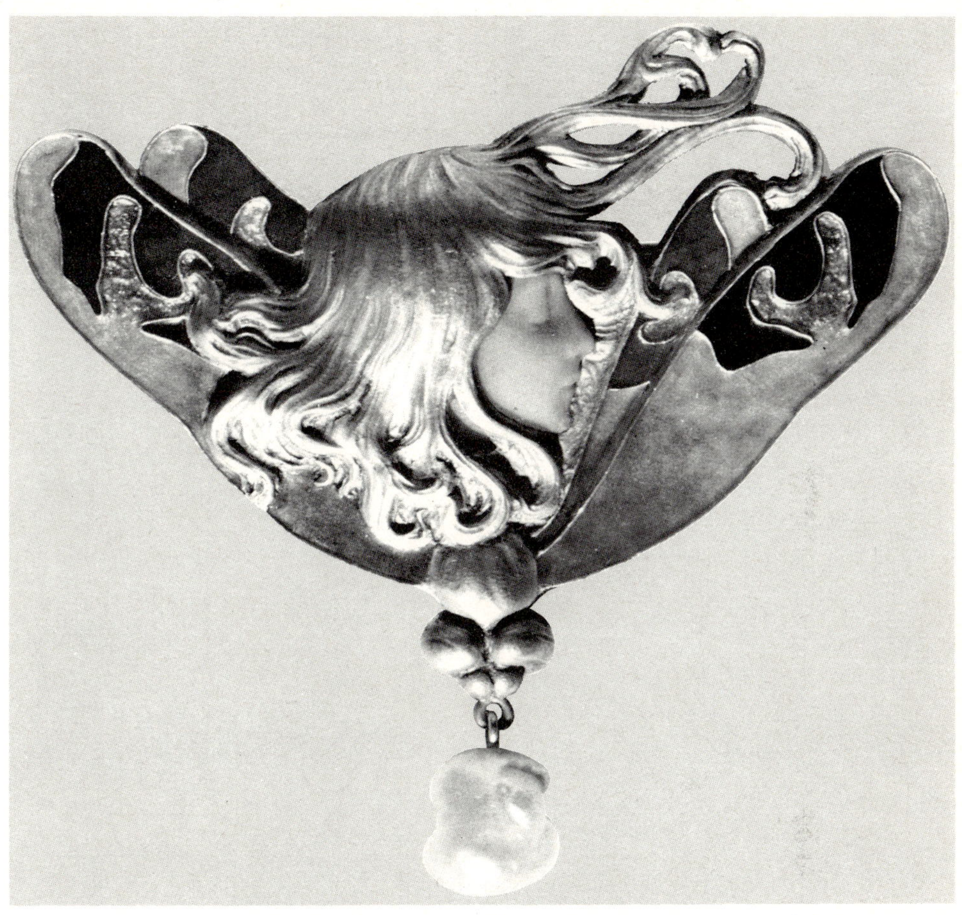

Rene Lalique   Carved horn brooch, ca. 1900

this René Lalique brought new wit, imagination, taste, and inventiveness which immediately revealed his complete mastery of the art. As soon as Lalique discovered that nature offered inexhaustible motifs, this became the revelation that enabled him to create a style which was so well suited to the elegance of current fashions, and to other forms of the decorative arts. For him, the invention of the subject, and the artistry with which it was treated, took precedence over all other considerations. Lalique did not set the precious gem according to the conventional formulas based on displaying its value to best advantage. Nor did he disdain the use of semiprecious stones, until then ignored — when they contributed to the effect he sought. In his view, the art and science of the master goldsmith gave the jewelry its importance;

231

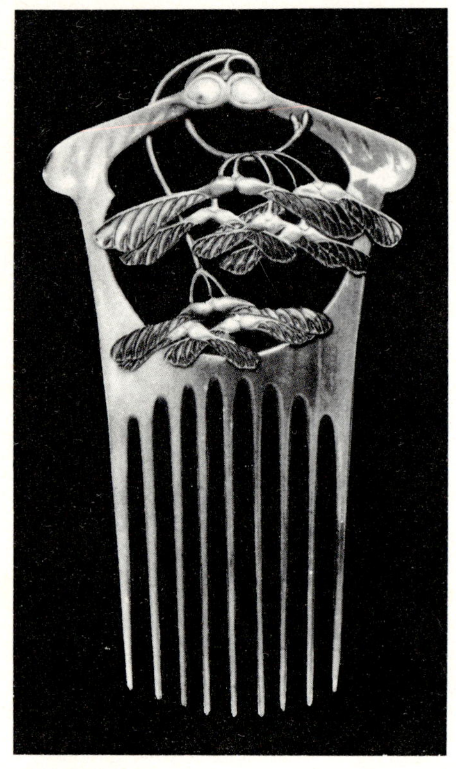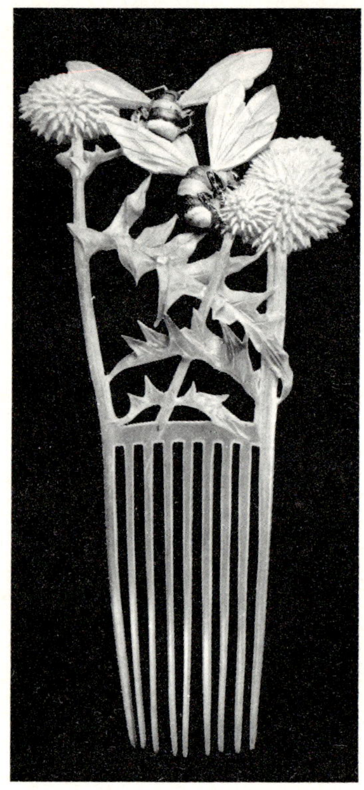

Lucien Gallard   (left) Carved horn comb, 1906; (right) Carved horn comb, 1902

in this spirit, Lalique used as models field flowers, insects, butterflies, snails, frogs, anything that walked, crawled, or flew, transforming them into pendants, bracelets, combs, or hairpins; into all of these he infused the breath of life, and always with a delicacy and restraint which seemed to smile slyly at the Parisian lady, her nerves, her "vapors," while offering in homage his rays of poetry.

Lalique's success grew in France and beyond, creating many imitators. Almost all jewelers now set to work making Modern Style products. Some, like Henri Dubret, made only leaves and flowers; others, like Wolfers, experimented with the bizarre, introducing bats, crabs, reptiles, ants, aphids, or naked women treated like miniature statues. The cases at the salons were filled with these odd pieces. Some jewelers engaged the masters of art nouveau as designers. Fouquet worked with Mucha; Ververt commissioned designs from Grasset and Colonna.

the expansion of art nouveau

We have seen how art nouveau came into being almost simultaneously in Brussels, Nancy, Paris, Vienna, Munich, London, and Glasgow. Nor did the style remain confined to these cities. We can distinguish, moreover, in its diverse modes of expression (taking into account the exceptions and reservations which such discriminations entail) a Latin current and a German current, which, using the same language, speak with their own particular accent.

Even though there were then many fewer exhibitions and artistic exchanges than there are today, artists still made an effort to be in touch with fellow artists in other countries who shared their ideas. From his gallery in Paris, Bing was in contact with Meier-Graefe, who became the founder in Berlin of the review *Pan*. In 1896, Brinckmann, the very active director of the Kunstgewerbe Museum in Hamburg, organized an exhibition of engravings and posters, inviting a cosmopolitan group to contribute: from Munich, Thomas Th. Heine; from Belgium, Van Rysselberghe; from England, Walter Crane, Dudley Hardy, and Beardsley; while Paris sent an entire battalion, among which were works by Toulouse-Lautrec, Chéret, Steinlen, Puvis de Chavannes, Vallotton, Grasset, and Mucha.

The World's Fair of 1900, in which several of the national pavilions seemed, in their disparate architecture, merely to affirm the triumph of eclecticism, still contained a decorative arts section where art nouveau held its own. France was the country with the largest exhibit of the new style. But the only presentation catalogue which, in its illustration, design, and typography was completely modern, and commissioned for the occasion, was the German one, designed by Bernhard Pankok. The text was a good indication that art nouveau was accepted in Germany only by a minority, and that the general public still preferred the old styles; onetheless, the mere fact of saying this in an official catalogue of such modern format was at least a gesture, and all the more remarkable as the catalogue was also a showcase for all aspects of the German economy.

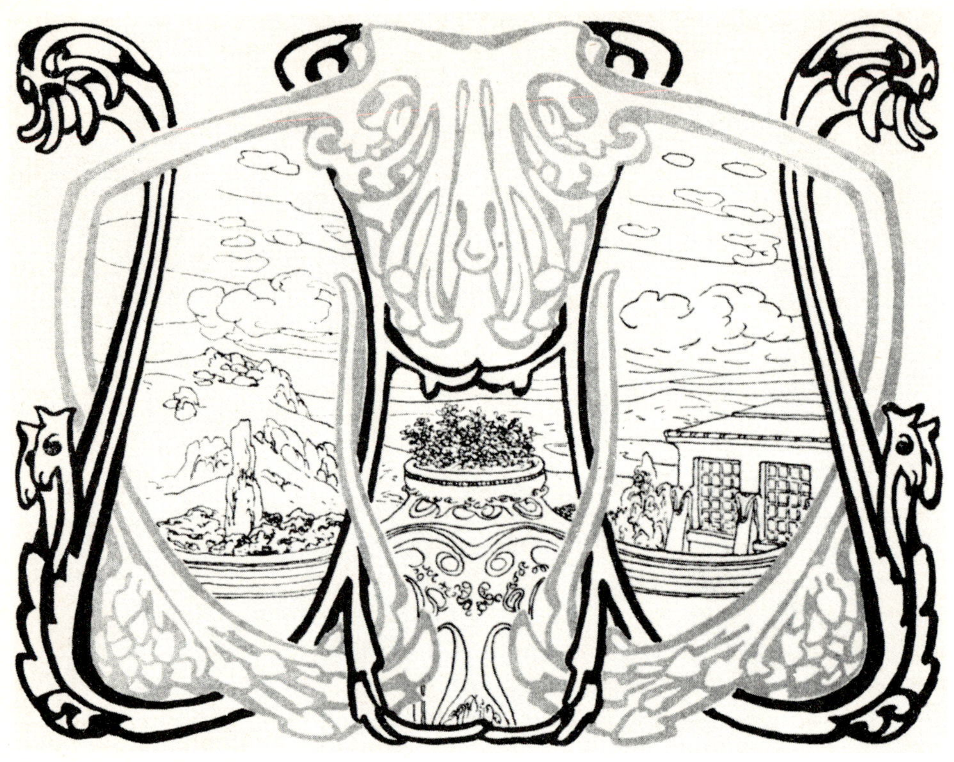

The proving ground of the World's Fair, let us not forget, took place when art nouveau reached the zenith of its popularity: thus, it attests to the limits of its influence. Beyond the capitals of art, and outside of a relatively limited public which accepted it, for reasons of either taste or snobbery, only useful objects of metalcraft, simple and practical, were copied. Whatever their origin, they were referred to as "English style." It is also true that there was a clientele almost everywhere in Europe who appreciated the new style before it became bastardized by industry. Innovators, too, in different technical areas were won over by the powerful attraction exerted by the new style.

Thus, the Bing and Groendal porcelain company in Copenhagen, with a world-wide reputation, modified its classic forms and highly naturalistic flower designs. The example of Johan Rohde (1846–1935) points to the precocious evolution which took place in the Scandinavian countries, directed toward purity of architecture and object. Beginning

234

his career as a painter, Rohde was a follower of the Pont-Aven school, and a friend of Maurice Denis. Then in 1897, he exhibited a cube-shaped armoire, devoid of ornament or molding, whose entire style was a function of its proportions and the quality of the cabinetwork — the first example of the kind of simplified furniture which would soon be all over the market in the twentieth century. Rohde subsequently designed metalwork for Georg Jensen, of equally austere appearance — a marked contrast to the overloaded period copies usual at this time. The movement he started in Copenhagen spread to the other Scandinavian countries. The Finnish architect Eliel Saarinen gave art nouveau a highly personal interpretation — World's Fair Pavilion, Paris; Architect's House, Kirkkonummi (1903); Helsinki Museum (1910) — before turning toward a new decorative order.

The Italians christened art nouveau *Stile Liberty*. The architect Aronco had a fertile imagination, but of a kind which led him to mix memories of the Sezession with a little Jugendstil, adding a few echoes of antiquity: the result could only be a more sophisticated version of an earlier eclectic style. After the 1899 earthquake, Aronco was summoned to Constantinople by the sultan; once there, on the pretext of accommodating to Mussulman tradition, he indulged in unrestrained eccentricity. The Milanese Giuseppe Sommaruga (1867–1917) had an altogether different idea of Liberty style. His facades, with their rectangular windows, would seem to have obvious roots in Italian tradition. They were covered, however, with sculptural reliefs, inspired by the baroque, but so protruberant that they no longer seem part of the building. The ensemble was handled with great care, particularly the conjunction of sculpture and ironwork. Among the buildings designed by Sommaruga in northern Italy were the Hotel del Campo dei Fiori, near Varese, and the Palazzo Castiglioni on the Corso Venezia in Milan (1903). The latter is distinguished by a completely classical structure, luxuriant with decorative motifs which reflect, not without a certain heavy-handedness, the new style of the period. Far removed from the formulas of these two architects is the surprising discovery in Florence, on the Via Scipione-Ammirato, of a house designed by Michelazzi, and related, in its felicity of expression, to the styles of Horta and Guimard. In Palermo, the architect Ernesto Basile tried to express a Stile Liberty that would be totally Sicilian. In his floral motifs, we find local vegetation, while his facades atempt to weld Modern to Byzantine, Arabic, and Gothic. They also reveal, in somewhat crude

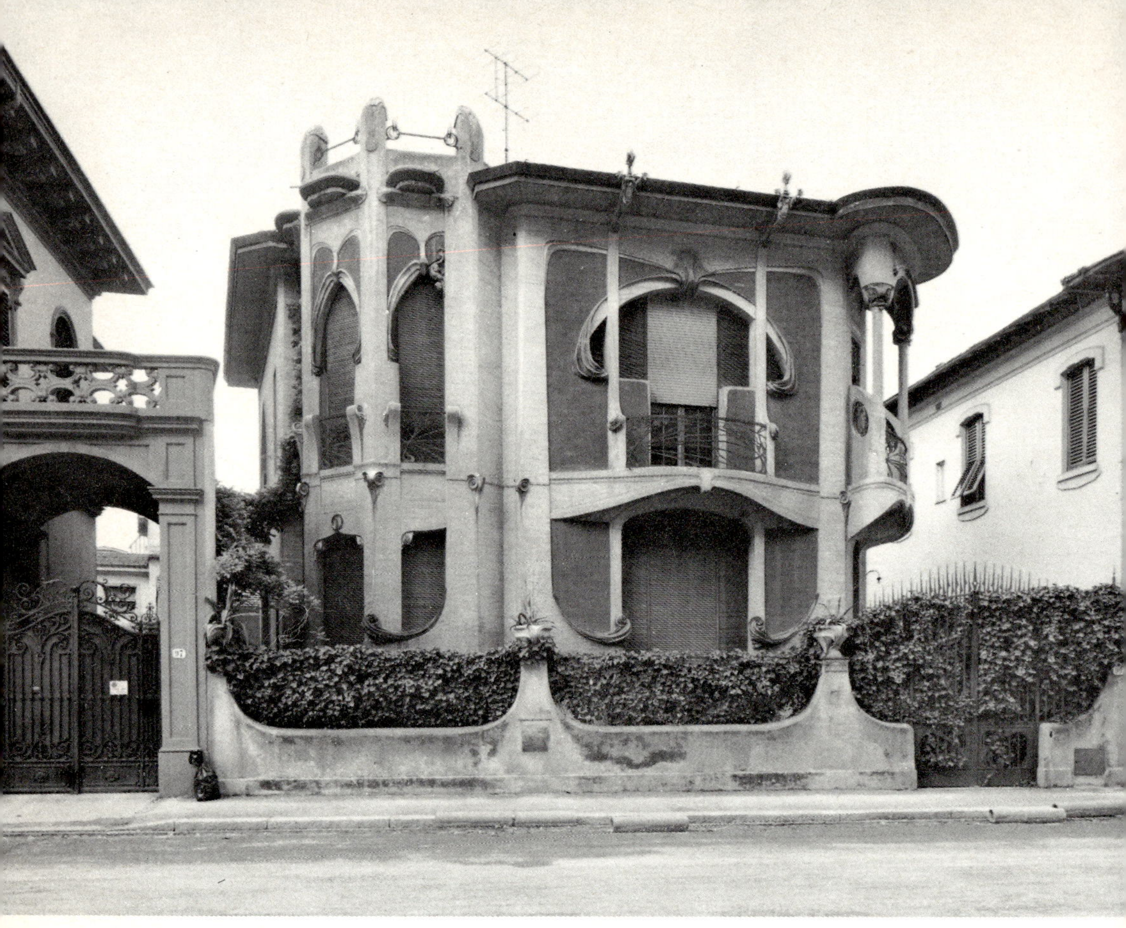

MICHELAZZI   Villa, Florence, 1901

form, the decorative influence of Guimard (Chapel of Santa Maria di Gesu, Villino Caruso). With its vast mural paintings and carved wood paneling, Basile's most accomplished building was the town house Villa Igiea (1899), which manages to avoid all reference to the antique.

First St. Petersburg, then Moscow entered a period of artistic ferment inspired by the Russian discovery of French painting — in particular, Seurat, Gauguin, and Van Gogh. France was the lodestar for artists. In 1895, Serge de Diaghilev paid a visit to Paris, accompanied by Alexandre Benois. Two years later, Diaghilev founded the review *Mir Iskousstva* which, along with examples of Russian folk art, heralded the new currents in art. Art and literary magazines burgeoned during this period. There were several hundred in Russia alone, which all disappeared with the Revolution. The example of Paris and the School of Nancy was disseminated through the textile designs of Yakouchivo;

the Fabergé workshops were in touch with Gallé, as were the crafts studios of Mamontov, whose products were very popular between 1898 and 1905. The Moscow Art Theater revealed new concepts in stage design which, executed by Bakst, Benois, and Gontcharova, were acclaimed shortly thereafter in Paris with the *Ballets Russes* of Diaghilev.

tiffany and company

The activity of Louis Comfort Tiffany (1848–1933) in the United States was, at least at the beginning, very dependent upon European art nouveau. Tiffany had studied painting in Paris, where he became particularly interested in design. His first real guidance came from E. C. Moore, who was a collector of exotic objects before becoming artistic director of Tiffany and Company. Moore had amassed a large collection of decorative objects — Turkish, Persian, Indian, Chinese, and Japanese — providing the designer with an inexhaustible repertory of models. Tiffany never tried to copy, or even to imitate; his inspiration came from the spirit of an object, pointing the way to new forms.

Tiffany began by experiments with ceramics, but, as soon as he exhibited his first glass objects, they were hailed with an acclaim which went far beyond the usual confines of connoisseurs, converting commerce and industry. This success obliged Tiffany to increase his production. When Bing was traveling through the United States, the two met and the Paris dealer immediately became as enthusiastic about Tiffany glass as the designer's compatriots. It was the impact of Tiffany's work which accounts for Bing's decision to give up, in part, his sales of Far Eastern objects, and to open his gallery, l'Art Nouveau, in the rue de Provence; here, he entered into a cooperative agreement with Tiffany, whose work he promoted in France through brochures, in which he gave his own impressions of the new aesthetic (*Culture artistique en Amérique,* 1896). And, soon, Tiffany objects were known throughout Europe.

Tiffany's art is contemporary with that of his compatriot Loïe Fuller; despite the opposition of a static and a dynamic art, we find in both the same spirals and flamelike movement. Tiffany gave Americans the illumination of pure fantasy, which had been totally lacking in their art. His gifts of assimilation, in contrast to so many others, fertilized his inventiveness; but since he was capable of doing anything he

wanted, he went from one style to another. The interior decorating
schemes which he designed and executed for rich New Yorkers were
a confusion of marvels. In his own house, surrounding a central fire-
place in a rustic style, suggesting present-day country houses, a multi-
tude of lamps were hung from the ceiling at every height; there were
oriental oil lamps, gothic censers, ostrich eggs. Tiffany was not attempting to create harmony from the juxtaposition of hangings, stained
glass, and bibelots. Moved by his horror of the conventional, he escaped
into the exotic disorder which was the orientalism of the time.

Mastering the art of stained glass led Tiffany to seek new materials
in the making of glassware. (At the Paris Salon of 1895, Tiffany
exhibited glass based upon works by Bonnard, Vuillard, Sérusier,
Lautrec, and Vallotton.) By 1892, he had perfected material which
could vary in degrees of opalescence; the glass might contain metallic

Louis Comfort Tiffany   Peacock vase, 1895

Louis Comfort Tiffany   Bowl, 1896

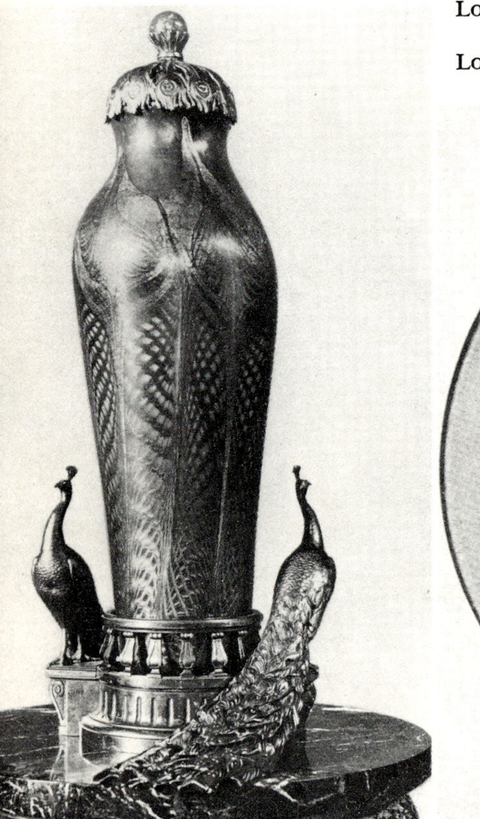

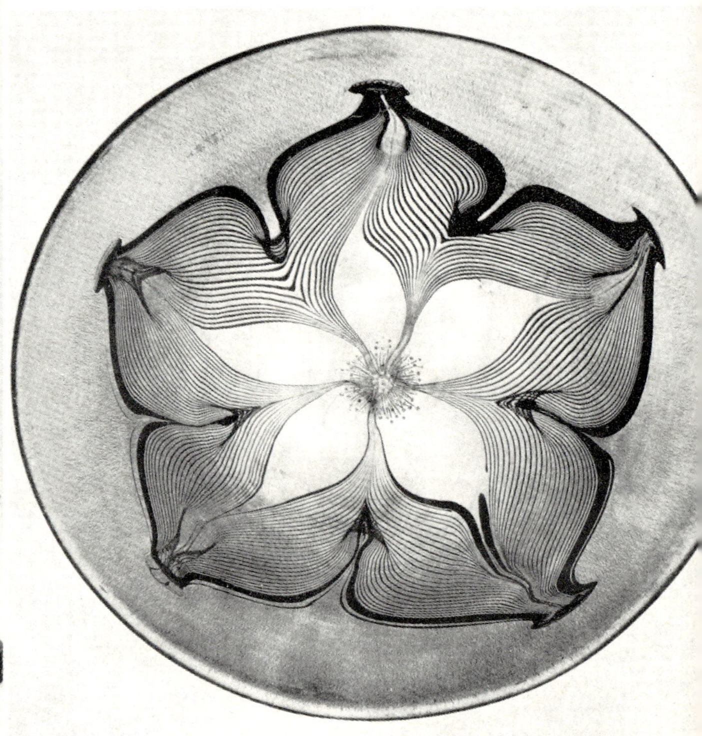

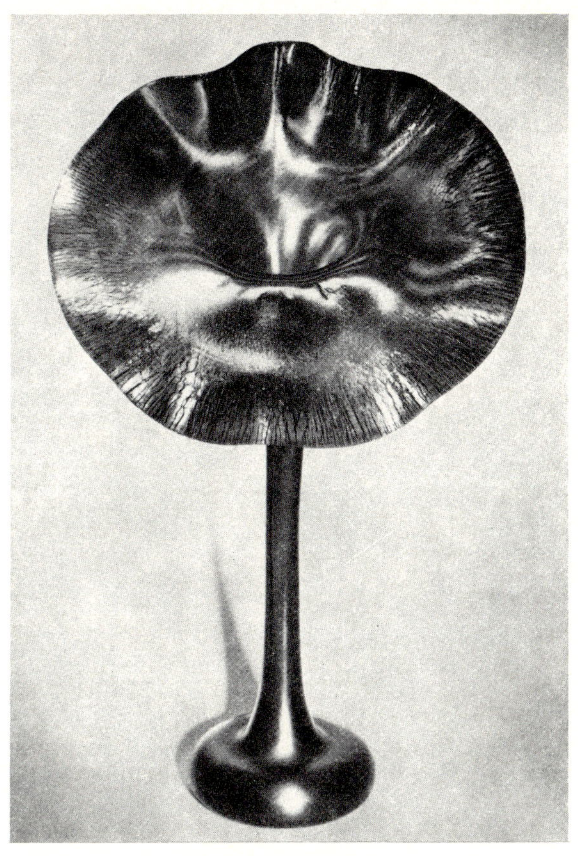

Louis Comfort Tiffany   Vase, ca. 1900

wire or filigree, or it could have a grainy patina made by blobs of
color run together, creating effects of delicate subtlety. Using these
techniques, Tiffany designed ornamental vases, then lamps in which
metal and glass mosaics were used to great effect, and which met with
immediate — and continued — success. He then began to experiment
with new forms, like the night lights in ogival shape, which were
adopted for the commercial market. Tiffany will inevitably be compared with Gallé, whose vases were made a decade earlier; Gallé glass
is the work of a poet, enamored of nature — the translucence reflects
nature's atmospheric nuances. Tiffany was more attracted by curvilinear geometry, as it could be applied to forms which, bolder than
those of Gallé, are less related to nature, and therefore better suited
to the quasi-industrial production of his "studios."

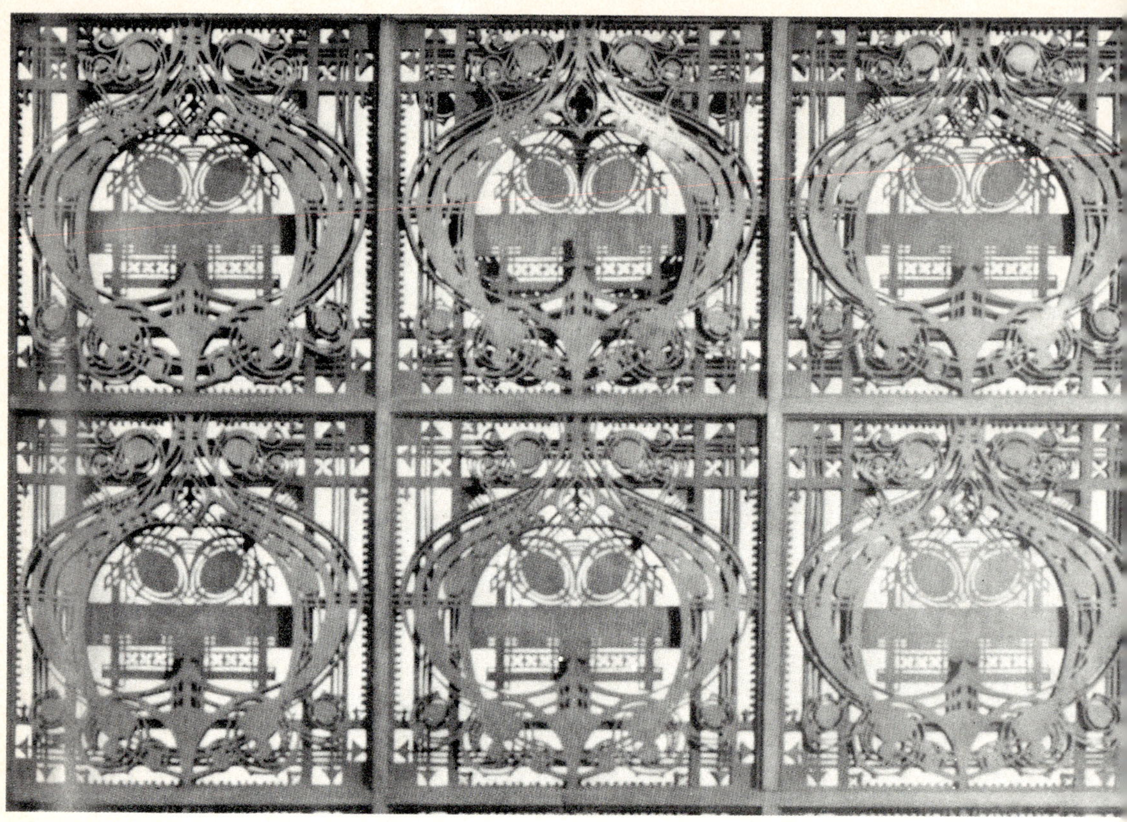

Louis Sullivan   Grill for Carson, Pirie, Scott Department Store, 1899–1904

The name of Louis Sullivan (1856–1924) is so closely associated with the first functional buildings of the Chicago School that his taste for design is too often overlooked. Trained at the Ecole des Beaux-Arts in Paris, he had worked for the architectural firm of Le Baron Jenney, where he learned the techniques of cast-iron scaffolding and glass sheathing. He hoped to combine a typically American commercial architecture with European design. The idea of this fusion was the direct influence of art nouveau, then in full flower. Sullivan restricted his ornament to the ground floor, the entrance ways, the staircases, or the top of his high-rise buildings (twelve to fourteen floors), which then only existed in the United States. Whether of stone or iron, Sullivan's buildings stood out, their wild exuberance a dramatic contrast to the rigid quadrilaterals of neighboring structures. In Sullivan's work we find, amplified and complicated, the interlace of curve and counter-curve analogous to the naturalism of Parisian Modern Style.

240

the graphic arts

When art nouveau moved beyond the enlightened circles of the sophisticated to reach a large public, it was through the intermediary of the graphic arts. The print was of interest to intellectuals and collectors whose curiosity was aroused by anything new. But the poster, by definition, reached everybody. The popularity of art nouveau coincided precisely with the first appearance of the illustrated wall poster used for publicity. This is the form of art nouveau which took to the streets, enjoined to conquer the masses. Since its goal was to attract the attention of passers-by, and to exercise its powers of persuasion, the poster had to communicate in a clear and easily understood language. This encounter proved a great opportunity. It showed those critics who had seen art nouveau as a diversion for aesthetes that it could also be a living art, capable of addressing the masses. For this task, moreover, manufacturers and businessmen were quick to give their blessing. Thanks to the poster, art nouveau was welcome everywhere.

engravings and books

We have already noted the attraction of the woodcut for artists in search of new forms. The famous frontispiece of Mackmurdo's book, *Wren's City Churches,* contains the seed of graphic inventions which nourished an entire area of art. This expressive page sets forth the pre-

cepts which will animate modern graphic arts; the title is incorporated
into a floral motif, to the point of being indistinguishable from it; the
lines of the drawing develop in semiparallels which follow all the inflec-
tions of the design, expanding and multiplying until they fill the entire
page with a wavelike pattern, opening up the central theme to infinity.

We find these same characteristics in more schematic engravings by
Van de Velde; these consist of a few basic curves, deeply incised, which
seem to reproduce one another. The same decorative method is used
by Peter Behrens, by Munch, by Ricketts, in Voysey's textiles, and in
some Tiffany glass. It should be noted that the principle of linear

ARTHUR HEYGATE MACKMURDO   Title page
for *Wren's City Churches,* 1883

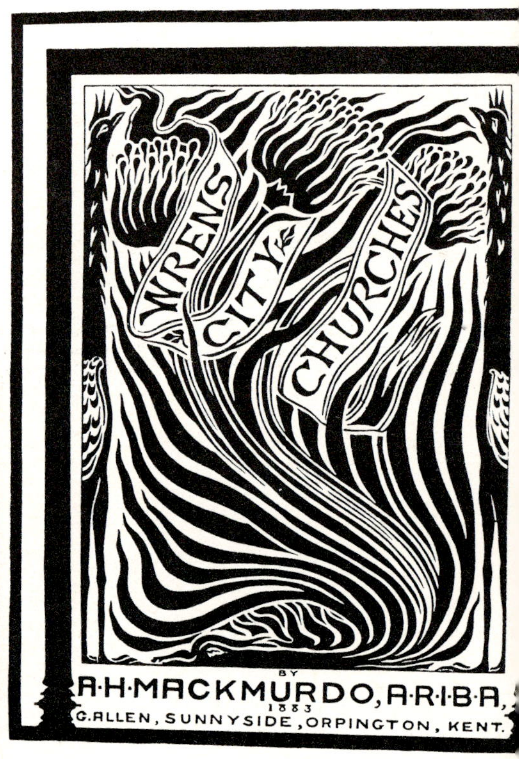

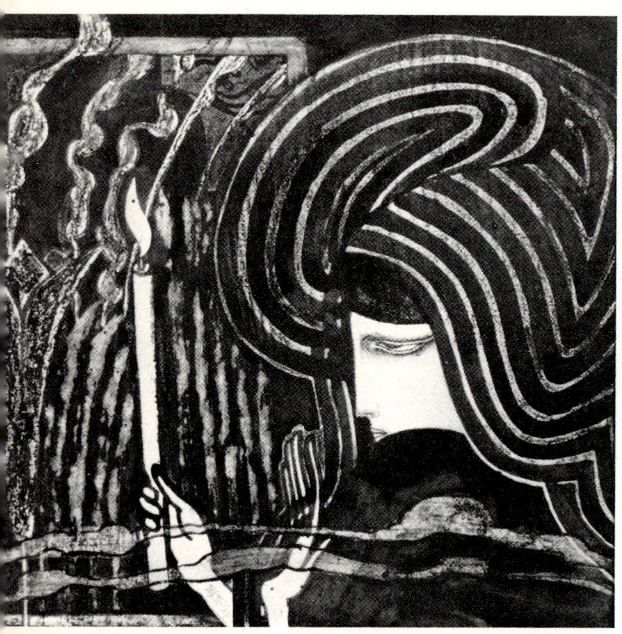

JAN TH. TOOROP   *Finding Oneself,* 1893

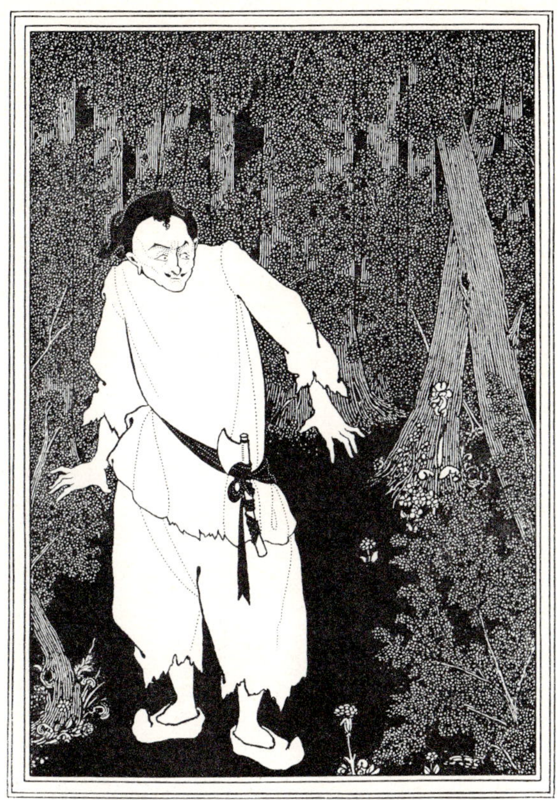

AUBREY BEARDSLEY *Ali Baba in the Forest,* 1897

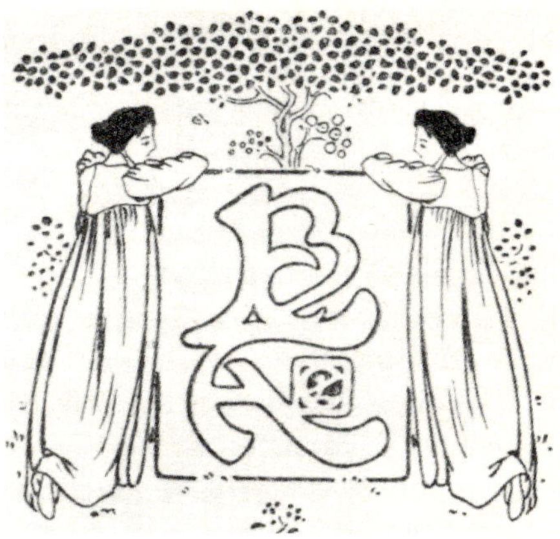

GEORGES AURIOL Monogram, 1901

repetition is also used, but less frequently, outside the graphic arts. Mackintosh furniture, for example, aligned slender verticals, creating a lyre-back effect. The technique was exalted in Toorop's lithographs and posters, quickened by a vibrating rhythm which is one of the more eccentric hallmarks of the period. The same motif appears, in more attenuated form, in the graphic work of Toorop's compatriot Thorn-Prikker, and in other German and Austrian engravers.

In England, turn-of-the-century engraving was dominated by Beardsley; he had evolved a new style perfectly suited to illustration and typography, which could absorb even a wild imagination undercut by ambiguities of humor and irony.

Like Beardsley, Charles Ricketts illustrated Oscar Wilde's works, although he is far removed from the perverse prodigy in both inspiration and technique. Ricketts had carefully studied and remembered the les-

243

sons of Blake's art. He was familiar with the decorative interlace of Irish illuminated manuscripts. In his complicated hatchings, which fuse the modern and the archaic, lascivious figures disport themselves with an innocent air.

Engraving led painters like Fernand Khnopff to stylize their draftsmanship; this proved to be true of many artists who moved naturally from symbolism to art nouveau. In Austria, Koloman Moser contributed to catalogues and posters of the Sezession. When Eckmann, a German artist, began working for the review *Pan,* he revealed a new decorative quality; the fluidity of his drawing seemed to lead inexorably toward abstract ornament.

Engraving moved away from the analytic art of the impressionists, to create the art of synthesis predicated by Gauguin and his disciples. Most of the illustrated books by symbolist writers are enriched by engravings which integrate with the typography, and are perfectly adopted to the lettering and ornamentation. Books, art magazines, even

Will Bradley   Poster, 1895

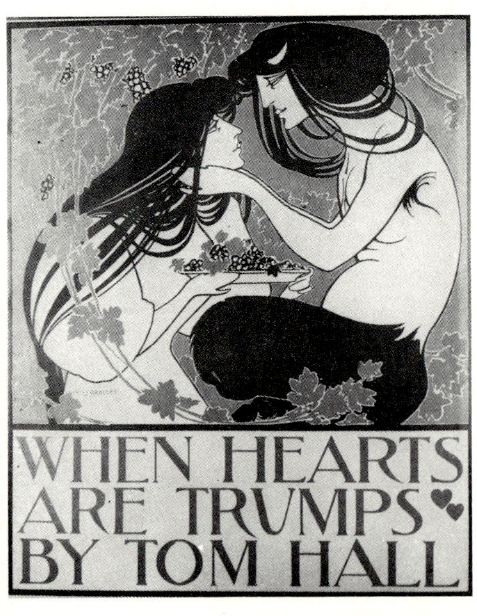

Henry Van de Velde   Binding for
Estampes et Livres, 1892

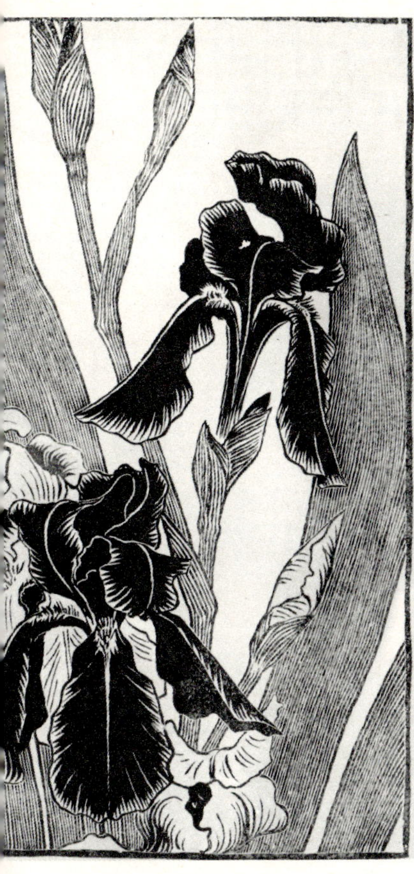

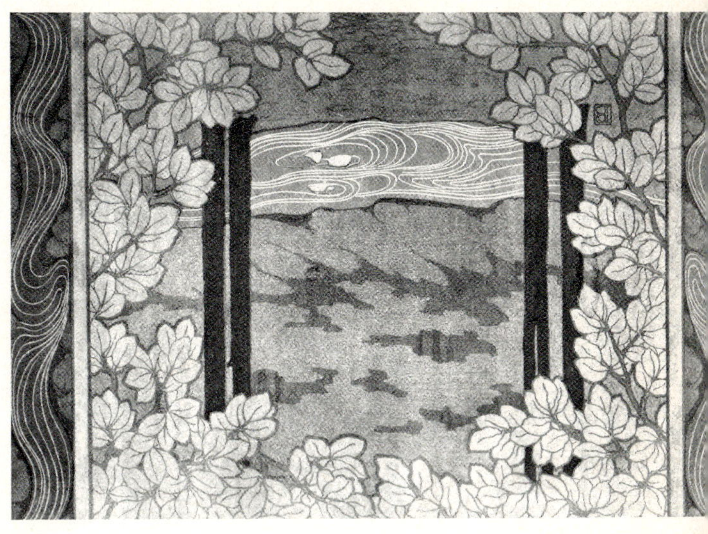

Peter Behrens   *Stream,* 1901

Otto Eckmann   *Iris,* 1896

their advertising brochures became, in their design, both a proclamation and artistic profession of faith. Collectively, they were the response to a need to affirm stylistic unity.

The development of color lithography also paved the way for a new vision of design. The engravers gleefully set to work using methods learned from the Japanese, which enabled them to discover and to evoke a hitherto unknown world of light and color. Mary Cassatt was the first, in a series of prints inspired by the Japanese technique, in which she "Europeanized" the subjects with exquisite taste.

The French painters who were reacting against impressionism found, in engraving, a medium through which they could forge a new style. We have shown earlier how much art nouveau owed to Gauguin and his followers. A seemingly instinctive rejection of the three-

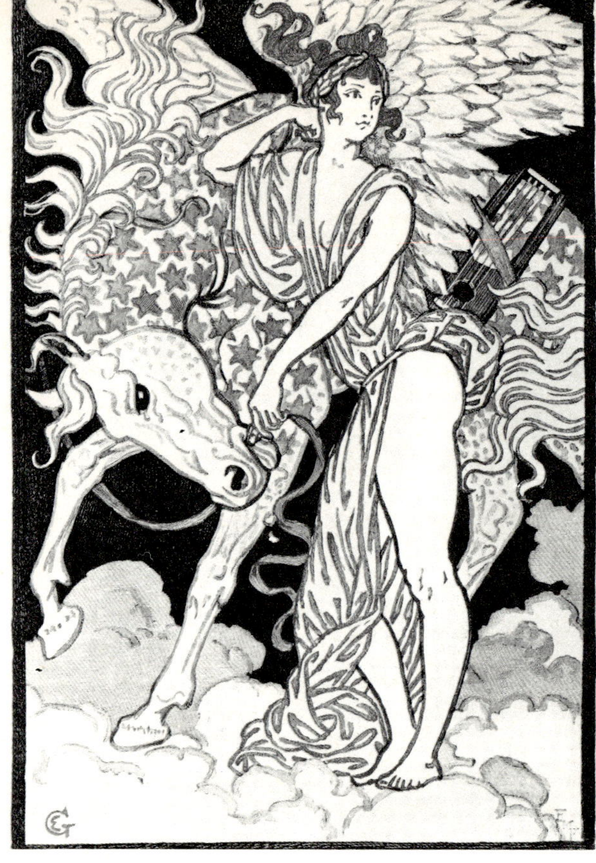

Eugène Grasset   Illustration for *l'Almanach du Bibliophile pour 1901*

dimensional, Manet's flattened volumes, suggested by drawing and his surfaces of contrasting colors, had really pointed the way; Maillol's woodcuts *(Daphnis and Chloe, Virgil's Eclogues)* reworked for too long, perhaps, the same terrain, but his works were always illuminated by the eternal youth of their author.

The ornamental signature called Modern Style had now become the subject of a body of teaching; its precepts were set forth by Eugène Grasset, whose *Méthode de composition ornementale* became a breviary. Grasset placed great importance on lettering, even inventing a typeface. Here, too, he wanted to strip away the decorative, which he called "encumbering archaeological accumulations." Georges Auriol also produced alphabets drawn in brush, vignettes, monograms and bookplates. Their fluid sinuous delicacy and impression of spontaneity all fascinated his contemporaries. "Auriol typeface" with its special ornamentation was used by the most important publishing houses.

246

the poster

In order to succeed, advertising has to seize on aesthetic currents when they are the height of fashion. From the beginnings of the illustrated poster this rule had been followed. Indeed, art nouveau and the poster seemed made for each other. The new style was an art of surface design, with flat areas of color; modeling suggested by the drawing, which might be condensed into outline; simplification of the motif; easily intelligible subject matter; silhouettes which could be grasped at a glance — all of these conditions were fulfilled, to the point that the very first art nouveau posters known were masterpieces. From an artistic point of view, technical perfection means nothing. Admirable pages of typography appeared immediately after the invention of Gutenberg's movable type. It is also worth noting that the illustrated poster was instantly accepted by artists themselves, as a medium worthy of their talents. An art magazine was named *L'Estampe et l'Affiche (Print and Poster),* which appeared from 1897 to 1900;

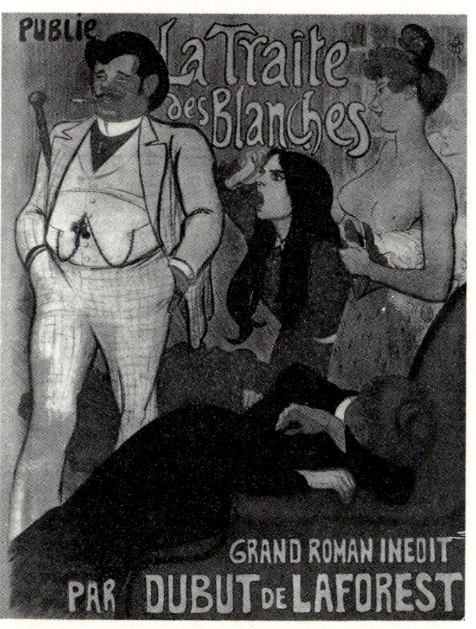

THÉOPHILE ALEXANDRE STEINLEN
Poster for the book
La Traite des Blanches, 1900

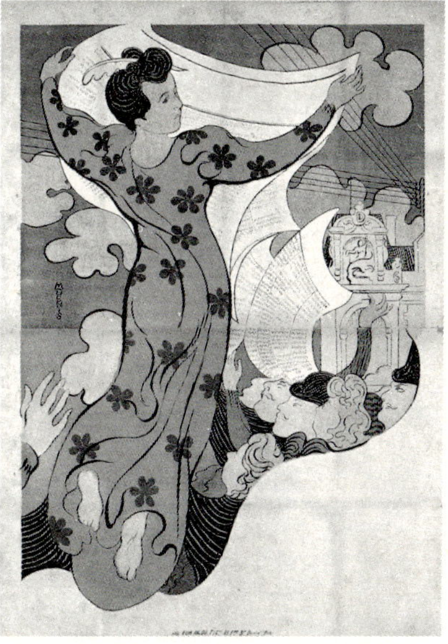

MAURICE DENIS
Poster for a magazine, 1898

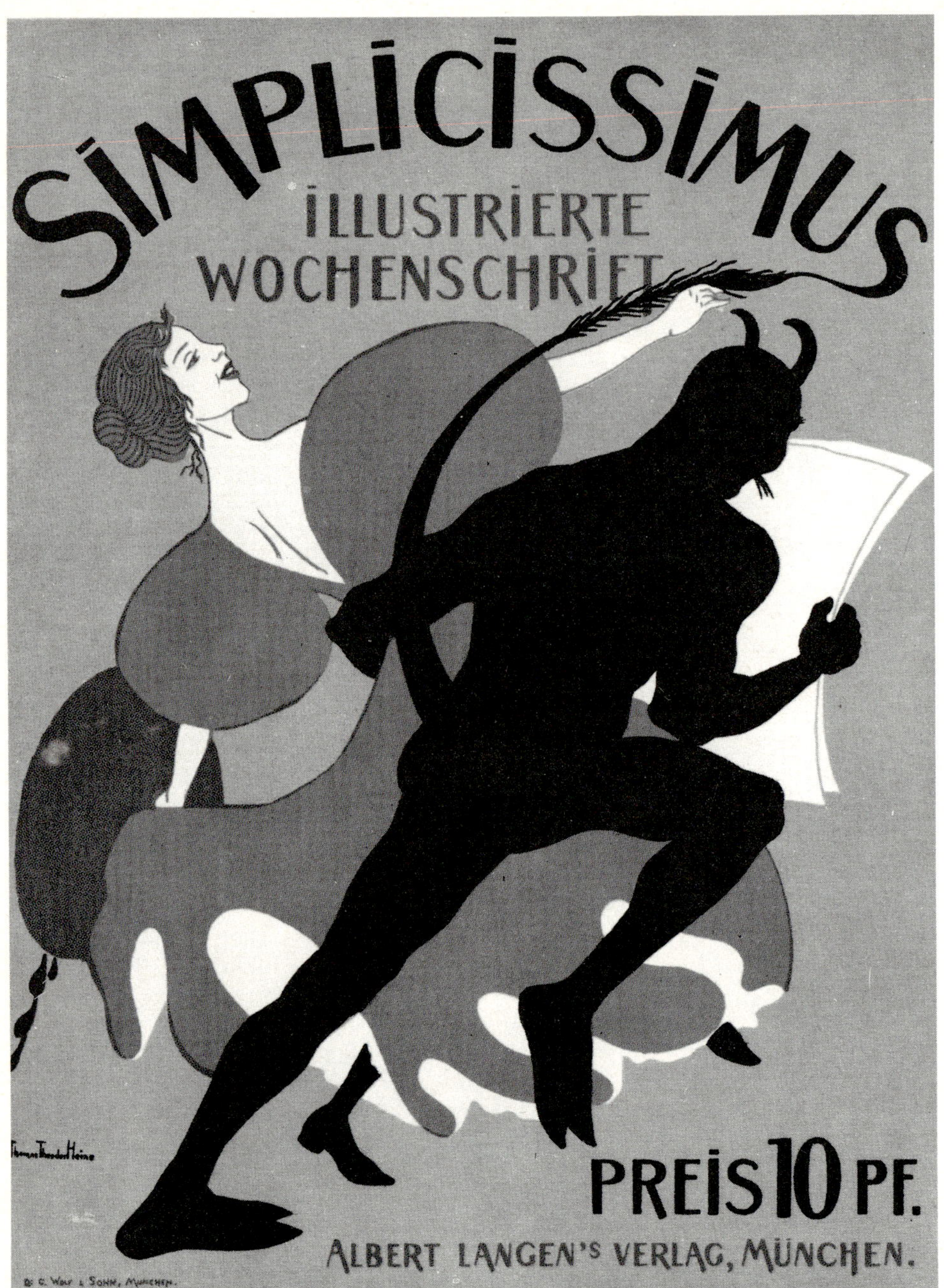

THOMAS THEODOR HEINE   Design for title page of *Simplicissimus,* ca. 1895

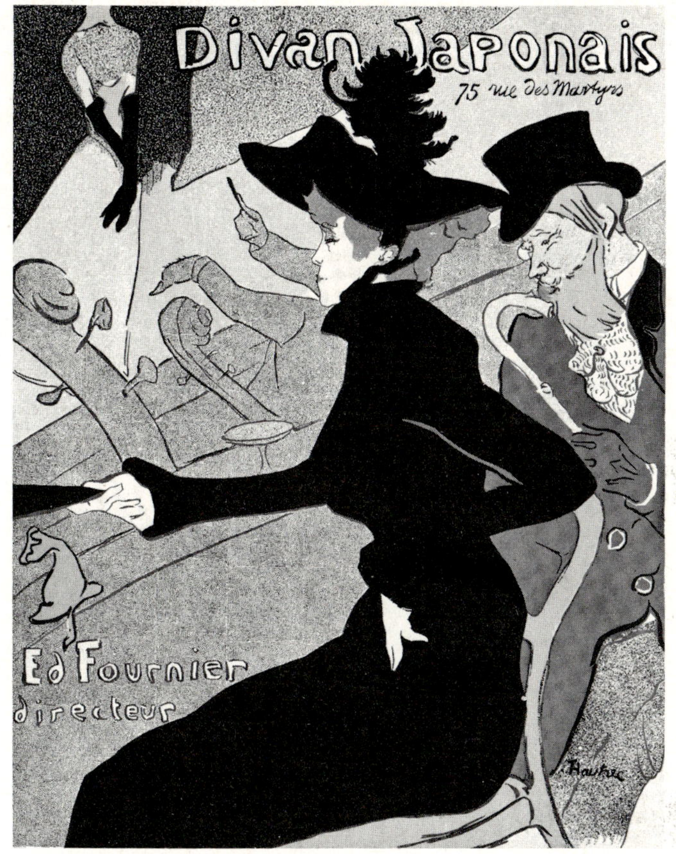

HENRI DE TOULOUSE-LAUTREC   Poster for *Le Divan Japonais,* 1895

the review itself was advertised by a poster — a rather confusing one, in fact — designed by Bonnard. Toulouse-Lautrec burst forth as the great painter of Parisian life, a great artist, *and* a great publicist. Posters like *la Goulue, Reine de Joie, May Milton, Jane Avril, le Divan jayonais, Aristide Bruant, Confetti, la Troupe de Mlle. Eglantine* make their impact through life force, a percussive power, and their own beauty. In 1891, Bonnard designed his poster *France-Champagne* in a lighter but similar style.

The poster is a joyful art form, and will be around for a long time to come. Far from trying to convince the viewer with a body blow, it usually tries to be attractive and memorable — at least, that is the idea. Why else is the poster the first amenity offered a customer?

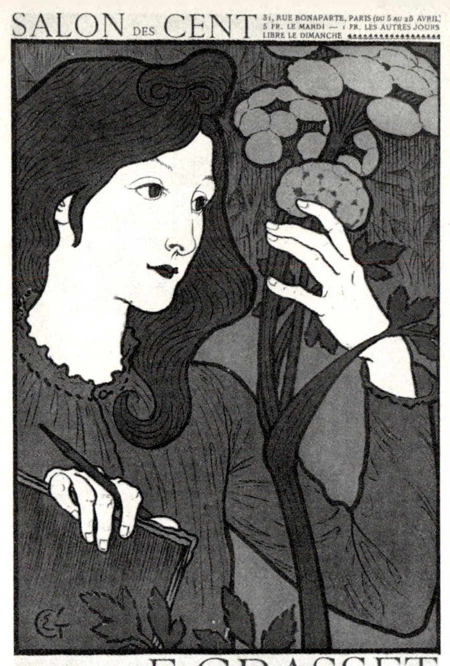

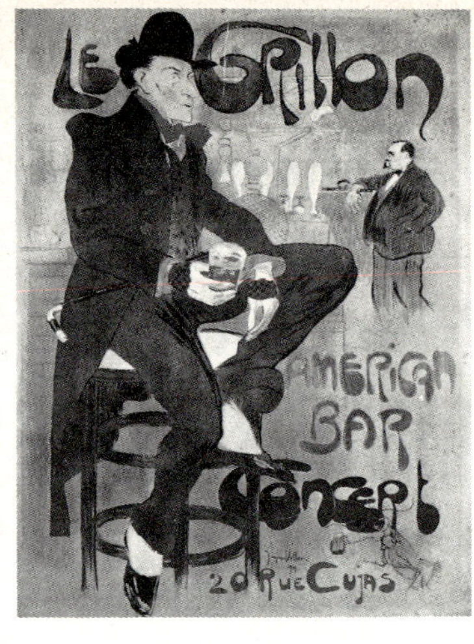

JACQUES VILLON   Poster
for *The Grasshopper,* 1899

EUGÈNE GRASSET   Poster for
Le Salon des Cent, 1897

Jules Chéret (1836–1930) exploited color lithography with exceptional brilliance in innumerable posters. His figures seem to whirl about to dance music, intoxicated by soft colors and sheer pleasure. Any commercial subject, no matter how unpromising — cigarette papers or kerosene — Chéret turned into a pulsating image with vitality and charm. He distributed color in large areas, but, in contrast to the convention of the day, his drawing was whimsical, gay, spontaneous, even frivolous. He is at the opposite pole from Lautrec, who always reveals a hard core of pitiless irony. If Chéret lacked the latter's authority and genius, he could still claim to have educated the public in a taste for bright, bold colors.

The poster had not yet made up rules designed to provoke and shock for the purpose of selling a product. Thus, the most admired painters did not consider it beneath them to ally themselves with commerce. And they were the ones who discovered the most effective means, by playing upon current fads and fantasies, of capturing the customer. Woman, "the eternal feminine" of the period 1900, was, of necessity, the primordial subject; attitudes, fashions, smiles played a large role. No one worried about naturalism; this was theater, in avowedly sophisticated form, a domain in which Modern Style became affectation,

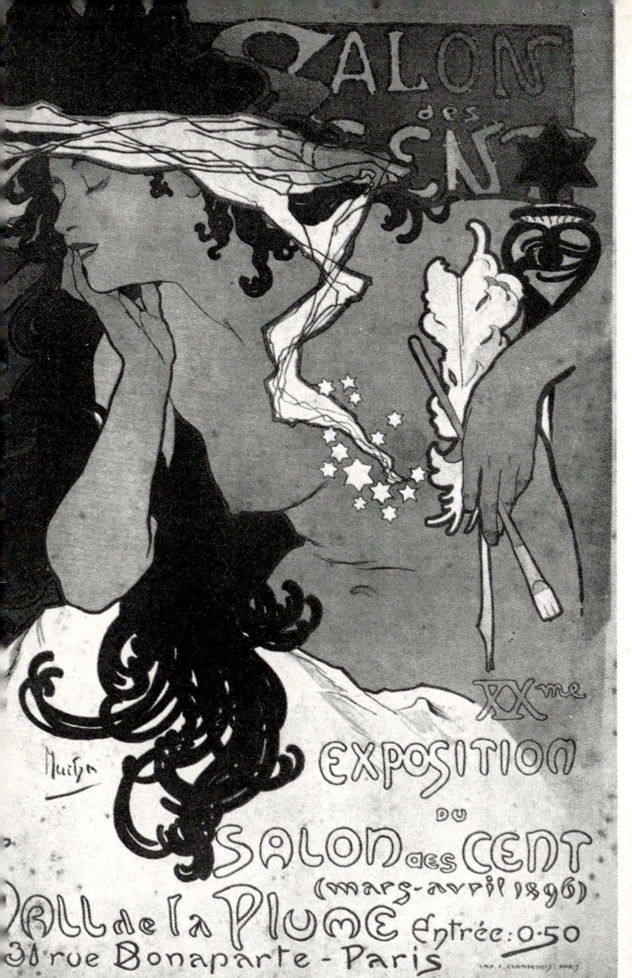

Alfons-Maria Mucha   Poster for
Le Salon des Cent, 1896

Alfons-Maria Mucha
Poster for *La Plume*, 1896

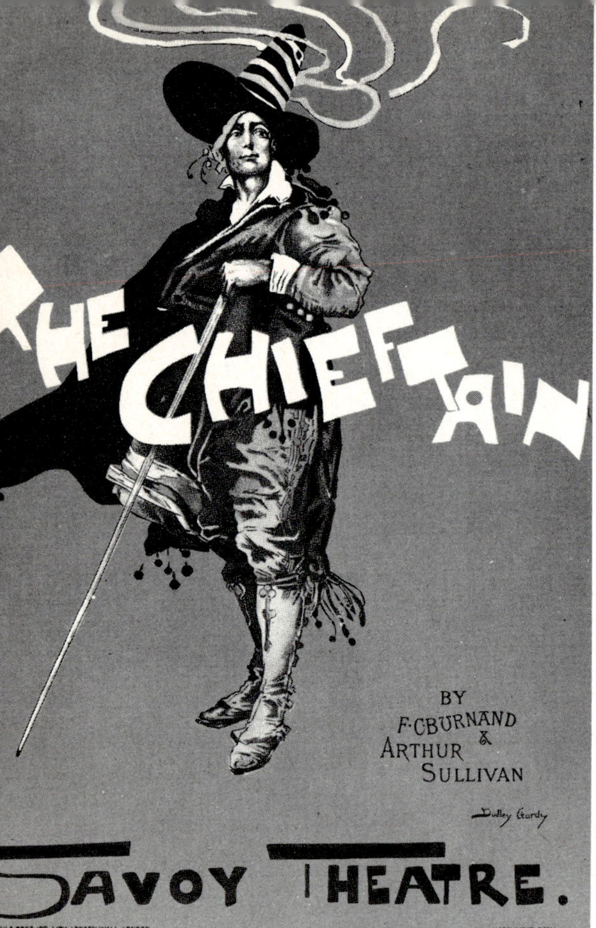

DUDLEY HARDY   Poster for
The Chieftain, 1896

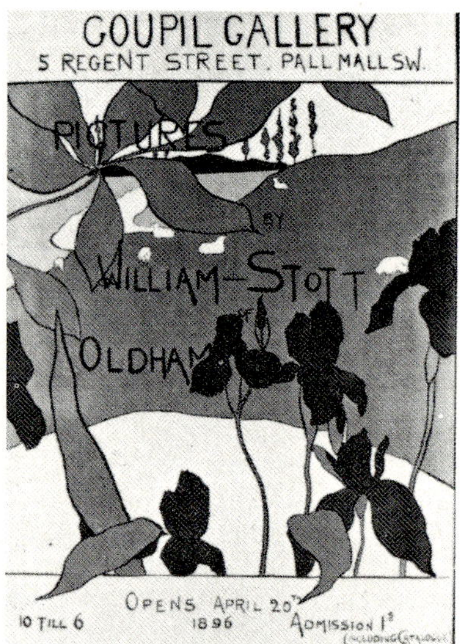

WILLIAM STOTT   Poster for
Goupil Gallery, 1896

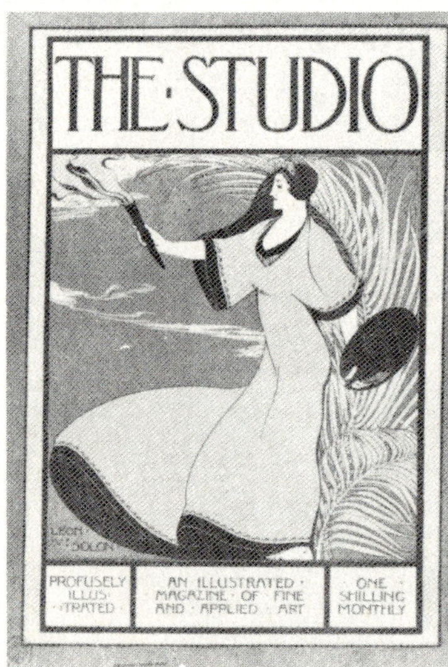

LEÓN W. SOLON   Poster for the
review *The Studio*, 1896

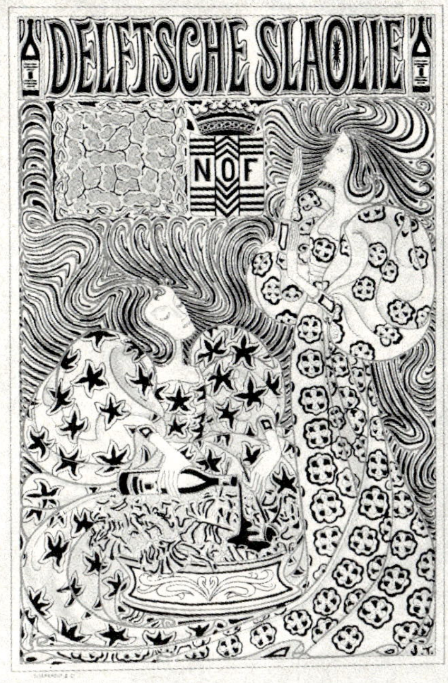

A. A. TURBAYNE   Cover for Peacock Edition, Macmillan's Illustrated Standard Novels, 1898

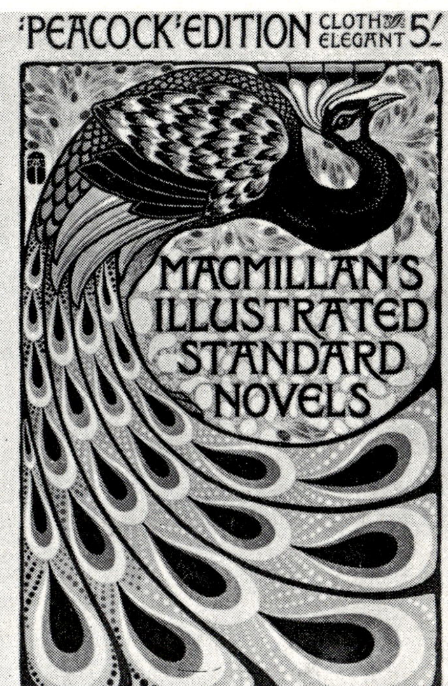

JAN TH. TOOROP   Poster for salad oil, 1897

turning into a caricature of itself. De Feure, the poet of flower-woman, Grasset, Willette, all followed this movement. Steinlein, too, more vulgar and more somber, remained faithful to its rules. With gentle curves, Maurice Denis made *la Depêche de Toulouse* famous, and Jacques Villon, whose beginnings were in commercial art, revealed the first phase of his talent in the poster.

The master of the art nouveau poster, the prince of elegant "Parisianism" was Mucha (1860-1939), a Czech by birth, who had come to Paris to work with Jean-Paul Laurens. He began, first of all, under the influence of his teacher, by becoming an honest history painter – until one event completely transformed his career: he was given the commission for a poster to advertise *Gismonda,* a play by Victorien Sardou,

253

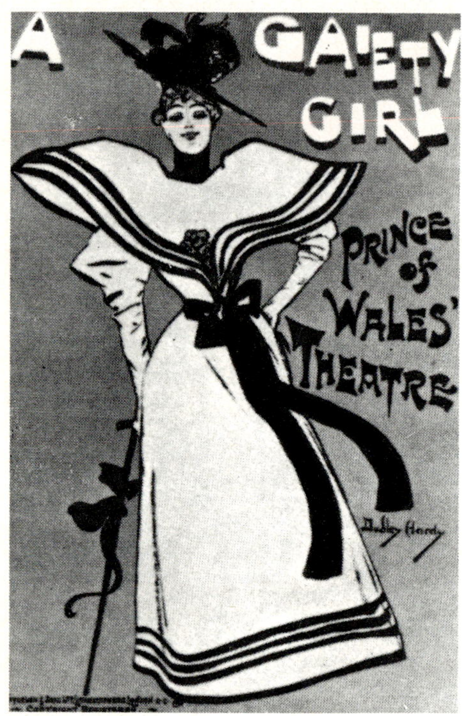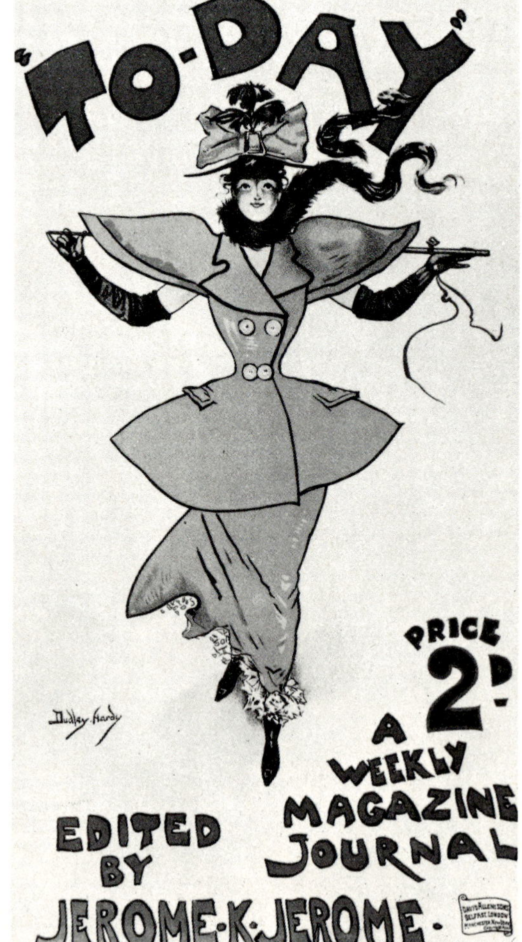

DUDLEY HARDY   Poster for
A Gaiety Girl, 1893

DUDLEY HARDY   Poster for the
newspaper *To-day,* 1893

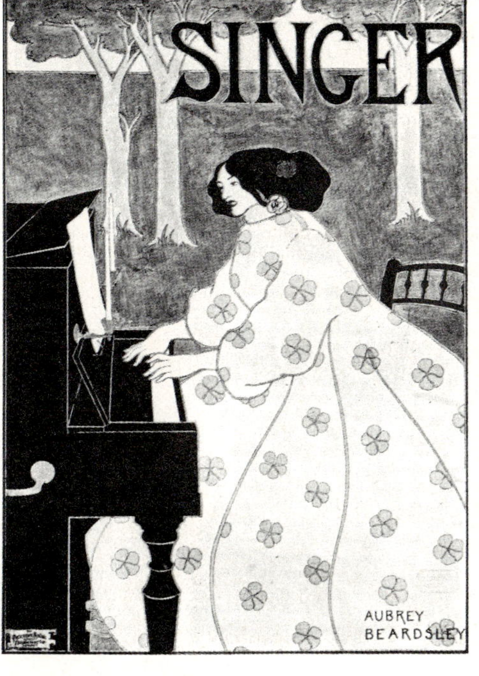

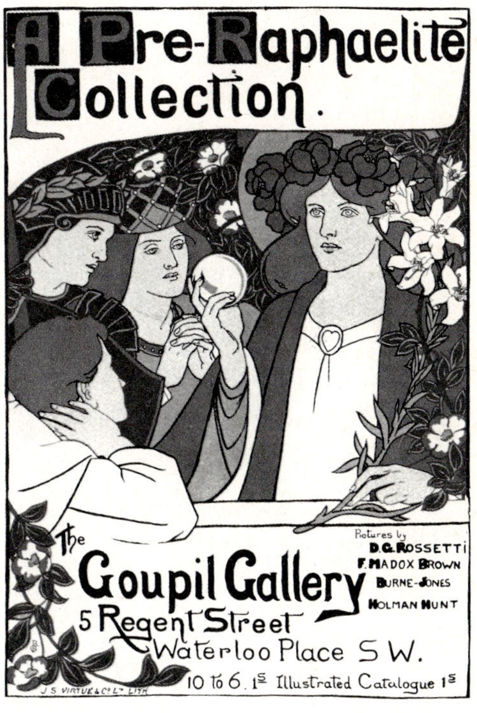

AUBREY BEARDSLEY   Poster for the
Singer Sewing Machine, 1898

WALFORD GRAHAM ROBERTSON   Poster for
the Pre-Raphaelite Exhibition, 1894

in which the starring role was played by Sarah Bernhardt (1895). The
great actress was captivated. It was Mucha, thereafter, in the posters
he did for most of her plays, until the final *l'Aiglon,* who immortalized
her fame on every wall in Paris. Mucha was part of the symbolist
cenacles, as well as an accolyte of groups devoted to the occult. If we
can no longer unravel the overlay of intentions hidden in the innumerable scrolls of Mucha's artificial decors, it is still impossible to resist
the charm of the highly personal style which quickens them. His style
remained his own, even when he did publicity for the large commercial
enterprises which clamored for his signature.

The English poster had its own special idiom: a somewhat rigid
linear quality, vast areas of unmistakable "English green" and vermilion,

Eugène Grasset   Poster for
the ink L. Marquet, 1892

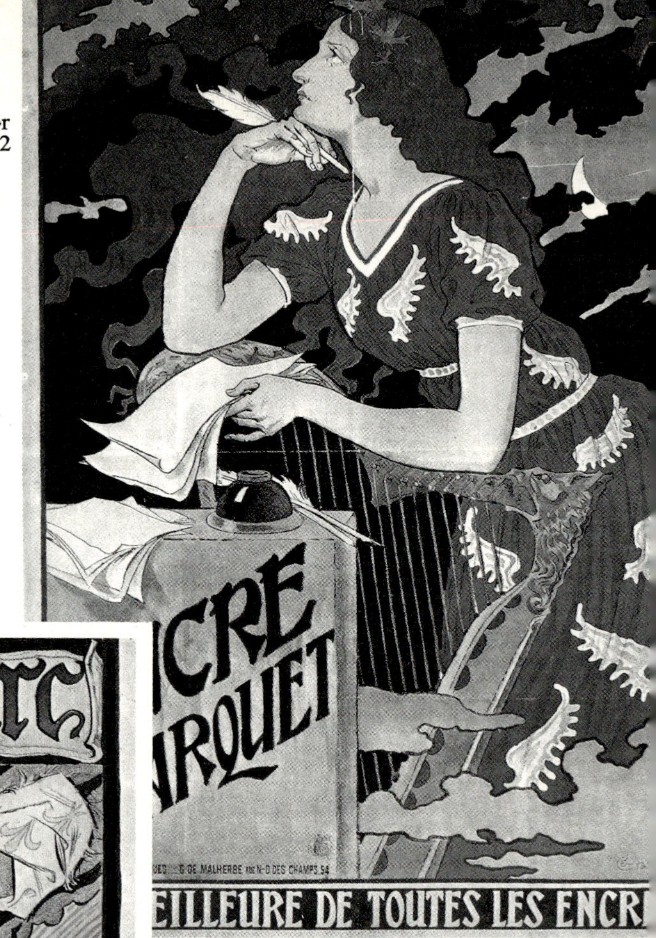

Eugène Grasset   Poster of
Sarah Bernhardt as Joan of Arc, 1893

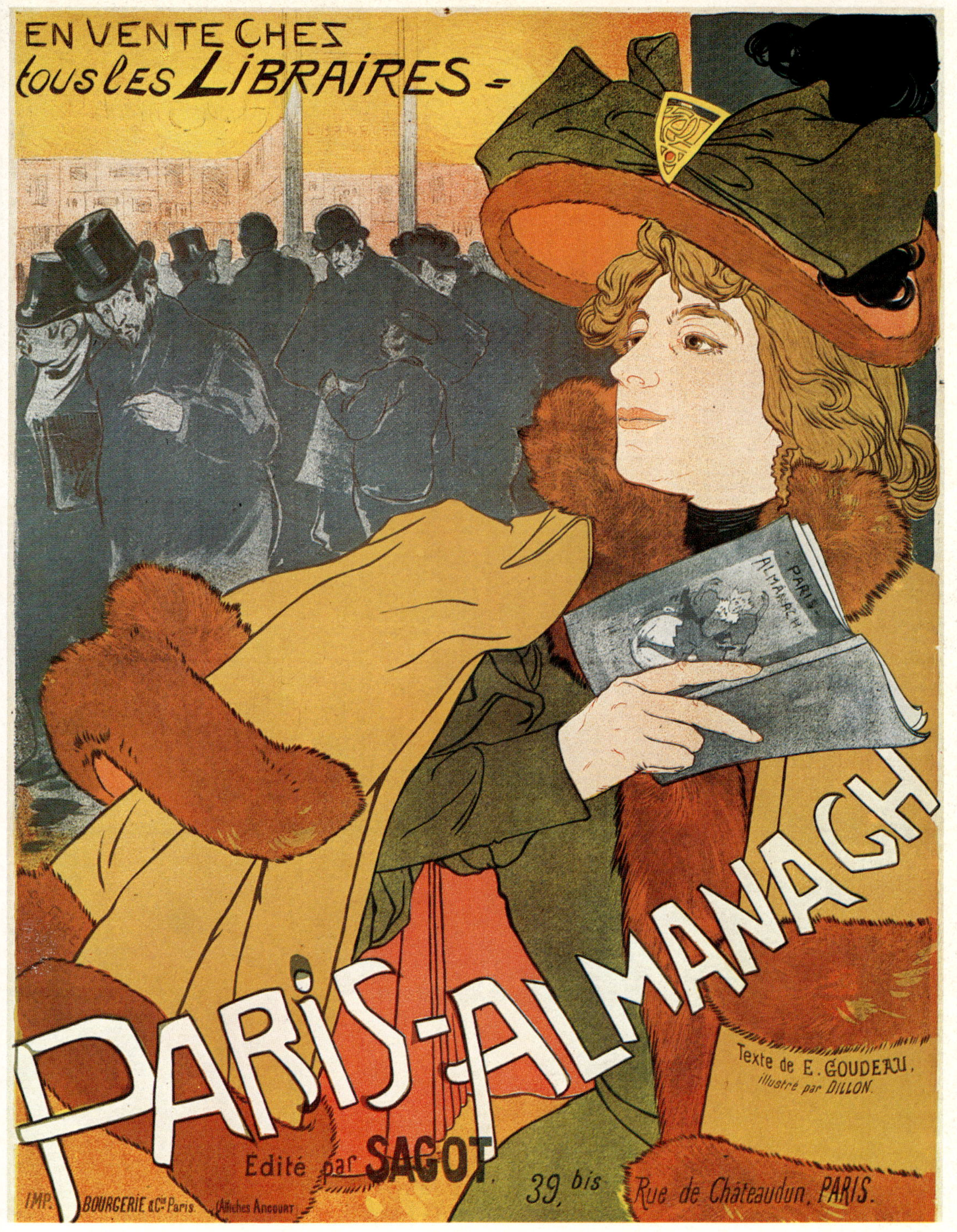

GEORGES DE FEURE   Poster for *Paris-Almanach*, 1895

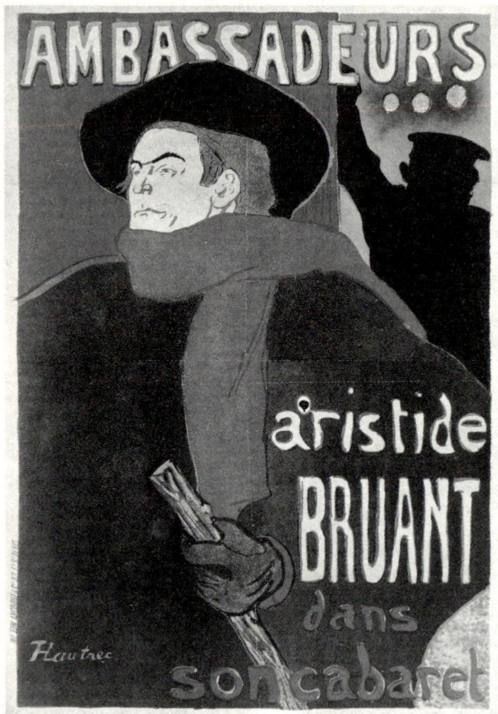

HENRI DE TOULOUSE-LAUTREC
Poster for *Reine de Joie*, 1892

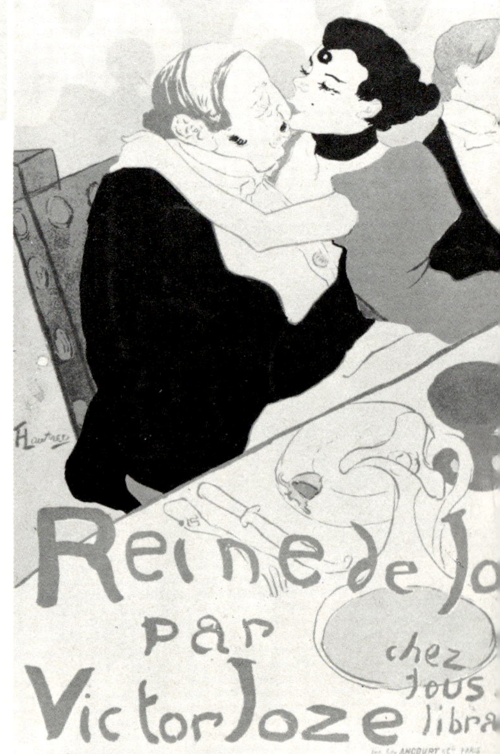

HENRI DE TOULOUSE-LAUTREC
Poster for Aristide Bruant dans
son Cabaret, Ambassadeurs, 1892

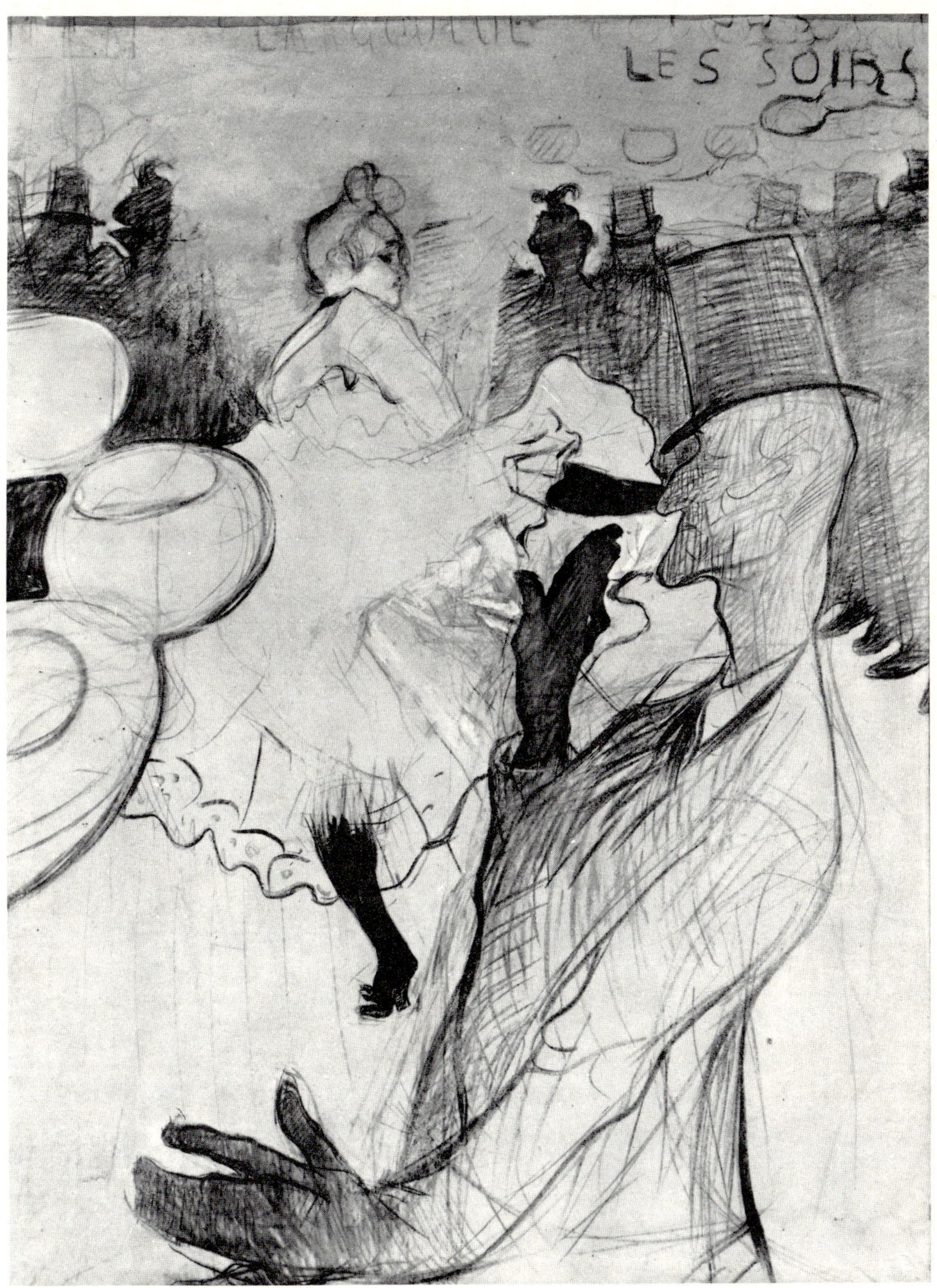

Henri de Toulouse-Lautrec   Poster for Au Moulin Rouge, La Goulue, 1892

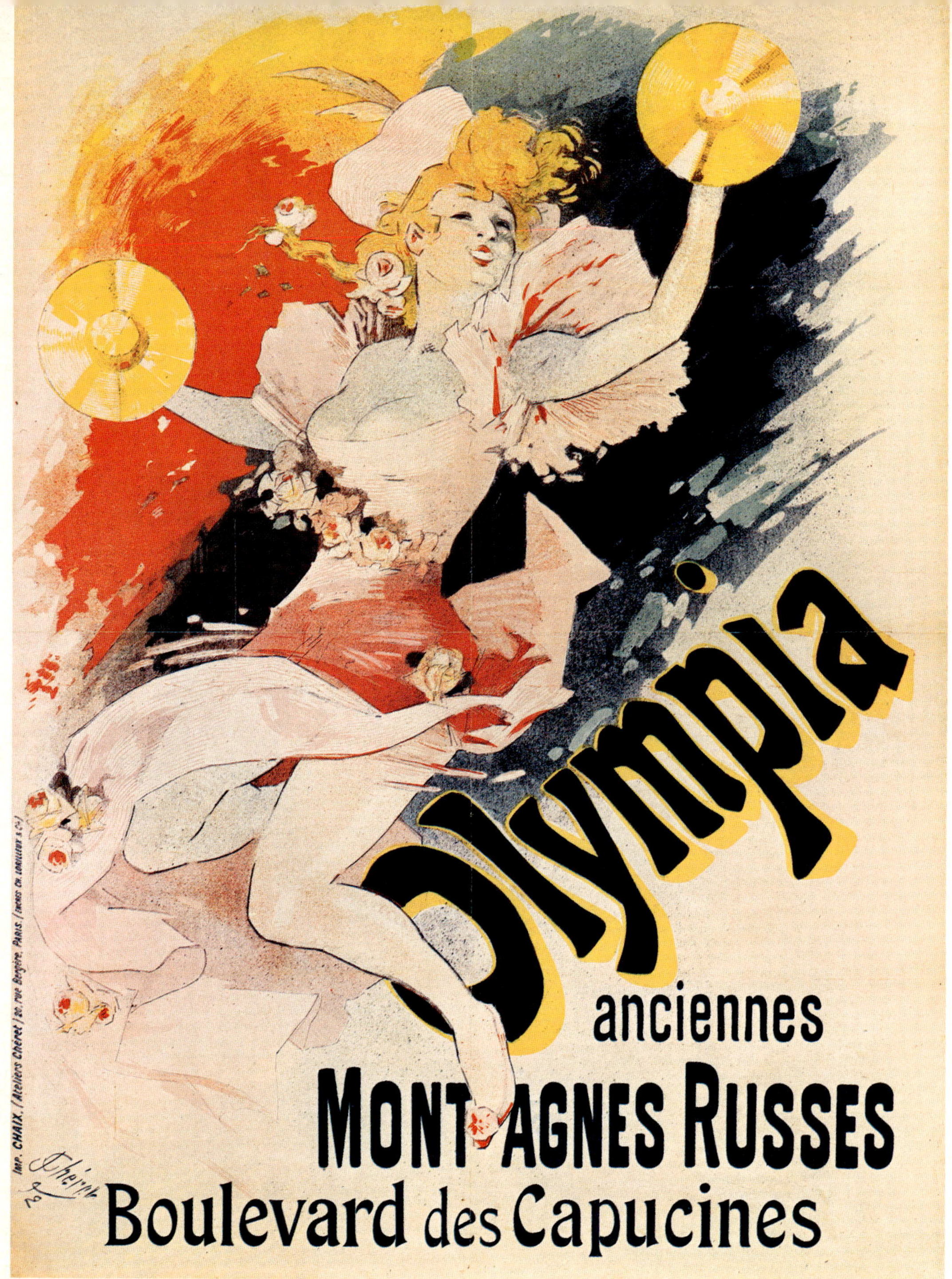

Jules Chéret   Poster for L'Olympia, 1892

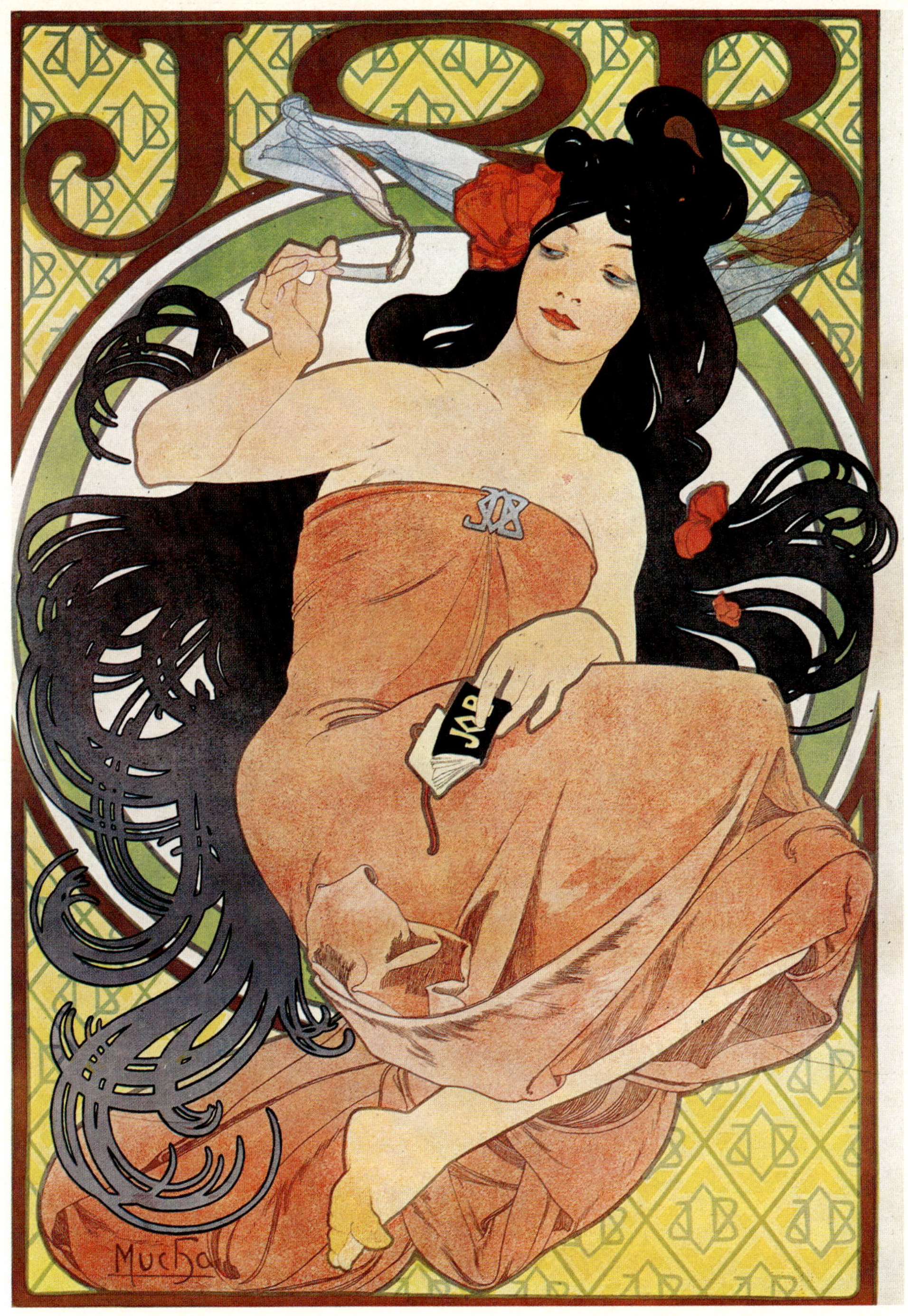

ALFONS-MARIA MUCHA   Poster for Job Cigarette Papers, 1898

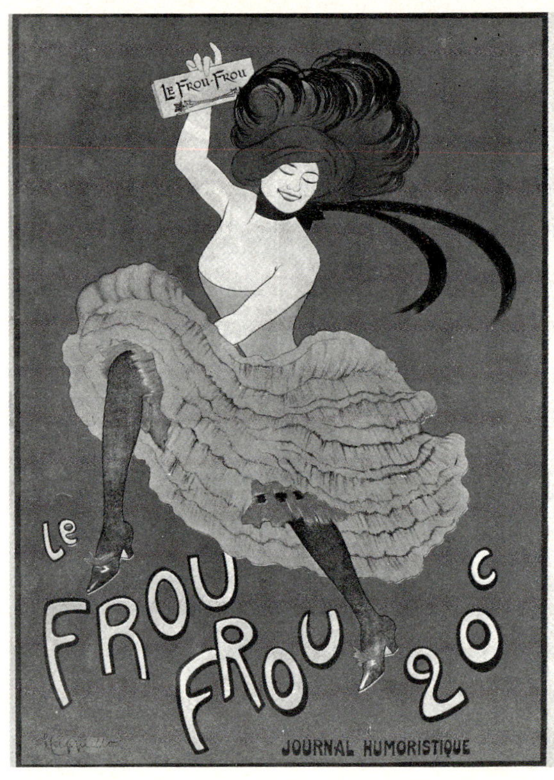

LEONETTO CAPPIELLO   Poster for the review *Le Frou-Frou,* 1899

along with unusual refinement in the choice of model and expression.
The art of Beardsley *(A Comedy of Sighs)* exemplifies the English
poster style. Dudley Hardy, who excelled in a marvelous play of arabesques, Greiffenhagen, William Nicholson, David Hallen, Hyland Ellys
were the masters of the poster in Great Britain during the last years of
the nineteenth century. Toorop took his linear fantasies to Holland. In
Belgium, Van de Velde was actually describing abstract art nouveau
symbols in his advertisements for the Tropon Company. The German
poster-makers were more austere, and consciously more dramatic. Their
humor, in the style of the review *Simplicissimus,* would emerge later.

In the first years of the new century, Cappiello did posters of demo-
nic vitality. The shriek of bright color, the dynamism of his forms —
and his elegance — animated this artist whose graphics grabbed the
viewer, and stayed in his memory. It was a publicity revolution; and
the power of Modern Style was thereby diminished.

gaudí

If we have left Gaudí for the last pages of this book, it is certainly not to award him the title of "last in class." He is, conversely, entitled to every honor — honors, moreover, of which he was deprived during his lifetime. He deserves a special pedestal for the proper appreciation of an architect possessed by the desire to make new discoveries and with the inventive genius to make them.

Gaudí is not like anyone else. He lived and worked only in Barcelona, never seeking to establish contact with colleagues abroad. Thus, in the annals of art nouveau, his work remains an inexplicable phenomenon.

Born near Tarragona in 1852, Gaudí died in Barcelona in 1926. Antoni Gaudí y Cornet at first followed the conventions of his craft. He was an excellent student at architectural school, where he studied with José Fontséré, who was himself in reaction against the hybrid buildings we have mentioned earlier, which were a mix of every European style and period. In 1880, a remarkable plan of expansion was adapted by the city of Barcelona. This was an opportunity for original work in architecture and city planning, and there emerged from this collective effort architects like Puig y Cadalfach, and particularly Domenech y Montaner, the first Spaniard to use pre-stressed concrete. Gaudí first worked on the restoration of historical monuments, notably the Abbey of Montserrat, which, situated in a landscape of scattered rock formations, helps us to understand the young architect's future work, as much inspired by geological as by organic forms.

Some critics have seen in Gaudí a pioneer of contemporary architecture even though, with his unbridled imagination and his love of

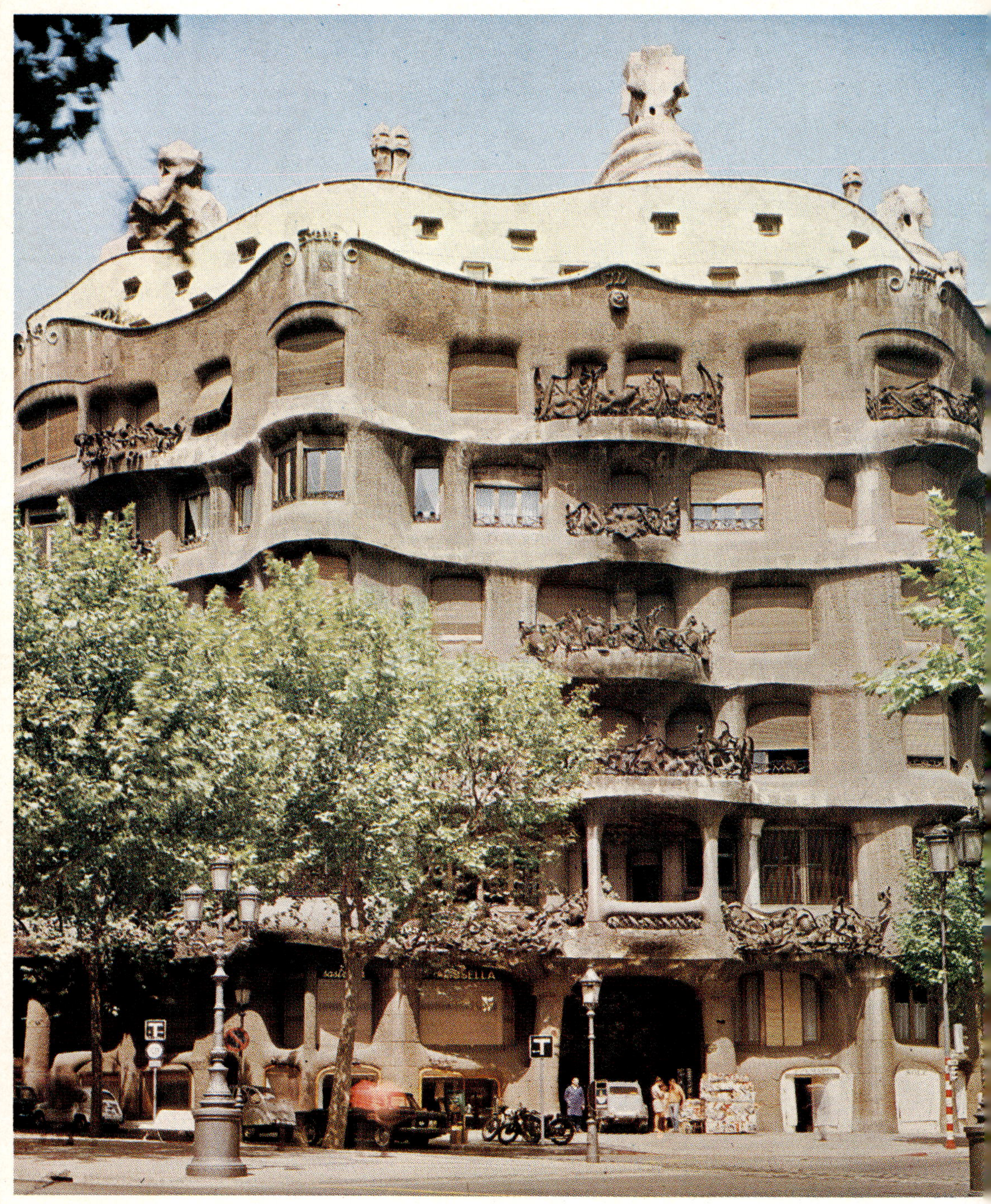

ANTONI GAUDÍ   Facade of the Casa Mila, 1905–1910

ornament, he is the antithesis of rationalism, and, given that he never repeated himself, he is also at the antipodes of all standardization. Gaudí was part of the age of concrete, but himself remained faithful to stone and especially to brick. He was equally loyal to the most traditional methods of handicrafts, which allowed him to change his designs as he went along. But, as a prodigious inventor, adding balance to extravagance, he was still the most revolutionary architect of his time. "The other architects of Modern Style," wrote Michel Ragon, "were really only concerned with the facing, or camouflage of a building. While Gaudí, whose decoration is by far the wildest, was also a structural innovator. His domes are architectural tours de force . . . . He studied shells, drawing ideas and inspiration from their combination of solidity and lightness, which he applied to his roofs and vaults."

Searching nature for models, Gaudí was not satisfied with surface and appearance, but sought fundamental architectonic principles. Everything seems decorative in his work, but every decorative element became an architectural one. And each structural component was transformed into poetic expression. Nikolaus Pevsner considered that Gaudí was "an individualistic craftsman, a lone amateur inventor and putterer," and that "he is part of art nouveau by virtue of an extreme individualism." He may have been a putterer, but a putterer possessed by the genius that conceived and built the Sagrada Familia.

It is more appropriate to see Gaudí in the context of that Spanish baroque which found its natural expression in the marvelous and fantastic, and, above all, to see him in that center of Catalan culture which would produce talents as startling as Dali, Miró, and Picasso. It is apparent that Gaudí was imbued with Catalan and Moorish traditions, although his work was his own invention, in which everything was translated into a personal language close to vision and dream. He seems to have been destined for magical décors, for fantastic stage or film sets; but, in fact, his architecture is solid and structurally sound, the work of a conscientious craftsman whose entire life was directed, with almost religious fervor, toward creations inspired by the impulses of his inner vision. It was through the medium of his prodigious skills as an architect that he was freed to translate the extraordinary content of his dreams.

The strangest aspect of Gaudí's work, and the one which lends itself to all sorts of interpretations, is the juncture of wild lyricism and hallucinatory fantasy with a perfectly organized sense of balance. The

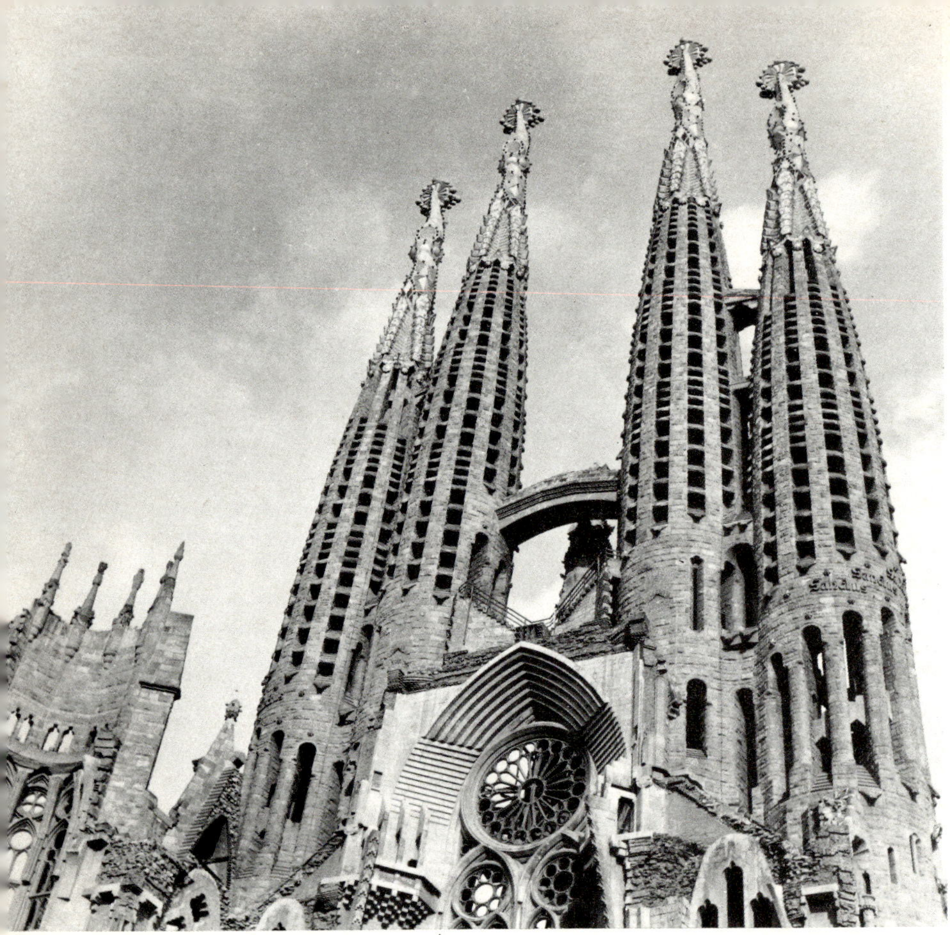

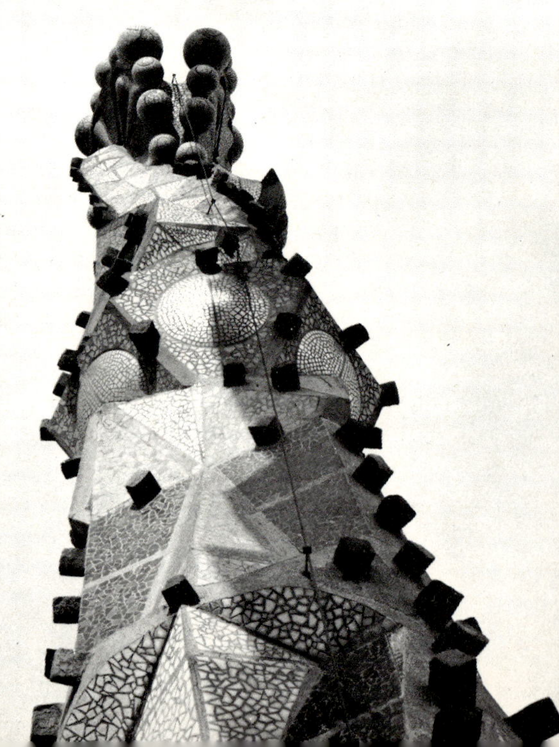

Antoni Gaudí
Church of the
Sagrada Familia, 1883–1926

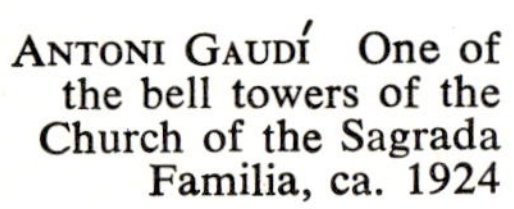

Antoni Gaudí   One of
the bell towers of the
Church of the Sagrada
Familia, ca. 1924

constraints of the material, the tours de force which he loved to pile one upon the other in his buildings — he managed to triumph over them all. The parabolic arches, the oblique pilons, the most daring technical complexities were always controlled by a flawless mastery of the craft of architecture.

Gaudí was twenty-four and had just received his degree when he presented the design for his first building, the Casa Vicens, to a manufacturer of ceramic tile. Although partly inspired by the Mudéjar style, this plan reveals his inventive mind and highly developed architectural identity. He made brilliant use of colored ceramic facing, of logical off-center and asymmetrical construction. The wrought-iron grill and entrance way display a profusion of interlace tracery which prefigures art nouveau. The organization of the interior of the house, in which naturalism is welded to Mozarabic abstract design, is so extravagant that one may well wonder that an ordinary businessman agreed to live in such a setting.

But, in fact, Gaudí's architecture often gives the impression that he worked primarily to please himself. Happily for him, he always managed to find clients in Barcelona who were not only wealthy, but enlightened enough to accept his wildest inventions, however expensive, and even to come back for more. His most important client was Count Güell, for whom he designed a number of his most significant works between 1884 and 1914.

The facade of the Güell House, with its narrow, tall windows, placed close to one another, would seem austere, were it not for the two large entrance ways in the form of demiparabolas, closed by a wrought-iron grill, whose design is described with freely drawn tracery. The grill is a masterpiece of art nouveau — before it was known as such. Covering the two centrally placed windows on the ground and first floors, another grillwork design transposes the arms of Catalonia, giving a seigneurial character to the building. The owner was a connisseur and art collector, and the disposition of the music rooms, the drawing rooms, their plan and lighting show a rational intelligence. The entire house is enlivened by various contrasting materials, like the brightly colored notes of ceramic tile and mosaic.

The Güell Villa, then in the suburbs, was an excuse for ornamental fantasies, in which Arabic motifs mingle with neighboring decorative figures, the creation of Gaudí's imagination alone. Among the latter is a monstrous ironwork dragon, executed with dazzling virtuosity.

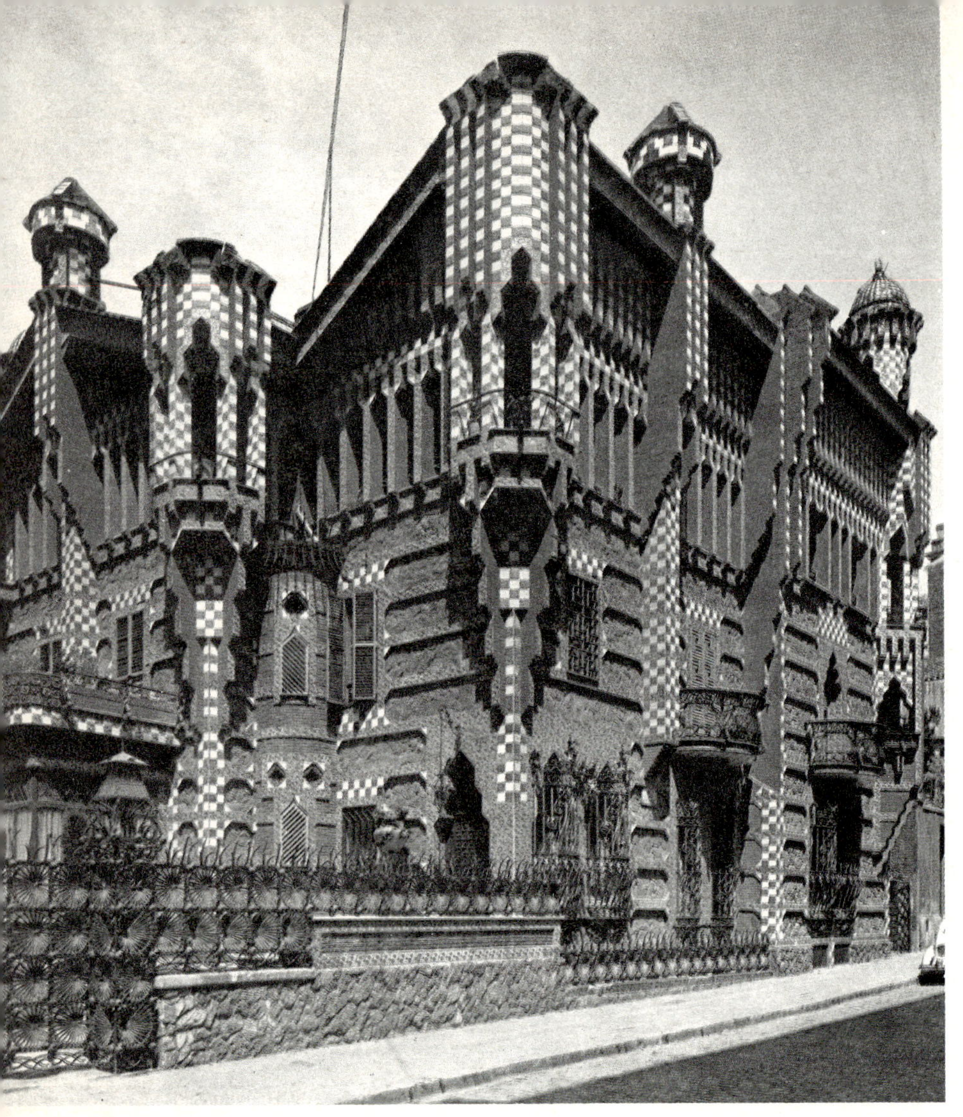

For the workers' housing project of Santa Colonia de Cervello, established by Güell, his patron commissioned Gaudí to design the church. For an assortment of reasons, the project was halted after only the crypt had been completed. But in this crypt and under the porch, open to nature, we find Gaudí's most inventive ideas. The piers bend in every direction, some of them scarcely hewn; others are made of brick, fitted together with the most precise and artful masonry. The twisted vaulting seems incoherent, at first sight; it is, in fact, the result of a meticulously planned system of construction.

In the Güell estate, on the slope of Mont Pelée, we are really in a kind of wonderland, populated with structures which look straight out of the Thousand and One Nights: fountains faced with *azulejos*, faïence petals, tree trunks made of brick, and carefree monsters — all the elements of a surrealist stage set. On the side of a hill, there is a long, comfortable bench; of serpentine form, it is covered entirely with shards of ceramic in strange designs; it has a seating capacity of five thousand persons.

Gaudí could also express himself simply when he wished, and when the circumstances compelled him to simplify. For the college of Santo Teresa de Jesus, part of a convent, the design was determined by the structure of the perfectly regular windows, and by the general use of the steeply sloping arch.

But he made up for it in his private houses. The Calvert House with its oriel windows of stone carved like metalwork, its interlace motifs, complicated patios, and furnishings (Gaudí also designed furniture for some of his projects) is a triumph of the boldest recasting of the baroque. The Batlló House compels our attention because it represents Gaudí's intervention with an earlier building, which he left unrecognizable: balconies in the form of masks are placed in front of the windows. The second floor and the roof are part of the play of undulating forms suggesting abstract sculpture. The facade is studded with glazed earthenware and colored glass.

In buildings intended as a source of income, Gaudí concentrated on practical problems like ventilation and lighting. In the Batlló House, the windows looking on the inner court become progressively narrower as they move closer to the sky. The Milá House rises like a mountain of stones. The scaffolding consists of thick piers and iron beams; balconies thrust forward like open lips, while enormous roof chimneys, barely visible, suggest anthropomorphic chimera. Everything curves and undulates; there is not the smallest surface area that does not seem to move. Gaudí's landscapes of sculpture-architecture are always tormented and troubling. They make the viewer feel in the grip of hallucinatory visions; then he discovers the reality of precise and solid forms, compelling in their strange beauty.

The Sagrada Familia proved to be Gaudís life work. He pondered it constantly, from the time he became an architect in 1883, until his death in 1926. From 1910 on, he turned down all commissions to devote himself exclusively to this project. All Barcelona saw him going to the site every day, when he was not actually living in a shed there.

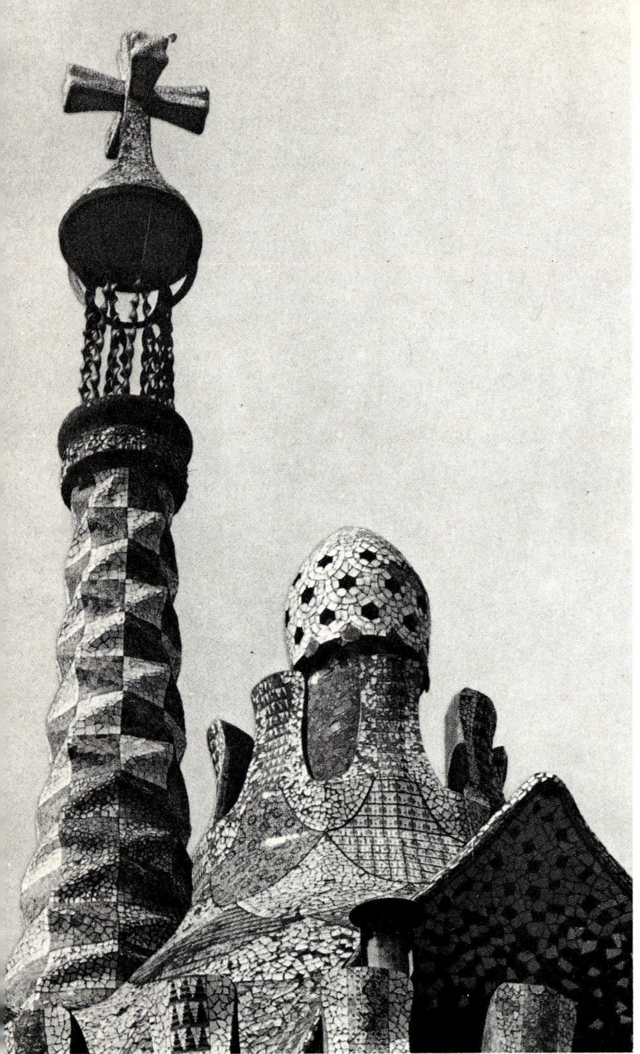

Antoni Gaudí Top of the
entrance pavilion for the
Güell Estate, 1887

Deeply religious and observant, Gaudí built a cathedral in a spirit as exalted as that of his Medieval forebears; like them, he felt obliged to invent every element. He understood Gothic perfectly, but felt that his mission was to surpass it. "Gothic," he said, "is a dead system. We must be the ones to breathe new life into it, and treat construction in a naturalist manner, so that it becomes the expression of the forces acting upon it."

In the meantime, Gaudí had been appointed Diocesan architect, succeeding a colleague who had begun the crypt of the Sagrada Familia, which was meant to support the building in the neo-Gothic style prevalent at the time. He began by raising the crypt so that it would

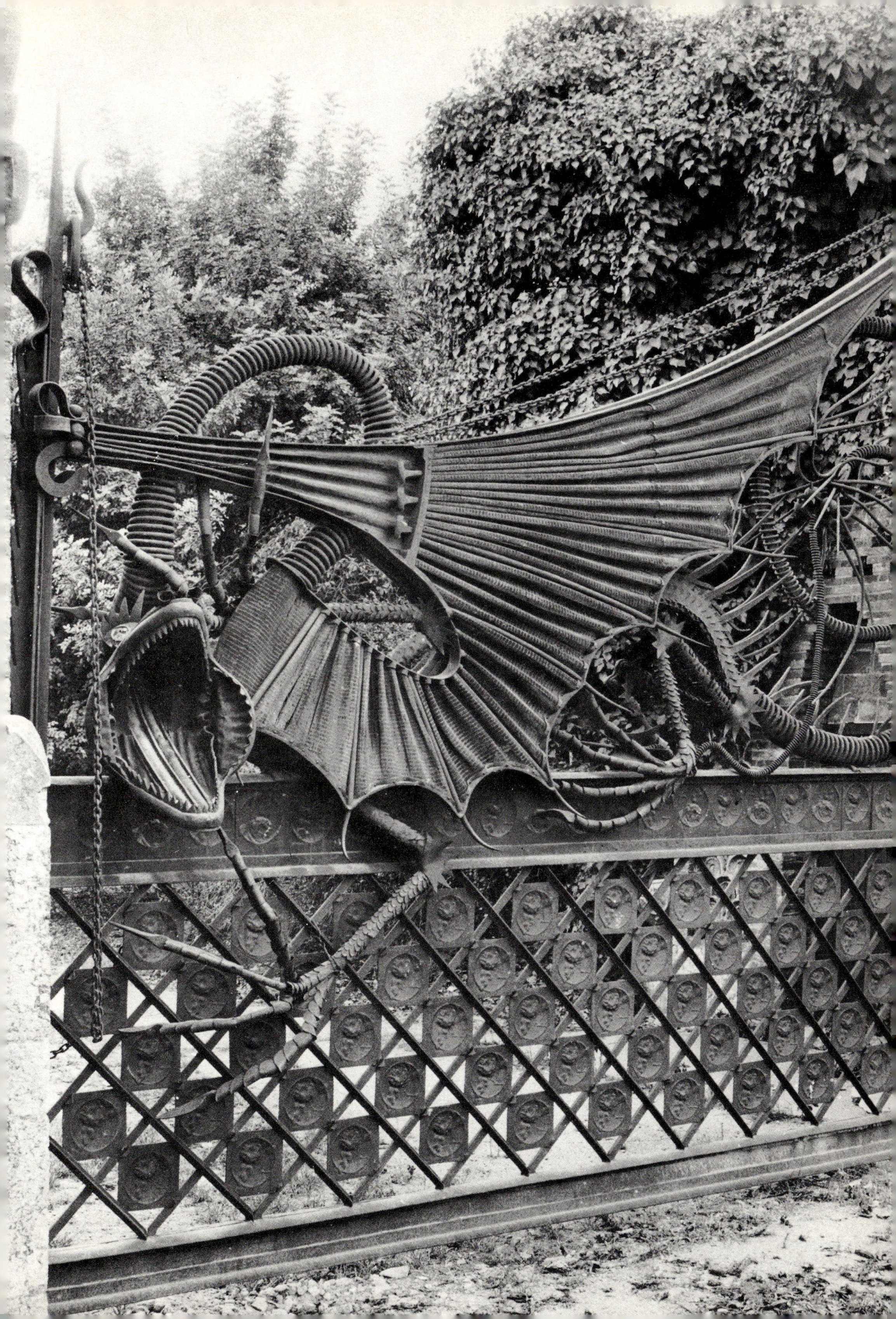

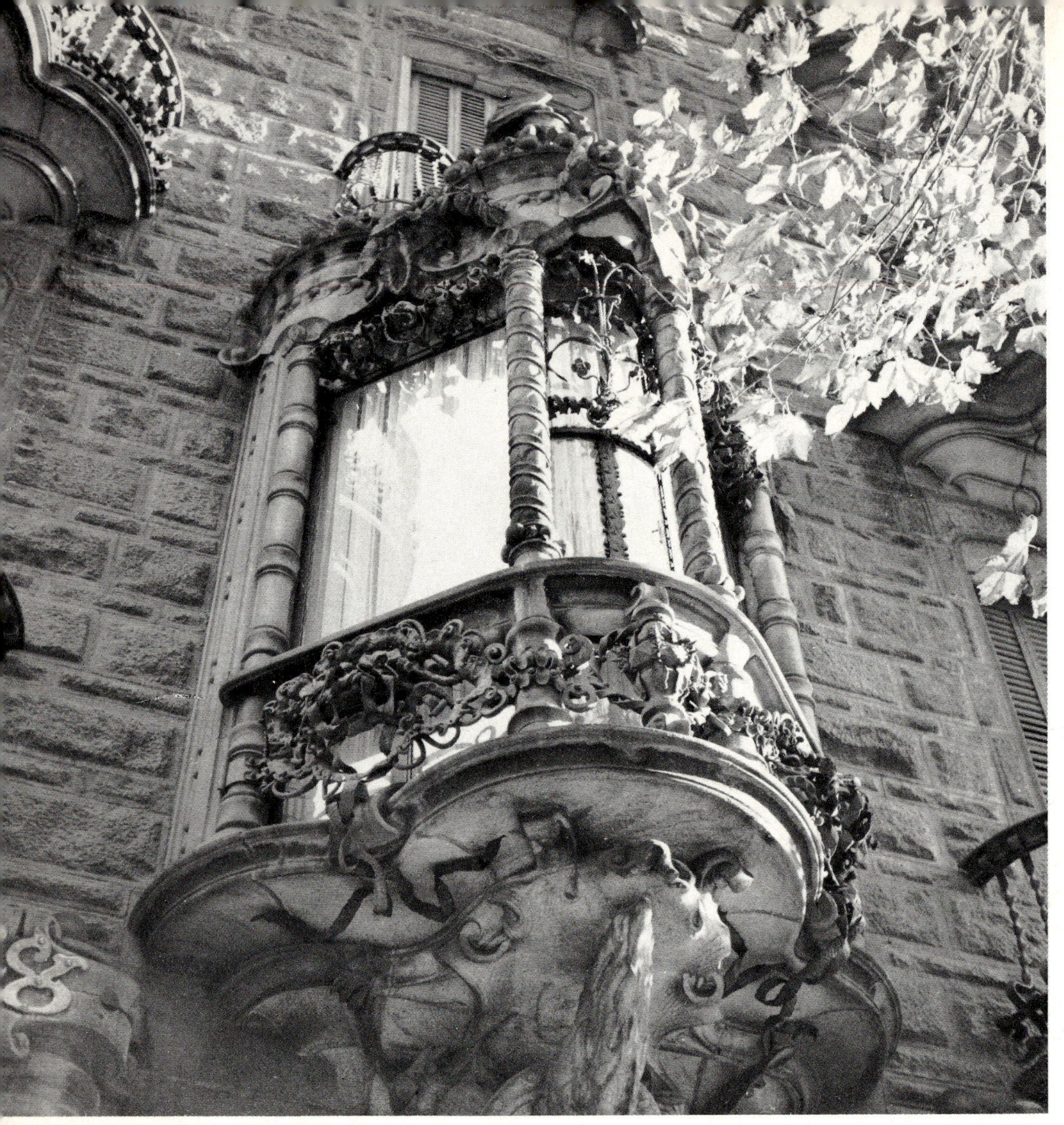

Antoni Gaudí   Detail of the Casa Calvet, 1898–1904

receive natural light. Money had been collected in various countries, especially South America, by the Association of the Devotos de San José for the church. The apse was completed in 1895, when a large donation enabled him to change the plans completely. Gaudí then conceived a monumental structure to be crowned with twelve spires. He next worked on the north transept and its facade, dedicated to the nativity. This is the only part that was completed, which we see today, with its four towers, each one-hundred meters (325 feet) high, that are so characteristic of Gaudí. He remained faithful to the total concept of the tripartite medieval portal, but, little by little, his imagination ran riot everywhere else. Above the portal with the *Coronation of the Virgin,* from the cluster of pinions, tall spires, in the shape of ears of corn, shoot up, the last work of Gaudí's lifetime. They carry heavenward the mesage "Hosanna" sculpted in stone, crowned by a cross of glory, like a deep cry of faith.

The architect of the church that has been called the "cathedral of the poor" himself lived and dressed like one of them. He could be seen in the street — an old man with a white beard, who ate only milk and fruit — rushing to finish the monument on which he had worked

Antoni Gaudí   Detail of the roof of Casa Batlló, 1905–1907

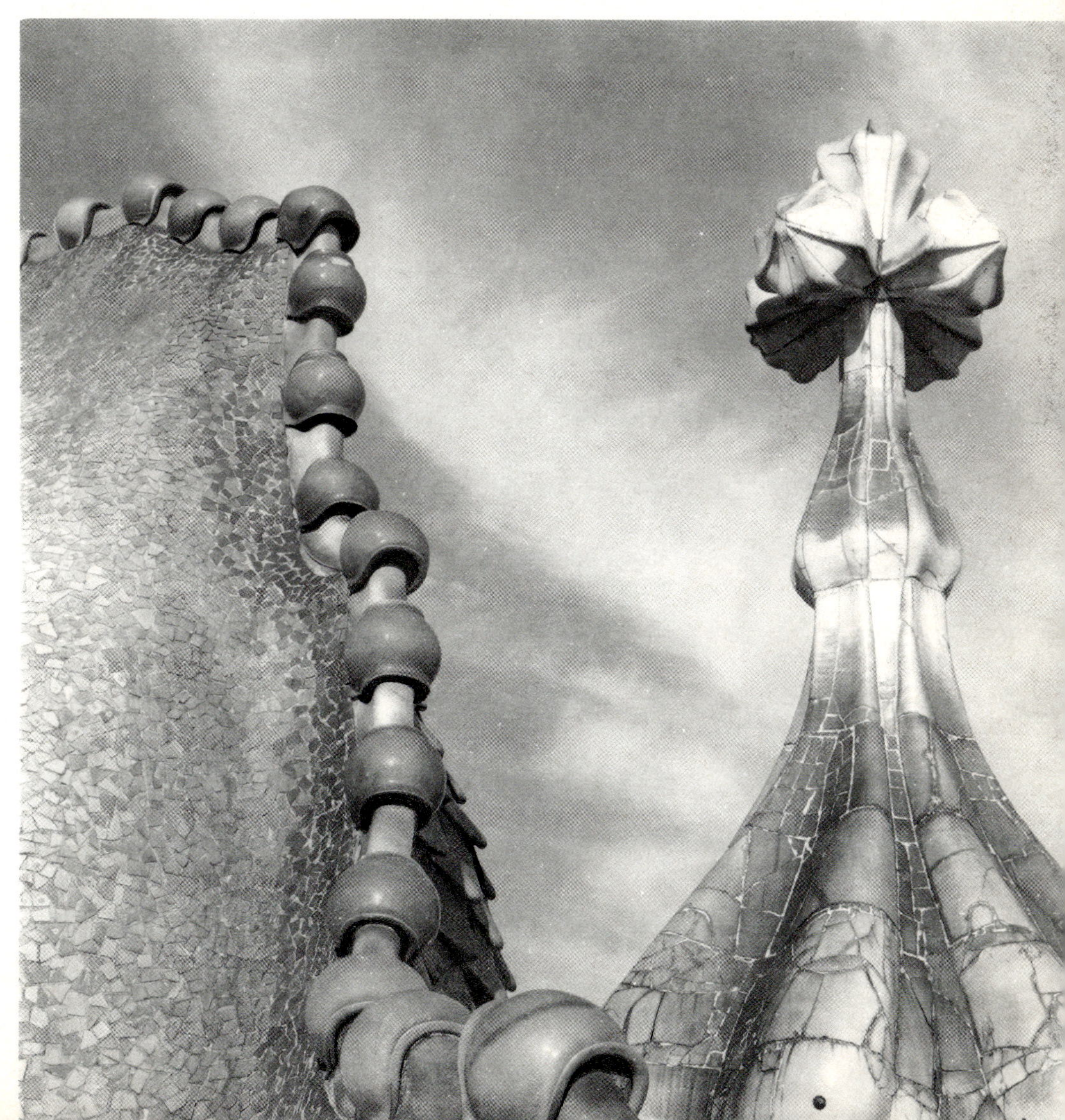

for forty-three years. For many of those years, he had given his fees back to the Catholic church and to the Catalan party.

One day in 1926, the building suddenly stopped. Gaudí had been run over by a trolleycar. He died three days later.

The Sagrada Familia, or at least, the part that is finished, is full of religious images and a whole world of symbolism, like the churches of the Middle Ages. The master did all the calculations of wind resistance himself, according to more or less empirical methods, not hesitating to change the plans as the construction went along. Thus, the highest parts of the steeples are encrusted with multicolored pieces of faience, ending in a style that is Gaudí alone, and which no longer bears any resemblance to Gothic. His naturalism did not always work for the architect. Gaudí populated the portals with statuary that would have to be called academic, of dubious proportions, despite the fact that these figures were generally molded on actual living or dead bodies. (Is this an example of the "creative bad taste" of which his great admirer Dali speaks?) The Sagrada Familia is composed of just this kind of paradox and antithesis; it took the vision of an inspired builder to unite them all in a single monument, albeit unfinished.

Incomplete, abandoned, the Sagrada Familia has taken on a ghostly appearance, and its unlikely monumental presence in a busy section of Barcelona is in itself compelling. In 1952, a resurgence of interest in Gaudí's work induced the government to classify his buildings as historical monuments. A Gaudí museum was established in Barcelona. The abandoned site of the Sagrada Familia became active once again. But the work continued in a spirit even more timid and conventional than was warranted by the fact that the original plans, drawings, and models had been destroyed during the Spanish Civil War. The work of Gaudí is the subject of scholarly theses and passionate exegeses in Spain today.

A visionary like Gaudí could not really have disciples. His work is too qualified by improvisation, by surprise and mystery, to be imitated. Because of his ingenious mind, which found practical solutions to problems of construction, no one has exalted his *functional* side. But the very word is a play on words. The forerunners of functionalism were building their skyscrapers with metal scaffolding in Chicago when Gaudí was building the Güell House. His architecture of transcendance is addressed to the spirit of man more than to his functions.

a new look
at art nouveau

Having reached its hour of glory around 1900, art nouveau soon began to show signs of fatigue. This was followed by terminal decline in the form of mechanical series, recopying the same models, and bastardized forms. The flourishing tree had withered, leaving only shriveled rejects.

But could art nouveau have survived the upheavals of the day much longer? In every domain, Europe and its ancient culture were being shaken at the roots. Economic and social metamorphoses, the advent of a new industrial society, the search for the utilitarian, the triumph of the machine and the decline of handicrafts — these were the ways taken by the twentieth century, while it rejected art nouveau as insignificant frivolity.

On the aesthetic level, it was already dead. The cubist explosion had shattered its fluid lines and emphasis on elegance. Even though art nouveau had given cubism its first breath of life, there was no accommodation possible between two such antithetical doctrines. The evolution of taste, following upon the technical revolution, the ever wider diffusion of models from the Bauhaus — that laboratory of forms geared to mass production — all led to the stripped-down aesthetic in building and furniture. The Exhibition of Decorative Arts in Paris in 1925 only accepted more moderate versions of these new *moderne* creations, recoiling in horror now from Modern Style; floral decoration was only permissible if expressed in stylized geometric form.

In the cities, now enthralled by the rigidities of mechanization, the very spirit behind art nouveau, its personal flavor and poetry, would have been meaningless. Its own theoreticians had felt obliged to renounce their movement. Horta, Van de Velde, Guimard, like the others, set to work designing unoriginal houses, expunging from their work any trace of the style which had made their reputation. Gaudí alone, indifferent to outside influence, conscientiously continued until his death to design motifs more extravagant than ever on the spires of his triumphant church. But it is also true that Spain generally remained outside of aesthetic and industrial developments.

In the thirties, memories of Modern Style contributed both to nostalgia for *la Belle Epoque* and to jokes about it. It became part of humorous subject matter, like the first lady cyclists, the modest bathing costumes, and the glamorous casinos of the period.

Serious study of a style once only spoken of as "amusing" is a recent phenomenon. The first sign of the new attitude was an exhibition held at the Kunstgewerbemuseum in Zurich in 1952. For the first time, art nouveau was presented in a scholarly way, with the references and studies usually accorded exhibitions of art of historical interest. Small, specialized museums of the period were established (for Horta and Van de Velde, respectively, in Brussels, Gaudí in Barcelona, the School of Nancy in its native city). Several exhibitions of Jugendstil were held in Munich. In 1960 the Council of Europe organized a marvelous exhibition in Paris, held at the Musée d'Art Moderne, called *Sources of the Twentieth Century;* it had the singular wisdom to place art nouveau, brilliantly, moreover, in the context of the whole of contemporary artistic creation. A traveling exhibition on Guimard was shown all over the United States. And in 1971, the Musée des Arts Décoratifs in Paris presented a series of exhibitions devoted to the major figures of art nouveau. For many viewers, these were a complete revelation.

Demoted, ridiculed, undervalued, art nouveau, for more than half a century exemplified the nadir of the unfashionable. Today, man, disoriented by the confusion of the present, seeks sustenance from all civilizations, from earliest history to periods nearest his own; these "revivals," however, are capricious and generally go together with a taste for the unusual, the legacy of surrealism. In short, art nouveau acquired new powers of seduction — ones which would certainly have surprised its creators. People rummaged in the refuse of attics and closets. Antique dealers combed the provinces, and in the auction rooms lots of objects and art soared to heights which would have seemed exorbitant but a few years earlier.

Students decorated their rooms with reproductions of Mucha posters. Trendy avant-garde jewelry imitated Lalique. Designers of fashion fabrics interpreted Modern Style, with modifications of their own. Advertising and commercial art all banged the drum for 1900, and their profits indicated that the public was captivated, once again. Needless to say, these are only reflections of art nouveau projected upon the decorative and commercial art of our day, adopted to contemporary taste and habits. But the nineteenth century was avid for just such imitations. We are well aware of the passion, during the Second Empire, for Louis XVI and Directoire. During the Third Republic, Henri II refectory tables appeared such as had never been seen during the reign of Henri II. The most paradoxical, for obvious reasons, is the creation of a "modernized Modern Style" when the original was itself a reaction against the modernizations of earlier periods.

The glittering page and brief stardom of art nouveau did manage to leave its intellectual legacy. And perhaps, more than a revival, we are now witness to a resurrection of its most valuable gifts — a rediscovery of the poetry of objects, their potential magic, the hypnotic fascination of color. It may also be that we are seeing art nouveau in the light of kitsch, of "camp," or with the sentimental nostalgia we harbor for styles left behind. The revival may also be a reaction against the constraints of the way we live today, against the unconscious rejection of the life rhythm by the machine. Living in the midst of blocks of concrete, art nouveau represents a breath of romanticism, the longing to escape into a past far enough away from us to be misted in dreams — and too close to have been forgotten.

list of artists and works illustrated

(Numbers in italics indicate color plates.)

photographic credits

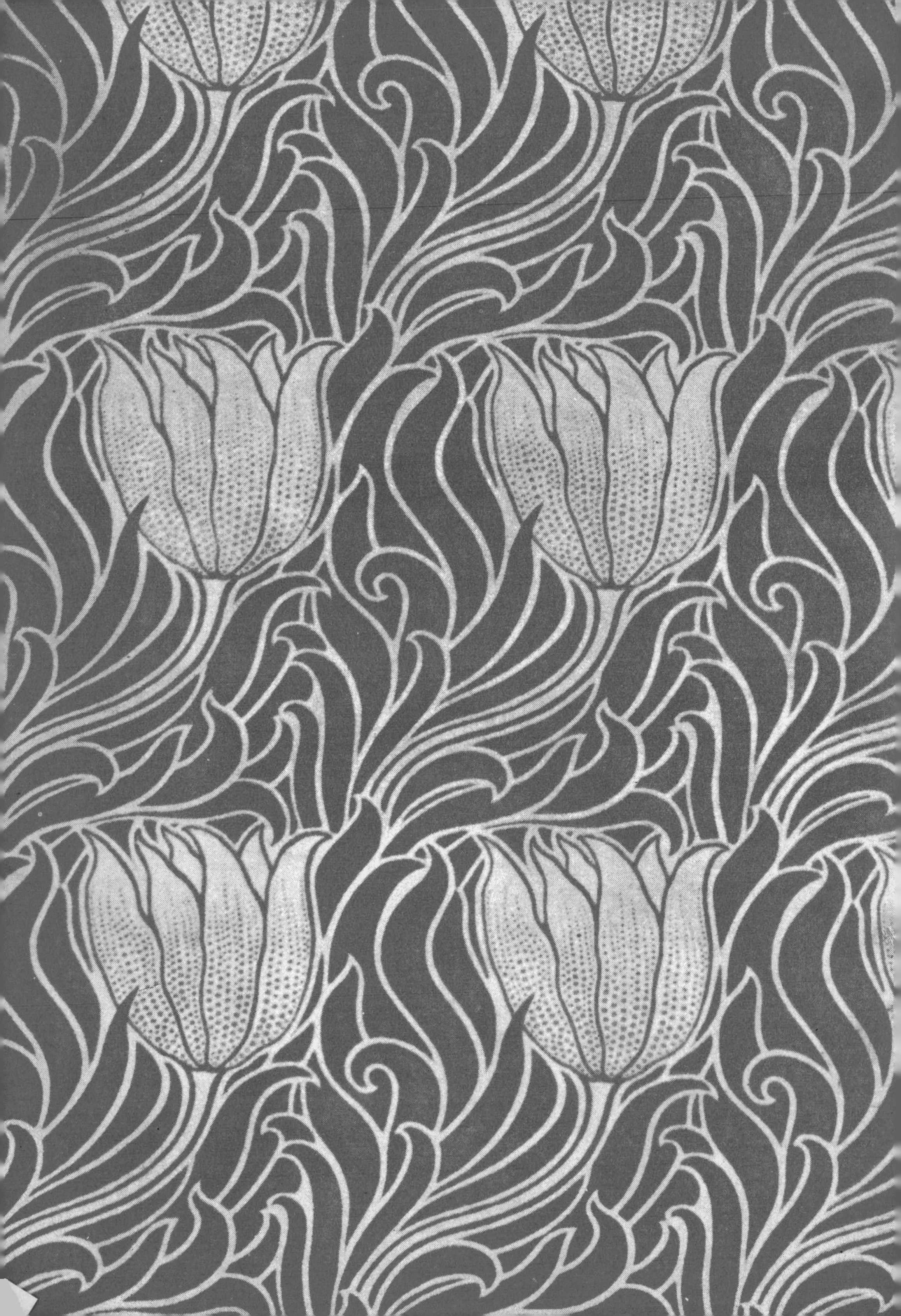